Corporate Valuation

The Wiley Finance series contains books written specifically for finance and investment professionals as well as sophisticated individual investors and their financial advisors. Book topics range from portfolio management to e-commerce, risk management, financial engineering, valuation and financial instrument analysis, as well as much more. For a list of available titles, visit our website at www.WileyFinance.com.

Founded in 1807, John Wiley & Sons is the oldest independent publishing company in the United States. With offices in North America, Europe, Australia and Asia, Wiley is globally committed to developing and marketing print and electronic products and services for our customers' professional and personal knowledge and understanding.

Corporate Valuation

Measuring the Value of Companies in Turbulent Times

MARIO MASSARI
GIANFRANCO GIANFRATE
LAURA ZANETTI

WILEY

Published by John Wiley & Sons, Inc., Hoboken, New Jersey.
Published simultaneously in Canada.

For general information on our other products and services or for technical support, please contact our Customer Care Department within the United States at (800) 762-2974, outside the United States at (317) 572-3993 or fax (317) 572-4002.

Wiley publishes in a variety of print and electronic formats and by print-on-demand. Some material included with standard print versions of this book may not be included in e-books or in print-on-demand. If this book refers to media such as a CD or DVD that is not included in the version you purchased, you may download this material at http://booksupport.wiley.com. For more information about Wiley products, visit www.wiley.com.

Library of Congress Cataloging-in-Publication Data is available:

ISBN 9781119003335 (Hardcover)
ISBN 9781119003359 (ePDF)
ISBN 9781119003342 (ePub)

Cover Design: Wiley
Cover Image: © Alicia_Garcia/iStockphoto

Printed in the United States of America

10 9 8 7 6 5 4 3 2 1

Contents

Preface

A ROADMAP FOR THIS BOOK

The value of a business is essentially related to three main factors: its current operations, its future prospects, and its embedded risk. The advent of globalization, new technologies, and the consequences of the recent financial crisis completely reshaped these elements, thus making more elusive the definition of company "value" and of the metrics to measure it.

Firstly, firms do business in a context becoming progressively faster, more diverse, and more interconnected so that also valuing their current operations is a task less straightforward than in the past. Secondly, forecasting future macro and business related dynamics is getting less standardized in a business environment characterized by inherent difficulty in predicting changes—both on the upside and on the downside—and by constant innovation for companies that are more and more exposed to hyper-competitive industry dynamics. Thirdly, new types of risks and competition, so far unknown (think for example of climate change risks), are shaping both the operational and the financial side of enterprises, redefining the importance of managing uncertainty as a key element to achieve success.

In this context, the book is organized in three parts. In the first part of the book (Chapters 1 to 4), the main focus is on the relationship between value and business/economic uncertainty. In an environment characterized by an increased complexity where the concept of value itself is challenged, we provide a definition of corporate value based on a holistic approach, thus encompassing both the accounting and the financial perspective (Chapter 1).

Moving to relationship between uncertainty and value, we focus on the business modeling tools available to forecast corporate results and determine company value. Depending on the level of uncertainty, on the information available, and the time and effort investable in the analysis, it is possible to pick one out of three possible approaches. We start from a standard situation when uncertainty is limited and there is a clearly dominant, likely scenario (Chapter 2).

When there is a significant amount of uncertainty and there is one or more scenario(s) that are alternative to the most likely one and that could have extreme—either positive or negative—consequences for company's value, the scenario-based approach is to be preferred (Chapter 3).

Stochastic simulation (Chapter 4) is to be used when detailed data is available (or assumed) regarding the probability distributions of key variables affecting future cash flows. This approach, as discussed, is mathematically complex but it can be handled by software packages easily available.

Having tackled the uncertainty modeling aspects, the second part of the book is focused on the main valuation approaches that can be used in practice. The chapters from 5 to 13 present therefore the main principles of corporate valuation starting from the reorganization of the financial statement data and business plan figures (Chapter 5). The relationship between financial leverage and corporate value is then presented (Chapter 6), followed by the discussion of how corporate growth and, financial leverage are interrelated (Chapter 7).

Chapter 8 presents the main techniques and tools to estimate the cost of capital. From Chapter 9 to Chapter 11, the discounted cash flow analysis is presented in depth highlighting the various approaches that can be used in practice.

Moving to relative valuation, Chapters 12 and 13 present respectively the theory and practice of multiple-based valuation for companies.

The third and final section of the book comprises Chapter 14 and 15, which introduce the main elements of valuations in the market for corporate control and models to structure corporate valuations in the framework of M&A transactions.

Chapter 16 features a topic, the valuation of right issues, seldom mentioned by corporate finance handbooks but which is becoming crucial in many financial markets.

Chapter 17 closes by introducing a topic that is receiving increasing attention by investors and policymakers, namely the incorporation of environmental risks in corporate valuation.

The key message of the book is that standard business planning and valuation, which assume high visibility of firms' future performances, tend to prove more and more inadequate. In the context of high market volatility and recurring disruptive economic events associated with the post-financial crisis business world, companies' operations face systematically new points of discontinuity and increased risks. As a consequence, traditional standard valuation techniques may provide insufficient information in an economic environment characterized by high uncertainty. This book treats risk not as one of the input variables used in the valuation process but as the main driver to be considered when approaching the estimation of corporate value.

Acknowledgments

Of course, we owe a very great debt of thanks to friends, colleagues, and students who have contributed to this work. First, we thank greatly Marco Villani, a valuation expert who read and commented on chapters. Second, Federico D'Agruma provided extensive and invaluable assistance for the preparation and revision of the manuscript. We would like to also thank Marco Ghitti who prepared the supporting materials for the book. We are also grateful to John Carusone, Alberto Maria Ghezzi and Kim Salvadori, who helped in the revision of some sections of the manuscript. We are immensely grateful to the Wiley team—especially to Meg Freeborn, Bill Falloon, and Caroline Maria Vincent—who assisted us in the book preparation and showed incredible patience with our consistent missing of deadlines.

About the Author

Mario Massari is Full Professor of Corporate Finance and former Head of the Finance Department at Bocconi University (Milan). He has written extensively on business valuation and corporate finance topics, and he is considered one of the leading experts in Italy in the field of Business Valuation. He serves as board member at several listed and unlisted companies and he is a member of the Executive Committee of the OIV (the Italian valuation principles setter).

mario.massari@unibocconi.it

Gianfranco Gianfrate is a Giorgio Ruffolo Fellow at the Harvard Kennedy School (Cambridge, MA) and a research affiliate of Tufts University (Medford, MA). He has authored several books and articles on business valuation and corporate governance issues.

Previously, he was a consultant at Deloitte (Milan), a manager at Hermes Fund Managers (London), and served as member of the Investment Committee at Eumedion (Amsterdam). He has also been a member of the IPO Best Practice Committee at the Italian Stock Exchange, co-authoring the official Listing Guide for going public companies.

g_gianfrate@hks15.harvard.edu

Laura Zanetti is Associate Professor of corporate finance at Bocconi University (Milan), where she teaches company valuation and is research fellow within CAREFIN, centre for applied research in finance.

She has been the director of the Master of Science in Finance at Bocconi, visiting scholar at Massachusetts Institute of Technology (Cambridge, MA) and London School of Economics and Political Sciences (London).

She published several books and articles on corporate governance, valuation, M&A, and industrial performance. She is a Certified Public Accountant, Certified Auditor in Italy, and board member of listed and private companies.

laura.zanetti@unibocconi.it

## CHAPTER 1

Introduction

1.1 WHAT WE SHOULD KNOW TO VALUE A COMPANY

This book is based on the idea that mastering valuation techniques is possible only after having gained a sound theoretical knowledge. But theory is not enough. In order to evaluate an enterprise or an acquisition, an analyst should have enough first-hand experience: such experience usually does not depend on the quantity of the previous valuations carried-out but on the quality of the work done.

A distinguishing feature of the valuation process is that to produce convincing valuations, analysts should master various areas of expertise, and three in particular:

1. *Industrial economics and business strategy* with reference to the analysis of the industry and competitive context devoted to understanding the validity of the company's business model, its past results, and its future plans
2. *Theory and techniques of finance* with regard to the basic principles of net present value, to the underlying links between leverage and value, to models that explain stock prices on financial markets, and finally to the techniques which correctly depict the business plan in terms of cash flow
3. *Economic theory,* in particular with regard to the relationship between uncertainty and value[1] in all those cases in which the simplifications assumed in the standard models presented in the finance textbooks do not permit the development of convincing valuations

Despite the fact that theoretical contributions in all three disciplines are widely known, valuation is more than a collage of knowledge and technique.

---

[1]One of the limitations of such models is the assumption of normal distributions of results. In such a case, the highest probable expected output is the average output. Quite often, though, prospective results are mutually exclusive, thus making expected "average" results unlikely. The very idea of *average* thus loses its significance.

1

In a valuation, critical drivers are so bound together that the real distinguishing element is the "glue" that holds them together. This glue consists of the ability to balance the different choices made in each phase of which the evaluation process is composed, of correctly weighing the empirical evidence, and of the ability to perform coherent estimates within the final objectives of the valuation work.

1.2 VALUATION METHODS: AN OVERVIEW

Finance textbooks offer several different options to perform the valuation of a firm or of an acquisition. Furthermore, financial institutions and consulting firms typically work out tailor-made models expanding the spectrum of available techniques. In the end, in assessing value of firms belonging to particular industries, several empirical techniques have gained quite a standing among practitioners.

Given the number of methodologies made available by theorists and practitioners, we find it useful, before getting into the core of this book, to explore a classification of the most widely used methodologies (Exhibit 1.1).

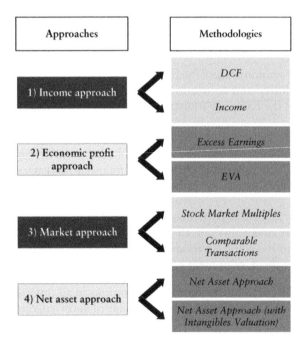

Exhibit 1.1   An overview of the main valuation methodologies/approaches

Exhibit 1.1 shows that the methodologies available (excluding simplistic empirical approaches) can be grouped into four fundamental approaches, each a function of the relevant link between corporate value and relevant value driver. A methodology is then a choice of the relevant driver, chosen out of the above-mentioned four approaches in order to assess value:

1. Income approach
2. Economic profit approach
3. Market approach
4. Net asset approach

The first approach expresses the value of a company or an investment as a function of the expected returns it generates. The so-called financial method (or, better, discounted cash flow, or DCF) falls into this approach and is the methodology most consistent with those found in standard finance textbooks.

The second approach is based on the idea that the value of a company is determined by two components: net asset value and earnings that exceed the "normal" return of the assets (economic profit is then the difference—when positive—between realized returns and "normal" industry returns).

The third approach is empirical: valuations are performed through a comparison with comparable assets traded on the market.

Finally, the fourth approach determines value from the estimation of the assets (tangible and intangible) that, net of the liabilities, constitute the net invested capital of the firm.

1.2.1 Common Practices in the Accounting and Financial Communities

Often, professionals separate methodologies into two main approaches to valuation: the first is the standard practice adopted by the financial community; the second one is the most widely used by accounting professionals.

The common practice in the financial community can be traced back to the methodologies adopted by investment and merchant banks—in particular:

- The DCF method based on the discounting of future cash flows derived from the company's business plan or assumed by the analyst
- Stock market multiples or multiples derived from comparable transactions

In other professional fields, the other methods set forth in Exhibit 1.1 seem to be preferred, partly because of cultural affinities and partly because of the specific goal of the valuation.

Indeed, some methods (particularly those based on excess earnings):

- better fit into some economic and accounting environment;
- follow, therefore, a logic more understandable to the actors for whose benefit the valuation is performed; and
- allow one to effectively and convincingly deal with special valuation problems, such as third-party interests or tax benefit valuations.

1.2.2 Approach of This Book

Despite the widespread use of alternative methodologies, most of this book will be devoted to the DCF analysis.

The reason for this choice is that DCF valuation processes allow a clear focus on the fundamental principles underlying valuation conditions that need to be met, and also when the professional believes a different methodology to better fit the final valuation objective.

In this chapter, we introduce, following a logical order that teaching experience has shown to be effective, the basic principles and themes that form the pillars of the DCF valuation approach:

- The net present value (NPV) principle
- How to deal with uncertainty
- The relationship between uncertainty and value
- The need for preventing, when possible, subjective judgments in value determination

1.3 THE TIME VALUE OF MONEY

Irving Fisher is considered the founding father of modern finance theory, not only for his market equilibrium model, which explains investment and consumption decisions, but also because of his almost-obsessive insistence on the need to determine any asset value exclusively as a function of its expected discounted cash flows.

Thanks to Fisher, since the early 1920s the main building block of valuation has been identified as follows: any asset value (financial or real) is a function of the cash flows it can generate and of the time distributions of the cash flows.[2]

Through Fisher's contribution, the concept of *time value of money* became solidified, thus building the rationale for the universally agreed need for a present value approach to valuation.

---

[2]Irving Fisher, *The Rate of Interest* (New York: Macmillan 1907) and *The Theory of Interest* (New York: Macmillan 1930).

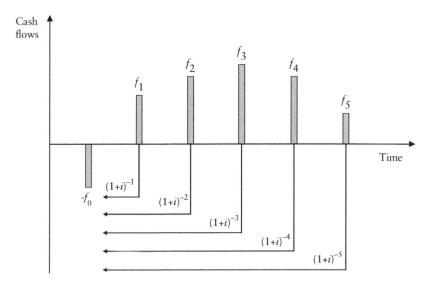

Exhibit 1.2   Investment cash flow profile and mechanics of discounting

So, without uncertainty, or, as it is often said, in a deterministic frame-work, an investment, firm, or more generally any asset value can be obtained by the following:

- Calculate the asset relevant cash flows and their time distributions.
- Discount any cash flows at a rate expressing the time value of money.

Typically, this rate is the return rate of investments whose issuers are virtually free of any insolvency risk, such as government bonds (so-called *risk-free* rate). Exhibit 1.2 shows the concept.

1.4   UNCERTAINTY IN COMPANY VALUATIONS

In order to set forth in an organized fashion the crucial problem of every eval-uation, it is necessary to understand the reasoning that guides the process of valuation in a context in which the results of an investment, or of a business, cannot be certainly determined in advance, but can only be estimated.

In order to introduce the problem of uncertainty with the pragmatic approach more suitable to the needs of a business or financial analyst, it is useful to start from some basic concepts:

- *The performance of industries is characterized by different degrees of predictability and, therefore, uncertainty.* For example, trend in demand in the public utilities sector shows a significant correlation with the trend in the GDP, or the total family income. In other sectors, demand is a function of different macroeconomic variables, such as industrial investments, interest rates, etc. Generally, though, these correlations are more weak because some factors, such as lifestyle evolution or consumer behaviour, can have a great influence on the demand. Further, some other industries are extremely sensitive to economic trends (typically, the intermediate sectors, investment goods sectors for which demand is formed by other industries). Finally, some industries are less cyclical (e.g., some food sectors, and the pharmaceutical industry).

■ *New ventures, or firms that develop innovative strategies, face a different kind of uncertainty than traditional or consolidated industries.* In fact, in traditional industries historical information helps to identify systematic correlations between the economic environment and a firm's expected results. In innovative ventures lacking significant historical comparisons, uncertainty can be associated with the idea of probability as an expectation of future events: therefore, estimates are largely subjective (uncertainty = belief).[3] Such a concept of uncertainty, in general, is contrasted by academics with the notion of probability that past events repeat themselves (in such case, the concept of probability is associated with that of frequency).

■ *Firms, as organizations of individuals competing on the market, generate evolutionary phenomena that constitute risk factors for other firms, which in turn react by generating new changes.* Therefore, we must abandon the idea, implicitly accepted by finance theorists, that uncertainty is a situation passively faced by firms. In the real world, uncertainty is managed by firms that seek to exploit favorable opportunities and limit the downside of unfavorable events. Management, indeed, by its own decisions continuously molds the risk profile characteristic of its core activity. That is, management style, interaction with the economic environment, and adopting innovative approaches rather than passive adaptation are fundamental factors in adjusting the degree of uncertainty associated with external factors, common to all the firms belonging to the same strategic business area.

---

[3] It's well known that the different phases of the life cycles of firms and industries are characterized by different levels of uncertainty. Scholars are of the opinion that there exists a stable and demonstrated relationship among the risk profile type of industry and life cycle of the very same industry. In the initial phases of the cycle (so-called "introduction" and "development"), the risks are particularly elevated, with the consequent possibility of huge losses of invested capital. In general, in the innovative sectors uncertainty and the difficulty of forecasting are well-known risk factors.

In the valuation of investments, acquisitions, or businesses, different forms of uncertainty can coexist—although, generally, one form tends to prevail over the others.

On the one hand, there are valuations of companies that operate in highly stable macroeconomic contexts, in highly predictable industry, and whose future performance is characterized by high visibility. Such cases of "easy" valuations become less and less frequent in the current context of erratic economies and turbulent financial markets.

1.4.1 Organizing the Analysis

Financial analysts approach the issue of uncertainty in forecasting by adopting logical tools and models developed in the area of industrial economics and of strategy. Exhibit 1.3 shows a simplified description of a typical analysis workflow.

Business Model Analysis Typically, analysts use the expression *business model* to assess the characteristics of the products or services offered by a firm, the marketing choices adopted, and the production decisions. In the business model analysis, analysts seek to understand the cost/revenues structure of the firm or of the investment project. An example can help clarify the concept.

Alpha is the European leader in automated equipment for manufacturing and packaging for the pharma industry (blisters, boxes, wrappers, case packers, and palletizers). In the pharma industry, a fundamental feature of production equipment is reliability while price is a secondary issue. Alpha has consolidated its leadership position by systematically investing a significant portion of its revenues in improving equipment for specific functions and researching innovative technical solutions. Non-core components production has been assigned to different companies. Equipment is marketed by a European and North American distribution network. Technical support, spare parts sales, and equipment updates represent a significant fraction of the overall gross margin.

Business Model Analysis

⬇

Market and Competitors Analysis

⬇

Risk Profile Analysis

Exhibit 1.3 Uncertainty analysis

This scant information defines the "business model" and lets us understand that the revenue share emerging from equipment sales, being related to the pharmaceutical industry, is only marginally affected by cycles and is complemented by further revenues, with high margins and no cyclicity (as, for instance, in the after-sales support business).

Under the cost structure planning, assembly, setup, and a significant share of the R&D costs are largely inelastic, because they require a highly specialized staff, which is a strategic resource of the company and is fundamental to the growth outlook for Alpha.

Production costs are, on the other hand, relatively flexible: as previously noted, Alpha assigns the manufacturing of noncore components of its own products to a small selected number of suppliers, mostly located in the same geographical area.

Market and Competitors Analysis   The next step consists of the analysis of the environment external to the company, in order to understand the firm's market positioning relative to competitors and therefore the prospects for growth and profit. At this stage the analysis focuses on the business lifecycle and the competitive pressure which characterize the industry, the threat of substitute products, the entry barriers and potential competitors, and the relationship between customers and suppliers.

In the Alpha case, the pharmaceutical industry is characterized by a sustained growth rate, both in Europe and in the USA (over 7% per year in real terms). Industry analysts believe this trend is destined to last in the future.

By examining balance sheets for the most important pharmaceutical firms, one observes a strong correlation between revenue growth rate and spending on technical investments.

Just a small number of competitors are active in Alpha's market niche. Potential supply is represented by packaging equipment firms, which generally develop less reliable technologies than the standard pharma industry requirements.

Risk Profile Analysis   Typically the assessment of risk profile begins with a classical SWOT analysis of the competitive environment and the competitors.[4]

The case under consideration doesn't show significant risk factors: entry in the industry is limited by specific technical competence needed to produce

---

[4]The most widely used models are the Porter five forces—Michael Porter, *Competitive Strategy* (New York: The Free Press, 1980)—and the strategies and competitive advantages matrices—M. Porter, *Competitive Advantage: Creating and Sustaining Superior Performance* (New York: The Free Press, 1985).

the equipment targeted for the pharmaceutical industry and by the market reputation of Alpha. Thus, there are no reasons to induce the analyst to delineate alternative competitive scenarios (for instance, the entry of a new-comer with resulting reduction of market share or margin squeezes). Yet, this approach can be easily shared provided Alpha can keep up with a growth rate consistent with the pharma industry rate and can complete its product range by acquiring competitors working in related market niches.

Consolidating Alpha's market share could allow for an extension of the product range offered: from mere equipment sales to planning the whole production cycle as a general contractor. Moreover, Alpha could step into the business machines used in the cosmetic industry that, although not as demanding in terms of the technological specifications as the pharma industry ones, show significant similarities.

1.5 UNCERTAINTY AND MANAGERIAL FLEXIBILITY

In a traditional approach, closer to financial modeling than strategic analysis, estimate of value stems from a passive attitude toward risk. Yet, we have observed that in reality businesses are by far more articulated: in fact, up to a certain level, the phenomena of change can be managed or turned to one's favor through opportune intervention.

1.5.1 Static versus Dynamic Assumption

As a first step, when facing the valuation of an investment plan, acquisition, or firm, it is worth asking which standpoint should be adopted:

- A static view assuming that the current business model will continue to work as it is
- A dynamic view which takes into account the adaptation of the business model to new scenarios

If we want to frame the issue in general terms, the valuation boundaries are determined—with regard to the choice of the correct standpoint—by two main factors:

1. The level of uncertainty, which characterizes the estimate measured as the impact that information unavailable at the time of the valuation can have on the valuation result itself; or, in other words, how far it is from the idea of probability based on the repetition of past results
2. Managerial flexibility—that is, how much the business model allows management to handle unfavourable scenarios or pick new opportunities in favorable situations

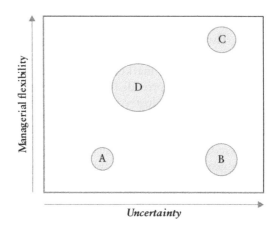

Exhibit 1.4   Valuation framework as a function
of uncertainty and managerial flexibility

Exhibit 1.4 presents a graph that permits us to frame the context that
drives the valuation with respect to the degree of uncertainty and management flexibility.

Limited Uncertainty and Flexibility   In Exhibit 1.4, area A identifies situations
in which the frame of reference of the estimate is delineable in clear terms and
the business model does not permit significant room to manoeuvre. A typical
example is the business of gas and electricity grids; in these business areas,
results emerge from a model in which relationships between macroeconomic
variables, tariffs, transported volumes, and costs are definable with a close
approximation and can be consistently projected in the future with a high
degree of credibility.

Uncertainty factors consist of the evolution of energy consumption that,
as is well known, is a function, in the short term, of climate factors and, in the
long term, of the general trend of the industry as a whole; changes in industry
regulations; and the intensity of competitive pressure from the supply side.

In these businesses, shifts in consumption translate directly into operating margin decreases/increases since the cost structure is extremely rigid and
management has very limited flexibility to keep up with unfavorable trends
in demand.

In the previously sketched framework, the representation of uncertainty
is consistent with the assumptions generally adopted by finance textbooks. In
particular, it is possible to forecast different scenarios and to expect credibly
that realized results of the business will fall in between the two most extreme
cases (the most and the least favorable).

To keep the analysis simple, analysts in general limit themselves to just three scenarios (optimistic, the most probable, and pessimistic). Therefore, uncertainty can effectively be depicted by means of a triangular distribution.

In the case of public utilities, the gap between scenarios is generally quite small; in other industries, the gap can significantly widen. Generally speaking, the scenario expected in average conditions is also the most likely to happen. Exhibit 1.5 graphically depicts the point.

In the framework similar to Exhibit 1.5, it is not unusual for analysts to work out only the most probable scenario[5] with respect to cash flow projections.

High Uncertainty and Limited Flexibility Area B in Exhibit 1.4 identifies those situations in which information useful to assess the performance of a business is not available at the time of the valuation, and flexibility to manage unfavorable events or to improve favorable ones is very limited.

For example, a company in the waste management industry had assumed the construction of a new landfill in its business plan. The project kickoff, though, was under litigation with the environmental groups that opposed the project, despite the fact that set-aside for dumping was a part of a regional plan.

The legal experts had identified a negligible risk of abandoning the project.

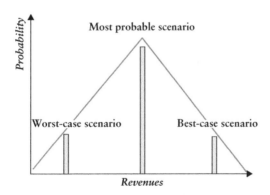

Exhibit 1.5 Moderate uncertainty scenario

---

[5]With asymmetric probability distributions, the most likely scenario is different from the expected scenario.

In similar situations, the following procedure could be adopted that has the merit of highlighting the risk profile of the venture:

■ Delineate the scenarios (in our case, accomplishment of the dumping or abandonment of the venture).
■ Calculate the net present value for each of the scenarios.

The procedure described has unquestionable effectiveness in terms of information transparency: it avoids the assessment of an "average" result (the mathematical average of two different scenarios) because this "average" event cannot, by definition, take place.

An example can clarify the idea. The existing landfill can generate returns equal to 400 per year, in the most probable scenario. The construction of the new facility can generate additional returns of 1,200. The total expected returns if the project is completed are therefore 1,600. Yet, the probability of making the second facility is 50 percent. Exhibit 1.6 depicts the situation.

One can see that the representation is very different than that presented in Exhibit 1.5. In this case, the uncertainty framework is closer to a coin toss: as a matter of fact, either you get the favorable scenario or the unfavorable one.

In valuating businesses, similar situations are rather frequent and involve:

■ The valuation of start-ups, of ventures in the initial phases of their life cycle, and of innovative businesses
■ The valuations with specific risk characters (e.g., license or contract renewals, environmental risks, strategic supplier dependence, high customer concentration, dependence on key persons)

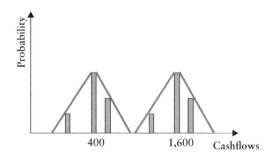

Exhibit 1.6   High uncertainty scenario

High Uncertainty and Flexibility Area C in Exhibit 1.4 depicts situations in which high uncertainty is accompanied by a wide range of managerial choices, which can, consequently, open new scenarios (in other words, some scenarios are extremely management decisions–related, decisions that can be the response to alternative scenarios).

Going back to the public utilities case, many analysts have approached the valuation of energy distribution firms by estimating the value of the growth opportunities offered by the option of using the commercial network to offer different services to the final users.

Given the uncertainty associated with such initiatives, it is reasonable to assume that a multiservice business model can be developed using a step-by-step process: the firm can, in an early stage, offer just services related to the core business (e.g., combine the energy distribution with the sale activities, installation and maintenance of home appliances), to further expand into a wider range of services in case of success of the *trial phase* (in-house insurance, consumer credit services, etc.).

Average Uncertainty and Flexibility In Area D in Exhibit 1.4 fall the situations that form the background of an evaluation: the scenarios can be credibly delineated and it is likely that management can take the necessary steps or seize the opportunity offered by change.

With regard to the situations referred to in Area C of Exhibit 1.4, change does not arise as a disruptive and intermittent phenomenon, but can lead back to the observable dynamics of the present.

As an example, in the valuation analysis of an important business in the spirit industry, the team doing the business analysis had described two scenarios. The first assumed decreasing sale volumes, consistently with the life cycle of a mature industry as observed in other firms within the same industry. The second one assumed instead, due to the strong brand value, a constant sale volume not affected by the general trend in the industry.

Given the notoriety of the brand and the strength of the commercial network of the business, it was unlikely to assume that management would have reacted passively to a reduction in sales. More realistically, it would have differentiated the products between the traditional ones and the new ones ("white" spirits, etc.).

Therefore, considering the operational flexibility permitted by the strength of the brand, the unfavorable scenario was modified assuming, after an initial decrease in sales, a return to the original levels with slightly lower margins given the increase in advertising costs.

The example shows a typical process of financial analysts, which translates into an upgrading of expectations in comparison to the industry due to the strength points of the business that confirm the hypothesis that the management can effectively react to unfavorable market conditions.

Obviously, the opposite reasoning also holds: when the firm under valuation is weaker than competitors, the average industry expectations can be modified and generate worse scenarios.

Growth opportunities for firm Alpha can also fall in Area D of Exhibit 1.4. Entering the business of packaging for cosmetic products and offering new services to pharmaceutical companies are a natural evolution of the core business of Alpha. Alpha has in fact adequate technological and managerial resources to sustain growth in those businesses which are similar to the niche in which it already has a leadership position.

1.5.2 Some Conclusions on Uncertainty and Managerial Flexibility

The approach outlined in the previous paragraph departs from traditional analysis since it tries to contemplate whether, with different scenarios, the firm's business model can be adapted to new assumptions and what those assumptions imply in terms of the creation of value.

From a historical standpoint, the first attempts to assess managerial flexibility, when future opportunities in the evolution of a business exist, have concerned themselves with R&D investments, brand and patent acquisition, development of new technologies, and the research and exploitation of natural resources. These attempts assume as a starting point the explicit representation of a firm's results as a consequence of managerial decisions expected to be taken in the future. Generally speaking, these methodologies today fall into the field of so-called real option valuation (ROV).[6]

---

[6]For introductory reading on applications of real options in capital budgeting and investment policies, see Chapters 1 and 2 of A. Dixit, R. Pindyck, *Investments under Uncertainty* (Princeton, NJ: Princeton University Press, 1994), and W. C. Kester, "Today's Options for Tomorrow's Growth," *Harvard Business Review*, 60 (1984): 153–160. For an in-depth presentation of the real option applications, see L. Trigeorgis, E. S. Schwartz, *Real Options and Investment under Uncertainty: Classical Readings and Recent Contributions* (Cambridge: The MIT Press, 2001); N. Kulatilaka, M. Amram, *Real Option: Managing Strategic Investment in an Uncertain World* (Boston: Harvard Business School Press, 1999); T. Copeland, V. Antikarov, *Real Options: a Practitioner's Guide* (Texere, 2001). Though the real option approach is extremely insightful in terms of the logic underlying investment decisions, its real-world applications are limited; therefore this book will not cover the real option issue.

In this framework, the value of a project is just the sum of two elements:

$$\text{PROJECT VALUE} = \frac{\text{Base value in a}}{\text{static framework}} + \frac{\text{Value generated by new}}{\text{choices and opportunities}}$$

1.5.3 Valuing Companies Assuming a Dynamic Standpoint

The dynamic approach was first used in valuations of Internet companies and Internet stocks.

Looking at the background in which the so-called *new economy*–related ventures originated at the end of the nineties, we can identify the typical characteristics referable to area C of Exhibit 1.4:

- The operators' expectations assumed strong growth in the market.
- A high degree of uncertainty characterized the assumptions about Internet users' behavior and technological evolution.
- Entry barriers on the market were modest: Internet companies could have adapted the business model to eventual shifts.

After the radical U-turn in scenarios and expectations with respect to high-tech stocks, in the first half of 2000, the dynamic valuation models have been harshly criticized. Despite many excesses, the euphoria that drove markets and the analysts has left us an important contribution: the models adopted and the debate that followed have brought attention, also out of the academic studies, to the fact that managerial flexibility can be an appreciable factor in the valuation of businesses and acquisitions, and not only in well-defined investment niches (R&D, natural resources search and development, etc.). On the practical side, the key issue of the dynamic approach is the need for restricting the analysis only to the credible development of a business model.

1.6 RELATIONSHIP BETWEEN VALUE AND UNCERTAINTY

The basis for the determination of the cash flow that best represents the future expected performance of the business lies in the analysis of the risk profile of the business itself. This section aims at classifying some typical situations of uncertainty, and at representing the cash flows that best describe them. Exhibit 1.7 provides us with a general initial reference framework, which by the way proves useful in multiple valuation settings as well by enabling the expert to carry out a more refined comparability assessment.

Exhibit 1.7   Risk profiles and cash flows modeling

Risk profile	Cash Flow Modelling	How to Structure the Valuation
Stable business model and continuity of the corporate strategy Risks are mostly related to the whole economy/market	Single dominant likely scenario	Valuation "as is": standard DCF valuation
Relevant changes of the business model/strategy are expected Risks are mostly related to firm-specific factors	Multiple scenarios	Scenario analysis valuation: average (weighted using scenarios' probabilities) value in each scenario
Managerial real options are embedded in the expected strategy	Event tree Decision tree	Decision Tree Approach (DTA) or Real Option Valoation (ROV) approach

Exhibit 1.7 shows how valuations of businesses whose financial results are driven mainly by market factors or macroeconomic parameters are based generally on a single cash flow profile, referring to the scenario that management deems the most likely one ("management scenario").

These valuations yield accurate results only when the distribution of expected results is symmetric. This condition is satisfied, for example, when the relevant risk factors depict a continuous distribution. Furthermore, it should be noted that such cash flow representation type requires historical data be both available and reliable. When there are multiple risk factors, the traditional representation centered on the management scenario may lead to undesired informational gaps.

Simulation techniques, like for instance the Monte Carlo, may in these cases improve the informational quality through the use of numerous combinations of the risk factors, yielding different expected results and different related results and valuations.

A second case is represented by the businesses subjected to idiosyncratic risks, which by their own nature are characterized by discrete (and at an extreme binary) outcomes distribution (e.g., businesses whose activity is based on the renewal of a concession). In these situations, the informational quality increases by projecting a cash flow pattern in each of the major scenarios that could take place. In practice, a final valuation can be obtained by weighting the valuations obtained in the different scenarios. As said, it is worth stressing the fact that this proceeding is sensible in those situations when risks have discrete distributions. Otherwise, the applicable case turns back to scenario A, which envisages the representation of the cash flow profile of only the most likely scenario.

For some businesses (case C of Exhibit 1.7), which are typically articulated along distinct sequential phases, risks depict a sequential structure in that value creation process is subordinated to the successful crossing of some key critical steps in the project life. This is the case, for instance, of some pharmaceutical businesses, or of the projects subjected to articulated authorization itinera (e.g., wind farms). In such situations, cash flow profiles linked to the business can be analyzed through the techniques of the event trees and of the decision trees. These techniques to deal with uncertainty have the advantage to highlight the key critical aspects in the formation of the value of a project along its life. Typically, during the initial phases idiosyncratic risks are the prevailing ones, and they can determine the survival or abandonment of an initiative. Once the uncertainty surrounding the first phases of the life cycle of an initiative has been solved, systemic (market) risk factors tend to emerge.

Such analyses on the risk profiles have important consequences on the choices regarding the determination of which is the most appropriate discount rate to be applied. Indeed, if the dominant risk is an idiosyncratic one, the risk-free rate can be used assuming a Capital Asset Pricing Model framework (Chapter 8). In the opposite case, some more complex techniques deriving from the valuation models of financial option should be used.

CHAPTER 2

Business Forecasting for Valuation

2.1 INTRODUCTION

The business plan is the document that represents both the management strategies and the results that management expects from their implementation. As a consequence, analysts carrying out the valuation should always include the business plan in their valuation report. When the business plan is provided by the company itself (or by its advisors), a careful assessment—from both a qualitative and quantitative point of view—is a phase of paramount importance within the valuation process. Bearing this in mind, we devote this chapter to illustrate, by means of several examples, three aspects:

- The key phases of any business plan preparation
- The structure of the business plan as a function of the nature and the features of the activities carried out by the company
- The main practical issues arising when preparing or assessing a business plan.

2.2 KEY PHASES OF THE BUSINESS PLAN ELABORATION

Business plan preparation consists of several interrelated phases:

- Thorough analysis of the company features, of the market(s) it competes in, of its positioning within such market(s), and of the past performance achieved

- Definition of the precise competitive strategies that the management is expected to pursue the future
- Definition of the actions that need to be implemented to pursue those competitive strategies
- Definition of the quantitative assumptions underpinning the forecast income statement, balance sheet, and cash flow statement
- Preparation of the forecast income statement, balance sheet, and cash flow statement

2.2.1   Markets, Competitive Positioning, and Past Results

In order to prepare accurate and reliable forecasts, it is necessary to deeply understand and analyze the markets the company is operating in.

The articulation and the complexity of the analysis to be carried out are a function of several variables, including the number of business segments the company operates. The following cases are indeed possible:

- The company operates in unrelated businesses (e.g., the case of the so called "holding companies");
- The company operates in different geographical markets. In case such markets differ because of nature and intensity of the competition, it is advisable to carry out in depth analyses for each of them.
- The business unit(s) targets different distribution channels (e.g., the company sells its products through both its proprietary website and a network of retail stores)
- Hybrid situations that mix the cases above.

2.2.2   Definition of the Competitive Strategies

The definition of the competitive strategies expected to implemented by the company over the business plan horizon is certainly a key aspect.

If the company operates in different sectors, the competitive strategies should be prepared both at the overall company level and at any single business unit level.

Competitive Strategies at Company Level   The definition of competitive strategies at the company level should include the following aspects:

- *The sectors in which the company is expected to operate in.* This element impacts on:
  - Shutting down or divesting business units

- Planning the entry in new segments/sectors (if appropriate via extraordinary corporate transactions such as M&A or joint ventures)

■ *The legal structure to adopt.* Some possible choices are:

- Comprehensive unique legal entity embedding all the operations regardless of the nature of the businesses
- Creation of a holding with coordination and headquarters functions; such parent company would own (entirely or partially) subsidiaries running the different business the company operates in
- Mixed structure where the parent company runs some operating activities and runs other activities via legally independent subsidiaries and

■ *The best way to get and structure financing.* Companies may decide, for example, to finance their growth by going public listing their shares on a stock exchange, opening their capital and raising primary proceeds that will be invested to carry out the growth plans. In the case of large corporations, there might be an "internal capital market" that provides financing for new business/projects via cash pooling arrangements with the subsidiaries. In general, companies can choose from these alternatives:

- Render the legal subsidiaries financially autonomous from the parent company, with the consequence that each subsidiary is free to arrange and procure autonomous financing on the private and public markets in the way it prefers.
- Manage the raising of financing at holding level, redistributing it through the group entities by means of intragroup loans.
- Use a mix of the two above.

■ *The tax strategy at corporate level.* For instance:

- Assessment of the opportunity to consolidate the fiscal incomes generated by the different legal subsidiaries.
- Definition of the transfer pricing policies (this is the most common choice of multinational corporations).

■ *The investment and management strategy of the corporate intangible assets.* For instance, the intangible assets could be:

- Controlled by the single legal entities that have developed or bought it.
- Concentrated in a unique legal entity created ad-hoc to develop, maintain, and protect the overall company intangible assets stock in

the best possible way. The other legal entities of the group can use the intangible assets legally owned by the above entity by means of license agreements.

■ *The role of the corporate structure.*

Exhibit 2.1 shows the structure of Alfa, a company controlling subsidiaries operating in the three following business sectors:

- ■ IT and media solutions: high-tech services for the sharing and broadcasting of events
- ■ Post-production and animation: digital content and graphical effects production for the cinema, television, and media advertising markets
- ■ Events media technology: planning and realization services for arts and exposition events

Exhibit 2.1   Competitive strategy at corporate level

Company	Strategy	Business Units	Business Plan Objectives
One Inc. Two Inc.	Grow	Post-production and Animation (One Inc.) IT & Media Solutions (Two Inc.)	Maximize portfolio value by expanding internationally and by innovating business models. Achieve the full potential over the business plan period.
Three Inc. Four Inc.	Maintain	Events media technology (Three Inc.) Post-production & Animation (Four Inc.)	Restructure the companies with low operational performance with the aim to: Bring them back to stand-alone profitability. Increase their attractiveness for their potential future sell down.
Five Inc. Six Inc. Seven Inc.	Sell	Events Media Technology (Five Inc.) Post-production (Six Inc.) Digital Content (Seven Inc.)	Get rid of the operational risk. Minimize the financial burden.

Exhibit 2.1 shows the strategies of Alfa Inc. management for the main businesses of the company.

Competitive Strategies at the Single Business Unit Level The main competitive strategies that can translated in business plan objectives consist of decisions regarding:

- The geographical markets where to sell company's products.
- The geographical markets to establish directly owned operations versus creating partnerships with independent local players.
- The competitive positioning to follow in the chosen market(s). As such, it is necessary to identify with precision:
  - Clients' needs to address
  - Type of reference client
  - Product/service to be offered
  - Price policy
- The distribution channel(s) to use.
- The nature of the business activity the company operates into. In this respect, the management may deem it necessary to implement the following measures:
  - Supply chain integration at the top/at the bottom of the chain. In other words, the company could decide to internalize and manage directly some activities or steps previously outsourced to suppliers, distributors, agents, and others.
  - Outsource some activities previously internalized in the company processes.
- The places in which to physically operate. Management could take these measures:
  - Start delocalization process, with the consequence that a portion of the activities is transferred to other production sites.
  - Develop new manufacturing plants/production sites.
  - Shut down some previously operating manufacturing plants/production sites.

Exhibits 2.2 and 2.3 show the competitive strategy studied by Alfa management with respect to, in particular, the "IT and media solutions" sector.

Exhibit 2.2 Competitive strategy at the single business activity level (the Alfa case, 1st part)

Business Model As Is	New Business Model
Based on **direct sales** of highly specialized and customized solutions, with a pricing model based on deployed human resources (FTE)	Add to the solutions already offered some standardized products that can be customized with low costs, with a pricing model based on licensing

Main Cons:	Main Pros:
1. High client risk: 70% of current revenue derives from the two major clients. 2. Saturation of traditional clients: limited margin for additional up-selling. 3. Profitability reduction: technological maturity reached by major clients and pressure on prices, driven by harsh competition.	1. Broaden the client base: consolidation by year t3 of a client portfolio in which no client accounts for more than 30% of total revenue. 2. Revenue growth: standardized products make it easier to approach new clients with offers scalable and easily adaptable to each client size needs and budget. 3. Maintain profitability in the long run.

2.2.3 Definition of the Actions Needed to Implement the Competitive Strategy

Once having defined the competitive strategies both at company and at single business activities level, it is then needed to focus on the actions needed in practice to implement them. For instance, let's hypothesize that the company management has opted to implement an internationalization strategy. In this case, the business plan will very likely envisage the opening of new branches, manufacturing plants, and so on in loco in those markets identified for the expansion. As a second example, let's assume the management has decided, in particular, to implement a cost-cutting program aimed at increasing the company profitability. In this example, the business plan could envisage, inter alia:

- Specific actions aimed at cutting labor costs (personnel cutting, delocalization of the production activity, etc.)
- Outsourcing of specific activities previously handled in-house
- Reengineering of the production process

Exhibit 2.3 Competitive strategy at the single business activity level (the Alfa case, 2nd part)

Key Strategic Guidelines in the Short Term	Key Strategic Guidelines in the Medium/Long Term

■ Opening of commercial branches in high-potential markets based on an opportunistic approach
■ Developing partnerships to explore new models of Go-to-Market in the short run
■ Completing the offer of online products
■ Taking part in potential auctions by client Gamma to secure more funding to the projects
■ Maximization of commercial opportunities deriving from the contacts and the references cumulated over the past projects
	■ Keep the relationship with the strongest traditional clients Gamma and Beta, which can ensure superior profitability, visibility in the market, and technological development
	■ Introduction of a new business model by means of:
	  ■ New commercial approach
	  ■ Evolution of product offer across the three business lines
	■ The new commercial approach is based on:
	  ■ Opening of branches in high-potential geographies to develop directly the major regional markets by focusing on high-profitability clients
	  ■ Adoption of new models of Go-to-Market (JVs, partnerships, models of indirect sale) to approach low-potential areas and less-profitable segments
	■ The evolution of these offers is based on:
	  ■ The realization of a new value proposition based on proprietary products (which can be integrated if needed to ensure the continued offer of complex solutions)
	  ■ Standardization of the production process, necessary in the product management activity

Each of these actions should be coupled with, at least, the following prescriptions:

■ Clear objectives that should be pursued
■ Impacts on income statement, balance sheet, and cash flow statement

- Expected realization timing
- The project manager responsible
- The potential problems linked with the implementation

The credibility of a business plan largely depends on how clearly the mapping of the actions to implement is set out from the very outset. Indeed, absent precise indications around the actions needed to implement the decided competitive strategy, the latter is jeopardized.

Exhibit 2.4 has been extrapolated from the business plan of Beta a company operating in the production and commercialization of luxury goods, whose management has decided to undergo an internationalization process. The exhibit shows, in particular, the detailed plan underpinning the opening of the new stores (both direct points of sale and stores in franchise), as hypothesized by the management. The schedule provides for each new store:

- The moment when raising of the financing needed for the setup of the new store activities is expected
- The moment when opening to public is expected

2.2.4 The Formulation of the Quantitative Assumptions

The output of the planning activity is represented by the income statement, balance sheet, and cash flow statement forecasts, which synthesize the outcome expected by the implementation of the competitive strategy set

#	Activity	t1				t2				t3			
		Q1	Q2	Q3	Q4	Q1	Q2	Q3	Q4	Q1	Q2	Q3	Q4
1	Store opening in NYC		■		▧								
2	WC financing	■	▧	▧	■								
3	Franchising store in Abu Dhabi			■									
4	Franchising store in China			■									
5	Store opening in Sao Paulo					■		▧					
6	Store opening in Macao							■	▧				
7	Franchising store in Dubai								■				
8	Franchising store in Russia								■				
9	Franchising store in China									■	▧		

Legend: ■ Fundraising   ▧ Kickoff activity

Exhibit 2.4 Definition of the necessary actions to implement the strategy (the Beta case)

up by the company management. Having said this, it is also worth noting that the development of such forecasts is based on a series of quantitative assumptions. The breadth of this in turn depends on the complexity inherent to the company for which the business plan has been prepared. As such, if the company operates in several business activities, the following should be defined:

- Macroeconomic assumptions which have to be formulated by distinguishing the different geographical areas where the company operates, and which concern in particular:
  - GDP real growth rates
  - Inflation rates
  - Exchange rates
  - Interest rates
- Assumptions on the business activity, concerning in particular the evolution of:
  - Revenues
  - Costs
  - Working capital
  - Capital expenditures
- Assumptions at the corporate level:
  - The evolution of the corporate costs structure
  - Financial management policy:
    - Financing costs
    - Raising/reimbursement of financings
    - Equity injections
    - Dividend distributions
- Fiscal policy
- The management of noncore (surplus assets) corporate activities

It is worth noting that:

- Assumptions shall be coherent with the competitive strategies formulated by the company management, as well as with the actual precise actions envisaged to implement the plan.
- Assumptions shall be coherent among each other. As a consequence, hypotheses on financing costs shall be in line with the forecasts on the interest rates evolution.
- All the assumptions shall be explicitly reported and, if possible, corroborated by independent data and supporting materials.

Exhibit 2.5 shows the business plan of Gamma, a company operating in the advertising industry. It shows the assumptions formulated by the

Exhibit 2.5 The definition of the quantitative assumptions (the Gamma case)

Market Stake	t-1	t0	t1	t2	t3	t4	t5
Traditional channel	12.8%	10.9%	9.6%	10.4%	12.9%	18.2%	22.5%
Online channel	17.4%	13.2%	10.4%	8.7%	8.4%	9.0%	9.3%

company management around the evolution of its market share with separate estimates for the off-line and on-line distribution channels.

2.2.5 Preparation of the Plan Forecasts

The last phase of the planning activity is represented by preparation of the forecasts for the income statement, balance sheet, and cash flow statement, which give a condensed representation of management's expected results on the back of the implementation of the chosen and pursued competitive strategies. When the company operates in multiple sectors of activity, it is necessary to take two steps:

1. Develop the forecasts for the income statement, balance sheet, and cash flow statement for:
   - Each business sector in which the company operates
   - The corporate headquarters
2. Integrate these prospects so as to give a holistic representation of the results expected.

2.3 WHAT DRIVES THE PREPARATION OF A BUSINESS PLAN?

In the previous sections we have gone through the main phases making up the activity of business plan preparation, which are common to all the business plan types. This, however, does not also imply that the logic and standpoint to be assumed when preparing the business plan are always the same. Actually, they vary in function of the nature and type of business activity carried out by the company.

Previously, we have represented the key areas of attention to consider with regard to the above aspect. Precisely, we have highlighted the necessity, in the case of companies operating in multiple businesses, to:

- Define the following:
  - Competitive strategies
  - Actions to carry out to implement the above strategies

- Quantitative assumptions necessary to develop the plan's forecasts (both at corporate and business unit level)
- Develop the forecasts for the income statement, balance sheet, and cash flow statement, with regard to:
  - Each business unit/activity
  - The corporate structure
  - The company as a whole

Bearing this in mind, over the next paragraphs we will focus on the logics and rationale that should underpin the business plan formulation and that are a function of the very nature of the company's business activity. In particular, we will distinguish among:

- Companies producing standardized goods on a large scale
- Commercial companies operating through a network of points of sale
- Companies working on order
- Companies operating in regulated sectors

For each of these categories we will present a case to show the most appropriate mechanics that should underpin the business plan preparation.

2.3.1   A Components Manufacturer

Company Delta operates in the mechanical components manufacturing sector, marketed to several end applications. The manufacturing activity is carried out in two plants, employing about 600 employees. The main geography to market the products is the national one. Its clients are industrial and distribution companies.

The company commercializes its products through agents. In order to define its competitive strategies, Delta has recently carried out some research aimed at detecting the key factors driving its clients' purchasing behavior. This study has shown that the following factors are the most important ones:

- Delivery speed (almost as much as punctuality)
- Price, above all in the cases of standardized products used for pretty straightforward applications
- Possibility to receive consulting services and assistance both prior to and after the purchase

The following paragraphs will analyze the main hypotheses formulated by Delta management to develop its plan (which spans a time horizon of five years).

Assumptions on Revenues Taking into account the activity carried out by Delta:

- Expected revenue forecast in t1, t2, and t3 has been quantified on the basis of the forecasts of:
  - Revenue volume and market price in the reference market, developed by some leading research provider companies
  - Delta market share
  - Revenue associated with the main clients (based on the commercial reviews carried out for the principal clients at the end of t0)
- Expected revenue has been obtained as the sum of:
  - Revenue as is: defined on a client-by-client basis, assuming that execution of the business plan commercial actions does not take place.
  - Additional revenue from new commercial activities: they concern both the old and the new (expected) clients, and are based on the expectations of Delta management around the effects of the implementation of the business plan (new applications, improvement of existing products, etc.). The quantum of this improvement has been estimated also based on the probability of success of the new commercial activities displayed in Exhibit 2.6.
- Revenues expected in t_4 and t_5 have been calculated based on the forecast for the volumes and prices in the reference market in the medium/long term.

Exhibits 2.7, 2.8, and 2.9 represent, for each category product, the expected evolution in sales volumes, unitary prices, and revenues.

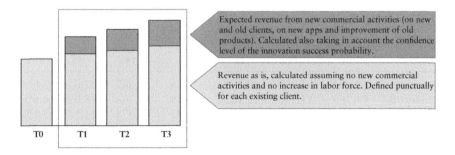

Expected revenue from new commercial activities (on new and old clients, on new apps and improvement of old products). Calculated also taking in account the confidence level of the innovation success probability.

Revenue as is, calculated assuming no new commercial activities and no increase in labor force. Defined punctually for each existing client.

Exhibit 2.6 Revenues as is vs. additional revenue from new commercial activities

Exhibit 2.7   Evolution in sales volumes (€)

Products	t0	t1	t2	t3	t4	t5	Cagr t0–t5
Product A	631,652	667,701	707,732	740,317	784,196	795,959	4.7%
Product B	79,687	82,703	87,127	91,455	96,444	97,891	4.2%
Product C	21,501	22,703	23,834	24,853	26,134	26,526	4.3%
Product D	2,694	2,837	2,990	3,085	3,276	3,326	4.3%
Product E	39,662	40,888	42,986	44,796	47,075	47,781	3.8%
Product F	172,512	182,462	191,921	199,933	211,234	214,403	4.4%
Product G	1,985,304	2,135,176	2,251,251	2,365,162	2,496,959	2,534,413	5.0%
Total	2,933,012	3,134,470	3,307,841	3,469,601	3,665,318	3,720,299	4.9%

Exhibit 2.8   Evolution in unitary prices (€)

Products	t0	t1	t2	t3	t4	t5	Cagr t0–t5
Product A	83.9	85.4	85.2	85.1	85.0	85.0	0.3%
Product B	180.3	185.1	184.8	184.3	184.2	184.2	0.4%
Product C	404.5	417.9	418.3	419.5	419.9	419.9	0.8%
Product D	429.1	434.5	433.7	435.2	433.2	433.2	0.2%
Product E	252.3	257.3	257.2	257.7	257.3	257.3	0.4%
Product F	67.3	69.3	69.4	69.3	69.4	69.4	0.6%
Product G	7.6	7.8	7.8	7.7	7.7	7.7	0.5%

Exhibit 2.9   Evolution in revenues (€)

Products	t0	t1	t2	t3	t4	t5	Cagr t0–t5
Product A	52,967	57,027	60,301	63,018	66,647	67,646	5.0%
Product B	14,369	15,305	16,102	16,859	17,768	18,034	4.6%
Product C	8,696	9,487	9,969	10,425	10,973	11,138	5.1%
Product D	1,156	1,233	1,297	1,343	1,419	1,441	4.5%
Product E	10,007	10,521	11,056	11,545	12,113	12,295	4.2%
Product F	11,603	12,642	13,310	13,851	14,662	14,882	5.1%
Product G	15,025	16,570	17,456	18,315	19,350	19,640	5.5%
Total	113,824	122,784	129,491	135,356	142,932	145,076	5.0%

Assumptions on Industrial Costs In the business planning process, Delta management has identified two types of industrial costs: variable costs and fixed costs.

Variable costs are linked to the industrial activity and can be ascribed, in particular, to:

- Raw materials
- Outsourced production
- Transportation
- Energy
- Direct labor costs

Variable costs account for over 70 percent of total operating costs each year (excluding the D&A), and have been quantified:

- Based on the expected production volumes for each product category (formulated to calculate the expected revenue as well)
- On a single product basis
- On the back of forecasts on the unitary cost for each production factor (cost per kilogram of raw material, cost per single manufacture, hourly cost for direct labor, etc.) (Exhibit 2.10)

Fixed costs can be mainly ascribed to:

- Indirect labor costs
- Services
- Maintenance
- Waste management

The above costs have been forecast by adopting different logics and drivers than the ones used to determine variable costs:

- Indirect labor costs have been quantified based on the forecasts on number of employees and unitary average cost per employee.

Exhibit 2.10 Evolution in the unitary cost for each production factor

	t1	t2	t3	t4	t5
Raw materials	0.0%	0.0%	1.0%	1.0%	1.0%
Manufacturing	0.0%	0.0%	0.0%	0.5%	0.5%
Transportation	0.0%	0.0%	0.0%	0.5%	0.5%
Energy	1.0%	1.0%	1.0%	1.0%	1.0%
Direct labor	2.0%	2.0%	2.0%	2.0%	2.0%
Other	0.5%	0.5%	0.5%	0.5%	0.5%

- Costs for external services and maintenance costs have been set equal to a percentage of the revenues.
- Waste management costs have been assumed to grow at a yearly rate equal to expected inflation factor.

Overall, fixed costs do represent approximately 30 percent of total operating costs (excluded D&A) over the forecast years.

Assumptions on the Commercial Costs   In the business planning process, Delta management has also identified variable and fixed commercial costs.
Variable costs are made up by:

- Transportation
- Agency services

These have been estimated based on the hypotheses used to forecast the sales.
Fixed costs can be ascribed to:

- Inventory management
- Commercial area employees

Personnel cost has been quantified on the back of the forecasts for:

- Employees number
- Average mean cost per employee

The other costs, instead, have been assumed to grow each year at the expected inflation rate.
Overall, commercial costs amount to about 7 percent of revenue, for each year over the business plan period. Fixed costs represent more than 80 percent of commercial costs.

Assumptions on the Working Capital   Delta net invested capital is for the major part represented by working capital, defined as the algebraic sum of trade credits and inventory, net of trade debts. Over the business plan period:

- Trade credits have been quantified based on the average days sale outstanding.
- Trade debts have been quantified based on the average days payable outstanding.
- Inventory stock has been quantified based on the average days worth of inventory (Exhibit 2.11).

Exhibit 2.11 Hypotheses underlying trade credit, trade debts, and inventory

	t0	t1	t2	t3	t4	t5	Cagr t0–t5
Days sales outstanding	120	118	115	115	115	115	−0.8%
Days payable outstanding	115	115	115	115	115	115	0.0%
Days worth of inventory	130	125	120	120	120	120	−1.6%

Conclusions Delta case shows us some general rules applicable to business planning for industrial companies manufacturing standardized products:

- Usually, planning process starts from the forecasts on sales volume and market prices evolution, developed by independent third parties (like research institutes and the like). Management assumptions are instead the ones about:
  - Company market share
  - Revenue streams linked to the major clients

It is then good practice to estimate analytically the effects (on the market share, sales volumes, and prices) deriving from the competitive strategies that management wants to pursue over the business plan period:

- The major portion of the operating costs is represented by the industrial costs, whose quantification is driven in particular by the hypotheses on:
  - Production volumes per product category (formulated to quantify the expected revenues)
  - Unitary cost per production factor
- Usually, another important component of the operating costs is represented by the commercial costs, which can be variable (transportation costs, agency costs, etc.) or fixed (inventory management costs, sales force costs, etc.).
- The relevance of the R&D costs is a function of the very products manufactured by the enterprise.
- The significance of the promotional activity costs is a function of the final client nature:
  - Generally speaking, if the product is marketed to the final consumer, it is necessary to heavily invest in promotional activities aimed at promoting the company product and direct final clients' purchasing choices to it.

- Conversely, if the product is marketed to another industrial company (this is the case of semi-finished products, or of manufacturing machinery), then the promotional activity financial burden will be minor.
- In general, industrial companies manufacturing standardized products do have relevant working capital stocks in their balance sheets. Usually:
  - Trade credits have been quantified based on the average days sale outstanding.
  - Trade debts have been quantified based on the average days payable outstanding.
  - Inventory stock has been quantified based on the average days worth of inventory.
- Capital expenditures (capex) are to be ascribed mainly to the industrial apparatus:
  - Maintenance capex, necessary to maintain the normal operations of the production apparatus, can be hampered by obsolescence.
  - Growth capex is aimed at upgrading the current manufacturing/production capabilities of the company PPE.

2.3.2 Commercial Companies Operating through a Network of Points of Sale

Zeta is a company distributing consumer electronics and white-goods products through a point-of-sale (173) network spread around the national territory. Main suppliers of Zeta are Samsung, LG, Sony, Apple, and Asus. The company manages logistics activities in a centralized way. Suppliers deliver the goods to the logistics center of Zeta, which in turn passes the received goods to the points of sale, based on the latter demands.

Promotional activity is managed partly by the central structure, which takes care, for instance, of the promotional campaigns with national diffusion, and partly of the single points of sale.

The following paragraphs will analyze the main hypotheses formulated by Zeta management to develop the company business plan (which spans a time horizon of five years).

Assumptions on Revenues Based on the activity performed by Zeta, the expected revenues over the business plan period have been quantified based on, in particular, the forecasts on:

- Commercial surface managed by the company, which is a function of the number and dimension of the points of sale. To this end, Zeta management has hypothesized:

- The closure of five points of sale (1 for each year of the business plan period) (Exhibit 2.12)
- The opening of 35 new points of sale (1 in t0, 4 in t1, 10 in t2, t3, t4, and t5) (Exhibit 2.12)
- The total managed surface to evolve, during the business plan period, from 282,061 square meters to about 325,561 square meters (Exhibit 2.13)
- Revenue per square meter for the managed surface. Zeta management has hypothesized that over the business plan horizon this KPI will evolve from €3,905 to €4,207 (Exhibit 2.14).

Exhibit 2.12 Evolution in the number of points of sale

	t0	t1	t2	t3	t4	t5
# of points of sale—BoP	172	173	176	185	191	197
# of points of sale closed		1	1	1	1	1
# of points of sale opened	1	4	10	7	7	7
# of points of sale—EoP	173	176	185	191	197	203

Exhibit 2.13 Evolution of managed commercial surface

	t0	t1	t2	t3	t4	t5
Managed commercial surface—BoP	280,561	282,061	286,261	299,461	308,161	316,861
Managed commercial surface—sqm closed		1,800	1,800	1,800	1,800	1,800
	1,500	6,000	15,000	10,500	10,500	10,500
Managed commercial surface—EoP	282,061	286,261	299,461	308,161	316,861	325,561

Exhibit 2.14 Evolution in revenue per square meter for the managed surface (€)

	t0	t1	t2	t3	t4	t5
Revenue per square meter	3,905	4,176	4,135	4,183	4,195	4,207

This dynamic is underpinned by the following:

- The expected competition level in the reference market is likely.
- The number of points of sale will change. In this respect, it is worth noting that:
  - Revenues per square meter of the points of sale for which closure is foreseen are far less than the average ones for Zeta points of sale.
  - Start-up phase of a new point of sale lasts about 1 year.
- Based on Zeta management experience, after a refurbishing intervention, the revenue per square meter KPI generally rises. In this business plan, the management has assumed that it will carry out renovation of 20 points of sale per year over the business plan horizon.
- Zeta has decided to undertake new promotional/commercial activities over the horizon plan.

Assumptions on the Contribution Margin As described, Zeta carries out a pure commercial activity by buying consumer electronics and white goods finished products from major international suppliers and reselling them through proprietary points-of-sale network for a profit. The contribution margin should be sufficient not only to outweigh the costs incurred in the business activity, but also to guarantee the desired rate of return on the capital invested in the business by the equity holders.

In this specific case, Zeta management expects over the business plan years a small contraction of the unitary average price per purchase from the suppliers. Accordingly, Zeta management has hypothesized the percentage contribution margin to expand over the business plan period (Exhibit 2.15).

As a direct consequence of the above, Zeta management expects the cost of goods sold to lie in the 71.5 to 71.7 percent (as a percentage of revenues) range.

In the business plan, the contribution margins for each of the business plan years have been constructed as the product between revenues and percentage contribution margin.

Exhibit 2.15 Evolution of the percentage contribution margin

	t0	t1	t2	t3	t4	t5
% Contribution Margin	28.2%	28.3%	28.4%	28.5%	28.5%	28.5%

Assumptions on Sales Force Employees Costs The major part of Zeta employees are engaged in the points of sale managed by the company and carry out commercial activities. As specified above, at the end of t0 Zeta managed as much as 173 points of sale. The sales force employees cost at t0 was €108 million (about 9.8 percent of revenues); over the business plan years it has been calculated as the algebraic sum of:

- Cost of sale force employees at t0, increase each year by 2.0 percent compound annual growth rate (CAGR)
- Additional cost of sale force employees deriving from opening of new points of sale
- Cost saving of sale force employees deriving from the closure of some points of sale

Assumptions on the Costs for the Location of the Points of Sale The number of points of sale managed by Zeta is expected to increase to 203 in t5. Points of sale are all rented, so that rental costs are a key item in Zeta's income statement. In t0, they amount to €58 million (5.2 percent of total revenues)—that is, about €205 per sqm.

Zeta management, taking into account the particular crisis currently afflicting the real estate market, believes the average rental cost per sqm can be squeezed down to €194 (Exhibit 2.16).

Assumptions on Promotional Activities Costs As said, Zeta promotional activities are managed by the central structure, which takes care of the advertising campaign with national reach and, partly, of the promotional campaigns at single points-of-sale level. In t0, Zeta has borne costs linked to promotional activities of €31 million (equal to about 2.8 percent of revenues).

For each year of the business plan, the promotional activities costs are calculated as the algebraic sum of:

- The costs of the promotional activities of t0, increase by 1 percent CAGR each year
- The additional costs deriving from the opening of new points of sale
- The cost saving from the closing of some old points of sale

Exhibit 2.16 Evolution of average rental cost per sqm

	t0	t1	t2	t3	t4	t5
Rental cost per sqm	205	203	196	196	195	194

Euro

Assumptions on the Logistics Management Cost   Zeta manages the logistics in a centralized way. As such, suppliers deliver their goods at the central logistics warehouse of Zeta, which in turn redistributes the goods to the points of sale. In t0, Zeta has borne logistics management costs of €62 million (5.6 percent of revenues).

For each year of the business plan the logistics management costs are calculated as the algebraic sum of:

* The costs of the logistics management of t0, increase by 2 percent CAGR each year
* The additional costs deriving from the opening of new points of sale
* The cost saving from the closing of some old points of sale

Assumptions on the Central Structure Costs   The activity of Zeta points of sale is coordinated in a centralized manner by the holding, which also manages, inter alia, the following activities:

* Purchase management
* Definition of the commercial strategy
* Business financial control
* Administration
* IT management

In exercise t0, central structure costs have been €21 million (equal to 1.9 percent of revenues). During the business planning, Zeta management has hypothesized that these costs grow by 2 percent CAGR each year.

Assumptions on Working Capital   At the end of t0, Zeta working capital is negative:

* Trade credits are practically zero, thanks to the very business activity of Zeta.
* Trade debts outweigh the value of inventory.

In preparing the business plan:

* Trade debts have been estimated based on the average days payable outstanding, which Zeta management estimates will decrease from 90 (t0) to 85 (t5).
* Inventory has been estimated based on the assumption that the company maintains about €850 of inventory for each commercial sqm managed.

Assumptions on the Capital Expenditures   The investments mainly relate to the points of sale. As anticipated, over the plan horizon, these are expected to evolve in number as an effect of management's opening and closing decisions. The capex envisaged in the plan relates to mainly three areas:

1. The maintenance capex necessary to guarantee the normal operations of the points of sale.
2. The growth capex aimed at improving some of the points of sale. As anticipated, Zeta management expects to renew 20 points of sale in each exercise.
3. The growth capex needed to open the new points of sale (35 in total over the plan, as explained above).

Conclusions This business case shows us some general rules applicable to the commercial companies selling goods through proprietary stores. Usually, the planning process starts from the forecasts on the evolution of the following:

- Commercial surface managed by the company, which is in turn a function of the number and dimension of the points of sale.
- Revenue per sq foot of managed commercial surface. In turn, this is forecast based on:
  - The expected evolution of the competition level among the different actors in the market.
  - The expected evolution of the number of the points of sale. For instance, the average revenues per sqm are positively influenced by the decision to close the points of sale underperforming versus the average. On the contrary, in the short run, they could be negatively affected by the decision to open some new points of sale, since the new points of sale can reach regime profitability only after a certain time lag (which depends on the industry features).
  - The frequency of the interventions aimed at renewing the points of sale. Generally speaking, after a renewal intervention, the average revenue per sqm soars.
  - The new commercial/promotional activities envisaged in the plan horizon.

The major part of the operating costs is represented by the costs incurred to purchase the finished goods to be sold in the point of sale. In general, their incidence (and their effect on the contribution margin) is a function of the forecasts on the evolution of average unitary prices paid to suppliers.

The other most relevant cost items attributable to the commercial activity are:

- *Sales force employees' costs*. For commercial companies operating through a points-of-sale network, most employees are engaged in the stores.

- *Rental costs.* These are factors when points of sale are not proprietary.
- *Promotional activity costs.* These consist of both advertising with local/national reach and initiatives carried out at the single point-of-sale level.
- *Logistics management costs.* Usually, suppliers deliver the finished goods to the central logistics warehousing of the commercial company, which in turn redistributes them to the different points of sale on the basis of their needs.
- *The points-of-sale activity is coordinated by a central entity/structure.* In the business planning phase, it is thereby necessary to carry out a series of forecasts also on the costs to run the central management structure.
- *Working capital available.* The nature of the business activity of commercial companies is such that working capital is usually very close to zero or even negative.
- *Capital expenditures.* Capex is mainly related to points of sale and is made up by three types:
  - Maintenance capex, necessary to guarantee the normal operations of the points of sale
  - Growth capex to better already existing points of sale
  - Growth capex to create new points of sale

2.3.3 Companies Operating on Order

Company Kappa activities are:

- The realization of feature animated movies in 3D
- The creation of new characters
- The development of the storyboards

Kappa activity is carried out by using digital technologies.

In general, each commission managed by the company is independent from the other ones the company is contemporarily working on. Duration of commissions is variable, and the most relevant ones can last as long as one year and more.

Lately, the reference business sector of Kappa has experienced solid growth, also thanks to the great monetary results achieved by the latest feature movies distributed on the market.

Kappa aims, over the next years, to do the following:

- Consolidate its positioning on the European market, within which it is among the major players.
- Increase its presence in the Canadian and U.S. markets.

The next paragraphs will offer an overview of the main assumption formulated by Kappa management to develop its business plan (which spans a three-year time horizon).

Assumptions on the Revenues Based on Kappa reference sector, revenues forecast have been developed on the basis of these expectations:

- *Revenues linked to already-earned orders.* Kappa has indeed a backlog of already-earned commissions, on which it is already working and already subjected to a final contract. Generally, the contracts signed by Kappa envisage fixed remuneration, whose payment is split in multiple tranches, based on the percentage of completion of the work. Moreover, the contracts precisely state the timeline of work completion status; as a consequence of this, there is usually a great visibility around both the quantum and the temporal distribution of revenues.
- *Revenues from the new orders under acquisition/auction.* In this respect, it is important to distinguish among:
  - *Orders for which negotiation with the counterparty is in already advanced phase.* In this case, there is good visibility around nature of the activity to carry out and quantum of the payments. In some cases, there can also be some commercial offers already submitted.
  - *Orders for which negotiation with the counterparty is in initial phase.* In these cases, the nature of the activity to carry out is known only partially, as is the compensation amount.
  - *Orders for which negotiation with the counterparty has not been initiated yet.* In these cases, both the activity type and the compensation amount are not visible at all, but can just be hypothesized.

    Clearly, the trustworthiness of the assumptions carried out on the revenues varies as a function of the commission under consideration: high in the first case above, very low in the third one. Expected revenues linked to future potential commissions have been weighted by the probability of winning the commissions.
- *Revenues from the orders that Kappa management thinks the company will win in the future.* This is based on its past experience and knowledge of market dynamics.

Exhibit 2.17 shows the composition of the revenues expected over the time horizon covered by the business plan.

Assumptions on the Direct Costs Kappa management has identified, in particular, three types of direct costs:

1. *Labor costs of internal staff:* specialized digital technicians working for Kappa under an exclusivity agreement

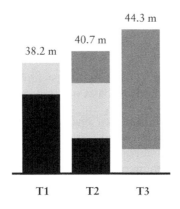

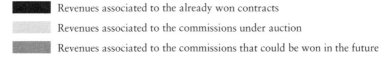

■ Revenues associated to the already won contracts
□ Revenues associated to the commissions under auction
■ Revenues associated to the commissions that could be won in the future

Exhibit 2.17   Expected revenues composition over business plan horizon

2. *Labor costs of external staff:* specialized digital technicians working for Kappa with no exclusivity obligations
3. *Services costs:* specialized activities that Kappa outsources to other companies

Having said this:

■ In the case of already-won orders, the company has carried out detailed costs budgeting activity and, as such, there is great visibility around the relevance of the expected costs and of their temporal distribution.
■ In the case of the orders under auction, the degree of precision of the estimated and, consequently, of their trustworthiness, is a function of how advanced the auction/negotiation with the counterparty is.
■ In the case of the orders that Kappa management believes the company will likely win, direct costs have been assumed equal to a fixed percentage of revenues (specifically, 70 percent).

Over the business plan years, the percentage incidence of direct costs over total revenues is equal to 68 percent (t1) and 70 percent (years t2 and t3).

Assumptions on Indirect Costs Kappa management has identified two types of indirect costs:

- Indirect personnel cost: employees taking care of the commercial activity, of the management of IT systems, of the day-by-day administration, etc.
- Structure costs

As anticipated, Kappa intends to expand geographically in the United States and Canada markets and this, based on management estimated, will translate into an increase of the commercial costs.

Assumptions on the Working Capital and on the Capex For Kappa, working capital has always been historically low. In particular, the inventory (represented by work-in-progress material for won commissions) has always been negligible. Bearing this in mind, over the business plan years the management has estimated:

- Trade credits based on average days receivable outstanding
- Trade debts based on average days payable outstanding

As anticipated, the activity is carried out by technicians specialized in digital techniques, who use IT systems and tools to perform their work. Accordingly, capex is made up by the investments for acquiring IT software and hardware materials.

Conclusions This business case provides us with some general rules, applicable to the case of companies operating on orders. In general, the panning process starts from the development of hypotheses around:

- The revenues associated with already-won orders, on which there is usually great visibility on both timing and size
- The revenues associated to orders under auction, for which estimates precision and trustworthiness is a direct function of how advanced is the negotiation between the parties
- The revenues from the orders that management is strongly inclined to believe, based on its past experience and knowledge of market dynamics, that the company will win in the future

The major part of the operating costs is represented by direct costs borne to complete the single orders. Obviously, the costs nature varies depending on the business activity of the company. In the case of company Kappa, specialized in the production of feature animated movies in 3D, direct costs are represented by the costs of the digital technicians. If we had analyzed a company operating in the naval construction sector, the nature of the direct costs to consider would have been totally different. Bearing this in mind:

- In the case of already-won orders, the company has carried out detailed costs budgeting activity and, as such, there is great visibility around the relevance of the expected costs and of their temporal distribution.
- In the case of the orders under auction, the degree of precision of the estimates and, consequently, of their trustworthiness, is a function of how advanced the auction/negotiation with the counterparty is.
- In the case of the orders that management believes the company will likely win, direct costs are usually assumed to be equal to a fixed percentage of the revenues.

The dimension and the dynamics of the working capital are a function of the sector in which the company for which the business plan is being prepared operates. In Kappa case, working capital has always been historically low. In particular, the inventory (represented by work-in-progress material for won commissions) has always been negligible. There are instead other sectors, like the naval construction one, where companies have to manage a commission process spanning a timeframe of multiple years, which implies the work-in-progress material and the working capital display very relevant sizes. Moreover, in this case the working capital depicts a nonlinear pattern as well, by steadily increasing during commission execution and sharply decreasing after completion.

Obviously, it is necessary to take into account these peculiarities during the business planning activity.

The capex size and dynamics as well depend on the sector where the company for which the plan is being prepared operates.

2.3.4 Companies Operating in Regulated Sectors

Company Sigma operates under a concession regime, with the current concession bound to contractually mature in t30. Based on the concession currently in place, Sigma manages a toll road system made up by three main roads: Road 1, Road 2, and Road 3.

When the current concession matures, Sigma will be forced to transfer the management of the toll road system back to the state authority responsible for it, with no monetary compensation for this.

Toll road tariffs applied by Sigma are determined based on a formula agreed on with the state authority. This formula is based on the following parameters:

- Capex spending—specifically, the bigger the capex, the higher the recognized tariff to Sigma
- Inflation rate

Over the first months of t1, Sigma management, as agreed with the State authority, has developed and presented to the latter a business plan, spanning the overall duration of the current concession (t30), which envisages:

- Powering interventions aimed at developing the infrastructure of roads 1 and 2
- €100m equity injection to fund growth
- €50m defiscalization measure

Based on the legal framework for toll roads currently in place in the state where Sigma operates, the business plan has been prepared in real terms. The following paragraphs will display the main assumptions underpinning the business plan.

Assumptions on Infrastructure Development In preparing the business plan, Sigma management made the following hypotheses:

- Total duration of the works: 4 years
- Total capex spent: €400 million
- Equity injection: €100 million
- Defiscalization measures: €50 million
- 30 percent of new infrastructure entering in operations in t2, with the remaining portion (70 percent) entering into operations in t4

Exhibit 2.18 shows the time distribution of capex and equity injection.

Exhibit 2.18 Time distribution of capex and equity injection

	t1	t2	t3	t4
Capex	100,000	120,000	130,000	50,000
Equity injection	25,000	25,000	25,000	25,000

Euro k

Assumptions on Revenues Revenues expected over the business plan time span have been estimated based on these expectations:

■ *Estimated traffic volumes.* Projections were arrived at with help from specialized market advisors, who have taken into consideration the expected effects stemming from the powering of roads 1 and 2 (Exhibit 2.19).
■ *Estimated tolls.* Sigma management has quantified, on the basis of the formula agreed on with the state authority, the expected future toll per km for each year, distinguishing among:
  ■ Light and heavy vehicles
  ■ The three roads managed

  Clearly, tolls evolution embeds the effects from the growth capex we have quoted before (Exhibit 2.20).

Hypotheses on the Toll Road Infrastructure Management Costs In the business planning process, Sigma management has identified primary typologies of costs that can be all condensed into the overall class of toll road infrastructure management costs:

■ Maintenance costs (excluding personnel costs): costs to maintain the efficiency and quality of road surface, machinery, safety systems, etc. Needed to ensure the normal business operations. In the business plan preparation, the management has distinguished among:

Exhibit 2.19 Traffic volume evolution (k km, for vehicle category)

	t1	t2	t3	t4	...	t29	t30
Light	2,451,894	2,497,380	2,511,420	2,566,661	...	2,716,847	2,733,896
Heavy	566,898	567,481	579,929	593,863	...	643,469	648,833
Total	3,018,792	3,064,860	3,091,348	3,160,525	...	3,360,316	3,382,729

Exhibit 2.20 Toll per km evolution

	t1	t2	t3	t4	...	t29	t30
Light	0.059224	0.063454	0.068113	0.072656	...	0.089054	0.089075
Heavy	0.095041	0.102002	0.109471	0.116604	...	0.143026	0.143069

Euro

- Costs related to already existing toll roads infrastructure (assumed to remain constant in real terms over the entire time span covered by the plan)
- Costs related to new assets to be realized in the context of the powering of roads 1 and 2
- Labor costs for the employees engaged in:
  - Toll collection
  - Security and safety
  - Maintenance

Labor costs have been forecast by carrying out assumptions on the:

- Number of employees
- Average cost per employee
- Services costs:
  - Bills for public utilities services (energy, water, etc.)
  - Collection costs

To prepare the business plan, Sigma management has hypothesized, in this respect, that:

- Collection costs evolve coherently with the increase in traffic volumes.
- Other services costs stay constant in real terms over the overall business plan time horizon.

Assumptions on D&A As anticipated, Sigma operates under a public concession (which will expire in t30). Afterward, the toll road infrastructure will need to be transferred back to the state authority with no remuneration envisaged for the termination. In light of this, D&A have been scheduled so book value of toll road assets at the end of the concession period gets to zero.

Assumptions on Taxes Business plan has been developed hypothesizing that Sigma will recognize a defiscalization tariff amounting to €50 million. This defiscalization tariff will take the form of a tax credit for Sigma, which will allow the company to not pay any taxes up to the above-mentioned cap of €50 million. Bearing this in mind, in the plan Sigma management has:

- Calculated the taxes expected based on the current legislation and absent any defiscalization measure
- Rectified afterward the above forecast to take into account the effects introduced by the defiscalization measure

Assumptions on Working Capital   The main items making up the working capital are:

- Trade credits and debts toward the companies managing the other toll roads concessions, arising from the fact that the toll roads managed by Sigma are interconnected to other ones
- Trade debts linked to the maintenance/development activity of the toll roads infrastructure

In the business plan:

- Commercial credits have been forecast based on receivable outstanding average days.
- Commercial debts have been forecast based on payable outstanding average days.

Conclusions   The previous paragraphs have analyzed the main hypotheses carried out to prepare the business plan of a toll road public concession. It is actually quite common to come across sectors that envisage, at least for some activities, the application of regulated tariffs:

- Transmission and dispatching of electrical energy
- Transportation of natural gas
- Storage and distribution of natural gas
- Supply of electrical energy, gas, and water
- Public transportation
- Telecommunications

The determination and formulas for the tariffs vary depending on the country of operations and the sector under consideration, but their forecast is the pivotal point in the business planning processes for any company operating in sectors with regulated tariffs. In this regard, regulated tariffs are determined by the public authorities, which means the companies operating in the regulated sectors are exposed not only to market risks and dynamics but also to the regulatory risk deriving from potential arbitrary and abrupt changes to the revenues formula by the public authorities.

Besides tariff-related assumptions, a key role is played by the ones related to volume:

- Traffic volumes (e.g., Sigma case)
- Volume of electrical energy sold
- Volume of gas sold

Forecasts on expected revenues over business plan years depend indeed on the interaction between tariffs evolution and activity volumes.

The nature of the operating costs and the technical solutions implemented to forecast them depends heavily on the business activity sector of the company for which the business plan is being prepared. For instance, in Sigma case, the operating costs are represented mainly by the costs linked to the maintenance of the infrastructure assets and by the personnel cost.

Sometimes, it may happen that these kinds of companies benefit from public contributions and/or ad-hoc favorable fiscal regimes, on the basis of the strategic relevance of the activities they carry out. In these cases, such features will need to be properly taken in account when preparing the company business plan.

2.4   THE MAIN METHODOLOGICAL ISSUES

In this paragraph we discuss the main methodological aspects of the business plan preparation. The consistency of the choices made before the plan is actually worked out determines the quality not only of the plan itself but also of the valuation process based on it.

2.4.1   Time Horizon Covered by the Plan

How long should the business plan time span be? A sound business plan should span a time horizon long enough to fully capture the effects expected from the implementation of the competitive strategies prepared by the company management. However, this is not always the case. Sometimes, indeed, the difficulties to extend the plan over a very relevant time frame are used as an excuse to limit the business plan time horizon to 3 to 5 years, even in those cases where a longer time frame would be highly desirable. In these cases, the business plan risks consequently to prove incomplete and, accordingly, useless. Indeed, in these cases:

- The business plan analysis gives representation to just a portion of the expected effects from the implementation of competitive strategies.
- It becomes impossible to extract from the business plan all the info needed to estimate the cash flows at regime to be used in the terminal value estimation. This is a direct consequence of the fact that the profitability levels that can be inferred from the plan are not representative of the long-term sustainable ones.

As such, to avoid the above problems, the most frequent solution is to extend the business plan horizon. Obviously, it is then required that over this time frame the company be run by the management that defines the competitive strategies upon which the business plan is built. If this were not the case, it would then be highly recommended that management vet at least the assumptions underpinning the extension phase of the business plan. In the contrary case, the business plan preparation would boil down to a mere numerical exercise with no sound background.

In some sectors, it is usual to determine the extension of the time horizon covered by the plan on the basis of the residual life of the tangible and intangible asset base controlled by the company. For instance:

- Business plans of companies operating by means of a concession (e.g., toll roads) last until its expiry.
- Business plans of companies operating in the naval industry are made up of a series of single plans for each proprietary ship, with the time horizons set to the relevant operational life of ships.
- Business plans of power companies have the same time-horizon of the proprietary PPE.

2.4.2 Real Business Plans versus Nominal Business Plans

The business plan can be developed in nominal or real terms. In the former case, the business plan takes into account inflation; in the latter, is does not.

In general, business plans are prepared in nominal terms, but there can be some special cases:

- Situations where it may be preferable or, in any case, sensible to develop forecasts in real terms as well. This is the case, for instance, for companies operating in settings characterized by high and persistent inflation.
- Sectors for which it is usual, or even legally binding, to prepare plans in real terms.

It is worth remembering that, in the context of the valuation process, cash flows and discount rates are coherent between each other. As such, cash flows in real terms shall be discounted with real terms rates, conversely nominal cash flows by nominal discount rates.

2.4.3 Aspects to Develop in the Phase of Business Plan Critical Analysis

The addressee of the plan, in order to formulate an assessment of it, should first ascertain whether the business plan ensures coherence among:

- The competitive strategies to implement
- The actions to concretely carry out

■ The quantitative hypotheses underpinning the income statement, balance sheet, and cash flow statement forecasts, and their expected results

Moreover, it is necessary to ascertain whether the competitive strategies, the actions to implement them, the hypotheses, and the expected results are coherent, in particular, with:

■ Company human, intangible, and financial resources
■ Reference competitive setting
■ Reference macroeconomic setting

In other words, the plan should depict a scenario that looks concretely attainable and realistic on the whole, also in the light of the company and reference setting features. When these points do not hold, the business plan ends up representing a main numerical exercise with no grounds on the reality.

Bearing these considerations in mind, in practice, in order to assess the feasibility/credibility of the business plan, it is useful to, for instance:

■ Verify the coherence between current results (first year of the plan) and historical results.
■ Compare the hypotheses underpinning the financial statements forecasts and results to the historical performances. In concrete, this means sense checking the evolution of the following ratios from historical values to forecast ones:
  ▪ Return on investment (ROI)
  ▪ Return on sales (ROS)
  ▪ Key performance indicator for production volumes[1]
  ▪ Average outstanding trade credit days
  ▪ Average outstanding trade debt days
  ▪ Average inventory days

  Some weird evolution in one of these ratios is a clear red flag to better analyze and scrutinize.
■ Carry out a benchmarking analysis on one or more key drivers, taking as a reference the most comparable players in the sector.

---

[1]For instance: (1) for an industrial company, the number of goods sold; (2) for a toll road concession, the traffic volumes; (3) for a commercial company operating through its points of sale, the revenues per sqm.

2.4.4 Sensitivity Analysis

As explained, the business plan is developed on the basis of several hypotheses, both quantitative and qualitative. Each hypothesis has an impact (more or less relevant) on the expected results. In general, several sensitivity analyses are carried out with the final aim of studying the variation in these key expected results following the modification of the hypotheses underlying the business plan. In order for the sensitivity analysis to be most efficient, it is key to spot the variables that have the greatest impact on the plan's forecasts. As such, a sound sensitivity analysis can be set up only after having thoroughly detected and studied the different hypotheses carried out in the business plan preparation process. Often, in practical applications, the sensitivity analysis exercise is misused, by just selecting a unique key variable and letting it change. Running in this way, the sensitivity analysis can turn out to be not only useless but even dangerous, since it implicitly assumes that changing one hypothesis of the business plan has no effect on the other hypothesized variables, which is almost never the case. Actually, to run properly the sensitivity analysis, it is needed to prepare some full real case scenarios versus the base one, by changing all the concatenated variables in the appropriate way.

The sensitivity analysis theme is interconnected with one of the main questions that shall be faced when preparing the business plan: how to deal with uncertainty in the valuation process.

As is well-known, the intrinsic value of a company is a function of:

- The cash flows expected in the future
- The uncertainty profile attached to the above-mentioned cash flows

To this end, it is necessary to consider that:

- The features of the performances of different companies are different as well and are accordingly exposed to different levels of uncertainty. Just to quote an example, it is well known that some sectors are more exposed to the evolution of the economic cycle than others are.
- The uncertainty affecting the new enterprises is totally different from the one characterizing the already established, consolidated activities.
- The uncertainty affecting the expected cash flows may arise from idiosyncratic factors, for instance:
  - The risk of a concession being not renewed
  - The risk of a license being not renewed
  - The risk that a turnaround process turns out to be unsuccessful

- The risk of failing to secure the financial resources necessary to kick off/continue a capex plan
- The risk of abrupt unexpected unfavorable changes in the legal reference framework

The uncertainty affecting the valuation process can be handled in different ways. One of these lies in performing, when feasible, a multiscenario analysis. With this exercise, the base scenario is complemented with one or more alternative scenarios (developed through the sensitivity analysis) to which a probability (summing up to 1 for the different scenarios) is assigned. The final outcome of the valuation will be equal to the weighted average of the valuations for the different scenarios. Obviously, performing a multiscenario analysis is feasible only if the different plans (one for each hypothesized scenario) are all available to the expert performing the valuation.

CHAPTER 3

Scenario Analysis[1]

3.1 INTRODUCTION

Chapters 1 and 2 introduced the tools and essential knowledge necessary to set up a meaningful valuation approach. Metaphorically, the reader is now provided with both the ingredients and the recipe needed to make a *valuation dish* in a very mechanical way.

The goal of this chapter is instead a different one. It is meant to provide the reader with the level of critical thinking that is necessary when valuing.

Due to the high level of subjectivity linked to the estimation of discount rates, to the choice of the appropriate valuation procedure, as well as to cash flow forecasting, scenario analysis is a useful tool that enables the analyst as well as the company's manager to better understand the risks associated with any given valuation.

In particular, many different factors could affect the results expected by a firm on the valuation date, leading to different realized returns. For instance, there are many hypotheses made during the valuation process that might depend on the state of the economy, on the current legislative and political systems, on a particular industry's situation, as well as on the current competitive environment. It would be important to consider possible future scenarios to arrive at the best valuation given future events. It is easy enough to imagine that there could be a sudden technological breakthrough that could cannibalize the business altogether. On the other hand, due to the impossibility of considering all future scenarios, it is useful to take into account only those scenarios that are reasonably likely to occur and that would influence value creation the most.

The first valuation the analyst carries out is usually assumed to be the base scenario of the analysis—that is, the circumstances and results to which every other scenario is compared.

---

[1] Elena Falcettoni is the author of this chapter.

We can generally categorize the assumptions underlying our scenarios into three main groups:

1. *Macroeconomic conditions:* Some industries are more influenced by this than others. Nevertheless, if assumptions on the sales growth as well as possible geographical expansions take the current economic situation into consideration, it could be interesting to look at how the valuation results would change if the economic situation were to change significantly.

2. *Industry-wide conditions:* There could be different factors influencing the industry-wide conditions that would in turn impact the company's results. The competitive environment as well as the importance of the industry as a whole can radically change throughout time. Kodak, the dominant firm in the photographic film business in the twentieth century, saw a rapid decline in the 1990s due to its inability to quickly adapt to digital photography, the new technology that was taking over the market.

3. *Company-specific conditions:* As addressed in the previous chapters, all the assumptions made regarding the firm's growth and development have to be feasible. That is, they have to be within reach of the firm given its resources, its historic performance, the situation of the industry it operates in, and so on. Nevertheless, the company might still experience issues that could prevent the realization of the base scenario both from an operating and a financial point of view. From an operating point of view, a clear example could be the firm's inability to obtain the expected market share assumed in the valuation, therefore leading to higher working capital needs due to higher inventory and lower payments than expected. Financially, the firm might find itself in need of a higher amount of financial resources despite the debt already undertaken. This might be a delicate situation if its D/E ratio is high enough that its cost of capital would increase greatly or that it could be denied further credit. Another important case is the one in which financing is linked to some clauses, often connected to the company's operating side. If the firm is unable to keep up with expectations regarding its operations, this could lead to the loss of financing, as well.

The analyst can therefore determine what are the main assumptions underlying the base scenario created for the company under interest in order to be able to run a scenario analysis. We will then be able to understand how the final result changes due to the variables hit by a shock.

The valuation process itself will sometimes inform the analyst of the uncertain situations underlying her projections. Anytime a *ceteris paribus* clause is essential for the valuation to be consistent, the elements supposed to stay constant should be subject to a scenario analysis following the valuation procedure.

3.2   WHAT IS SCENARIO ANALYSIS?

Scenario analysis is a tool that allows for the consideration of different future states of the world by specifically varying the different situations and assumptions underlying the base values to create possible new paths for the company's future. It is often used to analyze best, worst, and most likely outcomes. The uncertainty any business has to face leads to an unlimited number of futures to be considered.[2] Unfortunately, scenario analysis has to focus on a limited number of these.

Scenario analysis has been a very important tool for the private sector in the last 25 years for the development of strategies as well as for risk management. Due to its importance in decision making for both investments and corporate strategy, it has become more and more present as a medium-/long-term tool in strategic planning.

Moreover, this tool is not new in public policy. The public sector has used it for regional development as well as for the analysis of opportunities and risks in developing countries.

3.3   DIFFERENCE BETWEEN SCENARIO AND SENSITIVITY ANALYSIS

It is important to clearly differentiate between two different types of analysis to forecast variation in results: sensitivity analysis and scenario analysis. Even though we focus on the latter, the former is also often used and is not unrelated to the scenario analysis we perform. Sensitivity analysis requires the analyst to specifically identify the key variables underlying cash flow projections. In its simplest (and most used) approach, the analyst then identifies an optimistic and pessimistic value that the variables could take. However, sensitivity analysis does not consider that the variables could be interrelated. All it aims to calculate is the mathematical change in the final result when there is a variation in one of the key variables underlying the cash flow forecast. Scenario analysis takes all interrelations into account since it is meant to consider all the changes the firm would go through due to a change in assumptions or circumstances. A simple example can clarify the difference

---

[2]See, for example, H. G. Daellenbach, and D. C. McNickle, *Management Science: Decision Making Through Systems Thinking* (Palgrave MacMillan, 2005).

in the approaches taken. Imagine that the analyst wants to take a possible increase in a firm's market share into account. If the analyst runs a sensitivity analysis, he will increase the market share and recalculate the firm's final results. On the other hand, a scenario analysis would instead consider the fact that demand will probably be higher and the unit price will increase. If this is due to an inflationary effect, however, costs will increase as well. Another example is the rise in raw material costs. A sensitivity analysis would once again only consider the cost increase, leaving anything else unchanged. Analysts performing a scenario analysis would instead look at different simultaneous changes. First, they would look at possible substitutes if raw materials can be easily substituted. Otherwise, they would consider a possible pass-through of the increase in costs into an increase in price and, in turn, the effect of such price increase on the firm's final results. As can be easily seen, a scenario analysis gives a more realistic outcome, but it entails much more effort and knowledge.

3.4 WHEN TO PERFORM SCENARIO ANALYSIS

Scenario analysis can be used in a variety of specific ways, but we will focus on two main categories:

1. *Investment:* Scenario analysis is very useful to decide whether to undertake an investment in a company, whether we are talking about the acquisition of a new asset, a new project financing, or a business expansion.

   We know that the most common decision rule regarding an investment is the net present value (NPV), which has to be greater than zero for the investment to be undertaken. The NPV takes into consideration the future expected cash flows coming from the investment and the outflows needed to sustain it. Nevertheless, the calculation of these cash flows is often based on subjective elements and on the beliefs that those flows will be realized in the future.

   Scenario analysis can be applied in this case to consider the different possible outcomes of the investment. Instead of valuing only the most likely or rather the expected scenario (i.e., the one on which the choice is usually based), management could instead consider numerous possible realizations. The goal is then again to consider how likely it is for each scenario to happen and with what chance the investment could actually lead to results that would make the NPV negative.

2. *Valuation:* Similarly, as in the case with investments, the valuation of a company is extremely important to understand its current value.

Whether the valuation is carried out because the company is going public or due to an acquisition, the company basically becomes an investment for third parties. As such, therefore, investors expect the inflows coming from the company to be higher than the necessary outflow.

In a company valuation, we usually consider historic data, management's expectations, consensus estimates, as well as industry averages and macroeconomic factors to calculate the value of the company based on fundamentals.

Scenario analysis, similarly to the first case, provides a tool to investors and to the analyst to better understand what is the variance associated to the valuation process, and how much the final results calculated depend on the assumptions made. Moreover, it then provides the parties involved with the best and worst scenarios besides the most likely one. Finally, by anticipating what would happen to the firm's results in case of different shocks to the key variables involved, the interested parties have the possibility to set up a contingency plan if a particular scenario were to materialize.

3.5   WORST AND BEST CASES AND WHAT HAPPENS NEXT

A first approach to the use of scenario analysis is to restrict our attention on two paths that could be followed by the company under consideration: the best and the worst possible cases. In other words, it is often interesting to look at the firm's results both when everything works to perfection and every input variable is set equal to its best possible outcome and when, on the other hand, nothing works as expected and all input variables are set to their worst possible outcomes. While some papers or textbooks mention the idea that input variables should be maximized in the best-case scenario, we still hold feasibility into account. It is useless to build a best-case scenario that is a probability-zero event. A quick example could clarify this issue. When maximizing revenue growth, such a maximization could only be feasible with a reduction in prices, which would lower the firm's margins. Maximizing both variables is clearly an impossible event. If this is not taken into account, the final result could be higher than the one that could be feasibly obtained in the true best-case world.

The best/worst-case analysis is useful in two main ways.

In the valuation of an investment, despite the fact that either scenario has a very low chance of happening, the range between the best- and worst-case results yields an approximation of the risk of the investment itself. As a matter of fact, it is easy to imagine that a safe enough investment's results should be almost independent of changes in any other variables. Let us take an investment in a risk-free government bond compared to an investment in a company's stock. The former will provide the firm with coupons and principal regardless of the state of the economy, the firm's revenue growth, and so on, while the latter will not only depend on macroeconomic shocks but also on industry and company-specific variables. A scenario analysis would be useless in the first case, but definitely quite useful in the second one.

On the other hand, the second application is crucial both for investment and company valuations. As a matter of fact, the best/worst-case scenario analysis is particularly useful to understand how bad the worst-case scenario could truly be. In particular, when looking at an investment, the firm might be interested in fully comprehending the degree of spillover that the investment gone wrong could have on the firm's remaining operations. This is particularly useful when the company undergoing the investment has significant debt obligations. In this case, the company would be concerned with the worst-case scenario to understand whether the investment could lead it to default.

When valuing a company, on the other hand, the worst-case scenario gives an idea of the minimum value that the company will ever be able to achieve. In other words, it gives a minimum value of the firm when everything goes worse than expected, which is a particularly interesting element for an acquirer. It is quite easy to imagine that a buyer purchasing a company would be concerned with the worst outcome that the investment could materialize. It is important to mention that understanding the worst-case company value is not the same as setting a reservation price for the buyer. In a way, the value of the company is an expected value over all possible different scenarios, where each scenario occurs with a given probability.

3.6   MULTI-SCENARIO ANALYSIS

In general, the best/worst-case approach does not provide us with enough information. Besides providing us with an intuition on how much variance we can expect in the valuation's final results, such an analysis would not really produce the different paths into which the firm could likely fall in the future due to some macroeconomic or asset-specific shocks.

In a typical situation, the scenarios considered would be more than two. The analyst faced with the decision of running a scenario analysis has to take different elements into consideration:

1. The analyst must choose the factors on which to base the analysis. Going back to the introduction, we have already seen how the factors influencing the company's final results are linked to macroeconomic

conditions, to industry-wide elements, as well as to company-specific factors. The choice regarding the factors at the basis of the scenario analysis is definitely a subjective one. In general terms, as we specified in the introduction, any assumption that appears to be strong and necessary for the results to hold is a factor that should be analyzed to determine how strongly it could impact the final results. Analysts should usually narrow down their attention on two to three factors and build scenarios around these. A higher number of factors makes the process longer and less traceable. Keep in mind that there is always a trade-off between a higher number of factors and scenarios considered, which increase how realistic the analysis will be, and the ability to clearly differentiate across the effects of the different factors and scenarios analyzed.

2. The analyst must determine the number of scenarios to build. A greater number of scenarios clearly involve greater effort coming from the analyst. As we mentioned beforehand, a higher number of scenarios leads to a more realistic analysis. However, as the number of scenarios considered increases, it might become difficult to differentiate across them. The analyst will have to be able to collect information for each of the scenarios under consideration and to calculate the cash flow forecasts and final results from them. It is then obvious that such a process becomes cumbersome as the number of scenarios increases. The final choice will depend on how different the scenarios are from each other and on how easily the analyst can obtain the relevant information and calculate the necessary results. For each of the factors first chosen, the number of scenarios picked will be run. It is now even clearer, therefore, that the number of factors chosen in the first step should also be limited.

3. This third step is interesting in some applications. Once the scenario analysis has been run for all the factors first picked in all the scenarios chosen in the second step, it could be useful to calculate the probability with which each scenario could happen. Even though scenario analysis was born as a qualitative analysis based on quantitative methods (i.e., its main purpose was to convey the potential risks associated with a particular investment to the company's manager), this process—if run correctly—can yield very accurate values. In order to give a scale on how important each scenario is, a probability measure is necessary. This step is not particularly complicated for those factors that are related to macroeconomic conditions. For such variables, as a matter of fact, a probability with which shocks occur can be easily calculated from services that forecast these variables and that look at their historical trend and future expectations. For industry-wide or company-specific elements, it becomes more difficult to assign an objective probability to a variable shock and the analyst should then draw from his/her own expertise and knowledge.

3.7   PROS AND CONS

We have already mentioned many of the benefits that scenario analysis brings to a valuation process. Let us summarize them in a quick-to-access list:

- *Ease of comprehension:* The greatest advantage of scenario analysis is the clear message that it is able to convey to anyone involved in the transaction. Providing everyone with an expectation of the final results obtained in every scenario according to changes in the variable of interest, scenario analysis leads to a clear understanding of the importance of given variables on valuation and on their impact on the firm's results.
- *Risk measure:* As mentioned beforehand, scenario analysis can provide yet another measure of risk according to the difference between the results calculated in the worst and best scenarios possible. Unlike statistical measures (such as standard deviation or confidence intervals), scenario analysis provides managers with estimated (and hopefully accurate, as long as the process is run correctly) figures regarding the final valuation/cash flows of the investment considered.
- *Ease of use:* Despite the need for knowledge and expertise from the Analyst to input the right variables into the process in the right measure, scenario analysis is very easily applied in Excel, as we will see at the end of this chapter.
- *Interrelated variables:* Unlike sensitivity analysis, scenario analysis considers the whole new path taken by the firm due to changes in the key factors chosen by the analyst. Therefore, it does not simply calculate the change in the final results once one variable is varied, but it considers all the changes in the firm's behavior and outputs due to a change in one factor. Scenario analysis therefore realizes that variables are often interrelated and a change in one variable cannot leave everything else unchanged.
- *Decision making:* Besides providing the manager with a clear understanding of the risk and variance involved in the firm's final results, scenario analysis can be particularly useful to understand the probability with which a certain investment could lead a firm into default, or how likely it is for a valuation's expectations to be fulfilled in the future. Decision making becomes therefore clearer once a probability is attached to the desired value being created in the future.

Despite the benefits that scenario analysis can bring to a valuation process, it goes without saying that there are some drawbacks that should be considered during the process:

- *GIGO:* This very popular acronym stands for *garbage in, garbage out*. It is clear that this entire process depends on the analyst's choice of factors and cash flow calculations. If any step of the approach is wrong, the result will be wrong as well. Bearing in mind the fact that the process highly depends on the analyst's knowledge and experience, he has to particularly pay attention to the assumptions laid out. A scenario analysis performed in an excellent way will still yield unrealistic, unfeasible, and inaccurate results if the inputs are imprecise.

■ *Only a discrete number of scenarios can be considered:* As explained beforehand, it becomes cumbersome if not impossible to consider a very high number of scenarios. The analyst has to gather information and calculate the newly assumed firm's path in each of the possible scenarios. For continuous variables, it is impossible to consider all the possible values taken on by the factors. It is very common to discretize the values taken into value bins. For example, instead of considering the continuity of values that could be taken on by the growth rate, the analyst could classify the values into low growth, moderate growth, high growth and base his/her scenario analysis on these bins. Despite making life easier for the analyst, this restriction will make the analysis less realistic. In particular, we are assuming that the scenario calculations for each bin will be the same for each value taken on by the variable within that bin and different from the results obtained in the other bins. This will not be the case in general and it is obvious that variables' boundary values will always be more similar to the preceding or following bin, creating distortion in valuation. A solution to this problem is the randomization—instead of the estimation—of the values taken on by the variables under consideration. The most common random factor analysis is the Monte Carlo analysis, through which factor values are drawn from the probability distribution of the variables of interest.

■ *Double counting of risk:* Scenario analysis provides us with a very powerful qualitative tool based on quantitative methods to understand how likely it is that bad outcomes could hit our initial investment. Nevertheless, it is also crucial to consider risk only once in decision making. If the cash flows are already adjusted for risk through the discount rate, for instance, then a high probability of a bad scenario happening should not be counted as extra risk. The discount rate already includes that.

3.8 HOW TO PERFORM SCENARIO ANALYSIS IN EXCEL

This section is a step-by-step how-to guide for Mac and Windows. For the following examples, we will use Microsoft Office 365 Excel 2011 for OS X and for Windows.

We will work through a simple example to show how Excel Data Analysis works. The Excel spreadsheet is available as Scenario_Analysis.xlsx.

We will use a simple two-stage DCF model, in which we will therefore have a first-stage growth, a second-stage growth, and a terminal growth rate. We assume that the firm we consider, let us call it A, has the following characteristics:

Initial cash flow	$100,000
Debt level	$900,000
Shares outstanding	10,000

Moreover, we know that A is ready to expand geographically, something that will boost its revenues in the short term. We therefore consider that A will experience a high-growth first-stage period for 5 years, a moderate-growth 5-year period, and an inflation-based terminal growth period based on the going-concern assumption. In particular, we will consider the following growth rates:

First-stage growth rate (years 1–5)	8%
Second-stage growth rate (years 6–10)	5%
Terminal growth rate (years 11–∞)	2%

A faces a cost of capital equal to 10 percent, which we will use as our discount rate.

We therefore want to calculate the DCF for A, based on a 10-year forecasted period. We are interested in two values: the DCF itself (i.e., the present value of the cash flows estimated for the forecasted period summed to the discounted terminal value), and the intrinsic value (IV), equal to the ratio between the net value of the firm (DCF-debt) and the number of shares outstanding.

We input our data in Excel and calculate the DCF. The screen will appear as shown in Exhibit 3.1.

We are now ready to perform scenario analysis from our base case. As explained beforehand, the first step is to decide what variables to vary. This simplified example does not lead to many issues in our decision, but a real-life case would involve many more factors and this choice could in fact be quite challenging.

We decide to focus on the three different growth rates, on the discount rate, and on the debt level as our variables of interest.

The second step we perform is the choice of the number of scenarios to consider. As an illustration to the theory explained in this chapter, we will focus on a few cases: higher/lower growth than expected, higher/lower cost of capital than expected, higher debt level than expected, best-/worst-case scenarios.

	A	B	C	D	E	F	G	H	I	J	K
1	Initial Cash Flow:	$100,000.00									
2											
3	Years:	1-5	6-10	Terminal							
4	Growth Rate:	8%	5%	2%							
5											
6	Shares Outstanding:	10000									
7	Debt Level:	$900,000.00									
8											
9	Discount rate	10%									
10											
11											
12	Year	1	2	3	4	5	6	7	8	9	10
13	Growth	8%	8%	8%	8%	8%	5%	5%	5%	5%	5%
14	Flows	$108,000.00	$116,640.00	$125,971.20	$136,048.90	$146,932.81	$154,279.45	$161,993.42	$170,093.09	$178,597.75	$187,527.63
15	Value	$98,181.82	$96,396.69	$94,644.03	$92,923.23	$91,233.71	$87,086.73	$83,128.24	$79,349.68	$75,742.88	$72,300.02
16											
17	CF[10]*[1+g]	$191,278.19									
18											
19	PV of 10 year CF	$870,987.03									
20											
21	TV	$2,390,977.33									
22	Discounted TV	$921,825.26									
23											
24	DCF	$1,792,812.29									
25											
26	Value per share	$89.28									

Exhibit 3.1 The DCF valuation model in Excel

64

Exhibit 3.2 The assumptions for the scenarios

	Base Case	High Growth	Low Growth
1st stage growth rate	8%	10%	5%
2nd stage growth rate	5%	8%	2%
Terminal growth rate	2%	2%	1%

In particular, the higher/lower growth than expected scenarios will be characterized by these values—see Exhibit 3.2.

Notice that we do not increase the terminal growth rate in the high-growth scenario. The choice is not random. We do not believe that a firm could grow indefinitely at a rate faster than the inflation rate. We also would like the reader to notice that the high-growth scenario would be very suitable for a three-stage DCF model. We will maintain the simplification of a two-stage model throughout. Nevertheless, an analyst faced with such a situation should be as accurate as possible and add a third stage if needed.

For the cost of capital, the three scenarios are presented in Exhibit 3.3.

In the high-debt scenario, we assume that the firm has to take out more debt than expected, increasing the debt level from $900,000 to $1,300,000.

The best- and worst-case scenarios put the various elements together as shown in Exhibit 3.4.

We are therefore ready to create our scenarios. The first step is to click on the "Data" tab to then click on the "What-If" button in the "Analysis" section (see Exhibit 3.5).

Exhibit 3.3 The discount rate (cost of capital) for each scenario

	Base Case	High WACC	Low WACC
Discount rate	10%	13%	8%

Exhibit 3.4 Summing up the scenarios' assumptions

	Base Case	Best Case	Worst Case
1st stage growth rate	8%	10%	5%
2nd stage growth rate	5%	8%	2%
Terminal growth rate	2%	2%	1%
Discount rate	10%	13%	8%
Debt level	$900,000	$900,000	$1,300,000

Exhibit 3.5 Locating the What-if Analysis in Excel

Exhibit 3.6 The Scenario Manager command in Excel

A menu will appear with three different alternatives (see Exhibit 3.6). "Scenario Manager..." is the option you want to click on.

The Scenario Manager window will open next. No scenarios are present immediately. We can create as many summaries as we wish and Excel will be able to summarize all of them together in one sheet (Exhibit 3.7). In order to create scenarios, click on the "Add..." button.

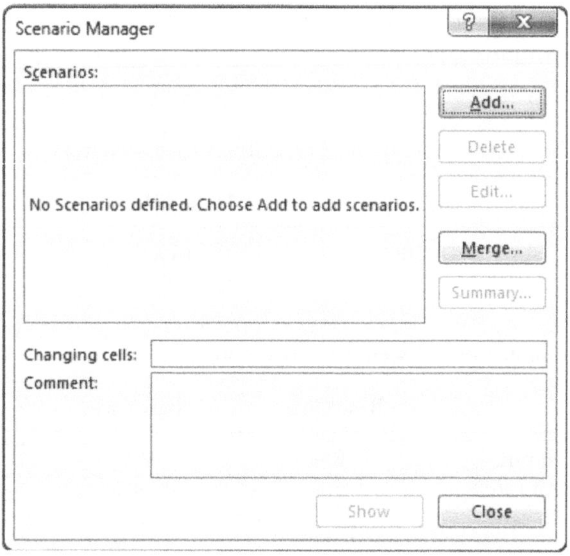

Exhibit 3.7 The summary of defined Scenarios

Scenario Manager will then ask for a Scenario Name to keep track of the different scenarios analyzed in the process. We will name ours in the following way: "High Growth," "Low Growth," "High Capital Cost," "Low Capital Cost," "High Debt Level," "Best Scenario," and "Worst Scenario."

The next step is to select the changing cells, that is, the variables of interest that will take on different values in our scenario. As we mentioned beforehand, the variables changing in the high-growth scenario are the three growth rates, shown in Exhibit 3.8.

Clicking on "OK," Scenario Manager will ask for the values taken on by the variables in the scenario under consideration.

Clicking on "OK," the scenario has been added to the list.

We run the same process for all the scenarios we want to consider, obtaining the complete list in Scenario Manager. Once all the scenarios have been created, all we need to do is to click on "Summary..." to obtain the results from the different scenarios, shown in Exhibit 3.9.

Scenario Manager in Windows is almost undistinguishable. For the sake of completeness, this is the same window that would appear in Windows, as shown in Exhibit 3.10.

Scenario Manager automatically selects "Scenario summary," which is the choice of interest, but prompts for the "Result cells"; that is, the values with the results that the manager/analyst wants to monitor to understand how they change following a change in the key variables. In our example,

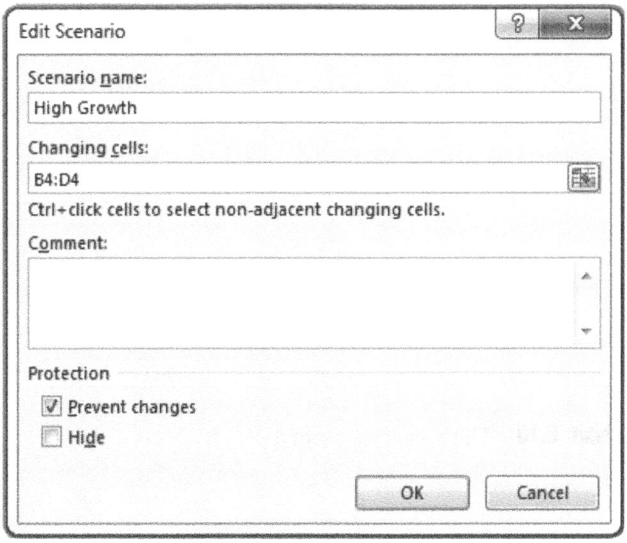

Exhibit 3.8 The editing command for Scenarios

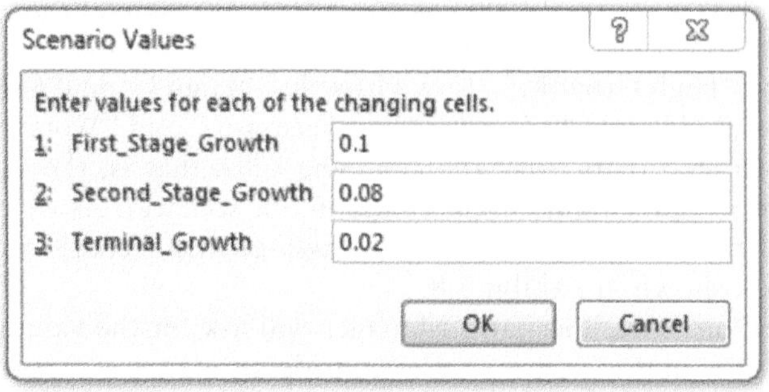

Exhibit 3.9 Entering the values for the changing cells

Exhibit 3.10 The Scenarios created

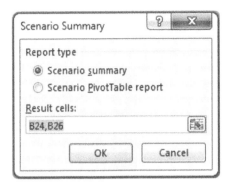

Exhibit 3.11   Entering the results cells

as mentioned beforehand, we want to keep track of the DCF value as well as of the intrinsic value, shown in Exhibit 3.11.

The "Scenario Summary" sheet is then finally created (see Exhibit 3.12). What can we learn from the analysis we have just performed?

First, we can see that there is a difference of almost 2 million between the best- and worst-case scenarios. The valuation is therefore highly dependent on the assumptions in place. Moreover, we can also see that the worst-case scenario leads to the firm's default, since the DCF, a little above a million dollars, is lower than the increased debt of $1,300,000.

We can also see that the high-growth scenario leads to very similar results to the low cost of capital case. In the same way, the low-growth scenario is highly comparable to the high cost of capital case. In both cases, however, the cost of capital seems to have a higher impact on A's DCF. Nevertheless, this is not a coincidence. Since we did not vary terminal growth in the high-growth scenario and we lowered it from 2 to 1 percent in the low-growth case, the growth scenarios impact the forecast period more than the terminal value. The discount rate, on the other hand, impacts all periods, since it is needed in the terminal value calculation as much as it is needed in the discount of the forecasted cash flows. However, the terminal value makes up for more than half of A's DCF value. The discount rate will therefore have a greater possibility to influence our results.

Finally, none of the scenarios are identical or really similar to the base case. This indicates the good choice of the factors to consider. On the other hand, however, this result confirms the subjectivity and the importance of accurate and well-thought-out inputs. It is clear how the wrong assumptions would lead to completely different results.

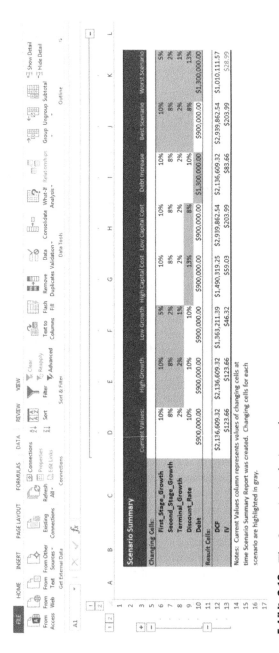

Scenario Summary	Current Values	High Growth	Low Growth	High Capital Cost	Low Capital Cost	Debt Increase	Best Scenario	Worst Scenario
Changing Cells:								
First_Stage_Growth	10%	10%	5%	10%	10%	10%	10%	5%
Second_Stage_Growth	8%	8%	2%	8%	8%	8%	8%	2%
Terminal_Growth	2%	2%	1%	2%	2%	2%	2%	1%
Discount_Rate	10%	10%	10%	13%	8%	10%	8%	13%
Debt	$900,000.00	$900,000.00	$900,000.00	$900,000.00	$900,000.00	$1,300,000.00	$900,000.00	$1,300,000.00
Result Cells:								
DCF	$2,136,609.32	$2,136,609.32	$1,363,211.39	$1,490,319.25	$2,939,862.54	$2,136,609.32	$2,939,862.54	$1,010,111.57
IV	$123.66	$123.66	$46.32	$59.03	$203.99	$83.66	$203.99	$28.99

Notes: Current Values column represents values of changing cells at time Scenario Summary Report was created. Changing cells for each scenario are highlighted in gray.

Exhibit 3.12 The Scenario Analysis result

In our simplified example, we did not consider as many variables in our scenarios. Nonetheless, this exercise should have already conveyed to the reader how useful scenario analysis can be, as well as the challenges that it entails.

3.9 CONCLUSIONS

The use and application of scenario analysis has been discussed in this chapter. We have outlined the main reasons underlying the growing importance of scenario analysis in firms' strategic planning and in valuation.

We have provided a roadmap for the application of this easy-to-use tool by highlighting the different assumptions underlying the valuation of an investment or of a company and by suggesting criteria to be used in the process. We have described the main differences between scenario and sensitivity analysis and then touched on the main applications of the former. In particular, we have explained the use of the best- and worst-case scenarios to then proceed to the multi-scenario analysis.

After a quick comment on the main pros and cons that characterize this analysis, we have illustrated how to implement it in Microsoft Office Excel under the two most used operating systems, OS X and Windows. Despite having provided a simplified example, we believe that it is already evident how useful yet challenging the described process can be.

In particular, despite its easy application through an Excel built-in tool, scenario analysis greatly depends on the analyst's information and experience, since he is in charge of selecting the most accurate values of inputs.

Scenario analysis can be a very important resource to understand how a given investment or valuation depends on the assumptions made and how variable the final results can be based on them. For a relatively safe investment, the different scenarios should not lead to highly different results; the opposite is true for a risky investment.

As mentioned beforehand, scenario analysis is unable to consider the continuity of values that could be taken on by some of the inputs. For this case, we invite the reader to refer to random factor analysis through the Monte Carlo analysis, through which factor values are drawn from the probability distribution of the variables of interest (addressed in Chapter 4).

CHAPTER **4**

Monte Carlo Valuation[1]

4.1   INTRODUCING MONTE CARLO TECHNIQUES

In recent years, the importance and the power of mathematical and numerical computation have increased noticeably both among academia and among financial practitioners. Financial assets derive their values from contractual claims and contractual claims are in turn linked to the occurrence of future events. Future events, however, are highly uncertain in the real world. Therefore, the ability to predict and describe them accurately is crucial to estimate the value of a financial asset with reliability. Modern computers have strengthened our ability to forecast future events and to produce accurate estimates through the implementation of complex mathematical and numerical methods that could not be applied without the support of sophisticated technologies. Several financial fields, including risk analysis, stress testing, and equity security valuation, have greatly benefited from these advances. The Monte Carlo method, probably the most intuitive and the most widely used among these approaches, finds wide support both in the financial literature and in practical implementations that require the estimation of uncertain processes. This chapter begins with a brief introduction to the Monte Carlo model; it then describes its interaction with the conventional fundamental valuation approaches, listing the advantages that Monte Carlo offers over its alternatives and explaining what drawbacks it is able to solve. Finally, an application of Monte Carlo in a real-case scenario is illustrated.

The implementation of the conventional discounted cash flow (DCF) model, as well as of any other fundamental valuation approach, has several advantages. First, it is a quantitative yet surprisingly simple method that still benefits from an economic rationale and a good level of precision. More importantly, however, it factors in the time value of money by discounting consecutive cash flows, it is roughly insensitive to different

---

[1]Roberto Vincenzi is the author of this chapter

72

accounting conventions, and it includes a basic risk structure, captured by the risk-adjusted discount rate. The conventional DCF model, however, has a major drawback: it is a deterministic model used to describe a stochastic world, a world characterized by continuous risk and uncertainty. In quantitative terms, stochastic and deterministic models are opposed because the former are characterized by a random evolution. In particular, while deterministic models are based on the assumption of a single way on how a process evolves over time, stochastic models assume that an unpredictable component and some kind of randomness will drive the future dynamics of a set of events. This random element implies that even if the original situation is known, there are many possible future evolutions for a process.

In the world of firms and investment, several factors interact and randomly affect outcomes and values. Not taking into account properly the variability and complexity of the world companies work in may result in severely flawed valuations.

First of all, traditional valuation approaches mostly assume that all the decisions about the future management of a firm (or of an investment) are made at the time at which the model is set up, not allowing future revisions of the management strategy over the life span of the firm. However, in the real world, firms are managed over their lifetime and on the basis of their achievements. The decision to invest in a new drug by a pharmaceutical firm, for instance, evolves during each of the development phases of the drug. Only if a project produces consecutively positive outcomes (e.g., only if the treatment proves effective, if tests made on human beings are conclusive, if the drug obtains regulatory approval), the pharmaceutical firm keeps the project in its pipeline and finances its development with a growing amount of resources. Second, traditional valuation techniques are based on the assumption that future cash flows are assumed to be highly predictable and deterministic. Nevertheless, the cash flows of an investment, and even more so a firm's cash flows, are stochastic and risky in nature. Not only can their amount be estimated only with a large degree of approximation, but also the precise timing of their occurrence is absolutely random. Finally, and perhaps most importantly, all risks are accounted for by a unique discount factor as mentioned in the first Chapter. However, such a discount rate is ambiguous in many instances and does not allow for a clear evaluation of the risks inherent to an investment. In fact, multiple sources of risk are present in the real world: they can be idiosyncratic to a firm (such as the effectiveness of its business strategy, the appeal of the firm's products, the aggressiveness of the competitive environment), or systemic, that is, more generally ascribable to the conditions and the externalities of the overall market in which a firm is and that interact and affect the measures of value (such as the macroeconomic risk and the country risk). It is clear, therefore, that the conventional risk-adjusted cash flow approach has some relevant limitations and that it is not able to realistically reproduce the uncertainty of the real world that it tries to describe. The Monte Carlo method is a valid support to overcome these difficulties, as it is an informative way to present and assess a firm's uncertain and risky environment. The approach indeed can be applied effectively to the modeling of stochastic processes and to the simulation of future uncertain scenarios on the basis of a given statistical distribution.

The Monte Carlo method, which owes its name to the city of Monte Carlo and to the random dynamics of gambling played in its casinos, was originally developed starting in the 1930s by physicists Enrico Fermi, John Von Neumann, and Stanislaw Ulam and was first applied to the study of the random neutron diffusion of the atomic bomb. Over the decades, the Monte Carlo approach found widespread application in areas such as chemistry, agriculture, medicine, and astronomy. Its methodology is based on the generation of random numbers, extracted from a predefined statistical distribution, and to their application to an experimental model that describes the real system under study. The Monte Carlo method, hence, first simulates thousands of future paths for an uncertain variable, repeatedly extracting values from a probability distribution (computer statistical sampling). Then it links each simulated path to a simulated scenario and to a simulated final outcome through mathematical formulas. The random simulation of thousands of different paths, scenarios, and outcomes replicates the uncertainty inherent to stochastic variables, allowing for many improvements into our modeling.

4.2 MONTE CARLO AND CORPORATE VALUATION

The features of the Monte Carlo method make it an appealing tool in the financial area to investigate stochastic variables in processes of risk analysis and forecasting. Modern financial economists initially showed that the price of a derivative can be obtained discounting its future expected payoffs, which can be modeled as continuous stochastic processes. On this basis, a common approach to derive the price of a derivative is to build a three-stage Monte Carlo procedure. First, the potential behavior of the underlying variables driving the future payoffs of the security under observation is simulated over thousands of different sample scenarios. Second, the discounted value of the payoffs of the security in each of these scenarios is computed. Finally, the average of the discounted values obtained in the sample scenarios is calculated to derive the simulated price of the security.

In recent years, the Monte Carlo technique also found application in the valuation of firms and other real investments. Indeed, in the process of valuing a firm, we need to investigate and factor into the valuation model the uncertain evolution of numerous economic value drivers, related both to the firm's idiosyncratic operations and to the overall market conditions in which the firm operates. For instance, the future growth rate of a firm's revenues, its industrial margins, and the future interest rates observed in the market are all key inputs to the value of a firm, but their future evolution is generally uncertain. These value drivers can indeed fluctuate sharply due both to the changes in the overall economic scenario and to the evolution of the firm itself, such as changes in the firm's capital structure or in its perimeter. In particular, these economic variables are not only impacted by predictable economic processes but are also driven by random components, and are therefore stochastic. The uncertainty surrounding their future occurrence, therefore, cannot be represented with one or a few data points but only through a more complex statistical distribution.

Financial analysts, however, frequently develop their valuation models only considering point estimates of economic stochastic variables. By doing this, however, they only investigate a single scenario, or a best-case and a worst-case scenario at most. In light of our previous observations, the approach that they use is excessively simplistic, as analysts can at best determine a range or a distribution of the expected values of a stochastic variable, but they are not able to produce reliable estimates at single point. Due to this extreme simplification, analysts fail to fully consider the uncertainty of real-world events and implement a deterministic analysis that partially ignores the information incorporated in the uncertain distribution of the different value drivers. In particular, analysts tend to consider the average of the distribution of stochastic economic variables as their best and most reliable estimate, even if the average is only one of the parameters describing the distribution and might not be representative of the entire set of values that the variable might take. In this regard, indeed, the average of the distribution of a stochastic variable might represent a situation that is in between different potential outcomes but that has no actual chance to occur. Therefore, analysts who rely on this approach lose important information about the degree of risk of the different variables, represented by their variance, and about their particular behavior—as in the case of variables with peculiar or nonsymmetrical distributions—and their valuations might therefore produce misleading results. By incorporating uncertainty in their valuation processes, analysts could largely improve the outputs of their model.

A clear example of a distribution for which the average value leads to almost no information is the beta distribution with alpha = beta = 0.5. In this case, the distribution takes on a very well-known U-shape, which is characterized by a high-probability mass in the tails of the distribution. In this case, the average value of the distribution would not only have a quasi-zero chance of occurrence, but the whole area surrounding such value will have a negligible probability mass. The mistake made by considering the average value in this distribution would definitely be much greater than the one made by looking at the average value in the normal distribution, for which 99 percent of the probability mass is contained within the first three standard deviations from the mean value.

A second important issue related to the behavior of stochastic variables in the process of valuing a firm concerns the variables' interdependency. In the real world, the occurrence of a company event is likely linked to the occurrences of other events affecting the firm's operations. For instance, it would be logical to expect that the growth in revenues and the gross margin of a manufacturing firm positively interact (i.e., they are positively correlated) on the basis of the enhanced economies of scale that follow from an increase in the production output. Therefore, to improve the accuracy of the economic inputs of a model and its final valuation, the value drivers' reciprocal interactions (correlations) should also be investigated and accounted for.

The Monte Carlo approach can be effectively applied to this framework, as it allows analysts to address the complexities generated by the random behavior and interaction of the main inputs of a valuation model with relative ease through the generation of thousands of artificial sample paths for important value drivers. The simulation repeatedly picks random values of the main inputs of the model from a predefined probability distribution and generates as output the distribution of the variable under study—that is, the investment value. By the replacement of point values with distributions, large improvements can be applied to financial modeling. Studying the behavior of each uncertain variable independently, simulating their potential occurrence on the basis of a defined distribution, and analyzing the joint influence of the stochastic variables on the outputs of the model provides much more insights about the valuation framework than the point estimate analysis. Overall, a valuation procedure that focuses on the entire statistical distribution of the value drivers and of the firm value rather than on a single point estimate allows for a more adequate description of the risk profile of the investment under study.

4.3   A STEP-BY-STEP PROCEDURE

Several steps need to be sequentially applied to properly build a valuation model enhanced via a Monte Carlo simulation. In *Step 1*, a conventional DCF model (or another fundamental valuation model that might be preferred on the basis of the investment valued) is set up. In this phase, precise mathematical relations are designed to link the value drivers of a firm (the inputs of the model) to the value measure (the output of the model).

In *Step 2*, the risk variables, which are all those value drivers that have a much deeper influence on the outcome of the valuation model (i.e., a higher impact on value), need to be identified. The identification of the most relevant value drivers is crucial to increase the clearness of the model. As a matter of fact, we will substitute the single point estimator with more complex probability distributions only for these selected value drivers, and not for all of them. The selection of the most critical value drivers is carried out through both a qualitative and a quantitative evaluation. Qualitatively, we will look at certain features of the variables under consideration, such as their past patterns and their future expected variability; quantitatively, we will use specific tools to estimate the impact of a change in each variable on the final valuation output of the model.

In *Step 3*, the probability distributions of the selected risk variables are investigated and defined. In this critical step, therefore, a full range of the possible values potentially taken by each of the risk variables is defined and probability weights are allocated to this range of values. Two main approaches can be applied to carry out this task. On the basis of the first approach, the probability distribution of a risk variable is derived considering the frequency distribution of the available *historical data*. Nevertheless, an obvious prerequisite to apply this methodology is the existence and availability of past data on the identified value driver. Before considering past data, furthermore, standard statistical procedures should be applied to determine whether available data are representative of the entire probability distribution of a variable and to check for potential outliers, which should be eliminated to preserve the reliability of the analysis. Finally, it is necessary to check that no structural changes have happened, making the past distribution of data unreliable. It should be noted, furthermore, that historical data do not necessarily need to be related to the operations of the firm that is valued, as they might, for instance, refer to a set of comparable firms and to investments that are similar to the investment analyzed (e.g., this is a very common approach when running an analysis based on multiples). When, on the basis of the available past observations, it is possible to assume that the empirical data come from a theoretically known statistical distribution, the Monte Carlo approach works by drawing values from the identified theoretical distribution. In such instances, therefore, the empirical distribution of past data is not directly used to draw random data and generate a random path. It is instead used only to identify the main parameters that will characterize the simulated observations, such as the average and the standard deviation. In the parametric approach, several theoretical distributions can be considered before identifying the one that best fits the available data. Typical examples are the normal and the lognormal distributions that are often used due to the ability for the central limit theorem[2] to kick in. In several circumstances, however, it is not possible to identify a conventional statistical distribution that meets the characteristics and the requirements of the probability distribution of a value driver. For instance, the industrial margin as a percentage of revenues is a value that cannot go above 100 percent. For this reason, many conventional statistical distributions (such as the normal one) cannot be adopted in order to preserve the reliability of the analysis (as such distributions are not cut at the range of values we need). When it is not possible to identify a conventional statistical distribution from the available data, it is not possible to derive conventional statistical assumptions about the future behavior of a risk variable and hence one more caveat applies. In these cases, nonparametric or distribution-free methods are used, and the Monte Carlo technique designs simulated future paths and scenarios drawing random values directly from the past observations rather than generating new data based on predefined statistical assumptions.

The second approach that can be effectively used to investigate and define the probability distribution of the relevant value drivers is merely based on experts' *opinions* and experience. On the other hand, in some circumstances, data about past occurrences of a certain variable indeed do not exist or are not available. In such instances, analysts can derive the probability distribution of stochastic variables on the basis of their or other experts' opinions. Nevertheless, this case also requires the identification of a parametric distribution to be used with the generation of simulated observations. However, differently from the approach already described, the parameters defining the distribution are not derived from observable data. On the contrary, these parameters are identified on the basis of the indications provided by the people acquainted with the firm and its environment and of their insights about the expected evolution of a value driver, its potential variability, and its worst- and best-case trends. A particularly popular distribution used in this framework is the triangular distribution that is built on the basis of three views coming from experts on the dynamics of the stochastic value driver under study: a pessimistic one, an optimistic one, and an average one. Furthermore, the estimates provided by more than one expert can be considered and weighted on the basis of each expert's reputation and track record. Overall, the choice of an appropriate probability distribution in the Monte Carlo procedure is likely the most relevant step and needs to be computed with great accuracy. Decision makers should approach this step with great caution in order to derive meaningful pictures of the risk of their investments and the volatility associated with their estimated values.

---

[2] See Amir Aczel and Jayavel Sounderpandian, *Complete Business Statistics*, 2008.

In *Step 4*, the important issue of interdependency among relevant value drivers is addressed and modeled. When the impact of the relationships among variables is negligible, it can easily be ignored. However, all relevant relationships should be measured and accounted for while modeling future scenarios. The importance of interdependency is particularly evident in the forecast of expected free cash flows (FCFs), which are required for the implementation of fundamental models. For instance, FCFs are a function of firms' growth, investment expenditure, and margins. However, the evolution of each of these variables is not independent of the evolution of the others in real companies. It would not be appropriate to model future scenarios ignoring these relationships. Indeed, as the growth rate increases, unit margins increase, since fixed costs are spread among more units being produced. The relationship between revenue growth and margins is therefore positive. Furthermore, revenue growth needs to be financed through increasing investments in production assets. Therefore, the relationship between growth and investments in current and fixed production assets is also positive. When past observations are available, the interdependency between different value drivers can be generally estimated through the Pearson's correlation coefficient—that is, with the typical ratio between the covariance between the two variables and the squared root of the product of the two variables' variances.

$$r = \frac{\sum_{i=1}^{n}(x_i - \overline{x})(y_t - \overline{y})}{\sqrt{\sum_{i=1}^{n}(x_i - \overline{x})^2 \sum_{t=1}^{n}(y_t - \overline{y})^2}}$$

The Pearson's correlation coefficient, however, is a parametric measure and can be used appropriately only when the correlated variables are distributed as a normal and their relationship is linear. When these conditions are not satisfied, the nonparametric Spearman's rank correlation is more commonly used. The Spearman's coefficient takes this particular form:

$$\rho = 1 - \frac{6 \sum d_i^2}{n(n^2 - 1)}$$

where:

$d_i = x_i = y_i =$ the difference between the ranks of corresponding values X_i
and Y_i.

$n =$ the number of values in each data set (same for both sets).

The Spearman rank correlation method is very useful when normality and/or linearity are not reasonable assumptions for our data. In particular, this correlation does not assume any specific distribution for the data under study and is therefore highly appropriate for data with large outliers and/or with very strong relationships among variables that are not normally distributed. The Spearman rank correlation method first takes the individual data points and assigns a rank number to each of them. It does not matter if the highest data point gets the lowest rank or vice versa, as only ranks—and not actual values—are used in the calculation. This is precisely why outliers have less of an effect on the Spearman calculation. If the ranks of the data of two series are the same, then there is a very strong relationship between the two series. The Pearson correlation, however, will not necessarily show this because it only shows the strength of the linear relationship among variables.

Once the correlations between the relevant variables have been estimated, they can be added to the model by connecting the parameters of their probability distributions in such a way that the occurrence of one variable in the simulation would influence the occurrence or the condition of the other. A final point that is important to underline is that when correlations among past observations are considered, we are making the implicit assumption that no changes in the structural behavior of the variables have happened over time. This is a crucial assumption that needs to be verified.

In *Step 5* of the Monte Carlo procedure, the cumulative distribution of all possible results is evaluated. Differently from the conventional DCF approach, a range of firm values is shown together with their associated probabilities. This output allows us to analyze both the average expected firm value and the degree of probability that an investment value will be above or below a critical value of interest (value-at-risk (VAR) analysis). This latter analysis is particularly useful when constraints on the value of an investment are in place (e.g., the regulatory capital restrictions of financial institutions) and the potential risk to violate one of them needs to be quantified.

4.4 CASE STUDY: OUTDOOR INC. VALUATION

As stated in the previous section, the Monte Carlo valuation process is carried out in such a way that

$$NPV = f(x_1, \ldots, x_n)$$

where NPV is the net present value of the investment in a firm or in other real project and $x_1, x_2, \ldots, x_n$ are the value drivers of the investment.

In the expression above, at least some of the value drivers are stochastic and, therefore, the net present value is also characterized by a random distribution. In the following part of the chapter we use the numerical power of a modern software (MS Excel and Crystal Ball) to generate a large number of outcomes for a set of risk variables and investigate their impact on the value distribution of a firm. Values of the risk variables, in particular, are simulated in accordance to prespecified probability distributions and take into account the dependences (correlations) among them. The recursive simulation of the value drivers generates a large number of outcomes for the output variables (cash flows and *NPV*), as well as their probability distributions. We analyze the distribution to identify the main descriptive parameters, as well as particular behaviors of the computed values.

The following example investigates the case of a company producing outdoor furniture, *Outdoor Inc.*, a global leader in its industry that mainly operates in the premium segment of the market. *Outdoor*'s ownership is shared among three entities, with the founder and the management team, respectively, owning a 10 percent and an 8 percent stake and an external private investor exercising control and owning the remaining 82 percent stake.

We analyze the position of a new private equity sponsor that is considering the option to carry out a management buyout on *Outdoor*. Negotiations are already at an advanced stage, and an accurate valuation of the firm is required to support a final agreement between the buyer and the existing shareholders.

Outdoor has gone through an important phase of restructuring over the previous years. It has increased its international exposure, with export currently representing more than 50 percent of its overall revenues, and has focused on a simplification of its cost structure. The firm's outputs pertain to three main product classes (furniture items, structures, and accessories), with revenues mainly driven by lumber (40 percent), iron (40 percent), and aluminum (15 percent) products. Sales are distributed across four major geographical regions: Italy is the largest market, accounting for approximately 45 percent of sales, France is worth 30 percent of revenues, while Germany and Spain each represent 10 percent of total turnover. *Outdoor*'s business is highly cyclical, with more than three quarters of its revenues arising during the spring, when clients concentrate the purchases of outdoor furniture items. To limit the effects of seasonality on working capital and achieve a more stable financial structure, specific agreements are in place with the main suppliers.

The outdoor furniture market in the countries in which *Outdoor* is present generates overall revenues of €2 billion per year (Germany is the largest national market with turnover amounting to approximately

€700 million) and has grown by a 6 percent CAGR[3] over the previous five fiscal periods. Approximately 20 percent of this market is represented by the premium segment, the one in which *Outdoor* mainly operates. The industry is highly fragmented with a large base of small and medium firms having an individual turnover rarely in excess of €10 million. Only a few players, including *Outdoor*, are able to offer a diversified set of products, while the majority of the firms active in the industry are specialized in the distribution of a limited range of articles, generally made of a single raw material, unlike *Outdoor's three material choice*.

Exhibit 4.1 summarizes *Outdoor's* historical financial information over the years 2011 to 2013 as well as the budgeted financials for the year 2014. Revenues increased by a 6.8 percent CAGR between 2011 and 2014, boosted by both the growth in size of the different geographical markets for outdoor furniture products and the firm's increasing market share in those regions, with only a limited trend reversal observed in 2013 due to adverse meteorological conditions. Purchases represent the most critical cost item in *Outdoor's* income statement as manufacturing operations are mainly outsourced, with 80 percent of the items coming from production centers located in Far East Asian countries. In particular, the incidence of purchases on revenues has largely increased recently due to an upward trend in the prices of raw materials. Transportation costs, mainly due to the naval shipments from Asia, also grew more than proportionally compared to revenues (see Exhibit 4.1).

Going back to our problem, we will use the aforementioned Monte Carlo valuation procedure to analyze the potential acquisition from a new private equity sponsor. In *Step 1*, we set up a DCF financial model. In such a model, we provide a detailed projection of the financial statements for the first 10 years after the potential acquisition and we assume a perpetual growth rate of 2.5 percent for the following period. We also assume that the management buyout will be financed through both equity and debt at a 30:70 ratio. In line with other similar transactions the deal is therefore assumed to be structured using a high degree of financial leverage. Base scenario assumptions on the evolution of the main items on the income statement and balance sheet are developed considering past trends and management estimates. In particular, we assume that the markets in which *Outdoor* mainly operates will grow to a certain extent between 2015 and 2019, as shown in Exhibit 4.2, and that *Outdoor* will be able to improve its presence in those markets by increasing its market share. In our base scenario, we assume that cost items will evolve following their past trend and that they

---

[3]Compound Annual Growth Rate.

Exhibit 4.1   Outdoor financials

		t-4 A	t-3 A	t-2 A	t-1 B	
Income Statement		t-4A	t-3A	t-2A	t-1B	CAGR 11-14
Revenues—Italy		27.2	30.1	28.7	32.3	5.9%
	%yoy		10.7%	−4.7%	12.5%	
Revenues—France		17.8	20.1	19.3	21.9	7.2%
	%yoy		12.9%	−4.0%	13.5%	
Revenues—Spain		6.5	6.7	6.6	7.2	3.5%
	%yoy		3.1%	−1.5%	9.1%	
Revenues—Germany		5.8	6.1	6.2	7.0	6.5%
	%yoy		5.2%	1.6%	12.9%	
Revenues—Other		1.2	1.5	1.7	2.8	32.6%
	%yoy		25.0%	13.3%	64.7%	
Total Revenues		**58.5**	**64.5**	**62.5**	**71.2**	**6.8%**
	%yoy		10.3%	−3.1%	13.9%	
Cost of Purchases		(11.0)	(13.0)	(17.1)	(21.0)	24.1%
	% revenues	(18.8%)	(20.2%)	(27.4%)	(29.5%)	
Transportation Cost		(3.0)	(3.6)	(4.4)	(5.3)	20.9%
	% revenues	(5.1%)	(5.6%)	(7.0%)	(7.4%)	
Total Variable Costs		**(14.0)**	**(16.6)**	**(21.5)**	**(26.3)**	**23.4%**
	% revenues	(23.9%)	(25.7%)	(34.4%)	(36.9%)	
Contribution Margin		**44.5**	**47.9**	**41.0**	**44.9**	**0.3%**
	% revenues	76.1%	74.3%	65.6%	63.1%	
Marketing		(6.0)	(6.2)	(6.5)	(6.8)	4.3%
	% revenues	(10.3%)	(9.6%)	(10.4%)	(9.6%)	
Personnel Cost		(8.1)	(8.3)	(8.3)	(8.4)	1.2%
	% revenues	(13.8%)	(12.9%)	(13.3%)	(11.8%)	
SG&A		(4.4)	(4.3)	(4.2)	(4.2)	(1.5%)
	% revenues	(7.5%)	(6.7%)	(6.7%)	(5.9%)	
EBITDA		**26.0**	**29.1**	**22.0**	**25.5**	**(0.6%)**
Amortization		(7.0)	(6.9)	(7.0)	(6.5)	(2.4%)
	% revenues	(12.0%)	(10.7%)	(11.2%)	(9.1%)	
EBIT		**19.0**	**22.2**	**15.0**	**19.0**	**0.0%**
	% revenues	32.5%	34.4%	24.0%	26.7%	
Cash Interests on Debt		(3.5)	(3.6)	(3.6)	(3.5)	
Cash Interests on ST Debt						
PIK Interests						
Extraordinary Gains (Losses)		(0.9)	(0.7)	(0.1)	(0.3)	
EBT		**14.6**	**17.9**	**11.3**	**15.2**	**1.4%**
Taxes		(5.6)	(7.0)	(4.8)	(6.4)	4.6%
Net Income (Loss)		**9.0**	**10.9**	**6.5**	**8.8**	**(0.7%)**
	% revenues	15.4%	16.9%	10.4%	12.4%	

Exhibit 4.2 Revenue growth for Outdoor

SALES																
Italy	Year	t-4	t-3	t-2	t-1	current	t+1	t+2	t+3	t+4	t+5	t+6	t+7	t+8	t+9	t+10
	Market size (€M)	81	90	85	96	103	113	120	124	135						
	Share	33.5%	34.0%	34.0%	34.5%	34.8%	35.0%	35.5%	35.5%	36.0%						
	Outdoor's turnover	27.1	30.6	28.9	33.1	35.8	39.6	42.6	44.0	48.6						
France	Year	t-4	t-3	t-2	t-1	current	t+1	t+2	t+3	t+4	t+5	t+6	t+7	t+8	t+9	t+10
	Market size (€M)	100	114	105	119	130	141	148	159	168						
	Share	17.8%	18.0%	18.3%	18.8%	19.0%	19.4%	19.8%	20.0%	20.2%						
	Outdoor's turnover	17.8	20.5	19.2	22.4	24.7	27.4	29.3	31.8	33.9						
Germany	Year	t-4	t-3	t-2	t-1	current	t+1	t+2	t+3	t+4	t+5	t+6	t+7	t+8	t+9	t+10
	Market size (€M)	99	100	98	100	103	104	105	110	115						
	Share	6.0%	6.1%	6.3%	6.9%	7.4%	7.7%	8.1%	8.5%	8.9%						
	Outdoor's turnover	5.9	6.1	6.2	6.9	7.6	8.0	8.5	9.4	10.2						
Spain	Year	t-4	t-3	t-2	t-1	current	t+1	t+2	t+3	t+4	t+5	t+6	t+7	t+8	t+9	t+10
	Market size (€M)	62	63	62	65	69	71	72	76	78						
	Share	10.5%	10.5%	10.5%	11.0%	11.1%	11.3%	11.5%	11.6%	12.0%						
	Outdoor's turnover	6.5	6.6	6.5	7.2	7.7	8.0	8.3	8.8	9.4						
Other	Year	t-4	t-3	t-2	t-1	current	t+1	t+2	t+3	t+4	t+5	t+6	t+7	t+8	t+9	t+10
	Outdoor's turnover growth rate (average)					10%	8%	6%	7%	8%						
Long-term sale growth	Year	t-4	t-3	t-2	t-1	current	t+1	t+2	t+3	t+4	t+5	t+6	t+7	t+8	t+9	t+10
											3.0%	3.0%	3.0%	3.0%	3.0%	3.0%

will absorb a constant percentage of overall revenues. We base the computation of passive interest rates on market rates and average spreads demanded by debt financing providers in similar management buyout deals, as illustrated in Exhibit 4.3. Our forecasts of working capital items are also linked to the firm's past performance. Since working capital is equal to the sum between inventories and receivables taking payables out, we will need the historical trends of these variables, which are shown in Exhibit 4.4. By analyzing past capital expenditures, we can easily observe that they generally absorbed between 3 percent and 5 percent of firm's revenue, with the exception of 2012, when a considerable amount of investments was dedicated to new showroom openings. Therefore, we assume that capital expenditures will follow a similar trend also in the forecasted years. The relevant discount rate, that is, the weighted average cost of capital (WACC), is calculated considering the risk-free rate and the market risk premium observable in the market at the time of the valuation. The unlevered beta of companies in the furniture industry, the cost of debt, and the pertinent tax rate are taken from available public sources at the time of the valuation. The detailed assumptions used to forecast operating and financial items, to compute the discount rate and the income statement, balance sheet, and cash flows projections at the basis of our original DCF model are displayed in Exhibit 4.5. Running the model, we obtain an equity value of 74€ million in this base scenario that, net of the initial 60€ million investment by the private equity firm, implies a 14€ million *NPV*. This valuation, however, is based on static assumptions and does not account for the variability inherent to important value drivers of our model.

In *Step 2* of the Monte Carlo valuation process, we address this issue and we investigate what value drivers have the strongest impact on the estimated cash flows and on the *NPV* of the investment. We consider that the future evolution of the revenues of *Outdoor* will highly impact future cash flows. The evolution of revenues in turn will mainly depend on the future size of the core markets of the company and on the ability of the firm to increase its relative market share in those regions. We therefore consider the outdoor furniture market in Italy, France, Germany, and Spain as well as *Outdoor's* market share in those countries as random risk variables to be investigated. We also observe that the cost of purchases and the transportation cost have absorbed a large portion of *Outdoor's* revenues over the past years (on average 30 percent of overall revenues in the period 2011–2014) and that these costs are highly correlated with two indices describing the price of raw materials used by the company, as shown in Exhibit 4.6. In particular, we observe that the cost of purchases benefit from a 0.9 correlation with the index representing the general prices of lumber, iron, and aluminum, which are the main materials used to produce *Outdoor's* products, and that transportation cost

Exhibit 4.3 Financing profile for Outdoor

OPERATING COSTS

		t-4	t-3	t-2	t-1	current	t+1	t+2	t+3	t+4	t+5	t+6	t+7	t+8	t+9	t+10
Cost of Purchases	Year	t-4	t-3	t-2	t-1	current	t+1	t+2	t+3	t+4	t+5	t+6	t+7	t+8	t+9	t+10
	% revenues	-18.8%	-20.2%	-27.4%	-29.5%	-24.0%	-24.0%	-24.0%	-24.0%	-24.0%	-24.0%	-24.0%	-24.0%	-24.0%	-24.0%	-24.0%
Lumber	Year	t-4	t-3	t-2	t-1	current	t+1	t+2	t+3	t+4	t+5	t+6	t+7	t+8	t+9	t+10
	Amount of purchases															
	% cost of purchase	43%														
	Average price past 4 years	307.3														
	Forecasted price					307.3	307.3	307.3	307.3	307.3	307.3	307.3	307.3	307.3	307.3	307.3
						-8.07	-8.83	-9.43	-10.00	-10.86	-11.19	-11.52	-11.87	-12.22	-12.59	-12.97
Iron	Year	t-4	t-3	t-2	t-1	current	t+1	t+2	t+3	t+4	t+5	t+6	t+7	t+8	t+9	t+10
	Amount of purchases															
	% cost of purchase	41%														
	Average price past 4 years	134.2														
	Forecasted price					307.3	307.3	307.3	307.3	307.3	307.3	307.3	307.3	307.3	307.3	307.3
						-7.68	-8.40	-8.97	-9.51	-10.33	-10.64	-10.96	-11.29	-11.63	-11.98	-12.34
Aluminum	Year	t-4	t-3	t-2	t-1	current	t+1	t+2	t+3	t+4	t+5	t+6	t+7	t+8	t+9	t+10
	Amount of purchases															
	% cost of purchase	17%														
	Average price past 4 years	2016.6														
	Forecasted price					134.2	134.2	134.2	134.2	134.2	134.2	134.2	134.2	134.2	134.2	134.2
						-3.15	-3.45	-3.68	-3.90	-4.24	-4.37	-4.50	-4.63	-4.77	-4.91	-5.06
Transportation Cost	Year	t-4	t-3	t-2	t-1	current	t+1	t+2	t+3	t+4	t+5	t+6	t+7	t+8	t+9	t+10
	% revenues	-5.1%	-5.6%	-7.0%	-7.4%	-6.3%	-6.3%	-6.3%	-6.3%	-6.3%	-6.3%	-6.3%	-6.3%	-6.3%	-6.3%	-6.3%
	Amount	96.4														
	Average price past 4 years	96.4														
	Forecasted price					2016.6	2016.6	2016.6	2016.6	2016.6	2016.6	2016.6	2016.6	2016.6	2016.6	2016.6
						96.4	96.4	96.4	96.4	96.4	96.4	96.4	96.4	96.4	96.4	96.4
						(5.0)	(5.4)	(5.8)	(6.2)	(6.7)	(6.9)	(7.1)	(7.3)	(7.5)	(7.8)	(8.0)

		t-4	t-3	t-2	t-1	current	t+1	t+2	t+3	t+4	t+5	t+6	t+7	t+8	t+9	t+10
Marketing	% revenues	-10.3%	-9.6%	-10.4%	-9.6%	-10.0%	-10.0%	-10.0%	-10.0%	-10.0%	-10.0%	-10.0%	-10.0%	-10.0%	-10.0%	-10.0%
Personnel cost	% revenues	-13.8%	-12.9%	-13.3%	-11.8%	-12.9%	-12.9%	-12.9%	-12.9%	-12.9%	-12.9%	-12.9%	-12.9%	-12.9%	-12.9%	-12.9%
SG&A	% revenues	-7.5%	-6.7%	-6.7%	-5.9%	-6.7%	-6.7%	-6.7%	-6.7%	-6.7%	-6.7%	-6.7%	-6.7%	-6.7%	-6.7%	-6.7%
Amortization	As from management forecasts		-3.5	-3.6	-1.8	-8.1	-8.1	-8.1	-8.1	-8.1	-7.6	-7.5	-7.6	-7.5	-7.5	-7.5
Depreciation & Amortization	% revenues	-12.0%	-10.7%	-11.2%	-9.1%	-10.7%	-10.7%	-10.7%	-10.7%	-10.7%	-10.7%	-10.7%	-10.7%	-10.7%	-10.7%	-10.7%
FINANCING																
Cash interests on debt	Interest rate (IRS Euribor 5Y = 0.7%)		-5.9%	-6.0%	-6.5%	-3.5%	-3.5%	-3.5%	-3.5%	-3.5%	-3.5%	-3.5%	-3.5%	-3.5%	-3.5%	-3.5%
Cash interests on ST debt	Interest rate					1.5%	1.5%	1.5%	1.5%	1.5%	1.5%	1.5%	1.5%	1.5%	1.5%	1.5%
PIK interests	Interest rate (IRS Euribor 5Y = 0.7%)					-5.5%	-5.5%	-5.5%	-5.5%	-5.5%	-5.5%	-5.5%	-5.5%	-5.5%	-5.5%	-5.5%
TAXES																
Taxes	% EBT	-38%	-39%	-42%	-42%	-40.5%	-40.5%	-40.5%	-40.5%	-40.5%	-40.5%	-40.5%	-40.5%	-40.5%	-40.5%	-40.5%

Exhibit 4.4 Working capital evolution for Outdoor

BALANCE SHEET																	
Accounts receivable	Year		t-4	t-3	t-2	t-1	current	t+1	t+2	t+3	t+4	t+5	t+6	t+7	t+8	t+9	t+10
Days	Days		4	3	3	3	3	3	3	3	3	3	3	3	3	3	3
Inventories	Year		t-4	t-3	t-2	t-1	current	t+1	t+2	t+3	t+4	t+5	t+6	t+7	t+8	t+9	t+10
Days	Days		80	114	119	96	102	102	102	102	102	102	102	102	102	102	102
	Min	98															
	Max	103															
Accounts payable	Year		t-4	t-3	t-2	t-1	current	t+1	t+2	t+3	t+4	t+5	t+6	t+7	t+8	t+9	t+10
Days	Days		−30	−57	−62	−55	−51	−51	−51	−51	−51	−51	−51	−51	−51	−51	−51
	Min	−50															
	Max	−55															
CAPEX	Year		t-4	t-3	t-2	t-1	current	t+1	t+2	t+3	t+4	t+5	t+6	t+7	t+8	t+9	t+10
							5%	5%	5%	5%	5%	5%	5%	5%	5%	5%	5%

Exhibit 4.5 The assumptions for Outdoor valuation

Key Assumptions

Valuation date	End of 2014
WACC	0.0%
Perpetual growth rate	2.5%

Management Scenario

Cash Flow Statement	t-3	t-2	t-1	current	t+1	t+2	t+3	t+4	t+5	t+6	t+7	t+8	t+9	t+10	Norm.
EBITDA	29.1	22.0	25.5	31.7	34.6	37.0	39.2	42.6	43.9	45.2	46.6	48.0	49.4	50.9	
Change in allowance	0.8	0.4	0.4	0	0	0	0	0	0	0	0	0	0	0	
Taxes on EBIT	(9.0)	(6.1)	(7.7)	(9.4)	(10.3)	(11.0)	(11.6)	(12.6)	(13.0)	(13.4)	(13.8)	(14.2)	(14.7)	(15.1)	
Change in other ST assets and liabilities	0.3	0.4	0.9	0	0	0	0	0	0	0	0	0	0	0	
Change in operating working capital	-2.3	0.8	5	(3.4)	(1.1)	(0.9)	(0.8)	(1.3)	(0.5)	(0.5)	(0.5)	(0.5)	(0.5)	(0.6)	
Change in net working capital	(11.0)	(4.9)	(1.8)	(12.8)	(11.4)	(11.9)	(12.5)	(13.9)	(13.5)	(13.9)	(14.3)	(14.8)	(15.2)	(15.7)	
Capex	(11.7)	(2.3)	(8.7)	(3.5)	(3.9)	(4.1)	(4.4)	(4.8)	(4.9)	(5.1)	(5.2)	(5.4)	(5.5)	(5.7)	
Extraordinary gains (Losses)	(0.7)	(0.1)	(0.3)	0.0	0.0	0.0	0.0	0.0	0.0	0.0	0.0	0.0	0.0	0.0	

(continued)

Exhibit 4.5 (*Continued*)

				current	t+1	t+2	t+3	t+4	t+5	t+6	t+7	t+8	t+9	t+10	
Operating FCF	-2.5	9.0	7.4	5.9	9.1	10.0	10.7	11.3	12.5	12.8	13.2	13.6	14.0	14.4	14.4
Year				current	t+1	t+2	t+3	t+4	t+5	t+6	t+7	t+8	t+9	t+10	
Discount factor				0.930	0.864	0.804	0.747	0.695	0.646	0.600	0.558	0.519	0.483	0.449	
Present value of FCFO				5.5	7.9	8.0	8.0	7.8	8.0	7.7	7.4	7.1	6.8	6.5	

Summary	(€m)
Present value of FCFO	81
Continuing value	293
Present value of continuing value	131
Enterprise value (value of operations)	212
Less net financial position	138
Equity value	74
NPV	14

Exhibit 4.6 Revenues–costs correlation

CORRELATIONS

	Lumber	Aluminum	Iron	Oil
Lumber	1			
Aluminum	0.085015364	1		
Iron	0.034669352	0.134884552	1	
Oil	0.102721406	0.413031384	0.087182052	1

is highly dependent on the cost of oil. Therefore, we consider the two cost items, that is, the index and the price of oil, as random risk variables that future evolution can be linked to the distribution of the prices of the relevant raw materials. We finally examine the short-term balance sheet items of *Outdoor* and observe a remarkably seasonal trend in sales that turns the evolution of net working capital into a critical factor for the sustainability of the firm. Indeed, deliveries from suppliers are generally carried out in the fourth quarter of each year and related cash outflows usually take place in the same period. However, *Outdoor* sells its products and collects cash mainly in the second quarter of each year. Therefore, the rotation of inventory is very slow and absorbs a considerable stake of capital, a particularly risky factor for a firm that is expected to grow quickly in the following years. We therefore consider two very common financial ratios, days inventory outstanding and days payable outstanding, as key random risk variables that can approximate how quickly the firm is able to have an inventory turnover on average and how quickly it is able to be paid by its customers on average. We then model their expected future distribution.

Hence, we recognize as random risk variables of the model:

- The size of the high-end furniture market in *Outdoor*'s core markets (Italy, France, Germany, and Spain) in the forecasted years 2015–2025
- *Outdoor*'s market share in the same markets over the years 2015–2025
- The evolution of the price of raw materials that are highly influential for *Outdoor*'s main cost items: lumber, iron, and aluminum (cost of purchases) and oil (transportation costs)
- The days inventory and days payable outstanding due to the highly seasonal trend in *Outdoor*'s turnover

In *Step 3* of the Monte Carlo valuation approach, we develop the distribution assumptions for the selected stochastic variables. To carry out this step, we rely both on the analysis of historical data describing the past behavior of the relevant value drivers and on the opinions of experts and management of the firm about the expected dynamics of these future value drivers. In particular, we assume the following distributions:

- *Size of core markets:* We select in Crystal Ball the Gumbel distribution to describe the random size of *Outdoor*'s core markets. This distribution is commonly used to describe the smallest value of a response over a period of time and is negatively skewed (i.e., it has a long tail extending toward more negative values). We select the Gumbel distribution to account for potential adverse meteorological conditions that can negatively impact *Outdoor*'s revenues in years characterized by bad weather in spring and summer, as in 2013. In particular, for each country/year observation, we choose a Gumbel distribution with an expected value equal to our base-case scenario, a minimum value equal to an 8 percent reduction of the expected value, and a maximum value equal to a 2 percent increase of the expected value. An example of a Gumbel distribution used for market size is displayed in Exhibit 4.7 and the minimum/maximum values assumed for each of these markets are reported in Exhibit 4.8.
- *Outdoor's market share:* We assume a normal distribution with standard deviation equal to 1 percent for the risky variable representing the market share controlled by *Outdoor* in each country/year. The expected value of the distribution coincides with our base case scenario. The 1 percent standard deviation has been selected according to expert

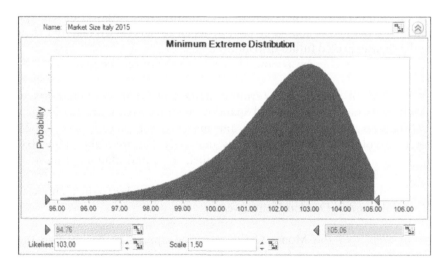

Exhibit 4.7 Gumbel distribution used for *Outdoor*'s market size

Exhibit 4.8 Min./Max. values assumed for each market

SALES

Italy	Year	current	t+1	t+2	t+3	t+4
	Market size (€M)	103	113	120	124	135
	Market size (€M) - Best	105.06	115.26	122.4	126.48	137.7
	Market size (€M) - Worst	94.76	103.96	110.4	114.08	124.2
France	Year	current	t+1	t+2	t+3	t+4
	Market size (€M)	130	141	148	159	168
	Market size (€M) - Best	132.6	143.82	150.96	162.18	171.36
	Market size (€M) - Worst	119.6	129.72	136.16	146.28	154.56
Germany	Year	current	t+1	t+2	t+3	t+4
	Market size (€M)	103	104	105	110	115
	Market size (€M) - Best	105.06	106.08	107.1	112.2	117.3
	Market size (€M) - Worst	94.76	95.68	96.6	101.2	105.8
Spain	Year	current	t+1	t+2	t+3	t+4
	Market size (€M)	69	71	72	76	78
	Market size (€M)—Best	70.38	72.42	73.44	77.52	79.56
	Market size (€M)—Worst	63.48	65.32	66.24	69.92	71.76

advisors' opinions to account for the uncertain future evolution of the market share.

■ *Cost of purchases and transportation cost:* We use an add-in function of Crystal Ball to fit the distribution of lumber, iron, aluminum, and oil prices based on past data from the raw material and derivative markets. Crystal Ball suggests *beta* distributions to describe the potential prices taken by lumber and oil and *gamma* distributions to describe the potential prices of iron and aluminum, as displayed in Exhibits 4.9 and 4.10.

■ *Days inventory and days payables:* Based on discussions with the management of the firm, we assume that attempts to improve *Outdoor's* net working capital structure will be carried out over the forthcoming years. Following this line of reasoning, we identify two triangular distributions and allow for potential improvements in the rotation of inventory and in the deferment of accounts payable, as shown in Exhibit 4.11.

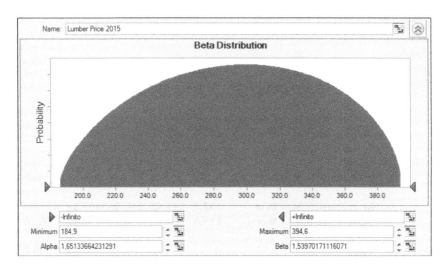

Exhibit 4.9   Potential prices of iron

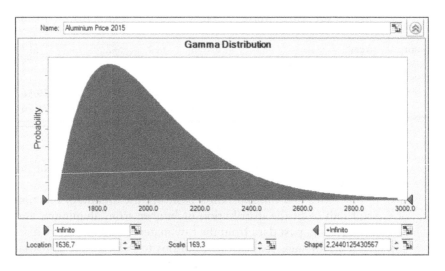

Exhibit 4.10   Potential prices of aluminum

In *Step 4* of the Monte Carlo procedure, we define relevant correlations among risk variables. In particular, we consider three main correlation dynamics:

- The correlation among the sizes of the markets in which *Outdoor* primarily operates is defined *cross-sectionally* within each of the forecasted

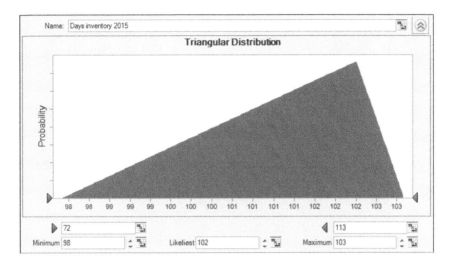

Exhibit 4.11 Modeling the working capital dynamics

year: Based on past evidence, we assume that meteorological conditions are correlated across neighboring European countries and we indicate a 0.8 correlation among the size of the Italian, French, German, and Spanish outdoor furniture markets.

■ The cross-sectional correlation among the market shares of the company in different markets is assumed to be negligible and is therefore set equal to 0. However, on the basis of the strength of the firm's brand in the premium furniture market, customer loyalty is assumed to hold over consecutive years. Therefore, a time series correlation equal to 0.7 is derived from past marketing data and is assumed to hold across consecutive years for each single core market.

■ The correlation among the changes in the prices of raw material is derived from past data in the 2011–2014 period and included in the model.

In *Step 5* of Monte Carlo, we run the analysis based on the model and on the assumptions defined in the previous steps. We ask Crystal Ball to run 5,000 simulations of the valuation procedure by generating sequences of random numbers for the selected risk variables. We define three forecast variables for the model:

1. Future expected cash flows, in the period 2015–2025
2. Equity value, equal to the value of the discounted expected cash flows plus the perpetuity value
3. *NPV*, equal to the equity value net of the initial equity investment

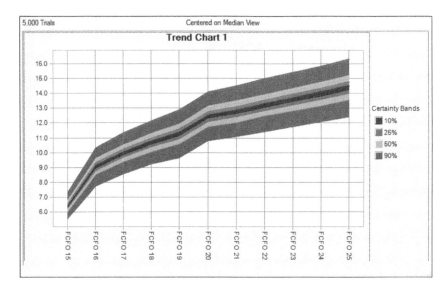

Exhibit 4.12   Future expected cash flows in the explicit forecast period

The output of the simulation generates several graphs and statistics that can be used to properly assess the profitability of the investment and its risk. Exhibit 4.12 provides an analysis of the future expected cash flows in the explicit forecast period. This trend chart displays different bands, each representing the certainty intervals into which the true values of the forecasts are expected to fall. For instance, the 80 percent certainty band shows the range of values between which the forecasted future cash flows are expected to fall 80 percent of the time. The bands grow wider as predictions move into the future as a result of the increase in uncertainty and in the forecasted standard deviation. As a matter of fact, while the cash flow forecasts for the first year of projections are contained in the interval €5.5 to €7.5 million, that is, a €2 million range, the cash flow forecasts for the final year of projections increase to a €4 million range, between €12.5 and €16.5 million.

The main results of our analysis are displayed in Exhibits 4.13 and 4.14, which show the distribution of the equity value and of the *NPV* of the investment from the private equity perspective. As stated previously, the Monte Carlo procedure produces a distribution of values based on recursively simulated random numbers. From the analysis of the outputs of Crystal Ball, therefore, we can infer the most likely outcome for the private equity's investment in *Outdoor*, and we can also assess the probability associated with each of the other potential outcomes. For instance, the private equity firm might be interested in knowing the probability with which the *NPV* of its

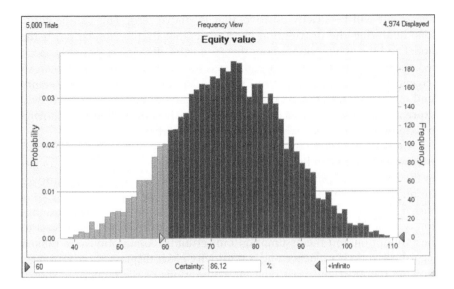

Exhibit 4.13 Distribution of the equity value

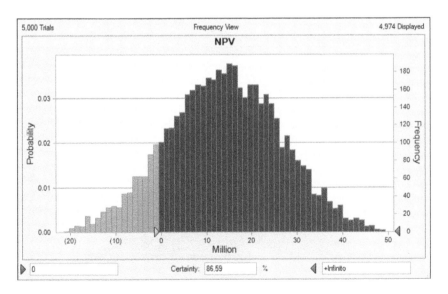

Exhibit 4.14 Distribution of the *NPV* of the investment

investment will be strictly positive, that is, above zero. This can be easily done analyzing the distribution chart generated by the simulation: if the model and the assumptions about the main value drivers are properly specified, the net value of the private equity investment will be positive with an 86 percent probability, as shown in Exhibit 4.14. Similarly, the private equity fund might be interested in knowing the probability that its investment will return an *NPV* larger than a certain amount, such as €10 million. As showed in Exhibit 4.15, this probability is equal to 60 percent.

Another interesting feature of the Monte Carlo procedure is the sensitivity analysis that can be run to show the impact that each assumption has on the forecast. In particular, a sensitivity analysis is very useful to answer the question, *What percentage of the uncertainty in the target forecast is caused by assumption X?* The overall sensitivity of a forecast to an assumption is a combination of two factors: the model sensitivity of the forecast to the assumption and the assumption's uncertainty. Assumptions are ranked according to their influence and a sensitivity chart displays these rankings, showing the most and least relevant assumptions of the model. As shown in Exhibit 4.16, the future trends in the French and Italian markets and the future dynamics in the cost of purchases are the risk variables that lead to the strongest impact on the simulated distribution of the net investment value in *Outdoor*.

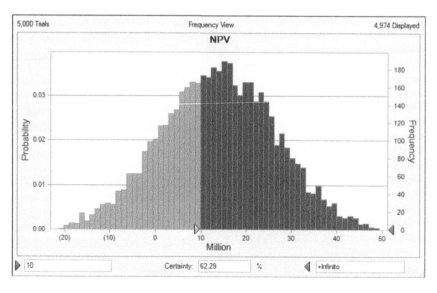

Exhibit 4.15   Probability of getting a return above a determined threshold

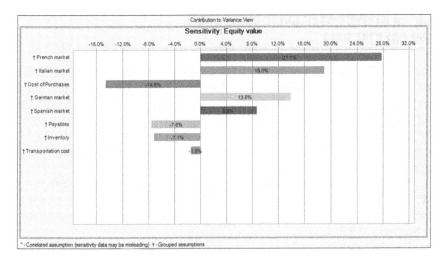

Exhibit 4.16 Variables with the strongest impact

As shown in this chapter, the Monte Carlo method leads to several improvements over the "pure" DCF methodology, in particular with regard to the consideration of uncertain and flexible scenarios. The Monte Carlo approach can be used to simulate a distribution for the return of an investment and to analyze its expected value as well as its volatility, rather than considering a simple point estimate. These features make the Monte Carlo model particularly suitable for situations in which the management of a firm needs to decide whether to take on an investment, allowing them to assess the investment's risk in terms of confidence levels and probabilities. It is also particularly useful to support a proactive strategy in the risk management of a real investment. Nevertheless, the Monte Carlo method also exhibits some drawbacks when compared to a conventional DCF valuation. In particular, the implementation of the model is more complex and time consuming than a simple DCF valuation and might discourage its use in situations characterized by a low level of uncertainty or at the initial stage of an analysis. Furthermore, the identification of proper assumptions for the model, in terms of the relevance of the selected risk variables, their distributions and correlations, becomes a crucial step in the process. If these steps are carried out without the required level of accuracy and sophistication, the final output of a Monte Carlo valuation might be less accurate and more subjective than the results of a conventional point estimate derived by the simple DCF model.

4.5   A STEP-BY-STEP GUIDE USING EXCEL
AND CRYSTAL BALL

For the following examples, we will use Microsoft Office 365 Excel 2011 for Windows. Crystal Ball is *Not* available for OS X. Anything reproduced in this chapter cannot be fully executed with a laptop running OS X without the Windows platform.

Crystal Ball does *Not* come with Microsoft Office. It needs to be downloaded as an add-in from: http://www.oracle.com/technetwork/middleware/crystalball/downloads/index.html.

We will now work through a simple example to show how we can run a Monte Carlo analysis in Excel. For simplicity, we will use the same example used in our example on scenario analysis. The Excel spreadsheet is available as Scenario_Analysis.xlsx.

For the sake of simplicity, let us reintroduce the example. We will use a simple two-stage DCF model, in which we will therefore have a first-stage growth, a second-stage growth, and a terminal growth rate. We assume that the firm we consider, let us call it A, has the following characteristics:

Initial cash flow	$100,000
Debt level	$900,000
Shares outstanding	10,000

Moreover, we know that A is ready to expand geographically, something that will boost its revenues in the short term. We therefore consider that A will experience a high-growth first-stage period for 5 years, a moderate growth 5-year period, and an inflation-based terminal growth period based on the going-concern assumption. In particular, we will consider the following growth rates:

First-stage growth rate (years 1–5)	8%
Second-stage growth rate (years 6–10)	5%
Terminal growth rate (years 11–∞)	2%

A faces a cost of capital equal to 10 percent, which we will use as our discount rate.

We therefore want to calculate the DCF for A, based on a 10-year forecasted period. We are interested in two values: the DCF itself, that is, the present value of the cash flows estimated for the forecasted period summed to the discounted terminal value, and the intrinsic value (IV), equal to the ratio between the net value of the firm (DCF-debt) and the number of shares outstanding.

We input our data in Excel and calculate the DCF as explained in previous chapters.

Similarly to what we did in scenario analysis, the first step consists in the decision on the variables to vary. This simplified example does not lead to many issues in our decision, but a real-life case would involve many more factors and this choice could in fact be quite challenging.

We decide to focus on the three different growth rates, on the discount rate, and on the debt level as our variables of interest.

Differently from scenario analysis, however, we do not have to pick a number of scenarios to run and give a discrete number of possible values taken on by the factors considered. Instead, we have to assume a distribution for our variables of interest and set the number of trials for our simulation. We will perform the first round of simulations assuming all variables to be drawn independently of one another and a second round of simulations in which variables are correlated. Both rounds are executed four times at 5,000, 10,000, 100,000, and a million trials.

We will try to set up our assumptions to create a high level of similarity between the example run with scenario analysis and the one run with Crystal Ball in order to be able to compare our results.

Once Crystal Ball is installed, a new tab will appear in Excel called "Crystal Ball." By clicking on it, a series of commands will appear, as can be seen in Exhibit 4.17. There are two main elements that we have to define: the assumptions (i.e., the variables that will be varied in the simulation), and the forecasts (i.e., the result variables in which we are interested).

As mentioned beforehand, therefore, our assumptions will regard the three growth rates, the discount rate, and the debt level, whereas our forecast will be the final DCF value and the intrinsic value, just as in our scenario analysis example.

In order to define our variables' distribution, we therefore click on our base case value of that variable and then on the "Define Assumption" icon (see Exhibit 4.18). We start from the first-stage growth rate, where base value is set at 8 percent. We will therefore click on the 8 percent cell, and then on the "Define Assumption" icon (see Exhibit 4.19).

Excel will then ask for a distribution type. According to the analyst's expectations, knowledge, and expertise, the best-fitting distribution should be chosen for any of the variables considered and inputs should then be plugged in accordingly.

In the case of the first-stage growth rate, we believe that a triangular distribution is the best-fitting choice, bounded by the low and high values that we discussed in the scenario analysis example—that is, 5 percent and 10 percent, and centered at the base value equal to 8 percent, as shown in Exhibit 4.20.

102

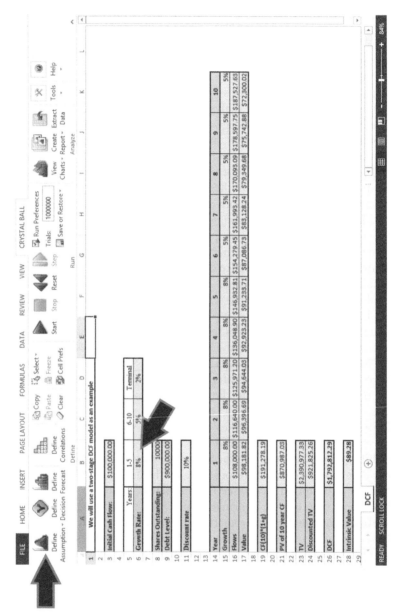

Exhibit 4.17 Main Crystal Ball interface

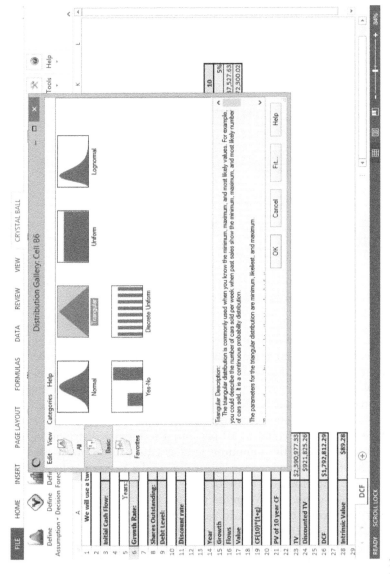

Exhibit 4.18 Defining assumptions in Crystal Ball

103

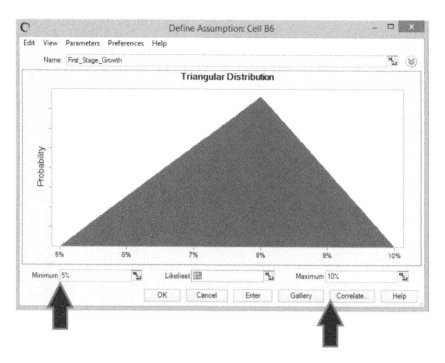

Exhibit 4.19   Entering assumptions in Crystal Ball

The same is done for the other variables. We choose a triangular distribution for the second-stage growth rate bounded between 2 percent and 8 percent and centered around 5 percent; a lognormal distribution for the terminal growth rate with mean equal to 2 percent, location parameter set to 1 percent, and standard deviation equal to 1 percent; a triangular distribution for the discount rate bounded by 8 percent and 13 percent with the most likely value equal to 10 percent; a triangular distribution for the debt level for which the minimum level is equal to the most likely debt level of $900,000, which is our base value, and a maximum level equal to $1,300,000. Therefore, debt cannot decrease from the base value, but it can be higher than expected. We invite you to check that we have maintained the best- and worst-case scenario values described in the scenario analysis chapter. Exhibits 4.20 to 4.22 illustrate the distribution assumptions made.

Once all the assumptions are set, the next step consists in the selection of the forecasts. We therefore first click on the DCF base value and we go back to the "Crystal Ball" tab and click on the "Define Forecast" icon.

A window will appear confirming the DCF value as a forecast value. We will press "OK" and do the same for the intrinsic value cell.

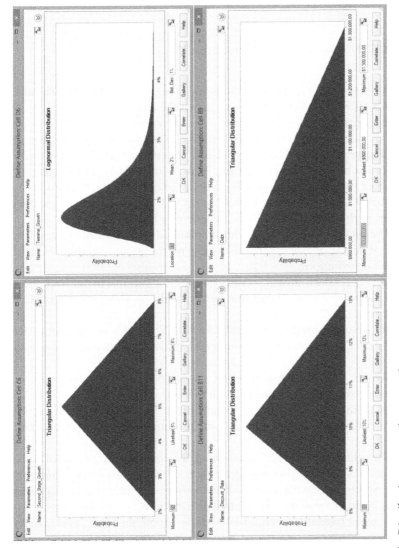

Exhibit 4.20 Distribution assumptions: case 1

Exhibit 4.21   Distribution assumptions: case 2

At this point, all the assumptions and forecasts are set and the simulation is ready to be run. The only choice left to the analyst is the selection of the number of trials. As mentioned beforehand, we will select 5,000 trials, then 10,000, then 100,000, and finally a million trials. In order to set the number of trials, we go back to the "Crystal Ball" tab in the "Run" section and type the desired number of trials in the "Trials:" tab, as shown in Exhibit 4.23.

Once the number of trials is chosen, the only thing left to do is to run the Monte Carlo analysis by clicking on the "Start" button of the "Run" section in the "Crystal Ball" tab, as shown in Exhibit 4.24.

The analysis will produce the simulated distribution of the result variables obtained drawing random values of the input variables from their defined distributions.

We obtain the following results for the DCF variable in our four different simulations at an increasing number of trials, as shown in Exhibits 4.25 to 4.28.

We obtain the following results for the IV variable in our four different simulations at an increasing number of trials, as shown in Exhibits 4.29 to 4.32.

We can immediately notice that a greater number of trials leads to the simulated distribution approaching a theoretical one much more accurately. Although the DCF distribution is still off at the peak of the distribution, the IV distribution almost perfectly fits the gamma distribution at a million trials.

Something is, however, still missing. The greatest advantage of scenario analysis was the ability to consider how the variables are interrelated to each other. So far, we have assumed all the variables to be drawn independently of one another from their respective distributions.

In order to enable Crystal Ball to draw "good" or "bad" events together more often, we can set up a correlation matrix across our assumptions. In order to do so, we click again on the first stage growth rate base value and on the "Define Assumption" icon once again. The assumption is already saved as we set it up beforehand, but we click on "Correlate..." this time, as shown in Exhibit 4.33.

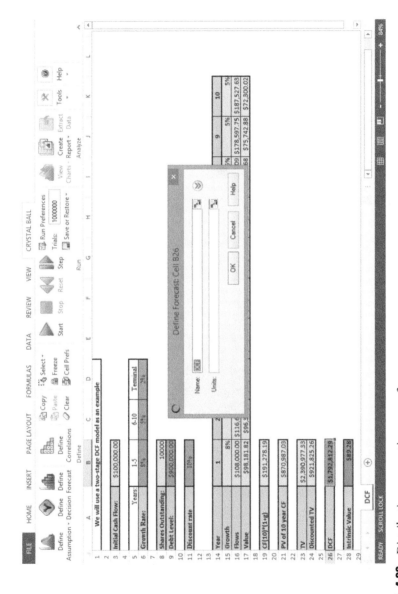

Exhibit 4.22 Distribution assumptions: case 3

107

Exhibit 4.23   Running trials in Crystal Ball

Exhibit 4.24   Starting trials

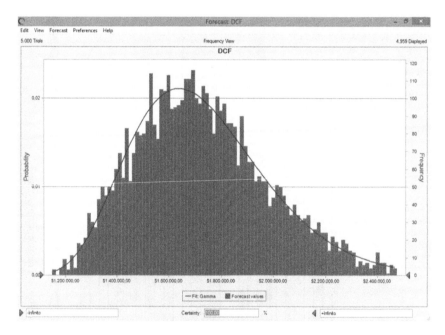

Exhibit 4.25   Simulation outcome depending on the number of trials

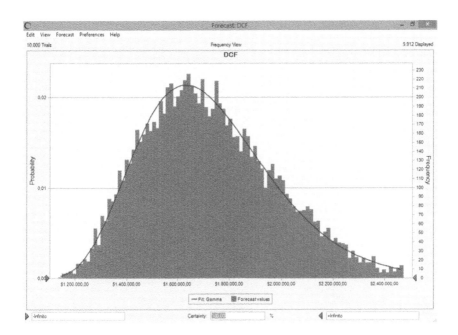

Exhibit 4.26 Simulation outcome depending on the number of trials

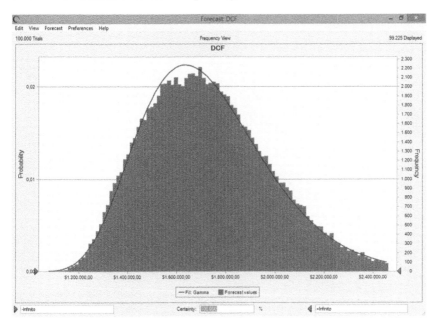

Exhibit 4.27 Simulation outcome depending on the number of trials

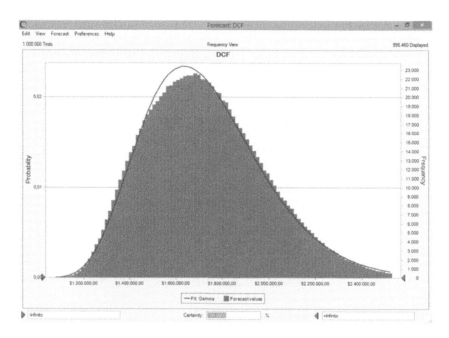

Exhibit 4.28   Simulation outcome depending on the number of trials

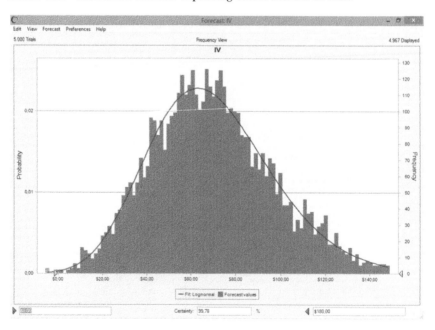

Exhibit 4.29   Simulation IV outcome

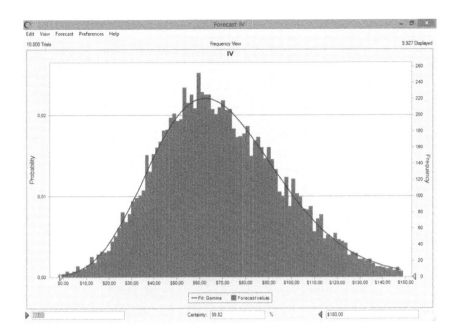

Exhibit 4.30   Simulation IV outcome

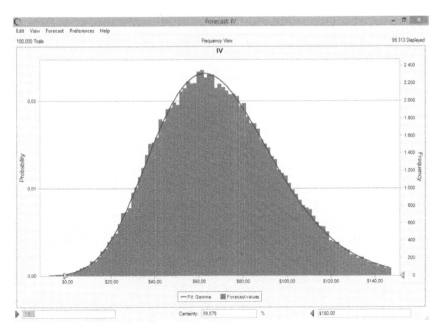

Exhibit 4.31   Simulation IV outcome

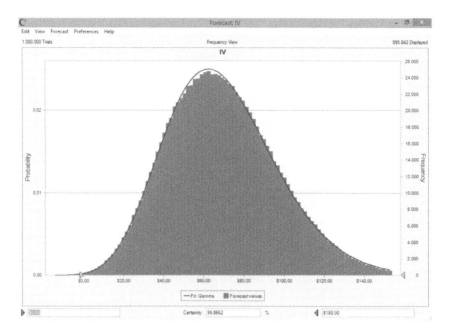

Exhibit 4.32   Simulation IV outcome

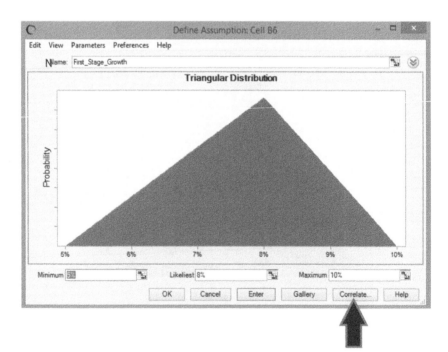

Exhibit 4.33   Correlation analysis in Crystal Ball

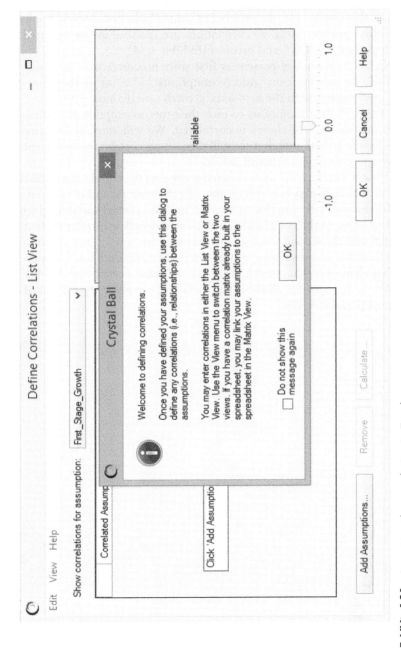

Exhibit 4.34 Accepting the correlation in Excel

A new window will now open. Excel will first explain how to define correlations and ask whether a correlation matrix already exists in the spreadsheet. In this simple case, the matrix can simply be linked. We will not worry about this situation, since no correlations are specified in our example. We will then click on "OK" and proceed (Exhibit 4.34).

No assumptions are present at first since no correlations are currently specified. We then click on "Add Assumptions . . . " to set up the other variables' correlations with the first-stage growth rate (Exhibit 4.35).

Excel will then prompt us to pick the other assumption variables with which our variable of choice is correlated. We will start by selecting the second-stage growth rate, but we will then set up correlation coefficients for all variables, as shown in Exhibit 4.36.

We will then have to write down the value of the correlation coefficient. Excel will also display a graph on the side showing the approximated relationship between the variable of interest and the selected variable, given the specified value of the correlation coefficient. We pick a correlation between the first- and the second-stage growth rates equal to 0.7, since it is intuitive that a firm that is able to grow very fast in the first stage is likely to experience a higher-than-expected growth in the second stage as well (Exhibit 4.37).

We do the same for all the other variables, obtaining the full list of correlations (Exhibit 4.38).

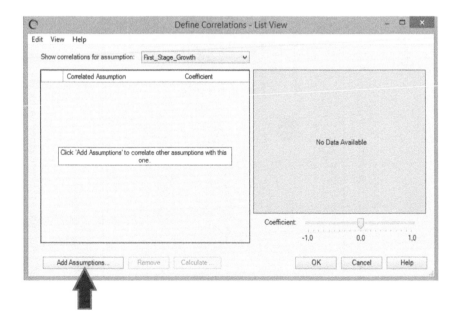

Exhibit 4.35 Adding assumptions

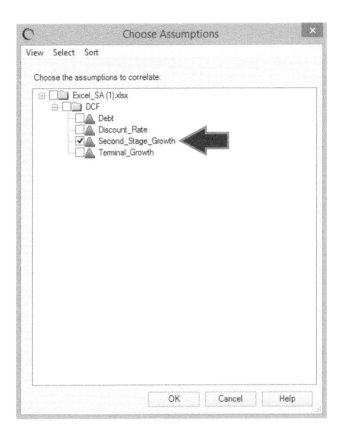

Exhibit 4.36 Setting up correlation coefficients

We now need to set the other cross-correlations. Excel will help us to build the correlation matrix in such a way that it is consistent. In more specific cases, when the correlation coefficients have to be set in a rigid way, we can simply input our own previously calculated correlation matrix. Since this is a simple example where we mostly care about the correlation signs being correct, we will illustrate how Excel takes care of this issue. We can then click on our second variable of interest, the second-stage growth rate, then on the "Define Assumption" icon, and on "Correlate . . . " once more. We then proceed to "Add Assumptions . . . " as we did before and we input some values for the correlation coefficients (Exhibit 4.39).

When we click on "OK" Excel will instead let us know that the values we picked are not consistent and ask if we would like Excel itself to adjust the correlations and create the matrix for us, as shown in Exhibit 4.40.

We therefore click on "Adjust" and we obtain the complete correlation matrix shown in Exhibit 4.41.

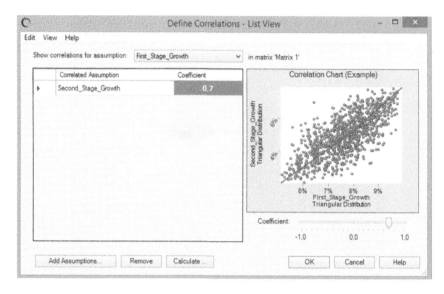

Exhibit 4.37 Choosing an adequate correlation

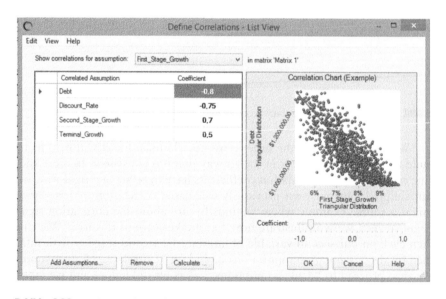

Exhibit 4.38 Full list of correlations

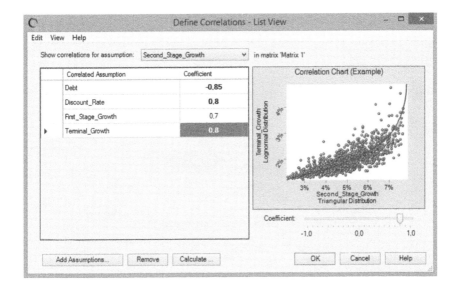

Exhibit 4.39   Entering values for the correlation coefficients

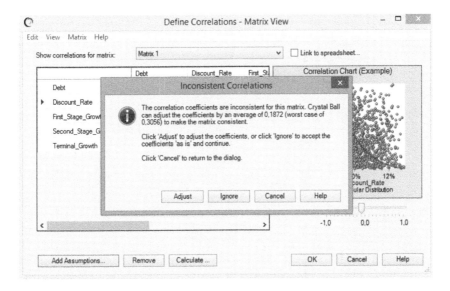

Exhibit 4.40   Choosing to adjust the correlations

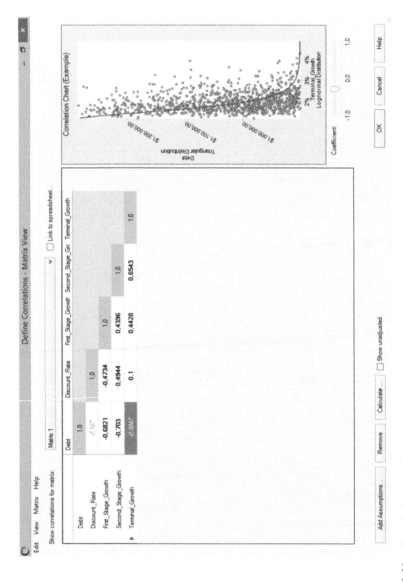

Exhibit 4.41 Correlation matrix

We can finally click on "OK" since all our variables are now correlated with each other. We invite you to check that a high draw of the first-stage growth rate is more likely to happen with a high draw of the second-stage and the terminal growth rates and with a low draw of the discount rate and the debt level. However, we do not want high growth rates in the future to lower discount rates, since the uncertainty is higher. If the growth rate is not high today, it will be more risky to obtain high growth rates in the future.

We can now finally rerun the simulations now that our variables are correlated with each other.

We obtain the following results for the DCF variable in our four different simulations at an increasing number of trials, demonstrated in Exhibits 4.42 to 4.45.

We obtain the results in Exhibits 4.46 to 4.49 for the IV variable in our four different simulations at an increasing number of trials.

What differences can we notice from the previous case of no correlation? It might seem that there is almost no effect, but the simulated distribution is actually more "well-behaved" once correlations are added in. In the IV case, the estimated distribution becomes smoother, whereas in the DCF case, it approximates the theoretical one more accurately.

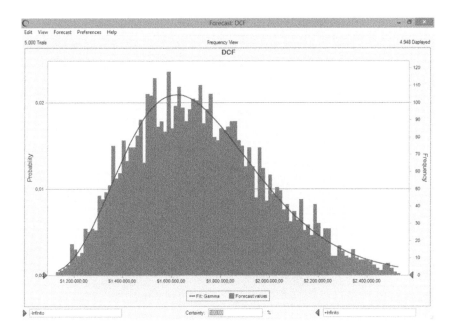

Exhibit 4.42 DCF results depending on the number of trials

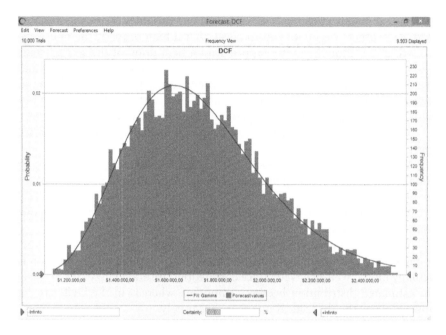

Exhibit 4.43   DCF results depending on the number of trials

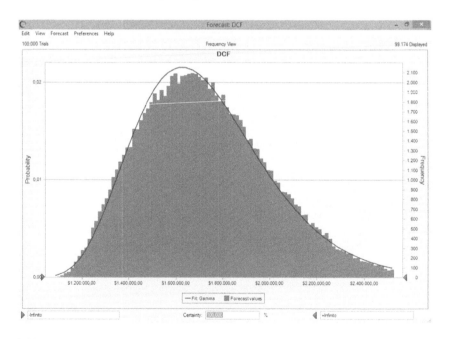

Exhibit 4.44   DCF results depending on the number of trials

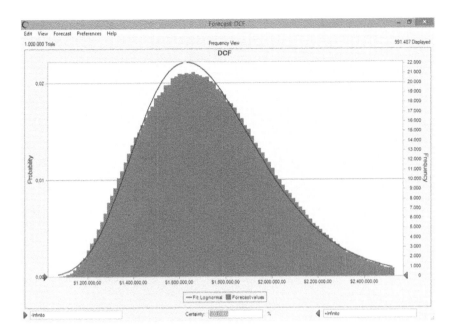

Exhibit 4.45 DCF results depending on the number of trials

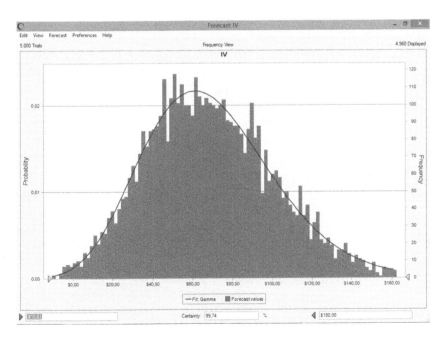

Exhibit 4.46 IV results depending on the number of trials

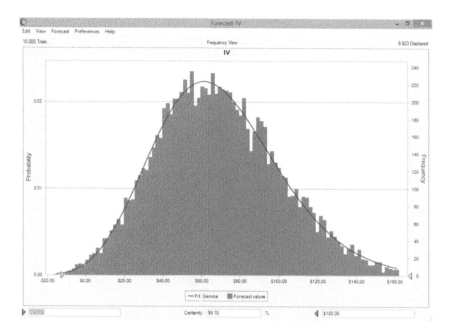

Exhibit 4.47 IV results depending on the number of trials

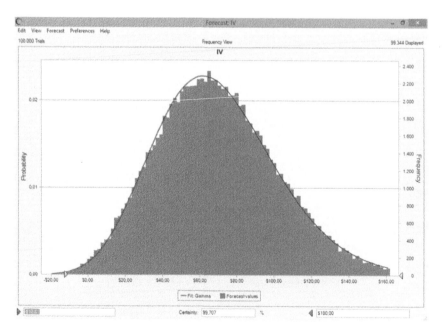

Exhibit 4.48 IV results depending on the number of trials

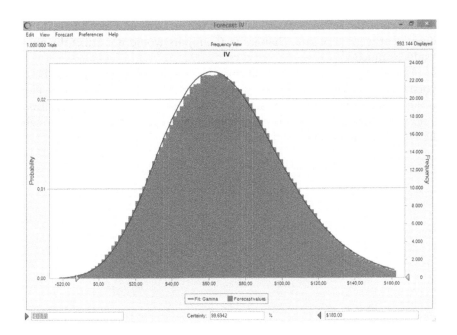

Exhibit 4.49 IV results depending on the number of trials

The most important takeaway from this exercise, however, is the many different realizations that a given investment could have in real life. If we take a look at our base scenario, with a DCF value of about $1.8 million and an intrinsic value slightly smaller than $90, we could be quite scared of finding out that these values will occur with a probability of less than 20 percent and less than 15 percent, respectively, with no correlation across variables at 5,000 trials. This probability drops for the DCF to 15 percent and increases to a value between 15 percent and 20 percent for the IV once correlation is added in. Increasing the trials all the way to a million, the probability becomes smoother at 20 percent and 15 percent, respectively, in the no-correlation case and is about equal for both variables to 15 percent when correlation is present across variables.

It is important to mention that this does not mean that the investment or the company is not as valuable as originally thought. The simulated DCF distribution is actually skewed to the right, indicating that it is more likely for a high outlier to happen than for a low one to be drawn. Nevertheless, a simulation exercise puts things into perspective. Even after having centered all our distributions around the base scenario values, the randomization is such that there is less than a fifth probability that those values will in fact materialize. It is true that better ones are likely to happen in the future, but this indicates the riskiness associated with the investment. Once again, if the investment were very safe, changes in the inputs would not affect the final results as much.

Therefore, this analysis confirms the results obtained in the best/worst-case scenario analysis, when we discussed the investment's risk due to the high gap between the best and worst possible results. This intuition is now supported by a much more solid mathematical reasoning through the DCF and the IV simulated distributions.

## CHAPTER 5

Determining Cash Flows
for Company Valuation

5.1 INTRODUCTION

As discussed in the previous chapters, valuing a company, an acquisition, or, more generally, any business investment requires some preliminary analysis in order to understand the business model under consideration and its potential growth. The next step considers the reorganization of the financial statement data and business plan figures to facilitate the application of the valuation methods hereafter discussed.

To this end, it is essential to recall the possibility to evaluate a company as a whole or as a sum of parts—that is, by evaluating the different business units the firm is composed of.

In particular, the sum-of-parts approach is more suitable when:

- The company operates in two or more business areas characterized by different underlying levels of uncertainty.
- The growth prospects differ significantly across the company's business units.

The need for separate valuations of the different business areas may arise also when the buyer, after the acquisition of control, is willing to spin off or sell some specific business units.

Management accounting provides the most important source of information to reorganize the company's data by business area. As a matter of fact, determining each business area's economic results is not enough: it is crucial to be able to account for each business's operating assets and liabilities. Such an operation can be particularly challenging whenever assets are common across different business units or when their allocation is not clear within the company.

We will assume throughout this chapter that the company operates in one business area only. This assumption allows a quick and effective introduction to the reorganization schemes generally adopted by analysts.

Our analysis focuses on the financial statements of the nonfinancial companies. Banks, insurance companies, and other financial firms are excluded from this chapter, as the criteria discussed herein are not always applicable to reorganization of their reported data.

Sections 5.2 and 5.3 will introduce common reorganization models of financial statements. In particular, we will focus on the two most important measures in valuation models: the *free cash flow from operations* (FCFO) and the *free cash flow to equity* (FCFE). We remind you that it is possible that other books could use different acronyms for the same measures that we will analyze. For instance, the FCFO is also called the *free cash flow to the firm* (FCFF) or the *operating free cash flow* (OFCF).

Section 5.6 concludes with a discussion on the main issues to tackle when moving from an analysis of historical data to a cash flow projection.

5.2   REORGANIZATION OF THE BALANCE SHEET

Across accounting systems and jurisdictions, the balance sheet model compliant with national regulations is in most cases not appropriate for corporate valuation applications. Bearing in mind financial statements have to convey information to various stakeholders (e.g., employees, shareholders, debt-holders, regulators) the main international accounting regimes tend to acknowledge two different guidelines on how balance sheets should be reorganized:

- *The financial principle,* which aggregates assets and liabilities based on their degree of liquidity and maturity. This principle allows the company's solvency to be evaluated by matching short-term assets with short-term liabilities.
- *The functional principle,* which aggregates assets and liabilities based on the business operations they belong to. This is particularly useful to measure the capital employed by the different business areas and the appraisal of the company's commercial and investment strategies.

The approach that we will illustrate in the following paragraphs follows the functional principle and has two main characteristics.

First, it points out several aggregations of value used in different approaches followed by several valuation techniques. It is about measures (such as net invested capital and working capital, etc.) that are used on a regular basis in the analyses made by investment banks and financial consultants.

Secondly, it introduces the distinction between core operating assets and assets related to noncore or complementary businesses (also referred to as *surplus assets*). Such assets are those employed by units that do not belong to the core activity of the firm. Despite this, nevertheless, they often reach considerable size relative to the value of total assets. By highlighting them, we can achieve two goals:

1. We can understand the amount of invested capital used in the company's core business and consequently correctly relate the resulting flows to the invested resources.
2. We can identify the asset values that are relevant for the projection of the future operational and financial dynamics.

5.2.1   Uses of Funds Related to Operating Activities

In order to show the financing needs associated with any business operations, we use a concise example assuming that a new manufacturing venture is launched. First of all, it will be necessary to sustain cash outflows to pay for the acquisition of the production structure—that is, for the purchase of facilities, machinery, operating departments if necessary, and so on. Second, once the company is active, production costs (employees, raw materials, services, etc.) and general costs have to be sustained. Generally, some inventories of raw materials and semi-finished goods will have to be maintained in order to ensure the continuity of the production cycle. In the same way, some inventories of finished goods will have to be maintained to quickly fulfill clients' orders.

After the sales are made, it typically takes a certain amount of time before payments are received. This will extend the financial exposure associated with production expenses and other operating outflows proportionally to the length of the average commercial credit collection period. However, it must be noted that a part of these expenses can be self-financed by delaying payments to suppliers.

This simple scheme allows us to identify the fundamental types of financial needs. For this purpose we have to distinguish between:

- The permanent needs related to the *operating assets* of the business.
- The net needs created by the cycle of the business operations (purchase of materials, manufacturing, selling), which are usually referred to as *working capital* needs. It mainly consists of the funds needed for inventory and commercial credit net of the financing received from suppliers.

The concepts explained above are displayed in Exhibit 5.1, which shows a balance sheet reorganized according to the functional approach.

Fixed Assets   When talking about fixed assets, we usually refer to a broad class of tangible assets (industrial buildings, facilities, machinery, etc.),

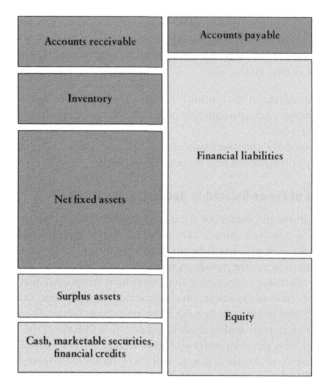

Exhibit 5.1   Balance sheet reorganized

intangible assets (brands, patents, etc.), and financial assets. Although there are typically no issues with the reorganization of the first two types of assets according to the operating area they are used in, the effective scope of financial assets has to be verified. Stakes held in commercial or industrial partnering companies can typically be considered *operating* financial fixed assets because they are part of the main "operations" of the company rather than mere short-term investments.

Working Capital   The categories related to the cycle of business operations (purchase of raw materials, manufacturing process, sale of finished products) consist of inventory, accounts receivable, and accounts payable (for goods and services related to the current cycle). The algebraic sum of these categories yields, as mentioned, the value of working capital.[1]

---

[1]To be complete, we should recall that there are other (less important) categories related to the buy-transform-sell cycle, such as accruals advances to suppliers for the purchase of materials and services, advances from clients, etc., which would also have to be considered.

Surplus Assets Surplus assets are defined as all those assets that could be alienated without compromising the requirements for the functioning of the core business. They normally consist of real estate properties that are not related to the company's core activity, stakes that represent financial nonoperating investments, and so on.

Cash and Cash-Equivalents In the reorganization model that we have introduced, cash and financial products equivalent to cash, securities held for trading and other financial receivables not related to operations are grouped in only one area.

This aggregation, generally used in valuation techniques, has the purpose of showing the company's net financial indebtedness or net financial position.

The Net Operating Invested Capital From Exhibit 5.1, we can now identify the areas related to operating activity and introduce the concept of net (operating) invested capital (NIC). Exhibit 5.2 shows the size of the company's NIC. It is composed of two aforementioned measures, net (operating) assets (NA) and working capital (WC).

The size of the *working capital*, keeping the business volume fixed, is directly related to the length of the *business operations' financial cycle (buy-transform-sell)*.

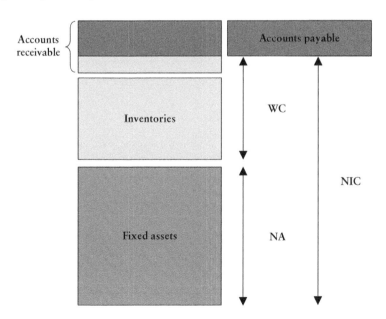

Exhibit 5.2 Representation of the net operating invested capital (NIC)

The length of the financial cycle is a function of the length of the several stages comprising the production process and of the company's policies relative to the collections and payment of its commercial credits and debits.

The size of fixed assets relative to the business volume depends on the capital intensity index and therefore on the business-technical characteristics of the productivity process, on the degree of vertical integration, and so on.

5.2.2 Sources of Financing

Let us now consider the structure of the financing sources of the NIC (and, if appropriate, of the nonoperating assets). Exhibit 5.3 gives a graphical representation of the relevant areas from Exhibit 5.1.

The net assets (both operating and nonoperating) are covered by financial liabilities negotiated by the company (in the short- and medium/long-term) and by its equity. The proportion of net financial debt with respect to equity determines the financial structure of the company. While the

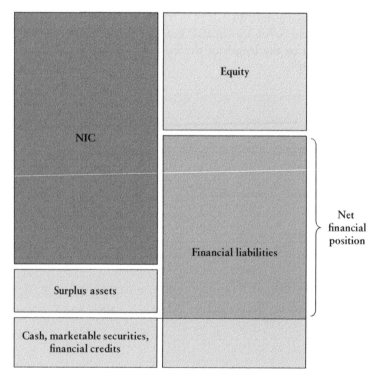

Exhibit 5.3   The structure of the financing sources

equity items of the balance sheet can usually be identified in a straightforward way, the liabilities and provisions pose several quantification issues.

The Pension Liabilities Problem In some countries, companies have to set aside a portion of employees' annual salaries as social security benefits. Depending on the country's regulations, the amount set aside can be revalued at the end of every year based on specific coefficients or indexes. The described mechanism can be interpreted in two ways, which lead to two alternative reclassifications of the pension liabilities item:

1. *As an element of the total cost of personnel, whose severance payment is delayed in time:* If this approach is followed, pension liabilities should be included in the working capital to be consistent with the previous discussion. As a matter of fact, the account would then be highly related to the buy-transform-sell cycle.
2. *As a way of financing granted by employees as frequently as their receipt of salaries and indexed on the capital:* Under this approach, pension liabilities should be included in the financial liabilities. To be consistent, the annual provision in the income statement should be divided into two parts: the first (current accrual) should be considered as a component of operating costs; the second (revaluation of the account) should be viewed as a financial liability and should be reorganized consequently.

In the example of *Printing Co.*, which is going to be discussed later, pension liabilities have been considered as operating assets, but in a different category outside of the working capital.

The Tax Liabilities and Provisions The tax liabilities and provisions represents another ambiguous reorganization item. If the tax payment happened right after the creation of income, we would not have any fiscal debits and credits in the balance sheet. Unfortunately, this is not usually the case.

The fiscal liability in the income statement summarizes fiscal debits and credits of all business areas as well as the extraordinary income components. This introduces a complication that has not been considered in the graphic representations of the balance sheet we have shown so far.

The correct solution to this problem would be to decompose the total fiscal debit (credit) into its basic components for each business area: this procedure, as we will soon discuss, is essential for the projection of net flows relative to each management activity.

In the analysis of historical balance sheets, this decomposition approach is too complicated for practical reasons. Therefore, we will instead highlight this account in an autonomous category of the financial coverage of the NIC (see Exhibits 5.1 and 5.2).

The Net Financial Position Exhibit 5.3 shows another measure commonly used by financial analysts: the net financial position (or net financial indebtedness). It is calculated as the difference between financial debt and financial assets. In some situations, the amount of financial assets could be larger than financial debt: in this case, the net financial position turns out to be positive.

The concept of net financial position is particularly useful for the measurement of the effective degree of indebtedness of companies that are part of a group and have relevant financial relations with the other members of the group. Indeed, it often happens that some companies of the group run into debt to mainly finance the other members; in this case, the size of the financial indebtedness tends to lose its significance.

In valuing a company, the size of the net financial position must always be compared to the normal structure of the working capital. If the suppliers' payment periods are extended, liquidity is freed-up, consequently reducing the company's net financial position. The same effect can be caused by seasonal trends in production and sales. Therefore, in order to understand the normal dimension of the company's net financial position, it is necessary to check that the payment schedules of clients and suppliers and the level of stock do not differ significantly from the industry standards and from values relative to normal business conditions.

In this regard, it is interesting to mention that when companies are sold, a covenant is generally added by the buyer requiring that the size of the working capital does not go below a predetermined level. This is due to the fact that the equity value is defined as the difference between the value of the company's assets and its net financial position. At the time of the execution of the contract, a lower working capital would imply a reduction of the net financial position, which in turn would lead to an increase of the consideration to be paid.

Clarifying a Few Points The reorganization scheme presented above for the balance sheet is particularly useful for financial valuation. However, it should not be confused with the schemes regularly used in textbooks of financial statement analysis, which address other needs.

In particular, the operating working capital concept is often confused with the net working capital used in the financial analysis literature. As a matter of fact, when analyzing financial statements, the net working capital is the difference between short-term assets and short-term liabilities, whether of a commercial or financial nature. A positive net working capital indicates an acceptable equilibrium between the maturity structure of the firm investments and the term maturity of the financial coverage. Thus, it can be seen as a measure of the firm's solvency.

In our view, however, the working capital only measures the resources involved in the current business operations cycle. As a matter of fact, the higher (lower) the level of working capital relative to the amount of sales, the higher (lower) the company's financial needs for the development of its activities.[2]

As explained in detail beforehand, the reorganization model introduced in this chapter cannot take the maturity structure of liabilities into account and it cannot be used as a tool to compare companies and their financial risks. As a matter of fact, two companies with the same net financial position relative to the NIC or to sales could potentially be exposed to very different financial risks if their liability maturities differ substantially. For a more comprehensive analysis that would take these differences into consideration, it is necessary to use schemes that highlight the maturity structure of the financial indebtedness.

5.2.3 Reorganization of the Balance Sheet of Printing Co.

Printing Co. is a company that operates in the printing and publishing services industry. Exhibit 5.5 shows Printing Co.'s balance sheet reorganized according to the functional principle explained in the previous paragraph. It is important to note that a relevant industrial (minority) stake has been reorganized as a surplus asset. Our choice comes from our earlier discussion and we therefore want to value such asset on its own. Exhibit 5.5 highlights in a more concise way the aforementioned reorganization.

A crucial element is that Printing Co. has taken out capital leases for the acquisition of facilities and machinery. Some of its contracts were still pending at the time the financial statement in Exhibit 5.5 was prepared.

According to international accounting principles, capital leases should be reported in the balance sheet according to the value of leased goods on the assets side and according to the indebtedness implicit in the projection of future lease payments on the liabilities side.

In Printing Co., the residual value (€5,712 million) of the leased goods and the relative implicit indebtedness has been added to the "Financial Tangible Assets" and "Bank Debts" respectively.

These amounts are reported on the asset side as tangible assets and on the liabilities side as financial debt.

---

[2]The two measures tend to be the same in equilibrium situations where:

- All credits and debits relative to commercial operations are liquidated within 12 months.
- No short-term financial debt exists.

Exhibit 5.4 *Printing Co.*'s Income Statement reorganized according to the functional principle (in Euro/000)

ASSETS	
Net Accounts Receivable	38,955
Other Credits	10,908
Inventory	7,924
Accruals and Deferrals	1,549
Current Commercial Assets	59,336
Fixed Tangible Assets	32,597
Fixed Intangible Assets	3,089
Net Fixed Assets	35,686
Cash and Cash-Equivalents	–
Surplus Assets	10,329
TOTAL ASSETS	105,351
LIABILITIES	
Accounts Payable	24,509
Other Debts	13,890
Accruals and Deferrals	1,601
Current Commercial Liabilities	40,001
Tax Payables and Provisions	5,861
Pension Liabilities	5,101
Bank Debts	18,979
SHAREHOLDERS' EQUITY	
Equity	20,658
Reserves	5,625
Net Income	9,126
Total Shareholders' Equity	35,409
TOTAL SHAREHOLDERS' EQUITY AND LIABILITIES	105,351

5.3 RELATIONSHIP BETWEEN A COMPANY'S BALANCE SHEET AND INCOME STATEMENT

One of the benefits of the "functional" reorganization model is the clear link between the account values found in the balance sheet and their respective flows in the income statement. Exhibit 5.6 shows an example of a reorganized income statement, highlighting the partial results for the different business areas. This scheme can be enriched according to the analyst's needs

Exhibit 5.5 *Printing Co.*'s net invested capital and coverage (in euro/000)

Commercial Assets	59,336
Commercial Liabilities	(40,001)
Net Invested Capital	**19,335**
Net Fixed Assets	35,686
Pension Liabilities	(5,101)
Net Operating Invested Capital	49,920
Surplus Assets	10,329
Total Invested Capital	60,249
NIC Coverage	
Tax Payables and Provisions	5,861
Net Financial Position	18,979
Equity	35,409
Total Coverage	60,249

Exhibit 5.6 Synthetic income statement reorganization model

+ Net sales
− Monetary cost of goods sold
= EBITDA
− Amortization and depreciation
= EBIT
+ Net result from noncore activities
− Net financial costs
± Extraordinary items
= EBT
− Taxes
= Net income

(i.e., pointing out the production value of the year or simply the operating costs structure, as in Exhibit 5.7).

Establishing a precise connection between balance sheet values and flow values allows us to make rigorous analyses of profitability and simplifies the construction of economic and financial plans. Moreover, the reorganization in a specific category of revenues and costs of noncore activities allows us to prepare the necessary data for the separate valuation of the company's core activity and surplus assets.

Once it is deemed convenient to evaluate the company as a sum of parts, it is necessary to proceed with the reconstruction of the costs relative to each

Exhibit 5.7 Printing Co.'s reorganized income statement (in euro/000)

Sales	101,923
Raw and Subsidiary Materials	(30,445)
External Manufacturing	(15,433)
Commercial Costs	(3,865)
Services	(1,277)
Contribution Margin	**50,903**
Personnel Costs	20,955
Pension Liabilities Provision	(979)
General Costs	(1,871)
Industrial Costs	(4,207)
Other Costs	(1,145)
Provisions and Markdowns	(1,871)
EBITDA	**19,875**
Depreciations	(3,521)
Amortizations	(773)
Property Leasing	(1,053)
Operating Leasing	(2,825)
EBIT	**11,703**
Net Financial Costs	(5,963)
Interests on Leasing	(2,738)
Positive Items	11,982
EBT	**14,984**
Taxes	(5,858)
Net Income	9,126

separate business area, normally up to the EBIT level. It does not usually make much sense to refer specific sources of financing and their costs to their use in specific areas.

5.3.1 Reorganization of Printing Co.'s Income Statement

Exhibit 5.7 shows Printing Co.'s reorganized income statement. As mentioned earlier, a relevant part of Printing Co.'s facilities and machinery has been acquired through capital leases. For reorganization purposes, lease payments have been divided into two parts. The first part, relative to the capital portion of the payments has been included in the operating costs as it can be considered as the depreciated value of the leased assets. The second part, relative to the interest paid on the leases, has been included in the company's financial expenses.

5.4 FROM THE ECONOMIC TO THE FINANCIAL STANDPOINT

The connection between the balance sheet and the income statement allows us to establish a relationship between specific flows of results and the specific assets used. We now go one step further to comment on the firms' results in financial terms. Our goal is now to consider all monetary inflows and outflows for all business areas, which conjointly determine the company's financial dynamics in a certain time period (to simplify this procedure, we will look at annual data in our exercise). In order to clarify the process underlying this analysis, it is necessary to precisely identify the forces that are at the base of a firm's financial dynamics:

- Continuing business operations (buy-transform-sell operations) and the relative investment/divestment in net working capital
- Investment and divestment in fixed assets
- The underwriting and repayment of financing instruments (including the issuance of equity capital)
- The payment of interests to debt-holders and of dividends to shareholders
- Net flows for the purchase or from the disposal of surplus assets (if any)

The forces we have just discussed can be merged to obtain a configuration of flows consistent with the reorganization model used in the balance sheet and income statement to represent the different business areas. They are reorganized as:

- Monetary flow of the operating area
- Monetary flow of the financial area
- Monetary flow of noncore businesses

5.4.1 Cash Flow from Operating Activities: Cash Generated from Current Operations

Looking at Exhibit 5.7, we can easily see that the cash generated from current business operations can be calculated by adding all the costs that do not have a financial impact on the company (i.e., those that do not generate monetary transactions) to the firm's operating result. These mainly consist of depreciation and amortization in industrial companies. In the framework of Exhibit 5.7, this item is referred to as EBITDA (earnings before interest, taxation, depreciation, amortization), a very popular acronym among financial analysts.

It is important to highlight that the EBITDA cannot always be used to finance the outflows unrelated to current activities (i.e., for the acquisition of assets, the repayment of expiring financing).

The actual availability of cash flow generated by current activities in unrelated areas depends on the changes in working capital in the period under consideration. A positive change in working capital mirrors an employment of cash resulting in a partial absorption of the EBITDA. As a matter of fact, when there is an increase in working capital, the flow generated from the sequence of buy-transform-sell operations turns out to be "frozen" due to the increase in commercial credits or in the inventory after having subtracted the possible credit increase agreed with suppliers. We can, therefore, determine the following fundamental relationship:

Monetary flow of current activities

= EBITDA ± Change in net working capital

Growing and Mature Firms When a business experiences high sales growth, the net working capital use can sometimes absorb most of the EBITDA. As a result, a typical example of financial crisis due to high growth can occur, which sometimes forces the firm to slow down its growth process in order to limit the need for new financing. On the other hand, mature companies characterized by sustained sales stability can generate lots of liquidity: there is no need to guarantee the coverage of net working capital increases for this type of company.

Finally, the monetary flow can be higher than the EBITDA in particular situations. This occurs in two cases: when the working capital decreases, either because of a contraction in the turnover or because of policies aimed at monitoring its value through a more careful management of inventory, and through changes in the strategies used toward clients and suppliers.

5.4.2 Cash Flow from Operating Activities: Investing Activities

The monetary flow coming from the operating business can be obtained by adding the level of investment and divestment carried out during the fiscal year to the flow of current activities, as in the following framework:

+ EBITDA

± Δ Net working capital

= Monetary flow of the current activities

± Change in the pension liabilities

− Investments referable to the operating area

+ Divestments referable to the operating area

= Monetary flow referable to the operating area

As already mentioned, this flow should be calculated net of the fiscal effects but taking into consideration the deductibility of depreciation and other provisions.

5.4.3 Cash Flow from Financing Activities

This value can be calculated on the basis of all monetary movements referable to debt and equity capital. This means that this value not only refers to interest repayment, but also to negotiations for new funds and to the repayment of existing financing, to dividend payment, to the increase and repayment of equity. In summary, the outline of the main elements to be considered for the financing cash flow can be written as:

- − Passive interest payment
- − Dividend distribution
- + New debt negotiations
- − Expiring debt repayment
- + Equity increases
- − Equity repayment
- = Flow referable to the financial area

For reasons we have already discussed, all the movements referable to the financial area should also be expressed net of fiscal effects.

5.4.4 Cash Flow from Surplus Assets

The cash flow from surplus assets is easily calculated due to the reduced number of elements that belong to this category. It is mainly composed of two fundamental components:

1. The income that derives from noncore businesses
2. The difference between new investments and divestments carried out in noncore businesses

The monetary flow of this business area should also be calculated net of fiscal adjustments.

5.4.5 Uses and Sources of Funds

Exhibit 5.8 represents the outline of a financial statement, which is particularly useful for the goal we have in mind. It gives a synthesized framework

Exhibit 5.8 Financial statement outline

+ EBITDA
± Change in working capital
= Monetary flow of the current activities
± Change in the pension liabilities account
− Operating investments
+ Operating divestments
= Monetary flow of the operating business
± Net flow of the noncore business
± Net positive (negative) interests
− Dividends
± Change in equity
− Taxes
± Change in the tax payables and provisions
= Change in the net financial position, which can be split up in:
− Debt repayments
− New financings
− Reduction of liquidity, negotiable securities, financial credits
− Increase in liquidity, negotiable securities, financial credits

of the forces that determine the financial dynamics that have already been mentioned:

■ Operating business, distinguishing between the flows linked to the current operations cycle and the flows used for investments
■ Noncore businesses
■ The financial management policies

Since the flows of these three business areas include fiscal debits and credits, two more categories appear in our outline:

■ Taxation
■ Change in the fiscal position

The effective financial outflow for tax payments is therefore represented by the algebraic sum of these two items shown in Exhibit 5.8.

It is crucial to highlight that the flows referable to the financial area are presented in Exhibit 5.8 in an order that draws attention to the change in the net financial position during the analyzed period.

The Nonmonetary Costs in the Working Capital We have assumed the equivalence between the working capital and the company's financial needs until now. It should be observed, however, that the firm's real financial exposure depends on the monetary costs effectively faced due to the buy-transform-sell cycle. Consequently, it is crucial to call for a more precise measurement that takes into consideration that:

- A partial recovery of costs due to the appraisal of semifinished and finished goods is considered to be a nonmonetary element. In particular, it is linked to the depreciation of the fixed assets that are part of the production costs.
- Sales credits, besides containing the nonmonetary costs found in the previous point, usually also include a given profit margin for the firm that does not contribute to its financial exposure.

We can therefore conclude that the firm's real financing need is smaller than the algebraic sum of the components of the working capital calculated according to their corresponding accounting values.

This distortion disappears if we switch from the working capital concept to the flow concept. As a matter of fact, the flow from current activities is always calculated in the following way:

Monetary flow from current activities

= EBITDA ± Change in net working capital

The nonmonetary components in the change of working capital are balanced by the nonmonetary elements in the EBITDA. They are nonmonetary costs recovered through the appraisal of semifinished and finished goods. The same is true for those margins (the difference between sales prices and operating costs) linked to sales for which there have been no collections yet. These margins are included in the EBITDA and in the change in accounts receivable during the period under consideration.

5.5   CASH FLOW DEFINITIONS AND VALUATION MODELS

The concepts introduced in the previous paragraphs have to be applied to flow projections in order to develop financial valuation techniques. The outline presented in Exhibit 5.8 has to be modified in a way that highlights the cash flows generated by the operating business (i.e., the free cash flow from operations, FCFO) and the net flows available to shareholders (i.e., the free cash flow to equity, FCFE).

Excluding noncore businesses, which should be valued autonomously, the structure of the FCFO and the FCFE are shown in Exhibits 5.9 and 5.10.

We can highlight the following points with respect to the outline of an ex-post financial statement presented in Exhibit 5.8.

Exhibit 5.9 FCFO calculation

+ EBITDA
± Changes in net working capital*
± Changes in the pension payables and provisions
− Operating investments
+ Operating divestments
− Virtual taxes on the operating income
= **FCFO (free cash flow from operations)**

*Includes the changes in the tax provisions

Exhibit 5.10 FCFE calculation

+ EBITDA
± Changes in net working capital*
± Changes in pension payables and provisions
− Operating investments
+ Operating divestments
= Operating monetary flow before taxes
− Net financial costs
− Income taxes
± Planned change in the net financial position
= **FCFE (free cash flow to equity)**

*Includes the changes in the tax provisions

In the calculation of the FCFO (Exhibit 5.9), the term *taxes* measures the theoretical fiscal outflow calculated on the operating result in a scenario of no debt and therefore with no deductible fiscal outflows (in this case, the operating result equals the EBT).

The value of the FCFE depends not only on the incidence of interest and income taxes but also on the change in the net financial position. Therefore, the projections set forth by the expert for the company's valuation need to include a limit (or a target) for the firm's financial structure. This is an important specification that draws attention to the fact that the cash flow to shareholders depends on the future financing operation choices involving the use of debt.

5.6   BUSINESS PLAN AND CASH FLOW PROJECTIONS

The structure and consistency of a business plan's assumptions determine the quality of the plan itself and of the whole valuation process. Therefore, it is of paramount importance to validate the assumptions used with the most accurate data and information available.

5.6.1 The Basic Assumptions

The projections of the firm's results, which are relevant for a firm valuation, are often (but not necessarily) derived from several provisional financial statements that are based on a system of basic assumptions (in the international jargon: valuation assumptions).

Since the setup of multiyear financial statements and flows is a technical procedure, the quality of the estimate exclusively depends on how sensible and consistent the valuation assumptions are with respect to the company's reality. Moreover, the valuation's disclosure and reliability always depend on how clearly the basic assumptions have been introduced and explained. It is useful to distinguish three categories of assumptions:

1. Assumptions on the general and financial economic environment. Depending on the specific needs of the estimate, they include factors such as:
   - GDP growth rate
   - Evolution of consumption (of final goods or investment)
   - Exchange rates
   - Interest rates
   - Expected inflation rate

2. Assumptions regarding the company's industry or the project that is being valued. Taking into consideration the specific needs of the estimate, they include factors such as:
   - Growth rate of the market (or niche) where the company is competing
   - Competitors' strategies
   - Evolution of fares (in the case of regulated prices)
   - Normative actions that affect the industry

3. More specific assumptions about the company or the project that is being valued. They include factors such as:
   - Evolution of the main sales prices and cost prices
   - Trend of working capital
   - Growth rate and the corresponding investment needs
   - Planned restructuring actions with respect to business lines, products, and employees
   - Trend of the debt ratio (this assumption is crucial for the estimate of the cash flows available to shareholders, FCFE)

- Benefits coming from post-acquisition actions (synergies obtainable through the integration of the target firm with the acquirer)
- Investment and the other expenses necessary to maintain the firm's position unchanged once an equilibrium has been reached

One can generally notice that the valuation of a company or a project is "easy" when the following happens:

- The general economic and industrial assumptions can be checked with data and information published by reliable sources.
- A proven correlation exists between the companies' results in the industry and some general industrial and economic key drivers.

If these conditions occur, the main problem analysts face is then the analysis of the consistency between the assumptions regarding the economy and the industry and the specific assumptions regarding the performance of the company under consideration. For instance, the main issue linked to the estimate of flows consists of respecting this consistency for firms in the commodities or utilities sectors.

On the contrary, valuations are "difficult" when the company-specific assumptions are largely independent of the evolution of general industrial and economic factors. In particular, this problem concerns the estimates of companies involved in new business areas, of start-ups, of companies whose success depends on a key person. We can thus conclude that it is generally much more difficult to value a small-sized company with respect to a company that has already consolidated its position in the market.

When the consistency between the company-specific and the general economy assumptions cannot be verified, the flows projections (and therefore the results of the estimates) have a strong subjective nature. In these cases, the analysts can only check for consistency between the assumptions made in the flow projection and the availability of company resources and competences at the organizational, managerial, technological, and marketing level.

When to Make Projections   In the valuation of companies and acquisitions, the need for projections depends on whether the activities are in a *disequilibrium* situation. As a matter of fact, a company's situation at the date of the valuation can be judged to not be in equilibrium according to two types of elements:

1. General factors, which concern the opportunity of rationalization, restructuring, and reconversion activities; the chance of gaining a more

favorable positioning in terms of sales, market share, etc. with the available resources; the dynamics of the economic cycle impacting the company's industry; the evolution of the competitive landscape.
2. Specific factors linked to plans and programs of acquisitions that involve a transfer of control.

If the aforementioned general or specific conditions do not occur, there is no need to project flows analytically, since in this case the company is already in an equilibrium situation and can be valued based on the most recent, at most normalized results.

The period of time over which the analytical flow has to be calculated depends on the time necessary for the company to reach an equilibrium condition. We will further discuss this topic in Chapter 6.

Assessing the Profitability of the Plan A simple but effective test of the sensibility of the assumptions made consists of the behavior of the ROS (return on sales) and ROI (return on investments) ratios in the same period of time as the explicit flow projection period.

It is possible to observe that the ROI sometimes tends to grow over the years until it reaches levels that are inconsistent with the industry's historical average and profitability. This depends generally on the very low size of investments. When the valuation is carried out through analytical financial methods with a terminal value, it is important to correctly estimate the level of both the investments necessary to sustain the growth assumed in the flow projection and the "renewal investments" necessary to keep the capacity in place unaltered. The value of these estimates can have strong consequences on the results of the valuation.

In particular, the flows of the last projection year, on which the terminal value calculation is based, have to be determined, paying close attention to the following:

- Estimating the right amount of renewal investment (it is often assumed that renewal investments are as high as the value of depreciation based on economic-technical standards)
- Estimating the right amount of costs to assure that the company can maintain its position in the market (marketing and research expenses, etc. according to their importance in the industry)

Consistency between the Company-Specific and the Industry/Market Assumptions In the first chapter, we have highlighted that the consistency between company-specific assumptions and assumptions concerning the industry and the economy is necessary to justify the use of opportunity-cost measures of capital that can be inferred from the market. One can think that the returns required by the market are based on assumptions on macroeconomic, financial, and industrial variables similar to the information available from the main research institutes. When this basic assumption system, which is accepted by the majority of operators, is modified significantly, we can no longer ensure consistency between the basic assumptions that are used in the valuation of the expected flows and the hypothesis underlying the valuation of the company's risk profile.

5.6.2   Projecting Cash Flows for Printing Co.

The printing industry in Europe is characterized by small- and middle-sized companies: only a minimal fraction of the printing companies employ more than 100 employees.

The demand is divided into three main segments: periodicals, catalogues, and books. These categories seem to be substantially stable and characterized by a need for cost reduction and by a progressive trend of segmentation circulation. The demand is requesting a progressively higher level of quality, which therefore becomes a prerequisite for the producer.

Printing Co. has been operating for more than 30 years in the industry and is able to offer high-quality products and services and to cover all the main product/market combinations. After a few important acquisitions, Printing Co. has started a restructuring program that is directed at operations and commercial improvement. The plan foresees both the concentration of production and a significant reduction in the number workers, a process that was facilitated by some legal concessions granted to the printing industry.

Flow Projection Assumptions

- The industry shows a moderate cyclical sensitivity, the competitive scenario is relatively consolidated, Printing Co.'s portfolio of contracts is balanced.
- The use of external manufacturing, particularly important in the restructuring stages, will be progressively reduced.
- Printing Co. has planned significant actions in order to rebalance its working capital (the current payment time granted to clients and by suppliers seems to be excessive).

■ Printing Co. has made a significant effort in the modernization of its machines also thanks to the use of some leasing contracts. Technical investments will be slowed down over the next three years but are planned to increase in the two following years.

The Cash Flow Projection   The analyst will create a five-year plan based on the starting financial situation shown in Exhibit 5.5 and on the previous general assumptions. The five-year length of the analytical flow projection enables us to completely highlight the effect of the investment cycle and of the normalization of the working capital on the monetary flows. Exhibit 5.11 highlights the other assumptions that have been used to build the plan.

Exhibits 5.12 and 5.13 show Printing Co.'s provisional financial statements built on the data in Exhibits 5.4 and 5.7 and on the assumptions summarized in Exhibit 5.11.

Exhibit 5.14 shows the projections of the monetary flow produced by the operating business, calculated from the provisional financial statements. It is worth mentioning that the flow produced by the operating business in t_1 is penalized by the significant increase in working capital caused by the

Exhibit 5.11   Printing Co. main assumptions

			Historical Data				
	t_{-2}	t_{-1}	t_1	t_2	t_3	t_4	t_5
Inflation rate	5.1%	4.7%	3.9%	3.5%	3.2%	2.8%	3.2%
Growth in sales	10.0%	−13.8%	−2.4%	4.1%	3.2%	2.8%	32%
Real growth in sales	4.9%	−18.5%	−6.3%	0.6%	0.0%	0.0%	0.0%
Cost impact (on sales)							
Raw materials		29.9%	29.9%	29.9%	29.9%	29.9%	29.9%
General costs		1.8%	1.9%	1.9%	1.9%	1.9%	1.9%
External manufacturing		15.1%	14.0%	14.8%	15.3%	15.8%	15.8%
Commercial costs		3.8%	3.4%	3.4%	3.4%	3.4%	3.4%
Industrial costs		4.1%	4.3%	4.2%	4.2%	4.2%	4.2%
Credit-days on sales	159	150	150	150	130	130	120	120
Inventory-days on costs	100	89	95	95	95	95	95	95
Debt-days on costs	183	209	195	190	160	160	150	150

Exhibit 5.12 Printing Co.'s provisional balance sheet

(€/000)	t_1	t_2	t_3	t_4	t_5
Assets					
Accounts Receivable	38,959	40,351	36,106	37,117	35,358
Other Credits	11,727	12,617	13,581	13,961	14.,08
Inventory	7,656	7,925	8,178	8,407	8,676
Accruals and Deferrals	1,549	1,549	1,549	1,549	1,549
Working Capital Assets	59,891	62,442	59,414	61,034	59,991
Net Tangible Fixed Assets	30,518	28,529	26,224	26,997	30,259
Net Intangible Fixed Assets	2,317	1,545	773	–	–
Net Fixed Assets	32,835	30,074	26,997	26,997	30,259
Surplus Assets	10,329	10,329	10,329	10,329	10,329
Total Assets	103,055	102,844	96,738	98,358	100,577
Liabilities					
Accounts Payable	18,998	20,083	19,635	17,811	21,047
Other Debts	13,783	14,268	14,723	15,135	15,619
Accruals and Deferrals	1,601	1,601	1,601	1,601	1,601
Current Liabilities	34,382	35,952	35,959	34,547	38,267
Tax Payables and Provisions	−577	407	2,192	134	−135
Pension Liabilities	5,786	6,502	7,248	8,021	8,824
Bank Debts	23,511	14,713	7,935	6,477	4,860
Equity	20,658	20,658	20,658	20,658	20,658
Reserves	14,751	19,295	15,606	21,405	21,249
Net Income	4,544	5,317	7,140	7,116	6,854
Shareholders' Equity	39,953	45,272	52,412	59,528	66,382
Total Liabilities and Shareholders' Equity	103,055	102,844	96,738	98,358	100,577

reduction of the suppliers' payment time while the flows in t_4 and t_5 mirror the new beginning of the investment cycle.

It is crucial to highlight that the calculation of the FCFO includes lease payments, but it also takes into account the tax shields linked to the deductibility of such payments.

Finally, Exhibit 5.15 shows the projection of the free cash flows available to Printing Co.'s shareholders. It is worth adding a few words on the evolution of the firm's tax fund. Printing Co. did not pay any tax advances at T_0 and included the entire value of taxes in a specific account

Exhibit 5.13 *Printing Co.*'s provisional income statement

(€/000)	t_1	t_2	t_3	t_4	t_5
Sales	99,523	103,622	106,962	109,697	113,207
Raw and Subsidiary Materials	−29,418	−30,448	−31,422	−32,302	−33,335
External Manufacturing	−13,922	−15,370	−16,357	−17,325	−17,879
Commercial Costs	−3,414	−3,533	−3,646	−3,748	−3,868
Services	−1,234	−1,277	−1,317	−1,355	−1,398
Contribution Margin	**51,535**	**52,994**	**54,220**	**54,967**	**56.727**
Personnel Costs	−21,401	−22,150	−22,859	−23,499	−24,251
Provision to Pension Liabilities	−1,118	−1,162	−1,206	−1,240	−1,323
General Costs	−1,856	−1,921	−1,983	−2,038	−2,104
Industrial Costs	−4,240	−4,389	−4,529	−4,656	−4,805
Other Liabilities	−1,121	−1,161	−1,199	−1,232	−1,272
Provisions	−1,856	−1,921	−992	−1,019	−1,052
EBITDA	**19,943**	**20,290**	**21,452**	**21,283**	**21,920**
Tangible Assets' Amortization and Depreciation	−3,629	−3,753	−3,862	−4,404	−7,067
Intangible Assets' Amortization and Depreciation	−773	−773	−773	−773	−
Operating Leasing	−2,669	−1,740	−323	−234	−
EBIT	**12,872**	**14,024**	**16,494**	**15,872**	**14,853**
Net Financial Costs	−2,617	−2,362	−1,184	−643	−208
Interest on Leasing	−545	−300	−54	−24	−
EBT	**−9,710**	**11,362**	**15,256**	**15,205**	**14,645**
Taxes	−5,166	−6,045	−8,116	−8,089	−7,791
Net Income	**4,544**	**5,317**	**7,140**	**7,116**	**6,854**

Exhibit 5.14 Printing Co.'s free cash flow from operations (FCFO) projection

(€/000)	t_1	t_2	t_3	t_4	t_5
EBITDA	19,943	20,290	21,453	21,283	21,920
Taxes (on the Operating Income)	−6,848	−7,461	−8,775	−8,444	−7,902
Changes in Working Capital*	−12,612	3	4,820	−5,090	4,494
Investments in Technical Assets	−1,551	−1,765	−1,558	−5,177	−10,329
Changes in the Pension Liabilities	685	716	746	773	803
FCFO	**−383**	**11,783**	**16,685**	**3,345**	**8,986**

*It includes the Tax fund.

Exhibit 5.15 Printing Co.'s free cash flow to equity (FCFE) projection

(€/000)	t_1	t_2	t_3	t_4	t_5
FCFO	−383	11,783	16,685	3,345	8,986
Taxes (on the Operating Income)	6,848	7,461	8,775	8,444	7,902
Net Financial Costs and Leasing Payments	−5,831	−4,402	−1,561	−901	−208
Taxes on Net Income	−5,166	−6,045	−8,116	−8,089	−7,791
Change in the Net Financial Position	4,532	−8,798	−6,778	−1,458	−1,617
FCFE	0	−1	9,006	1,341	7,272

(see Exhibit 5.4). It is also important to notice that the tax payables and provisions as shown in Exhibit 5.12, could be negative. These variations are mainly due to the erratic pattern of Printing Co.'s performance, which causes a mismatch between tax advances and actual tax burden.

## CHAPTER 6

Choosing the Valuation Standpoint

6.1 DEBT AND VALUE

The next two chapters will cover the relationship between debt and value creation. Understanding this relationship is fundamental for the valuation process as well as for the calculation of the cost of capital to be used.

We first introduce the relationship between leverage, opportunity cost of capital, and value in a static context, where cash flow is perpetual and the level of debt is held constant.[1] These topics are presented in all corporate finance textbooks. We specifically focus on their implications in the valuation of companies and M&A transactions. We describe two methods that analysts may follow while valuing a company with debt or a debt-funded acquisition. Pros and cons of alternative methods are also highlighted.

The methods of financial valuations currently used are based on the present value of the *free cash flow from operations* (FCFO) at the average weighted cost of capital. Such an approach results in an adequate solution for the majority of capital budgeting problems. However, it is much less satisfactory in the valuation of companies and acquisitions. In such cases, for the sake of transparency of the estimate, a separate estimate of the unlevered value of the firm and of the value of its tax shields conveys more complete information.

If companies were unlevered, or if acquisitions were just equity-funded, analysts could avoid many technicalities. In fact, the absence of debt would also eliminate three crucial problems that will be discussed in this chapter:

1. Does leverage create value for shareholders, and to what extent?
2. What are the valuation methods that account for the benefits of debt? We present two methods: the *unlevered value adjustment* and the *discount*

---

[1]Next chapter describes the relationship between leverage, opportunity cost of capital, and value in a growth scenario.

rate adjustment. The former method is the one that we prefer (and we will explain why); the latter is the most commonly used by professional analysts (despite its pitfalls).
3. How should the most effective perspective for the development of the valuation procedure be chosen? Determine the criteria for choosing between calculating: (a) the value of the company's assets, and (b) the value of the company's equity (i.e., the value of its shares).

6.2 FIRST PROBLEM: THE RELATIONSHIP BETWEEN LEVERAGE AND VALUE

The question of whether financial leverage does affect the value of the company is, in a way, one of the central questions for financial theory discipline (especially thanks to the theorems by Franco Modigliani and Merton Miller that are the very basis of modern corporate finance). In this section, we will focus on the valuation implications of leverage from a practical point of view.

6.2.1 Some Definitions

As already discussed, cash flows should be discounted at a proper rate (the *opportunity cost of capital*) in the valuation process. This rate has two functions:

1. It accounts for the financial value of time, following the rules of present value calculation.
2. It adjusts the expected cash flow for the risk of the project (RADR: risk-adjusted discount rate).

Indeed, the *opportunity cost of capital* has a double meaning:

1. For managers, it represents the minimum return that a company should reach in order to attract and retain capital in a competitive environment, where the investors can compare a number of investment alternatives.
2. For investors, cost of equity and cost of debt represent their expected returns on the resources invested in the company.

Using the approach common to financial markets, we can say that the cost of capital represents the return that investors expect and consider fair with respect to the risk they are taking.

The bondholders of a firm expect a return that we will indicate as K_d (cost of debt); its shareholders, instead, demand a return that we will denote as K_e (cost of equity).[2]

The expected return over the whole capital invested in the company, the return on its total assets, can be expressed as a weighted average of the expected return on debt and on equity. In the calculation of such average, we use as weights debt's and equity's respective contribution to the company's total amount of funds. This rate of return is called the *weighted average cost of capital,* usually indicated with the acronym WACC.

In valuing an investment or a company, we can highlight the following relationships between cash flows and discount rates:

- Free cash flow to equity (FCFE) $\longrightarrow$ K_e
- Free cash flow from operations (FCFO) $\longrightarrow$ WACC

If the valuation is based on the cash flow available to shareholders (FCFE), we should use K_e as the appropriate discount rate. If the valuation is based on the free cash flow from operations (FCFO), the appropriate discount rate is the weighted average cost of capital.

6.2.2 Relationship between Leverage and Discount Rates

One of the most debated topics in corporate finance is the relationship between leverage and value, or, to put it another way, between leverage, K_e, and the WACC. Before focusing on this topic, it is useful to define two essential concepts: operating risk and financial risk.

We have discussed at length the reasons why operating cash flow can change over time. While operating risk is related to this variability, *financial risk* depends to a great extent on capital structure decisions. Return to shareholders is subordinated to the obligations toward owners of debt capital. Holding the level of operating capital constant as well as the FCFO, any increase in the level of debt amplifies the impact of economic changes on the cash flow to shareholders (FCFE). In other words, *leverage amplifies the typical business risk of an economic venture.*

This idea can be easily expressed using a well-known relationship between financial ratios. Ignoring taxes, we can say that:

$$ROE = ROI + (ROI - K_d) \times D/E \qquad (6.1)$$

---

[2]How to appraise K_e and K_d is discussed later in Chapter 8.

where:

$$ROE = \text{Return on equity}$$
$$ROI = \text{Return on investment}$$
$$K_d = \text{cost of the debt}$$
$$D/E = \text{leverage (Debt/Equity ratio)}$$

When the ROI is greater than i, an increase in leverage causes an increase in the ROE. In negative scenarios, when the ROI is lower than i, an increase in leverage produces a decrease in the ROE greater than the one we would see without the additional debt.

We illustrate what we have just discussed with an example. The next table shows the value of the ROI in three different scenarios. The expected value of the ROI is 15 percent, calculated as the weighted average of the three scenarios. Note that we have considered the three scenarios to be equally likely, but this does not have to be the case in other applications.

Scenarios	I	II	III
ROI	5%	15%	25%
Scenario probability	1/3	1/3	1/3

Without debt or taxes, the values of the ROI are the same as the shareholders' return (ROE). Assuming a leverage ratio equal to one ($D/E = 1$) and a cost of debt equal to 10 percent, using [6.1], the expected ROE becomes:

$$E(ROE) = 0.15 + (0.15 - 0.10) \times 1 = 0.20$$

In our examples, the values of the ROE in the three scenarios will be:

Scenarios	I	II	III
ROE ($D/E = 0$)	5%	15%	25%
ROE ($D/E = 1$)	0	20%	40%

This example shows how a greater variability of results, and a consequent greater level of risk, corresponds to an increase in the expected ROE. Moreover, it allows us to rephrase the original problem in more understandable terms: *Does this increase in the expected ROE, which is linked to greater variability of results, create or destroy value?*

6.2.3   The Law of Conservation of Value

The *law of conservation of value*[3] is based on a simple assumption: if we ignore taxes, *the value of a company only depends on its operating cash flow*. The way the cash flow is shared between shareholders and bondholders is not relevant. This argument is illustrated in Exhibit 6.1.

If the law of conservation of value holds, changes in leverage have no impact on the value of assets. The cost of capital will be calculated later in this chapter relying on the assumption that the value of assets stays constant.

Since the value of A does not change, the discounting rate for the FCFO is not affected by leverage. We have stated earlier that the proper discounting rate for the FCFO is the WACC. Therefore, we can say that the WACC is independent of capital structure in this situation (because of the law of conservation of value). It only mirrors the return that the market expects for the operating risk related to that company or business. We can assume the following relation

$$WACC = K_{eu}$$

This relationship states that, without taxes, the WACC does not change due to changes in leverage. In this situation, the WACC represents the return

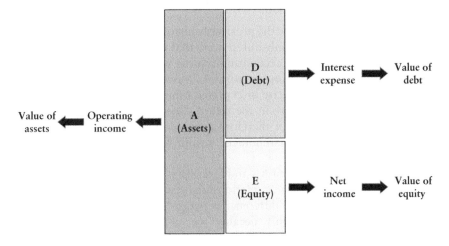

Exhibit 6.1   Balance sheet items and related flow (without taxation)

---

[3] J. B. Williams was the first scholar to talk about the "law of conservation of value," in a well-known finance textbook: *The Theory of Investment Value* (Boston: Harvard University Press, 1938).

requested by shareholders to invest in a firm funded only by equity. We will refer to this return as the *unlevered K_e: K_{eu}*.

We can now define the relationship between K_e and leverage, starting from the formula of the weighted average cost of capital *without taxes*:

$$WACC = K_{eu} = K_{el} \times \frac{E}{E + D} + K_d \times \frac{D}{E + D} \qquad (6.2)$$

K_{el}, where *l* stands for *levered*, is the return expected from shareholders when the company is levered; $E/(E + D)$ and $D/(E + D)$ are the "weights" for *equity* and debt, respectively, equal to their contributions to the total capital invested in the company. These "weights" must be determined using the market value (and not the book value) of *equity* and *debt*. Indeed, the return to investors should be expressed as the ratio between expected results and capital invested (both equity and debt), measured at its current price (market value).

K_{el} can be determined from [6.2]:

$$K_{el} = K_{eu} + [K_{eu} - K_d] \times \frac{D}{E} \qquad (6.3)$$

Therefore, the value of K_{el} *without taxes* stems directly from the law of conservation of value.

Equation [6.3] looks like the previously introduced relationship between the ROI and the ROE. The only difference is that we have investors' expected returns here instead of the accounting returns we used in [6.1]. From this comparison, we can infer one important consequence of the law of conservation of value: the increase in expected returns due to leverage is completely offset by the increase in the return expected by investors due to a higher level of risk. We can therefore conclude that leverage is not relevant in the calculation of shareholders' wealth: leverage neither creates nor destroys value.

The relationship between K_{el} and leverage is illustrated in Exhibit 6.2.

Exhibit 6.2a shows a *linear* relationship between K_{el} and D/E. The slope of the curve depends on the difference between K_{el} and K_d.

K_d is held constant only because we assume that cash flow from operations is always enough to repay debt obligations. If we removed this hypothesis, the cost of debt would increase with an increase in leverage. Nevertheless, the law of conservation of value and the formulas derived while holding this hypothesis as true are still valid. In this case, business risk is shared between shareholders and debt holders. As a consequence, the increase in K_d is balanced by an increase in K_{el} that is lower than the one shown in Exhibit 6.2a, where shareholders hold all the business risk. Exhibit 6.2.b shows this situation.

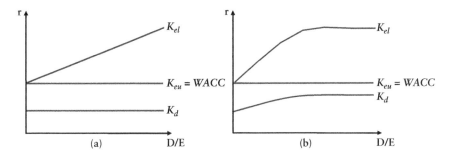

Exhibit 6.2 Relationship between K_{el} and leverage (D/E)

Proof of the Law of Conservation of Value The most famous proof of the law of the conservation of value is in an article by F. Modigliani and M. Miller,[4] which represents a cornerstone in corporate finance theory. Their main idea is that in a competitive market, two identical goods must have the same price. As an example, we can consider two companies (X,Y), with the same operating structure, but with a different capital structure. We also assume that there are no taxes and that the two companies are financed only by the issuance of shares and bonds.

Exhibit 6.3 illustrates how buying respectively 1 percent of equity and 1 percent of debt of X and Y leads to identical portfolios, with the same *payoff* (1 percent of the FCFO of the two hypothetically identical firms) and the same operating risk (the companies hypothetically bear the same operating risk). Therefore, the two portfolios must have the same value. If they were priced differently on the market, arbitrageurs would act, restoring the equilibrium between the total value of X and Y.

The proof by Modigliani & Miller relies on the assumption that we are in perfect capital markets. All the conditions associated with the theoretical concept of "perfect" capital markets are seldom met in real financial markets. Nevertheless, many researchers believe that the law of conservation of value is the most rational approach in the determination of cost of capital.

Is the "Law of Conservation of Value" Always True? The law of conservation of value introduces a significant principle: without fiscal benefits, the value of a company or an investment solely depends on its business and not on any financial features. Many think this is not correct in extreme situations—that is, when leverage is either very low or very high.

---

[4]F. Modigliani and M. Miller, "The Cost of Capital, Corporate Finance, and the Theory of Investment," *American Economic Review* 48 (June 1958): 261–297.

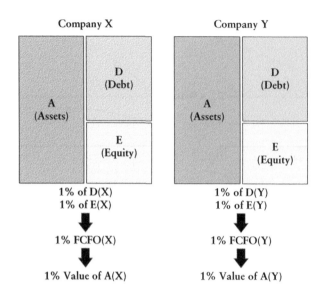

Exhibit 6.3   Proof of the law of conservation of value

In the first case (i.e., in the case of a company with extremely low leverage), it is argued that a small increase in debt would not change the return required by shareholders. Therefore, a low level of *leverage* could create value. This could mean that some investors might perceive risk not as variability of results, but as the probability with which very negative events affect shareholders' wealth. Nonetheless, even if this reasoning were true, it cannot be proved. We therefore prefer to rely on more rational laws, such as the law of conservation of value, in the valuation of companies and investments.

The second case is more relevant. When a company has a high leverage ratio, it can weaken its competitive position or fall into insolvency. If we consider these potential negative effects, the relationship between K_{el} and D/E is no longer linear. After a certain level of leverage, K_{el} increases more than D/E does.

Accepting this reasonable critique would result in a subjective and arbitrary estimation of K_{el}. We prefer, as many other researchers do, to think that the "law of conservation of value" is true even in this case. This has two practical consequences. First, we will consider the relationship between K_{el} and leverage to always be linear. Second, we will evaluate potential costs of financial distress separately.

6.2.4   Tax Advantages of Debt

If we consider corporate taxes, the previous conclusions—on the irrelevance of capital structure to value—do not hold anymore. To understand how

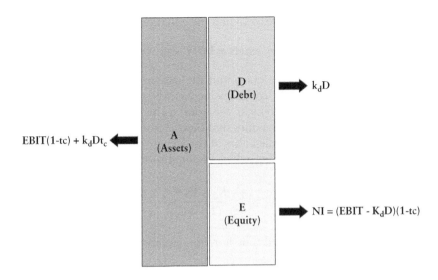

Exhibit 6.4   Company's flow and corporate taxes

things change, we can refer to Exhibit 6.4, where flow is illustrated both for the *assets side* and the *liabilities side* of the balance sheet, In particular, we define:

K_d = Cost of debt (for simplicity equal to company interest rate)
NI = Net income
$EBIT$ = Operating income
D = Debt
E = Equity
t_c = Marginal corporate tax rate

Flow related to debt and equity can be calculated as:

- D (debt) $\rightarrow K_d \times D$
- E (*equity*) $\rightarrow NI = (EBIT - K_d \times D) \times (1 - t_c)$

By definition, the sum of the flows that belong to shareholders and to debt holders should equal the total cash flow generated by *assets* (A):

Cash flow generated by assets $= K_d \times D + (EBIT - K_d \times D) \times (1 - t_c)$

By rearranging the terms on the left-hand side of the equation, we have:

$$K_d \times D + EBIT - EBIT \times t_c - K_d \times D + K_d \times D \times t_c$$

By canceling terms and rearranging the equation, we finally have:

Cash flow generated by assets $= EBIT \times (1 - t_c) + K_d \times D \times t_c$

If we consider corporate taxes and the tax benefits linked to interest expenses, the total flow of the company increases by the amount $K_d \times D \times t_c$.

Thanks to these tax savings, the total value of the company also increases. Shareholders are the ones that benefit from this increase.

Exhibit 6.5 shows how the value of the levered firm W_L increases with an increase in leverage by W_{TS}, which is equal to the present value of tax savings:

$$W_{TS} = \sum_{t=1}^{n} \frac{K_d \times D_t \times t_c}{(1 + K_{TS})^t} \qquad (6.4)$$

If we assume an unlimited time horizon, equation [6.4] becomes:

$$W_{TS} = \frac{K_d \times D \times t_c}{K_{TS}} \qquad (6.5)$$

In corporate finance textbooks, it is commonly assumed that the discount rate for tax savings (K_{TS}) is equal to K_d, since the cash flows necessary to exploit these tax benefits have the same level of risk as the debt itself.[5]

Under this assumption, equation [6.5] becomes:

$$W_{TS} = D \times t_c$$

In Exhibit 6.5, $(D/E)_1$ represents the degree of leverage where potential costs of debt (the shaded area) start to offset tax benefits. $(D/E)_2$ indicates

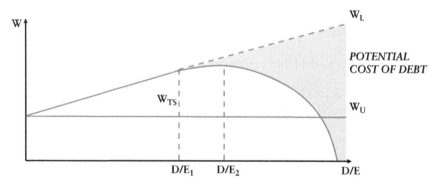

Exhibit 6.5   Increase in value due to tax savings

---

[5]This assumption will be further investigated in Chapter 7.

the leverage that maximizes shareholders' value. Any point beyond $(D/E)_2$ is characterized by the negative consequences of debt overcoming its benefits. When referring to negative consequences of debt, we refer not only to distress costs but also to the loss of managerial flexibility, which can seriously weaken the competitive position of a company.

Exhibit 6.5 can also provide useful insights on the valuation of highly levered companies. In such a situation, it is very difficult to apply traditional techniques, since these companies will not be able to entirely exploit the tax benefits of debt.

The Creation of Value for Shareholders To better show how tax savings create value for shareholders, we introduce the following example, where—for sake of simplicity—cash flow is assumed to be perpetual.

1. EBIT   200
   Corporate tax rate (t_c) 33%
   Net Income   134
   K_{eu} 10%
   Value of firm A:

$$W_U = \frac{200 \times (1 - t_c)}{0.10} = 1.340$$

2. Company A **buys shares, issuing new debt for 600:**

   D   600
   K_d 5%

   Present value of tax benefits calculated using [6.5]:

$$W_{TS} = \frac{630 \times 0.33 \times 0.05}{0.05} = 198$$

   Total value of firm A Levered, W(L):

$$W_U + W_{TS} = 1,340 + 198 = 1,538$$

   Value of the equity of the firm (Levered)

$$W_L - D = 1,538 - 600 = 938$$

Increasing leverage, shareholders' wealth changes in the following way:

- $D/E = 0$ Equity value: 1,340
- $D/E = 0.67$ Equity value: 938
                       + Shares buyback: 630
                       Total shareholders' wealth: 1,538

Compared to the initial situation, shareholders' wealth is increased by an amount *equal to the present value of the tax benefits linked to debt.*

6.3 SECOND PROBLEM: ALTERNATIVE VALUATION TECHNIQUES WHEN DEBT BENEFITS FROM A FISCAL ADVANTAGE

When tax advantages of debt are present, we can use two methods to value companies or investments:

- Alternative A: the unlevered value adjustment method (adjusted present value, or APV)
- Alternative B: the *discount rates adjustment* method

6.3.1 First Alternative: Adjusting the Unlevered Value (Adjusted Present Value, or APV)

The unlevered value adjustment method evaluates a company as the sum of the value of the tax benefits and its *unlevered* value, calculated using K_{eu} as the proper discount rate.

With this method, the *levered* value of a company can be found using the following equation:

$$W_L = W_U + W_{TS}$$

W_L = Value of the *levered* firm
W_U = Value of the *unlevered* firm
W_{TS} = Tax benefits arising from the deductibility of interest

The unlevered value adjustment method is better known as the adjusted present value (APV) approach. Meyers first used this approach in the valuation of investments.[6] More recently, this method has been applied to the valuation of companies and acquisitions. Meyers's approach is a little bit more complicated. In his original formulation, the value of a company is the sum of its *unlevered* value and all the *side effects* of the debt (i.e., the present value of tax benefits, financial distress costs, and agency costs).

---

[6]See S. Myers, "Interactions in Corporate Financing and Investment Decisions: Implications for Capital Budgeting," *Journal of Finance*, 29 (March 1974): 1–25.

6.3.2 Second Alternative: Adjusting Discount Rates for Leverage

The adjusting discount rates for leverage method is based on adjusting the discount rates calculated in [6.2] and [6.3] to take the value of tax benefits into account.

If cash flow is perpetual and if we keep leverage constant and static, equation [6.3] used to calculate K_{el} should allow for corporate taxes and related tax benefits as follows:[7]

$$K^*_{el} = K_{eu} + [K_{eu} - K_d] \times (1 - t_c) \times D/E \qquad (6.6)$$

K^*_{el} means that this rate has been adjusted to consider tax benefits.

Starting from [6.6], we can derive a new equation for the weighted average cost of capital:

$$WACC^* = K^*_{el} \times \frac{E}{E + D} + K_d \times (1 - t_c) \times \frac{D}{E + D} \qquad (6.7)$$

The symbol $WACC^*$ indicates that this rate has also been adjusted for tax benefits.

$WACC$ is constant and is equal to K_{eu} without tax benefits. In this particular case, $WACC$ can also be derived using the following equation:[8]

$$WACC^* = K_{eu} \times \left(1 - t_c \times \frac{D}{D + E}\right) \qquad (6.8)$$

Equations [6.6], [6.7], and [6.8] include the present value of tax benefits using K_d as the appropriate discount rate.

Exhibit 6.6 shows how discount rates change with the introduction of tax benefits linked to debt.

Without tax benefits (case A), the $WACC$ remains constant and equal to K_{eu}. When we allow for corporate taxes, the $WACC^*$ decreases as leverage increases.

You should also note that the slope of the K^*_{el} curve is lower than the one in case A. This difference in the slope is due to tax benefits and equal to $(1 - t_c)$.[9]

---

[7]This proof is shown in Chapter 7, Appendix 1 (A.2).
[8]This proof is shown in Chapter 7, Appendix 1 (A.1).
[9]The slope of the curve which represents K^*_{el} as a function of D/E is equal to $(K_{eu} - K_d) \times (1 - t_c)$.

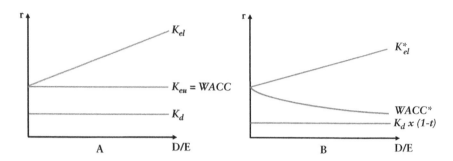

Exhibit 6.6 Discount rates, leverage, and tax benefits

Shortcomings of the Adjusting Discount Rates for Leverage Method If we use the *adjusting the discount rates for leverage* method in the valuation of companies or M&A operations, it is important to be aware of some of its shortcomings:

a. It does not allow us to separately assess the *present value of tax savings,* which are instead directly included in the final value of the company.
b. It brings in a circularity problem. K^*_{el} and the $WACC^*$ depend on the leverage ratio, which should be calculated using the market values of debt and equity. At the same time, we need K^*_{el} and the $WACC^*$ to determine the *market value of equity,* which represents the final result of the valuation process.
c. It assumes that the leverage ratio remains constant over time. This implies that the level of debt should change in order to balance changes in the equity value of the company. This might not necessarily happen in many companies.
d. Finally, if cash flows are perpetual, our results are not accurate. The error can be estimated by comparing these results with the ones obtained using the APV method. In the next chapter, we will show that these results can coincide if and only if the discount rate of tax benefits is chosen properly.

Using an iterative method to assess the leverage ratio can solve the problem mentioned in point (b). We can also overcome the problem set forth in point (c) by allowing the discount rates to vary over time according to company's forecasts of future leverage ratios. However, we should highlight that both solutions make the valuation process more complex.

In the next chapter, we will see also that the problems linked to the discount rate adjustment method become more complex once we take growth into consideration.

For all these reasons, we advise to use the unlevered value adjustment method, where the value of tax savings can be assessed separately.

6.4 THIRD PROBLEM: THE CHOICE BETWEEN AN ASSET-SIDE VERSUS AN EQUITY-SIDE PERSPECTIVE

Without debt, the choice between the asset-side and the equity-side approach is not even an issue. In this particular case, the FCFO is equal to the FCFE and one single discount rate can be used. The discount rate would be K_{eu}, the opportunity cost of *equity* for an unlevered company.

If we have to take debt into consideration, we must deal with two issues:

- Whether we prefer to value *assets* or *equity*. These two perspectives should lead to the same value of equity, as long as we use consistent criteria in the determination of all the input variables. Exhibit 6.7 illustrates these two alternatives.
- Whether we want to determine one value only that directly includes tax benefits or the *unlevered* company value and the value of tax benefits separately.

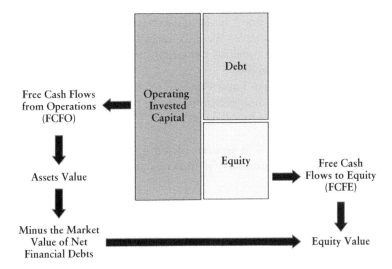

Exhibit 6.7 Assets-side and equity-side perspective

Exhibit 6.8 Different approaches in valuing the equity of a company

Asset side	$\displaystyle\sum_{t=1}^{n} \frac{FCFO_t}{(1+WACC^*)^t} - W_D$ (1)	$\displaystyle\sum_{t=1}^{n} \frac{FCFO_t}{(1+K_{eu})^t}$ $\displaystyle+ \sum_{t=1}^{n} \frac{D_t \times K_d \times t_c}{(1+K_{TS})^t} - W_D$ (2)
Equity side	$\displaystyle\sum_{t=1}^{n} \frac{FCFE_t}{(1+K_{el}^*)^t}$ (3)	$\displaystyle\sum_{t=1}^{n} \frac{FCFE_t - (D_t \times K_d \times t_c)}{(1+K_{el})^t}$ $\displaystyle+ \sum_{t=1}^{n} \frac{D_t \times K_d \times t_c}{(1+K_{TS})^t}$ (4)
	Discount rate adjustment method	**Unlevered value adjustment method**

Exhibit 6.8 highlights these alternative approaches.

The procedure shown in sections 1 and 2 describes the approach based on the asset-side perspective.

The method in section 1 is the most widely used by practitioners and is based on the idea that assets should be valued first while the equity value is derived as the difference between W_{assets} and the value of financial debt.

The approach in section 2 is the unlevered value adjustment method from the asset-side perspective. We have already introduced this method, known as the APV in the previous paragraph; it will be discussed in more detail in the following chapters.

The methods in sections 3 and 4 instead refer to the estimation of equity based on the FCFE. The "disaggregated" model from the asset-side perspective is only introduced here for completeness.[10] This method is never used in practice.

In the methods shown in sections 3 and 4, the resulting equity value should be identical if the necessary parameters are determined using consistent criteria.

---

[10] The first part in the equation in section 4: $\displaystyle\sum_{t=1}^{n} \frac{FCFE_t - (K_d \times D_t \times t_c)}{(1+K_{el})^t}$ represents the equity value without tax benefits; the second part $\displaystyle\sum_{t=1}^{n} \frac{K_d \times D_t \times t_c}{(1+K_{TS})^t}$ measures the present value of tax benefits. To be consistent, when we calculate K_{el}, the equity value used in the leverage ratio (D/E) should not include tax benefits.

6.5 FROM THE ASSET VALUE TO THE EQUITY VALUE

We can determine W_{equity} by subtracting the value of financial debt from W_{assets}. In the process, some problems may arise. Exhibit 6.9 highlights them.

In Exhibit 6.9, liabilities include financial debt, debt "substitutes" (financial leases and operating leases) and "hybrid" securities (such as convertible bonds and warrants).

The difference between W_{assets} and net financial debt represents the value to the current and potential shareholders (subscribers of warrant and convertible bonds or owners of stock option).

The purpose of the valuation process is usually to determine the current value of the equity (i.e., the value of the shares already issued when the valuation is carried out). If this is our objective, the value of the new shares embedded in issued financial instruments (e.g., warrant rights) or in approved option plans (to remunerate the management and the employees) should also be subtracted from W_{assets}. To determine accurately the value of such embedded equity, we suggest using option-pricing techniques.

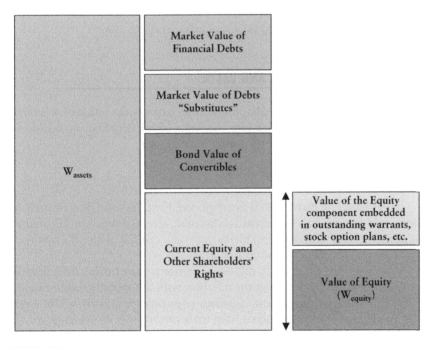

Exhibit 6.9 W_{assets} and W_{equity}

## CHAPTER 7

Leverage and Value in Growth Scenarios

I n this chapter we introduce the relationship between *leverage*, opportunity
cost of capital, and value assuming a growth scenario.
  This assumption will allow us to:

- Point out the hypotheses commonly used by professionals in their *discounted cash flow* (*DCF*) valuations[1] and the pitfalls that their model entails;
- Provide useful insights on the estimation of tax benefits.

7.1   GROWTH, LEVERAGE, AND VALUE

As discussed in the previous chapter, we can express the value of a levered company as its unlevered value plus the value of tax benefits (tax shield). In paragraph 6.2, we presented the following equation:

$$W_L = W_U + D \times t_c$$

  It was based on three crucial assumptions. First, the cash flow from operations was assumed to be perpetual. Second, leverage was not allowed to change over time. Finally, tax shields were discounted at the K_d rate (i.e., their cost was the same as the cost of debt).
  Once we allow for growth, this equation needs to be further investigated, even if we are merely adjusting for inflation with a nominal growth rate.
  In this situation, cash flow increases over time at a growth rate equal to *g*. At this point of the analysis, it is irrelevant to specify whether we are

---

[1] Many professionals assume a steady growth scenario in their valuation processes.

adjusting for nominal or real growth. In this newly specified growth scenario, *assuming that the ratio between debt and equity stays constant*, the value of a company can be expressed as:

$$W_L = \sum_{t=1}^{\infty} \frac{FCFO_0(1+g)^t}{(1+K_{eu})^t} + \sum_{t=1}^{\infty} \frac{(D_0 \times K_d \times t_c)(1+g)^{(t-1)}}{(1+K_{TS})^t}$$

where K_{TS} is the proper discount rate for tax benefits (and is not necessarily equal to the cost of debt anymore).

It is important to mention that, according to our assumptions, interest expenses can be defined in three different ways:

a. $D_1 \times K_d$, using the level of debt at the end of the period.
b. $D_0 \times K_d$, using the level of debt at the beginning of the period.
c. $\frac{(D_0 + D_1)}{2} \times K_d$, using the average level of debt during the period.

For sake of simplicity, we use the definition mentioned in b.[2]
The cash flow in the previous equation will then converge to:

$$W_L = \frac{FCFO_0(1+g)}{K_{eu} - g} + \frac{(D_0 \times K_d \times t_c)}{K_{TS} - g}$$

We can therefore calculate the value of a levered company in a growth scenario as:

$$W_L = W_U + D_0 \times t_c \times \frac{K_d}{K_{TS} - g}$$

where W_U is the *unlevered* value of a growing firm, while the remaining part of the equation represents the present value of tax benefits.

7.2 NOMINAL AND REAL DISCOUNTING

In our discussions in this textbook, we will always use nominal values. This means is that cash flows will take expected inflation into consideration while discount rates will be observed in financial markets and will therefore naturally include inflationary expectations.

---

[2]The same assumption is found in J. A. Miles and J. R. Ezzel, "The Weighted Average Cost of Capital, Perfect Capital Markets, and Project Life: A Clarification," *Journal of Financial and Quantitative Analysis*, 15 (September 1980).

If growth is only nominal and is therefore exclusively determined by inflation, equation [7.1] can be simplified. As a matter of fact, in the case of anticipated and neutral inflation, the value of a company can be calculated by discounting cash flows in real terms (i.e., without considering expected inflation) at a rate that is also expressed in real terms.

We can prove this statement starting with the well-known Fisher's equation, which expresses the relationship between nominal rates (i.e., market rates) and real rates:

$$i_r = \frac{1 + i_n}{1 + p} - 1$$

where:

i_n = nominal rate

i_r = real rate

p = expected inflation

Using this equation, we can rewrite nominal rates as:

$$i_n = i_r + p + i_r \times p$$

This relationship implies that—within an inflationary context—lenders will require not only an interest rate $i_r + p$, but also an additional amount, which allows for the conservation of the purchasing power of their funds.

The term $[i_r \times p]$ is what allows for this, adjusting the required real interest rate in terms of purchasing power.

We can then go back to equation [7.1] and rewrite the nominal rates K_{eu}, K_d, and K_{TS} using Fischer's equation and expressing p in terms of the nominal growth rate g_n:

$$W_L = \frac{FCFO_0(1 + g_n)}{K_{eu\_real} + g_n + K_{eu\_real} \times g_n - g_n} + \frac{(D_0 \times K_d \times t_c)}{K_{TS\_real} + g_n + K_{TS\_real} \times g_n - g_n}$$

We then perform some algebra to finally obtain:

$$W_L = \frac{FCFO_0(1 + g_n)}{K_{eu\_real} + K_{eu\_real} \times g_n} + \frac{(D_0 \times K_d \times t_c)}{K_{TS\_real} + K_{TS\_real} \times g_n}$$

$$W_L = \frac{FCFO_0(1 + g_n)}{K_{eu\_real} \times (1 + g_n)} + \frac{(D_0 \times K_d \times t_c)}{K_{TS\_real} \times (1 + g_n)}$$

$$W_L = \frac{FCFO_0}{K_{eu\_real}} + \frac{\frac{D_0 \times K_d \times t_c}{(1 + g_n)}}{K_{TS\_real}}$$

Equation [7.3] supports the well-known rule of consistency between cash flows and discount rates: the value of a company can be equally determined by discounting nominal cash flows using nominal rates or real cash flows using real rates.

This equation also points out that:

- Tax shields are usually greater with high inflation.
- Tax benefits only depend on the level of *real* rates. Therefore, these benefits can be high even when inflation is low if and only if *real rates are very low.*[3] We show this case in the following example, where the tax shields are discounted using K_d.

7.2.1 Nominal versus Real Terms

Analysts usually prefer to use nominal values, since the use of real values does not allow them to account for the impact of inflation on working capital and on the company's net financial position.

---

[3]To understand why this can happen, we should note that under the following hypotheses (1 and 2), equation [7.3] can be rewritten in this way:

Hypothesis 1: $K_{TS\_real} = K_{d\_real}$

Hypothesis 2: $K_d = K_{d\_real} \times (1 + g_n) + g_n$ (Fisher's Equation)

$$W_L = \frac{FCFO_0}{K_{eu}} + \frac{D_0 \times t_c \times [K_{d\_real} \times (1 + g_n) + g_n]}{K_{d\_real} \times (1 + g_n)}$$

$$W_L = \frac{FCFO_0}{K_{eu}} + \frac{D_0 \times t_c \times [K_{d\_real} \times (1 + g_n)]}{K_{d\_real} \times (1 + g_n)} + \frac{D_0 \times t_c \times g_n}{K_{d\_real} \times (1 + g_n)}.$$

Once we delete terms and rearrange the equation, we finally have:

$$W_L = \frac{FCFO_0}{K_{eu}} + D_0 \times t_c + \frac{D_0 \times t_c \times g_n}{K_{d\_real} \times (1 + g_n)}$$

The term $[K_{d\_real} \times (1 + g_n)]$, according to Hyp. 2, can be substituted with $[K_d - g_n]$. The levered value of a firm with inflation can be expressed as the sum of:

$$W(L) = \underbrace{\frac{FCFO_0}{k_e(U)}}_{\text{Unlevered value}} + \underbrace{D_0 \times t_c}_{\substack{\text{Value of tax advantages} \\ \text{due to the deductibility} \\ \text{of interests payable}}} + \underbrace{\frac{D_0 \times t_c \times g_n}{k_d - g_n}}_{\substack{\text{Value of tax advantages due} \\ \text{to the deductibility of interests} \\ \text{referable to the revaluation of the debt}}}$$

Exhibit 7.1   Scenarios' assumptions

	Scenario 1	Scenario 2
Prime rate	4.54%	17.15%
Inflation rate	3.0%	10.0%
Real rate	1.5%	6.5%
t_c	36%	36%
Tax shields (derived using [7.3]) relative to actual debt	1.06	0.84

However, we prefer real values when the time horizon is very long and we can safely assume that an increase in operating costs can be directly reflected in sales prices. For this reason, the valuation of an oil company is usually performed using real values, assuming that changes in raw materials costs are automatically reflected in sale prices.

Such a real terms approach is also used in the valuation of real estate investments as it can be very difficult to forecast real estate prices over a time horizon of 5 to 10 years.

7.3   PROBLEMS WITH THE DISCOUNT OF TAX BENEFIT

We stated earlier that, in a no-growth scenario, tax shields should be discounted using K_d, since their risk can be assumed to be the same as the risk of the debt they are applied to.

Other experts do not share this opinion. Miles and Ezzel[4] argue that if a company keeps its debt/equity ratio constant, the level of its debt depends on the value that its *equity* has in different scenarios. Therefore, the risk of tax shields can be assumed to equal the risk of the company's *assets*, and, for this reason, we should use K_{eu} as the appropriate discount rate (see the example in Exhibit 7.1).

Many issues can be found with the use of K_d as the discount rate for tax shields in growth scenarios. In this case, the issuance of new debt and the tax shields that stem from it are subordinated to being able to obtain a realized growth level equal to the assumed one. For this reason, we could assume the

---

[4] I. Miles and R. Ezzel, "The Weighted Average Cost of Capital, Perfect Capital Markets, and Project Life: A Clarification," *Journal of Financial and Quantitative Analysis*, 15 (September 1980): 719–730.

risk of tax shields to be the same as the operating risk of the whole company, which is priced at K_{eu}.[5]

Some other researchers believe that K_{TS} should be priced at some estimate within the range of values between K_d and K_{eu}.

We can conclude that experts are inclined to agree that K_{TS} should be higher than (or equal to) K_d and lower than (or equal to) K_{eu}:

$$K_d \leq K_{TS} \leq K_{eu}$$

We will show later in Chapter 8 how using K_d or K_{eu} or a value between them for K_{TS} can lead to very different results.

7.4   COST OF CAPITAL FORMULAS IN GROWTH SCENARIOS

As already discussed, if the cash flows were perpetual and constant, and if the level of debt stayed constant, the formula to compute K_{el}^*, assuming a discount rate for the tax benefits equal to K_d, is:

$$K_{el}^* = K_{eu} + [K_{eu} - K_d] \times (1 - t_c) \times D/E$$

On the other hand, in a no-growth scenario, the relationship between the WACC and K_{eu}, is:

$$WACC^* = K_{eu} \times \left(1 - t_c \times \frac{D}{D + E}\right)$$

Exhibits 7.2 and 7.3 summarize the relationships between K_{el}^* and K_{eu} and between the WACC and K_{eu} in a scenario with or without growth. Tax shields are discounted either using K_{eu} (on the left-hand side of the tables) or K_d (on the right-hand side of the tables). We prove all these equations in Appendix 1.

---

[5]Many authors suggest following this approach. R. A. Taggart, "Consistent Valuation and Cost of Capital Expressions with Corporate and Personal Taxes," *Financial Management* (Fall 1991): 8–20. S. Kaplan and R. Ruback, "The Valuation of Cash Flows Forecast: An Empirical Analysis," in *Journal of Finance* 50, 4 (September 1995). R. Ruback, "Capital Cash Flow: A Simple Approach to Valuing Risky Cash Flow," *Financial Management* (Summer 2002): 85–103.

We define the unlevered value adjustment method also as APV (adjusted present value), regardless of the rate used in the discount of tax benefits. Some authors, instead, define as capital cash flow (CCF) or compressed APV (CAPV) the unlevered value adjustment method, where tax shields are discounted using K_{eu}.

Exhibit 7.2 Relationship between K_{el}^* and K_{eu}

	K_{eu} as tax shield discount rate	K_d as tax shield discount rate
Steady state	a) $K_{el}^* = K_{eu} + (K_{eu} - K_d) \times \dfrac{D}{E}$	b) $K_{el}^* = K_{eu} + (K_{eu} - K_d) \times \dfrac{D}{E} \times (1 - t_c)$
Steady growth	c) $K_{el}^* = K_{eu} + (K_{eu} - K_d) \times \dfrac{D}{E}$	d) $K_{el}^* = K_{eu} + (K_{eu} - K_d)$ $\times \left[1 - t_c \times \left(\dfrac{K_d}{K_d - g} \right) \right] \times \dfrac{D}{E}$

Exhibit 7.3 Relationship between $WACC^*$ and K_{eu}

	K_{eu} as tax shield discount rate	K_d as tax shield discount rate
Steady state	a.1) $WACC^* = K_{eu} - K_d \times t_c$ $\times \dfrac{D}{D + E}$	b.1) $WACC^* = K_{eu} \times \left(1 - t_c \times \dfrac{D}{D + E} \right)$
Steady growth	c.1) $WACC^* = K_{eu} - K_d \times t_c$ $\times \dfrac{D}{D + E}$	d.1) $WACC^* = K_{eu} - \dfrac{(K_{eu} - g)}{(K_d - g)} \times K_d$ $\times t_c \times \dfrac{D}{D + E}$

We introduced all these equations adjusted for growth for sake of completeness. It is important to mention that they are never actually used by professionals and they are often not even introduced in many finance textbooks.[6]

In the previous equations (Exhibits 7.2 and 7.3), we used either K_d or K_{eu} as the discount rates for the tax shield. Just as we discussed while calculating the present value of tax benefits, different approaches can be followed. Among these, we want to point out the following two:

- Miles and Ezzel's[7] approach. The two authors suggest discounting the first-year tax shield using K_d (since we know the exact level of outstanding debt) and the following ones using K_{eu}. The formula then becomes:

$$WACC^* = K_{eu} - K_d \times \frac{(1 + K_{eu})}{(1 + K_d)} \times t_c \times \frac{D}{D + E}$$

---

[6]An exception is T. Copeland, T. Koller, J. Murrin, *Valuation: Measuring and Managing the Value of Companies*, 3rd ed. (New York: John Wiley & Sons, 2000).
[7]See J. A. Miles and J. R. Ezzel, "The Weighted Average Cost of Capital, Perfect Capital Markets, and Project Life: A Clarification," *Journal of Financial and Quantitative Analysis*, 15 (September 1980).

- The $WACC^*$ formula (as introduced in equation b.1 in Exhibit 7.3) applied to a *steady-growth* scenario implies rather complex hypotheses:
  - Tax shields that apply to already existing debt are discounted using K_d.
  - Tax shields relative to new debt following the company's growth are discounted using both K_{eu} and K_d (refer to Appendix 1, paragraph C, for more details).

The $WACC^*$ approach gives you the same results of the APV[8] if and only if cash flows are *perpetual*.

In the case of *cash flows projected for a limited period of time or cash flows which vary over time,* the $WACC^*$ approach bears results consistent with those obtained with the APV model if and only if both tax shields and cash flows are discounted using the same rate, K_{eu}.[9]

Recalling that the $WACC^*$ approach relies on the assumption that the ratio between the company's value and the value of its debt is held constant over time. This is rarely true in acquisitions or in *private equity* deals. The following example highlights the shortcomings of the $WACC^*$ approach in such situations.

7.4.1 An Example

We already pointed out that the equations for the determination of the costs of capital ($WACC^*$ and K_{el}^*) rely on the assumption that the ratio between the value of debt and the company's value remains constant.

In real situations, this ratio usually changes because:

- Capital structure decisions cannot be reverted in the short-term.
- Debt cannot be higher than a given threshold proportionally to invested capital.
- Acquisitions or *private equity* transactions are designed assuming a different capital structure for the transaction itself.
- Companies that generate cash flows tend to reduce their leverage over time.
- When the company's value decreases, leverage usually increases.

In order to illustrate the use of the $WACC^*$ (or K_{el}^*) formula, we will use a simple example. Assume that a *start-up* company is expected to generate the cash flows (FCFO) presented in Exhibit 7.4.

---

[8]As already pointed out, the APV approach gives you more accurate results since it allows you to value separately *tax shields.*

[9]Note that Miles and Ezzel's approach (which discounts the first-year tax shield at K_d and only the following flow at K_{eu}) can lead to results consistent with APV.

Exhibit 7.4 Expected cash flows

t_0	t_1	t_2	t_3	t_4	t_5
(10,000)	1,000	1,500	10,000	12,000	12,500

This company is financed for half of its need with debt equal to 5,000, which will be repaid in one installment at the end of year five. The parameters for the cost of capital estimation are presented in Exhibit 7.5.

Exhibit 7.5 Cost of capital parameters

K_{eu}	10%
K_d	6%
t_c	34%
K_{TS}	6%

Using the APV model, the value of this company is:

$$W_U = \sum_{t=1}^{5} \frac{FCFO_t}{(1 + K_{eu})^t} = 25,619.59$$

$$W_{TS} = (D_0 \times K_d \times t_c) \times a_{5 \neg K_d} = 429.66$$

$$W_L = W_U + W_{TS} = 26,049.25$$

We will compare this value with the one obtained from the $WACC^*$ approach. With this approach, the first issue we face is to choose the level of leverage to use in the equation.

If we assume that the financial analyst chooses the leverage using book values (thereby making a big mistake), he will use 50 percent ($D = 5,000$; Total Invested Capital $= 10,000$). In this case we can determine $WACC^*$ using equation b.1 in Exhibit 7.3:

$$WACC^* = K_{eu} \left(1 - t_c \times \frac{D}{D + E} \right)$$

$$WACC^* = 0.10 \times (1 - 0.34 \times 0.50) = 0.083$$

Using this discount rate, the value of the company is:

$$W_L = \sum_{t=1}^{5} \frac{FCFO_t}{(1 + WACC^*)^t} = 27,187.93$$

With the $WACC^*$ approach we obtain a higher value than the previous one using the APV. The difference comes from the fact that we assumed

Exhibit 7.6 Actual leverage and debt

	t_0	t_1	t_2	t_3	t_4	t_5
Actual leverage	0.19	0.18	0.17	0.23	0.44	0
Leverage assumed using $WACC^*$	0.50	0.50	0.50	0.50	0.50	0
Actual debt	5,000	5,000	5,000	5,000	5,000	0
Level of debt implicitly assumed using $WACC^*$	13,320	13,996	14,486	10,776	5,737	0

leverage to be constant and equal to 50 percent in the $WACC^*$ approach. In Exhibit 7.6 and in Exhibit 7.3, we compare this level of leverage with the actual one.[10]

It is crucial to highlight that the higher company's value comes from the higher debt (and therefore the higher tax shields) assumed using the $WACC^*$ approach.

We can now calculate the company's value with the APV model, using the same debt level assumed through the $WACC^*$ approach:

$$W_U = \sum_{t=1}^{5} \frac{FCFO_t}{(1 + K_{eu})^t} = 25,619.59$$

$$W_{TS} = \sum_{t=1}^{5} \frac{D_{t-1} \times K_d \times t_c}{(1 + K_d)^t} = 1,020.15$$

$$W_L = W_U + W_{TS} = 26,639.73$$

This result shows that the $WACC^*$ approach leads to different (even if not by much) values than those obtained through the APV model when cash flows are not perpetual.

Exhibit 7.7 Debt and tax shield value

D_{t-1}	$D_{t-1} \times K_d \times t_c$	$(1 + K_d)^{-t}$
13,320	272	0.943
13,996	286	0.890
14,486	296	0.840
10,776	220	0.792
5,737	117	0.747

---

[10]Since leverage also changes from one year to the next, the $WACC^*$ should therefore also be modified.

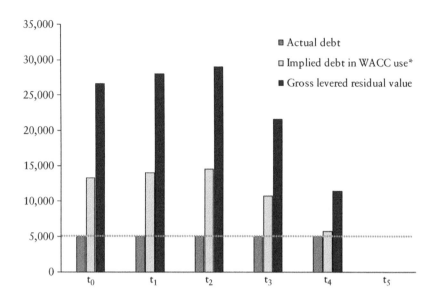

Exhibit 7.8   Levered company's value and debt

Exhibit 7.2 shows the levered company's value and the level of debt obtained using the $WACC^*$ approach. With this approach, debt adjusts year by year to the value of the company and, in the case of projects with a limited lifetime, to their remaining value.

7.5   THE WACC: SOME REMARKS

In *capital budgeting* decisions, the weighted average cost of capital plays an important role. As a matter of fact, the use of the $WACC$ allows managers to better understand:

- How debt can affect the value of an investment
- That an investment should be assessed on the basis of the company's long-term capital structure and not on the basis of the financial mix used to fund that particular investment

We can basically rely on the use of the $WACC$ to value an investment whenever the following conditions are true:

- Leverage is determined using market values rather than book values.
- The target capital structure is set effectively. Some companies surprisingly determine their $WACC^*$ assuming high leverage, even if they hold

a high level of cash, they have a positive net financial position, and no relevant acquisition is planned.

The preceding considerations refer to the valuation of an investment. The valuation of a company or an acquisition is a completely different story.

We can analyze the following substantial differences between the valuation of an investment and the valuation of either a company or an M&A transaction:

- The time horizon should be longer. This makes it more difficult to set the expected leverage to be used in determining K^*_{el} and the $WACC^*$.
- Leverage can dramatically change during the period of valuation. This requires more accuracy in the assumptions about the company's capital structure.
- Growth (at least the nominal one) should always be considered. If the FCFO does not adjust for inflation, the company is bound to fail.
- The value of tax shields can be very high, especially in levered acquisitions.

Therefore, it is worth highlighting the following elements:

- When valuing companies or acquisitions, methods that rely on K^*_{el} and on the $WACC^*$ can lead to inaccurate values even if these methods can be properly used in capital budgeting decisions.
- Using these methods makes it difficult to understand what proportion of the final value comes from operations and what proportion comes from mere tax benefits.

We do not find any reason why these methods should ever be preferred to more clear and simple ones, such as the adjusting the unlevered value method or the APV.

We think that the APV method will become the standard method in the valuation of companies and M&A or private-equity transactions.

The $WACC^*$ method will still be used in some cases:

- At the very beginning of M&A transactions, when we need to quickly and easily determine a rough value of the target company, on the basis of which we can begin the negotiation process.
- In valuations done in connection with corporate guarantees or for fiscal reasons. The purpose of these valuations is, indeed, to provide a prudential value of the company in a *stand-alone* scenario and not to value it based, at least partially, on its business plans.

In these two situations, it is better to use the $WACC^*$ method, which relies on a future capital structure typical of an average or normal situation. Nonetheless, you should be very careful when determining the average leverage level using market values of both equity and debt.

7.6 REAL DIMENSION OF TAX BENEFITS

We have assumed that the amount of tax shields is linked to t_c, which is assumed to be equal to the marginal corporate tax rate. Many scholars argue that the tax benefits of debt can be different and that t_c has to be adjusted in order to allow for:

- Personal taxes
- Alternative tax shields in cases of uncertainty due to factors other than those linked to the level of debt

7.6.1 Personal Taxes

If our purpose is to determine the value of the company for its shareholders, our analysis must also consider the specific gains and costs associated with the personal taxation (on dividends and capital gains) of the individual shareholder herself.

This issue is illustrated in Exhibit 7.9, which shows how the company's cash flows change if we introduce personal taxes.

If we assume that a company issues only bonds and shares, the after-tax flow to its bondholders and shareholders can be expressed as:

- Bondholders:

$$K_d \times D \times (1 - t_{pd})$$

where: t_{pd} is the personal tax rate on interest receivable;

- Shareholders:

$$NI \times (1 - t_{pe}) = (EBIT - K_d \times D) \times (1 - t_c) \times (1 - t_{pe})$$

where: t_{pe} is the personal tax rate on dividends (we assume that the entirety of the company's net income is distributed to investors).

As already stated, the sum of the cash flows distributed to shareholders and bondholders should equal the total cash flow generated by the company's *assets*.

The company's total cash flow can be written as:

$$(EBIT - K_d \times D) \times (1 - t_c) \times (1 + t_{pe}) + K_d \times D \times (1 - t_{pd})$$

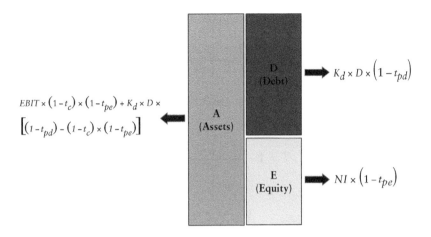

Exhibit 7.9 Cash flow with corporate and personal taxes

Rearranging terms, we have:

$$EBIT \times (1 - t_c) \times (1 - t_{pe}) - K_d \times D \times (1 - t_c) \times (1 - t_{pe}) + K_d \times D \times (1 - t_{pd})$$

As shown in Exhibit 7.3, we finally obtain:

$$[EBIT \times (1 - t_c) \times (1 - t_{pe})] + K_d \times D \times [(1 - t_{pd}) - (1 - t_c) \times (1 - t_{pe})]$$

The first term of this expression represents the after-tax flow of an unlevered company while the second term expresses the tax benefits of issuing debt instead of equity. If this flow is discounted using K_d, we obtain:
Present value of tax shields:

$$W_{TS} = \sum_{t=1}^{n} \frac{K_d \times D \times [(1 - t_{pd}) - (1 - t_c) \times (1 - t_{pe})]}{[1 + (1 - t_{pd}) \times K_d]^t} \qquad (7.4)$$

With personal taxes, the levered value of a company can be written as the sum of:

- *Its unlevered value*, obtained discounting $EBIT \times (1 - t_c) \times (1 - t_{pe})$ using an *unlevered* rate, K_{eu}. We assume that K_{eu} represents the return required from shareholders after personal taxes. This is the same as discounting $EBIT \times (1 - t_c)$ using K_{eu} expressed before personal taxes.
- *Present value of its tax benefits*. This value should be determined using a tax rate that represents the advantage that comes from distributing the cash flow from operations as interest payable instead of dividends.

If all the flows are perpetual, equation [7.4] can be rewritten as:

$$W_{TS} = \frac{D \times [(1 - t_{pd}) - (1 - t_c) \times (1 - t_{pe})]}{(1 - t_{pd})} \qquad (7.5)$$

Dividing both sides of this equation by D, we get the *tax advantage of issuing a unit of debt*, T:

$$T = 1 - \frac{(1 - t_c) \times (1 - t_{pe})}{(1 - t_{pd})} \qquad (7.6)$$

Consequently:

$$W_{TS} = T \times D$$

After determining T, we can now adjust equations [3.6] and [3.8] for personal taxes:

$$WACC^* = K_{eu} \times \left(1 - T \times \frac{D}{D + E} \right) \qquad (7.7)$$

and

$$K_{el}^* = K_{eu} + [K_{eu} \times (1 - T) - K_d \times (1 - t_c)] \times \frac{D}{E} \qquad (7.8)$$

Equations [7.7] and [7.8] are derived assuming that cash flows are perpetual.[11] Nevertheless, they can be used without difficulty even when assessing investments with a limited lifetime.

7.6.2 Uncertainty and Alternative Tax Shields

The use of debt can generate tax shields only if interest expenses effectively lower before-tax profit. These tax shields do not occur if the EBIT is lower than interest expenses. The risk of this happening, as already pointed out, is implicitly included in the discount rate K_{TS}. It is worth mentioning that some companies may exploit other tax shields, not necessarily linked to debt. Examples of alternative tax shields are deductible capital expenses, accelerated depreciation and tax benefits ad hoc tax reliefs to incentivize investments.

---

[11]Examples related to these equations are in S. Benninga, O. Sarig, *Corporate Finance: A Valuation Approach* (New York: McGraw-Hill, 1997).

Many researchers suggest that the discount rate t_c should be prudently reduced in the case of a company exploiting alternative tax shields if its operating profits are very volatile.

APPENDIX 7.1: DERIVATION OF THE FORMULAS TO CALCULATE THE COST OF CAPITAL

In parts A and B of this Appendix, we prove the formulas introduced in Exhibits 7.2 and 7.3.

In part C, we show how the equations related to K_{el}^* and $WACC^*$ rely on the assumption that different tax shield discount rates are used in growth scenarios.

A. Using K_d as the Discount Rate for Tax Benefits

A.1 $WACC^*$ in No-Growth Scenarios By assuming that the *levered* value (*asset side*) assessed with the discount rate adjustment method and the *levered* value calculated with the APV method are equal, we obtain:

$$W_L = \sum_{t=1}^{\infty} \frac{FCFO_t}{(1 + WACC^*)^t} = W_U + W_{TS} = \sum_{t=1}^{\infty} \frac{FCFO_t}{(1 + K_{eu})^t} + \sum_{t=1}^{\infty} \frac{D_{t-1} \times t_c \times K_d}{(1 + K_d)^t}$$

$$W_L = \frac{FCFO}{WACC^*} = W_U + W_{TS} = \frac{FCFO}{K_{eu}} + \frac{D \times t_c \times K_d}{K_d}$$

$$\frac{FCFO}{WACC^*} = \frac{FCFO}{K_{eu}} + \frac{D \times K_d \times t_c}{K_d}$$

Substituting D with $\frac{D}{(D+E)} \times W_L$ [where W_L is equal to $(D + E)$] and rearranging terms, we can determine the $WACC$:

$$D = \frac{D}{(D + E)} \times (D + E) = \frac{D}{(D + E)} \times \frac{FCFO}{WACC^*}$$

$$\frac{FCFO}{WACC^*} = \frac{FCFO}{K_{eu}} + \left[\frac{D}{(D + E)} \times \frac{FCFO}{WACC^*} \times \frac{K_d \times t_c}{K_d} \right]$$

$$\frac{1}{WACC^*} = \frac{1}{K_{eu}} + \left[\frac{D}{D + E} \times \frac{1}{WACC^*} \times t_c \right]$$

$$\frac{1}{K_{eu}} = \frac{1}{WACC^*} \times \left[1 - \frac{D}{D + E} \times t_c \right]$$

$$WACC^* = K_{eu} \times \left[1 - t_c \times \frac{D}{D + E} \right]$$

A.2 K_{el}^* in No-Growth Scenarios Recalling that:

$$WACC^* = K_{el}^* \times \frac{E}{E+D} + K_d \times (1 - t_c) \times \frac{D}{E+D}$$

and substituting $WACC^*$ with the equation found in (A.1), we can express K_{el}^* in no-growth scenarios as:

$$K_{eu} - K_{eu} \times t_c \times \frac{D}{E+D} = K_{el}^* \times \frac{E}{E+D} + K_d \times (1 - t_c) \times \frac{D}{E+D}$$

$$K_{el}^* \times \frac{E}{E+D} = K_{eu} - K_{eu} \times t_c \times \frac{D}{E+D} - K_d \times (1 - t_c) \times \frac{D}{E+D}$$

$$K_{el}^* = K_{eu} \times \frac{(E+D)}{E} - K_{eu} \times t_c \times \frac{D}{E} - K_d \times (1 - t_c) \times \frac{D}{E}$$

$$K_{el}^* = K_{eu} + K_{eu} \times (1 - t_c) \times \frac{D}{E} - K_d \times (1 - t_c) \times \frac{D}{E}$$

$$K_{el}^* = K_{eu} + (K_{cu} - K_d) \times (1 - t_c) \times \frac{D}{E}$$

A.3 WACC* in Growth Scenarios[12]

$$W_L = \sum_{t=1}^{\infty} \frac{FCFO_0 \times (1+g)^t}{(1 + WACC^*)^t} = W_U + W_{TS} = \sum_{t=1}^{\infty} \frac{FCFO_0 \times (1+g)^t}{(1 + K_{eu})^t}$$

$$+ \sum_{t=1}^{\infty} \frac{D_0 \times t_c \times K_d \times (1+g)^{t-1}}{(1 + K_d)^t}$$

$$W_L = \frac{FCFO_0 \times (1+g)}{WACC^* - g} = W_U + W_{TS} = \frac{FCFO_0 \times (1+g)}{K_{eu} - g} + \frac{D_0 \times t_c \times K_d}{K_d - g}$$

$$\frac{FCFO_0 \times (1+g)}{WACC^* - g} = \frac{FCFO_0 \times (1+g)}{K_{eu} - g} + \frac{D_0 \times t_c \times K_d}{K_d - g}$$

---

[12] We assume that interest expenses in time t, determined as $K_d \times D$, are generated by debt of the previous year $(t - 1)$. The same hypothesis is in J. A. Miles, J. R. Ezzel (see footnote 2 in this chapter).

For this reason, the series expressing present value of tax shields (last addend of the expression W_L) converge to $\frac{D_0 \times t_c \times K_d}{K_d - g}$.

Substituting D_0 with $\frac{D}{E+D} \times W_L$ (from this point on, we will indicate $\frac{D_0}{E_0+D_0}$ with $\frac{D}{E+D}$) and rearranging terms, we can obtain $WACC^*$ in growth scenarios:

$$D_0 = \frac{D}{(D+E)} \times (D_0 + E_0) = \frac{D}{(D+E)} \times \frac{FCFO_0 \times (1+g)}{WACC^* - g}$$

$$\frac{FCFO_0 \times (1+g)}{WACC^* - g} = \frac{FCFO_0 \times (1+g)}{K_{eu} - g}$$

$$+ \left[\frac{D}{(D+E)} \times \frac{FCFO_0 \times (1+g)}{WACC^* - g} \times \frac{K_d \times t_c}{K_d - g} \right]$$

$$\frac{1}{WACC^* - g} = \frac{1}{K_{eu} - g} + \left[\frac{D}{D+E} \times \frac{1}{WACC^* - g} \times \frac{K_d \times t_c}{K_d - g} \right]$$

$$\frac{1}{K_{eu} - g} = \frac{1}{WACC^* - g} \times \left[1 - \frac{D}{D+E} \times \frac{K_d \times t_c}{K_d - g} \right]$$

$$WACC^* - g = (K_{eu} - g) \times \left[1 - \frac{D}{D+E} \times \frac{K_d \times t_c}{K_d - g} \right]$$

$$WACC^* = K_{eu} - K_{eu} \times \frac{D}{D+E} \times \frac{K_d \times t_c}{K_d - g} + g \times \frac{D}{D+E} \times \frac{K_d \times t_c}{K_d - g}$$

$$WACC^* = K_{eu} - \frac{(K_{eu} - g)}{(K_d - g)} \times K_d \times t_c \times \frac{D}{D+E}$$

This equation can also be expressed as:

$$WACC^* = K_{eu} - \frac{(K_{eu} - g)}{(K_d - g)} \times K_d \times t_c \times \frac{D}{D+E}$$

$$WACC^* = K_{eu} + \frac{(K_d - K_d - K_{eu} + g)}{(K_d - g)} \times K_d \times t_c \times \frac{D}{D+E}$$

$$WACC^* = K_{eu} + K_d \times t_c \times \frac{D}{D+E} \times \left[\frac{K_d}{K_d - g} - \frac{K_{eu}}{K_d - g} - \frac{K_d - g}{K_d - g} \right]$$

$$WACC^* = K_{eu} - K_{eu} \times \frac{D}{D+E} \times \frac{K_d \times t_c}{K_d - g} + K_d \times \frac{D}{D+E} \times \frac{K_d \times t_c}{K_d - g}$$

$$- K_d \times t_c \times \frac{D}{D+E}$$

$$WACC^* = K_{eu} \times \left[1 - \frac{K_d \times t_c}{K_d - g} \times \frac{D}{D+E} \right] + K_d \times \left[\frac{K_d \times t_c}{K_d - g} - t_c \right] \times \frac{D}{D+E}$$

$$WACC^* = K_{eu} - K_{eu} \times \frac{D}{D+E} \times \frac{K_d - t_c}{K_d - g} + K_d \times \frac{K_d - t_c}{K_d - g} \times \frac{D}{D+E} - K_d$$

$$\times t_c \times \frac{D}{D+E}$$

$$WACC^* = K_{eu} - K_{eu} - t_c \times \frac{D}{D+E} - (K_{eu} - K_d) \times \frac{K_d - t_c}{K_d - g} \times \frac{D}{D+E} \quad ^{13}$$

A.4 K_{el}^* in Growth Scenarios By substituting $WACC^*$ in growth scenario (see A.3) in the following equation

$$WACC^* = K_{el}^* \times \frac{E}{E+D} + K_d \times \frac{D}{E+D} \times (1 - t_c)$$

we can derive K_{el}^* in growth scenarios:

$$K_{eu} - K_d \times t_c \times \frac{D}{E+D} - (K_{eu} - K_d) \times \left(\frac{K_d \times t_c}{K_d - g} \right) \times \frac{D}{E+D} = K_{el}^* \times \frac{E}{E+D}$$

$$+ K_d \times (1 - t_c) \times \frac{D}{E+D}$$

$$K_{el}^* \times \frac{E}{E+D} = K_{eu} - K_d \times t_c \times \frac{D}{E+D} - (K_{eu} - K_d) \times \left(\frac{K_d \times t_c}{K_d - g} \right) \times \frac{D}{E+D}$$

$$- K_d \times \frac{D}{E+D} \times (1 - t_c)$$

$$K_{el}^* = K_{eu} \times \frac{(E+D)}{E} - K_d \times t_c \times \frac{D}{E} - (K_{eu} - K_d) \times \left(\frac{K_d \times t_c}{K_d - g} \right) \times \frac{D}{E}$$

$$- K_d \times (1 - t_c) \times \frac{D}{E}$$

$$K_{el}^* = K_{eu} + K_{eu} \times \frac{D}{E} - K_d \times t_c \times \frac{D}{E} - (K_{eu} - K_d) \times \left(\frac{K_d \times t_c}{K_d - g} \right) \times \frac{D}{E}$$

$$- K_d \times (1 - t_c) \times \frac{D}{E}$$

$$K_{el}^* = K_{eu} + (K_{eu} - K_d) \times \frac{D}{E} - (K_{eu} - K_d) \times \left(\frac{K_d \times t_c}{K_d - g} \right) \times \frac{D}{E}$$

$$K_{el}^* = K_{eu} + (K_{eu} - K_d) \times \frac{D}{E} \times \left[1 - t_c \times \left(\frac{K_d}{K_d - g} \right) \right]$$

---

[13]The same equation is in T. Copeland, T. Koller, J. Murrin, op. cit.

B. Using K_{eu} as Discount Rate for Tax Shields

B.1 *WACC** in No-Growth Scenarios By assuming that W_L (*asset side*) obtained by applying the APV method and W_L determined with the discount rate adjustment method are equal, we derive:

$$W_L = \sum_{t=1}^{\infty} \frac{FCFO_t}{(1 + WACC^*)^t} = W_U + W_{TS} = \sum_{t=1}^{\infty} \frac{FCFO_t}{(1 + K_{eu})^t} + \sum_{t=1}^{\infty} \frac{D \times t_c \times K_d}{(1 + K_{eu})^t}$$

$$W_L = \frac{FCFO}{WACC^*} = W_U + W_{TS} = \frac{FCFO}{K_{eu}} + \frac{D \times t_c \times K_d}{K_{eu}}$$

$$\frac{FCFO}{WACC^*} = \frac{FCFO}{K_{eu}} + \frac{D \times K_d \times t_c}{K_{eu}}$$

$$D = \frac{D}{(D + E)} \times (D + E) = \frac{D}{(D + E)} \times \frac{FCFO}{WACC^*}$$

$$\frac{FCFO}{WACC^*} = \frac{FCFO}{K_{eu}} + \left[\frac{D}{(D + E)} \times \frac{FCFO}{WACC^*} \times \frac{K_d \times t_c}{K_{eu}} \right]$$

$$\frac{1}{WACC^*} = \frac{1}{K_{eu}} + \left[\frac{D}{D + E} \times \frac{1}{WACC^*} \times t_c \times \frac{K_d}{K_{eu}} \right]$$

$$\frac{1}{K_{eu}} = \frac{1}{WACC^*} \times \left[1 - \frac{D}{D + E} \times t_c \times \frac{K_d}{K_{eu}} \right]$$

$$WACC^* = K_{eu} \times \left[1 - t_c \times \frac{K_d}{K_{eu}} \times \frac{D}{D + E} \right]$$

$$WACC^* = K_{eu} - K_d \times t_c \times \frac{D}{D + E}$$

B.2 K_{el}^* in No-Growth Scenarios By substituting $WACC^*$ in no-growth scenario (see B.1) in the following equation, we can obtain K_{el}^* in no-growth scenarios:

$$WACC^* = K_{el}^* \times \frac{E}{E + D} + K_d \times \frac{D}{E + D} \times (1 - t_c)$$

$$K_{eu} - K_d \times t_c \times \frac{D}{E + D} = K_{el}^* \times \frac{E}{E + D} + K_d \times (1 - t_c) \times \frac{D}{E + D}$$

$$K_{el}^* \times \frac{E}{E + D} = K_{eu} - K_d \times t_c \times \frac{D}{E + D} - K_d \times (1 - t_c) \times \frac{D}{E + D}$$

$$K_{el}^* = \left(K_{eu} - K_d \times \frac{D}{D + E} \right) \times \frac{(E + D)}{E}$$

$$K_{el}^* = K_{eu} \times \frac{E + D}{E} - K_d \times \frac{D}{E}$$

$$K_{el}^* = K_{eu} + K_{eu} \times \frac{D}{E} - K_d \times \frac{D}{E}$$

$$K_{el}^* = K_{eu} + (K_{eu} - K_d) \times \frac{D}{E}$$

B.3 *WACC** in Growth Scenarios

$$W_L = \sum_{t=1}^{\infty} \frac{FCFO_0 \times (1+g)^t}{(1 + WACC^*)^t} = W_U + W_{TS} = \sum_{t=1}^{\infty} \frac{FCFO_0 \times (1+g)^t}{(1 + K_{eu})^t}$$

$$+ \sum_{t=1}^{\infty} \frac{D_0 \times t_c \times K_d \times (1+g)^{t-1}}{(1 + K_{eu})^t} \,{}^{14}$$

$$W_L = \frac{FCFO_0 \times (1+g)}{WACC^* - g} = W_U + W_{TS} = \frac{FCFO_0 \times (1+g)}{K_{eu} - g} + \frac{D_0 \times t_c \times K_d}{K_{eu} - g}$$

$$\frac{FCFO_0 \times (1+g)}{WACC^* - g} = \frac{FCFO_0 \times (1+g)}{K_{eu} - g} + \frac{D_0 \times K_d \times t_c}{K_{eu} - g}$$

$$D_0 = \frac{D}{(D+E)} \times (D_0 + E_0) = \frac{D}{(D+E)} \times \frac{FCFO_0 \times (1+g)}{WACC^* - g}$$

$$\frac{FCFO_0 \times (1+g)}{WACC^* - g} = \frac{FCFO_0 \times (1+g)}{K_{eu} - g}$$

$$+ \left[\frac{D}{(D+E)} \times \frac{FCFO_0 \times (1+g)}{WACC^* - g} \times \frac{K_d \times t_c}{K_{eu} - g} \right]$$

$$\frac{1}{WACC^* - g} = \frac{1}{K_{eu} - g} + \left[\frac{D}{D+E} \times \frac{1}{WACC^* - g} \times \frac{K_d \times t_c}{K_{eu} - g} \right]$$

$$\frac{1}{WACC^* - g} = \frac{1}{K_{eu} - g} \times \left[1 + \frac{D}{D+E} \times \frac{K_d \times t_c}{WACC^* - g} \right]$$

$$K_{eu} - g = (WACC^* - g) \times \left[1 + \frac{D}{D+E} \times \frac{K_d \times t_c}{WACC^* - g} \right]$$

$$K_{eu} - g = (WACC^* - g) + K_d \times t_c \times \frac{D}{D+E}$$

$$WACC^* = K_{eu} - K_d \times t_c \times \frac{D}{D+E}$$

---

[14] As already pointed out, the series that expresses the present value of tax shields converges to $\frac{D_0 \times K_d \times t_c}{K_e(U) - g}$.

B.4 K^*_{el} in Growth Scenarios

$$WACC^* = K^*_{el} \times \frac{E}{E+D} + K_d \times \frac{D}{E+D} \times (1-t_c)$$

$$K_{eu} - K_d \times t_c \times \frac{D}{E+D} = K^*_{el} \times \frac{E}{E+D} + K_d \times (1-t_c) \times \frac{D}{E+D}$$

$$K^*_{el} \times \frac{E}{E+D} = K_{eu} - K_d \times t_c \times \frac{D}{E+D} - K_d \times (1-t_c) \times \frac{D}{E+D}$$

$$K^*_{el} = \left(K_{eu} - K_d \times \frac{D}{D+E}\right) \times \frac{(E+D)}{E}$$

$$K^*_{el} = K_{eu} \times \frac{E+D}{E} - K_d \times \frac{D}{E}$$

$$K^*_{el} = K_{eu} + K_{eu} \times \frac{D}{E} - K_d \times \frac{D}{E}$$

$$K^*_{el} = K_{eu} + (K_{eu} - K_d) \times \frac{D}{E}$$

The equations so far introduced can be expressed as:

$$WACC^* = K_{eu} - \left(\frac{K_{eu} - g}{K_{TS} - g}\right) \times K_d \times t_c \times \frac{D}{D+E}$$

$$K^*_{el} = K_{eu} + \left[K_{eu} \times \left(1 - \frac{K_d \times t_c}{K_{TS} - g}\right) - K_d \times \left(1 - \frac{K_{TS} \times t_c}{K_{TS} - g}\right)\right] \times \frac{D}{E}$$

where K_{TS} is the tax shields discount rate.

C. Discounting Tax Shields Linked to Actual Debt (D) with K_d and Tax Shields Linked to Growth with K_{eu}.

$$W_L = \frac{FCFO_1}{K_{eu} - g} + D \times t_c + \sum_{n=1}^{\infty} \frac{D \times g \times t_c \times (1+g)^{n-1}}{(1+K_{eu})^n} \quad ^{15}$$

$$W_L = \frac{FCFO_1}{WACC^* - g}$$

---

[15]The numerator of the term that expresses the value of tax shields with growth expresses the series of tax shields linked to an annual funding activity. The tax shields of each phase of funding are determined using K_d as the proper discount rate.

$$\sum_{n=1}^{\infty} \left(\frac{\frac{D \times g \times t_c \times K_d \times (1+g)^{n-1}}{K_d}}{(1+K_{eu})^n}\right) = \sum_{n=1}^{\infty} \frac{D \times g \times t_c \times (1+g)^{n-1}}{(1+K_{eu})^n}$$

$$\frac{FCFO_1}{WACC^* - g} = \frac{FCFO_1}{K_{eu} - g} + D \times t_c + \frac{D \times g \times t_c}{K_{eu} - g}$$

$$\frac{FCFO_1}{WACC^* - g} \times \frac{D}{D + E} = D$$

$$\frac{FCFO_1}{WACC^* - g} = \frac{FCFO_1}{K_{eu} - g} + \frac{FCFO_1}{WACC^* - g} \times \frac{D}{D + E} \times t_c + \frac{FCFO_1}{WACC^* - g}$$

$$\times \frac{D}{D + E} \times \frac{g \times t_c}{K_{eu} - g}$$

$$\frac{1}{WACC^* - g} = \frac{1}{K_{eu} - g} + \frac{1}{WACC^* - g} \times \frac{D}{D + E} \times t_c$$

$$+ \frac{1}{(WACC^* - g) \times (K_{eu} - g)} \times \frac{D}{D + E} \times g \times t_c$$

$$K_{eu} - g = WACC^* - g + (K_{eu} - g) \times \frac{D}{D + E} \times t_c + \frac{D}{D + E} \times g \times t_c$$

$$WACC^* = K_{eu} - K_{eu} \times \frac{D}{D + E} \times t_c - \frac{D}{D + E} \times t_c \times g + \frac{D}{D + E} \times t_c \times g$$

$$WACC^* = K_{eu} \times \left(1 - t_c \times \frac{D}{D + E}\right)$$

APPENDIX 7.2: PATTERN OF K_{el}^* IN A GROWTH CONTEXT: SOME REMARKS

The following example shows how K_{el}^* changes according to changes in the growth rate. We assume K_d as the discount rate of tax shields.

The input data are the following:

K_{eu}	12%
K_d	7%
t_c	36%

Allowing for different growth rates and different leverage levels, using the input data and the adjusted equations presented in Appendix 1, we obtain the values for K_{el}^* shown in Exhibit 7.10:

Exhibit 7.10 Leverage, growth, and cost of capital

D/E	K^*_{el}		
	$g = 0$	$g = 2\%$	$g = 5\%$
50%	13.60%	13.24%	11.35%
80%	14.56%	13.98%	10.96%

In the first two cases (no growth and $g = 2\%$), K^*_{el} increases as leverage increases. In the last case, with $g = 5\%$, K^*_{el} instead decreases as leverage increases.

These results, apparently contradictory, can be better understood looking at the curve that shows the relationship between K^*_{el} and leverage. In particular, they depend on the relationship between the slope of this curve and the growth rate g, the tax rate, and the cost of debt K_d.

From the equation for K^*_{el}, we see that an increase in g causes a decrease in the slope of the curve. This slope can even become negative if g is greater than $K_d \times (1 - t_c)$.

In the previous example, the trigger value of the growth rate beyond which the cost of capital decreases with an increase in leverage is equal to 4.4 percent.

Exhibit 7.11 shows the relationship between K^*_{el} and D/E, assuming K_d as the proper discount rate for tax shields.

The slope of this curve decreases if we introduce taxes. It decreases more and more as the tax rate increases.

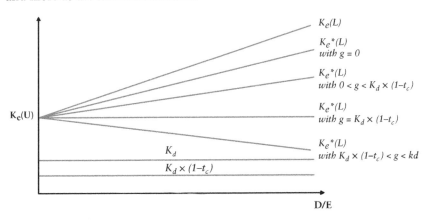

Exhibit 7.11 Patterns of K^*_{el} under different assumptions

In growth scenarios, this effect increases by the amount $\frac{K_d}{K_d - g}$.[16]

The slope of the curve is positive (therefore, K_{el}^* increases with leverage) until the point shown in Exhibit 7.12[17]:

$$g < K_d^*(1-t_c)$$

Exhibit 7.12

If K_d is equal to 5 percent and t_c is equal to 36 percent, the slope of the curve is positive until the growth rate is lower than 3.2 percent. It becomes negative (K_{el}^* decreases with an increase in leverage) for growth rates between 3.2 and 5 percent.[18]

---

[16] Because of the assumption that $K_d > g$, this amount is always greater than 1.

[17] As already shown, the relationship between the cost of equity and leverage (assuming K_d as the proper discount rate for tax benefits) is represented by the curve:

$$K_{el}^* = K_{eu} + (K_{eu} - K_d) \times \frac{D}{E} \times \left[1 - t_c \times \left(\frac{K_d}{K_d - g}\right)\right]$$

we set the slope to zero

$$(K_{eu} - K_d) \times \left[1 - t_c \times \left(\frac{K_d}{K_d - g}\right)\right] = 0$$

and we then obtain the corresponding value of g:

$$\left[1 - t_c \times \left(\frac{K_d}{K_d - g}\right)\right] = 0$$

$$\frac{K_d - g - K_d \times t_c}{K_d - g} = 0$$

$$K_d - g - K_d \times t_c = 0$$

$$K_d \times (1 - t_c) - g = 0$$

$$g = K_d \times (1 - t_c)$$

[18] Assuming a long term time horizon, g has to be lower than K_d (in this case, equal to 5%). We must highlight that this assumption is realistic in practice. As a matter of fact, even in the presence of inflation, higher growth rates are not sustainable for an indefinite time period. The temporary growth case is a different case, since it can be higher.

Note that the relationship between K_{el}^* and leverage *without taxes* assumes an economic meaning. As a matter of fact, in this case, K_{el}^* grows as shareholders' risk (both operating and financial) increases.

With taxes and tax shields, the meaning of K_{el}^* changes. In this case, it is also affected by tax shields and by the corporate tax rate t_c.

In growth scenarios, K_{el}^* should also express the value of tax shields due to growth (as already pointed out, the formulas of K_{el}^* and the $WACC^*$ are based on the assumption that leverage is constant and, therefore, debt increases proportionally to the increase in equity).

Therefore, whenever tax shields are high in an environment with growth, K_{el}^* can also be lower than K_{eu}, as shown in Exhibit 7.10.

CHAPTER **8**

Estimating the Cost of Capital

8.1   DEFINING THE OPPORTUNITY COST OF CAPITAL

In the previous Chapters we have discussed the calculation of the proper discount rate for cash flows by introducing formulas that are consistent with the *asset* and *equity side* standpoints and with the different definitions and derivations of the tax benefits associated with debt. All these formulas stem from two basic parameters referred to as the opportunity cost of capital of a firm with no debt (K_{eu}) and the opportunity cost of debt (K_d).

K_{eu} measures the rate of return that is considered acceptable by investors in the *equity* of a firm with no debt. The return should reflect only the risk profile associated with corporate assets regardless of the financial structure. As we are dealing with an opportunity cost, this return should be estimated taking into account the alternative returns that could be obtained from other investments characterized by similar risk profiles.

On the other hand, K_d measures (again, as an *opportunity cost*) the rate of return that is deemed acceptable by the holders of the firm debt. The risk for the underwriters of corporate financial liabilities is mostly a function of the likelihood of the firm not being able to timely fulfill its obligations along the agreed debt service schedule.

8.2   A FEW COMMENTS ON RISK

For economists, risky situations are usually associated with cases in which an "objective" probability (i.e., based on meaningful retrospective observations) can be attributed to a range of possible events. "Uncertain" situations, on the other hand, are characterized by the apparent inability to attribute an objective probability to a certain event.

Following the general practice, going forward we will use the terms *risk* and *uncertainty* interchangeably, but from a scientific point of view they are two distinct concepts. As a matter of fact, the scenarios underlying the valuation of a firm rarely allow for the estimation of probabilities based on "objective" findings strictly speaking. Intermediate situations or situations of real uncertainty, on the other hand, are much more common.

From a psychological point of view, risk generally carries a negative connotation for most individuals. On the contrary, in the financial world the phenomenon is usually seen more neutrally as the *dispersion (variability)* of the results of an investment.

In practice, a preliminary question should be addressed first regarding the reasons underlying the variability of the results in any investment. In other words, we must determine the risk factors based on which investors determine a suitable remuneration.

In a nutshell, we can state that the typical situations of risk/uncertainty underlying a valuation can be classified as follows:

- Situations in which the results of a firm or a venture mostly depend on the trend of some macroeconomic parameters (such as GDP growth, interest rates, private consumption)
- Situations in which the uncertainty depends on an innovative business idea
- Situations in which the results depend on macroeconomic parameters but it's possible to identify and quantify additional specific factors that can positively (*upside risk*) or negatively (*downside risk*) change those results

8.2.1 Scenario Driven by Macroeconomic Factors

As a starting consideration, we should point out that some industries are more exposed to the general dynamics of the economy than others. In the so-called *cyclical* industries companies' proceeds from sales tend to undergo sharper variations in the context of favorable and unfavorable phases of the economic cycle. This occurs especially in the materials, steel, building, and machinery industries. On the other hand, other sectors are less sensitive to economic trends, such as the pharmaceutical industry.

We can therefore assume that, in the sectors and companies affected mainly by this *systematic risk*, the analysis of their past performance allows us to formulate a reliable estimate of the dynamics of future results in both favorable and unfavorable macroeconomic conditions. Furthermore, it allows us to devise parameters indicating the level of exposure to market risk.

A second issue to be addressed when assessing risk concerns the sensitivity of operating results (measured in terms of EBITDA, EBIT, and net income) to revenues. It is well known that this depends on the level of inelasticity of structural costs (operating leverage) and, in terms of net result, on the financial burden (financial leverage). Thus, both the operating leverage and the financial leverage amplify revenues' variability, therefore acting as multipliers of the market risk.

8.2.2 Innovative Initiatives

Let us now consider the scenario in which the uncertainty depends on an innovative business idea. It is characterized by the possibility of radical changes in the business plan developed according to assumptions that cannot be objectively checked and that are formulated only on the basis of expectations (sometimes very hopeful ones). This is typically the case of technology start-ups and of innovative technology projects developed at established companies.

In textbooks[1] on strategic analysis, emerging sectors (and usually *start-ups*) are characterized by the presence of high risk due to technological uncertainties, forecasting difficulties, the likely competitions of new emerging companies, and the need for large investments in R&D.

The ability to manage risk then becomes a fundamental factor for the firm's survival, for its ability to raise capital, and eventually for the achievement of its sustainable profitabilty.

8.2.3 Presence of Specific Risks

Finally, there are cases where there are detectable signs or features pointing toward events that could significantly alter the expected results of a predetermined business plan. Some examples can clarify this concept.

The companies that operate under some licenses are subject to the risk of their licenses not being renewed. In this case, the presence of a terminable contractual agreement is a sign of discontinuity that could have a major impact on the firm prospects.

Small companies dominated by the personality of their entrepreneurs (*one-man companies*) often enter a period of crisis once the entrepreneur leaves. In this case, the sign of a performance discontinuity is suggested by the absence of an autonomous managerial structure.

Companies that depend on a single strategic supplier or make a large part of their sales from one or two customers are subject to the risk of drastic reductions in activity levels. In this case, the alarm signals lie in the concentration of purchases from one strategic supplier and/or in a limited market presence.

---

[1]See, for example, R. M. Grant, *Contemporary Strategy Analysis*, 5th ed. (New York: Blackwell, 2004).

The previous examples are intuitive. In other cases, the signals could be much weaker and less intelligible. For example, technological innovations can lead to great discontinuity for follower companies. Also, the growing concern for the environment and health can have disruptive effects on the performance of some companies. Such risks can be spotted sometimes—but not always—thanks to thorough *due diligence* covering legal, environmental, and technological, and production aspects.

8.3 PRACTICAL APPROACHES TO ESTIMATE K_{eu}

Although in practice many methods to estimate the cost of capital are commonly used, the procedures to estimate the cost of capital lead back to three fundamental approaches. Each of these approaches in turn can be developed through different methods. The fundamental approaches are:

- The use of historical records on past returns
- The extraction of the expected returns implicit in current market prices
- The application of risk *pricing* models as a function of a sector's or a company's sensitivity of results to other risk factors (so-called risk–return models)

Exhibit 8.1 summarizes the outlined approaches and the estimation methods associated with each of them.

8.4 APPROACH BASED ON HISTORICAL RETURNS

The simplest solution for anchoring the estimate of K_{eu} to objective parameters lies in the use of historical records of returns from stock investments characterized by comparable risk profiles.

Exhibit 8.1 Approaches/methods to estimate opportunity cost of capital

Type of Approach	Method
a. Historical records of past returns	– market returns – accounting returns
b. Returns embedded in current market prices	– *dividend discount model* – P/E model
c. Models based on results' sensitivity to one or more risk factors	– one factor (CAPM) – more factors (APT and other models)

In general terms, the use of historical records can be a sound decision to estimate K_{eu} if two assumptions hold:

1. *Ex post* returns are an acceptable approximation of the returns sought by investors. This implies that investors must be able to obtain returns that they deem suitable with respect to the risk they are taking.
2. The business risk profile is constant, meaning that no significant new factors emerge to increase (or decrease) the variability of past results.

8.5   ANALYSIS OF STOCK RETURNS

The return on a stock investment consists of two components: dividends and appreciation of the stock during the holding period:

$$r_t = \frac{P_t - P_{t-1} + Div_t}{P_{t-1}}$$

where:

r_t = return of the security in period 1
Div_t = dividend cashed during the holding period
P_t and P_{t-1} = price of the stock at the end and at the beginning of period $t-1$ to t

In order to compute the mean return, some choices have to be made that may significantly affect the result of the analysis. These concern the following:

1. *Arithmetic versus geometric mean.* The first problem concerns the choice between the arithmetic mean and the geometric mean of stock returns. The discussion developed here will also apply to calculation of the *equity risk premium* based on historical records.

    The main textbooks on valuation of investments and firms do not agree on a uniform choice on this point. For instance, Tom Copeland states that for the purpose of discounting expected *cash flows*, the appropriate measure is the geometric mean of the stock returns. The geometric mean is a suitable indicator to estimate the performance of an investment in a certain time period in the past (the geometric mean is the compound rate of return that balances the initial and final value of the investment). According to Copeland the performance of an investment in the past also represents the best approximation of the return expected by investors and therefore it is also the proper estimate for the opportunity cost of capital.[2]

On the other hand, Ibbotson[3] claims that the arithmetic mean return is the appropriate rate of return for the discount of expected cash flows. Ibbotson makes the assumption that the arithmetic mean represents an indicator of the returns obtained in the single unit periods that form the period under analysis. For this reason, he believes it to be the correct measure of returns behaving as a *random walk*.

The fundamental difference between these two approaches lies in the fact that the use of the arithmetic mean implies independence of returns over time while the geometric mean implies that the trend observed in the past is the best estimate for future returns.

Since numerous empirical analyses clearly show that the trend in stock prices does not follow a purely random process and that significant phenomena of self-correlation are instead observed, we are inclined to think that the long-term geometric mean represents the best estimation of future returns. Therefore, this estimate should also be used to determine the opportunity cost of capital.

2. *Reference period.* In principle, the longer the reference period, the more credible the mean value will be. On the other hand, lengthening the duration of the period also increases the possibility that the conditions determining certain returns have radically changed over time (due to evolving competition, changes in consumer behavior or in important environmental variables, etc.).

Despite these issues, experts usually believe that increasingly long periods lead to returns' convergence toward "normalized" values. In short periods of time, returns can instead be excessively low or excessively high, depending on two factors:

- The presence of growth or restructuring that affects a sector or a company
- The phase of the market cycle to which the statistics refer

3. *Real and nominal returns.* Although flow projections are usually made in nominal terms, it is useful to start our analysis with an estimate of "real" rates of return. As a matter of fact, monetary depreciation changes over time. Hence, the forecasted inflation (embedded in the flow used for the

---

[2]In the later version of his popular valuation manual, Copeland subsequently supported an approach that mixed elements from both the geometric mean and the arithmetic mean: see T. Copeland, T. Koller, and J. Murrin, *Valuation: Measuring and Managing the Value of Companies*, 4th ed. (Hoboken, NJ: Wiley & Sons, 2005).
[3]SBBI, *Valuation Edition* (Chicago: Ibbotson Associates, 1999), pp. 44–46.

valuation) does not usually coincide with the average inflation experienced in the past.

To solve this problem, the inflation can be filtered out of nominal returns per annum through the Fisher formula already mentioned:

$$r_{\text{real}} = \frac{1 + r_{\text{nominal}}}{1 + \text{inf\_rate}} - 1$$

The annual rate of inflation can be estimated, for example, using the consumer price index.

The real (average) return thus obtained can be turned into nominal rates consistent with the hypotheses on inflation made for the cash flow projection. Once again the Fisher formula is used:

$$\text{Nominal discount rate} = (1 + \text{Real discount rate})$$

$$\times (1 + \text{Forecasted inflation}) - 1$$

8.5.1 The Effect of Leverage

The rates of return we are discussing usually refer to indebted companies: that is, they are *levered* rates. Since our objective is K_{eu}, some adjustments should be made.

Taking tax benefits into consideration, we can obtain unlevered rates. Recalling that the value of a *levered* firm is equal to the sum of the value of the *unlevered* firm, W_{U}, and the value of tax shields, W_{TS}, we obtain:

$$K_{\text{eu}} = K_{\text{el}}^* \times \frac{E}{E + D \times (1 - t_{\text{c}})} + K_{\text{d}} \times (1 - t_{\text{c}}) \times \frac{D}{E + D \times (1 - t_{\text{c}})}$$

In the previous equation, K_{el}^* represents the return observed in the market that is considered equal to the opportunity cost of risk capital of an indebted firm. This equation can be better understood by adding a couple of comments. The two terms express the weight of debt and of *equity* in the company's financial structure. We can easily notice that the denominator is equal to the total value of the firm $(D + E)$ net of the current value of the tax benefits associated with the deductibility of interest payments. As a result, the cost of capital is expressed net of fiscal shields.

The formula is based on the hypothesis that all flows are perpetual and that the proper rate for the tax shields is K_{d}. If these hypotheses did not hold, the more complex formulae discussed in the previous Chapters should be used instead, moving therefore to a growth scenario. In the same way, however, the adjustments aimed at neutralizing the leverage effect are always approximate and are based on hypotheses that are difficult to verify.

Once K_{eu} is known, the values of K_{el}^* and the $WACC^*$ consistent with the financial structure of the venture under consideration can be calculated using the formulae in Chapter 6 if required by the estimation procedure.

8.6 ANALYSIS OF ACCOUNTING RETURNS

Fluctuations in market prices often deprive *ex post* returns of their meaning even when calculations are extended to more than 10 or 15 years. Consequently, accounting returns are sometimes preferred in the professional practice.

Such a choice is acceptable if it is assumed that accounting returns tend to align themselves with expected returns in the long term. In fact, there is a tendency toward reaching homogeneous return profile for the capital invested across different business sectors.

The use of accounting returns offers the advantage of avoiding any manipulation of rates. As a matter of fact, K_{eu} can be directly derived from the ratio:

$$K_{eu} = ROI \text{ after taxes} = \frac{\text{Operating return after taxes}}{\text{Net operating capital invested}}$$

The reference period for the calculation of the ratio should be long enough to embrace an entire economic cycle. This is due to the need for an estimation of the average return of capital invested in different economic phases.

Accounting returns certainly suffer from some limitations—mainly, the fact that they are not linked to the economic value of the invested capital and can be influenced by discretionary policies. Nevertheless, the validity of this procedure cannot be ruled out *a priori*. The significance of the results obtained must be assessed case by case considering the relevant competitive dynamics affecting the sector under consideration (i.e., the existence of entry or exit barriers, price competition). For example, in case of excess yield due to monopolistic returns, the method we have discussed could overestimate expected returns in the estimation of the opportunity cost of capital for a company likely to experience strong pressure from new competitors.

8.7 ESTIMATING EXPECTED RETURNS FROM CURRENT STOCK PRICES

If the background conditions under that historical returns realized have changed, or if historical returns do not represent an acceptable approximation for expected returns, it may be useful to instead use the information embedded in current market prices. Two techniques are usually proposed to determine expected returns according to this approach:

- The dividend discount model
- The P/E model

8.7.1 Dividend Discount Model (DDM)

The DDM is based on an extremely simple idea: those who purchase stock acquire the right to receive a future constant stream of dividend payments. For this reason, the value of stock must equal the current value of the stream of dividends, which matches the return that investors expect from investing on assets characterized by a similar level of risk.

If the dividends grow at rate g, the price of a stock can be derived from the following formula:

$$P_0 = \sum_{t=1}^{\infty} \frac{Div_0 \times (1+g)^t}{(1+r)^t} = \frac{Div_0 \times (1+g)}{r-g}$$

Thus, the cost of capital can be derived from the formula above, as follows:

$$r = K_{el}^* = \frac{Div_0 \times (1+g)}{P_0} + g$$

Since companies are usually indebted, the return r corresponds to the *levered* cost of capital K_{el}^*. K_{eu} can then be obtained through the delevering procedure already presented.

It is worth highlighting that the DDM is based on the following assumptions:

- The discount rate adjusted to the appropriate level of risk for the business is constant in the long term and the rate's maturity curve is therefore flat.
- The growth rate for the flow generated by the business is constant in the long term.

The key variable for the application of the DDM for the estimation of the cost of capital is therefore the rate g. Two procedures can be adopted at this point for its estimation:

- Calculation of the historical average dividend growth rate
- Analysis of the *consensus forecasts* published by specialized data providers

If the first procedure is used, the historical growth rate should be net of past inflation and subsequently re-expressed in nominal terms according to the inflation rate expected at the date of the valuation.

8.7.2 Two-Stage DDM

To refine the hypothesis on the perpetual growth of dividends, a two-stage DDM can be used:

$$P_0 = \sum_{t=1}^{n} \frac{Div_0 \times (1+g_1)^t}{(1+r)^t} + \sum_{t=n+1}^{\infty} \frac{Div_n \times (1+g_2)^{t-n}}{(1+r)^t}$$

In this case, g is differentiated as a function of two subperiods: $(t_1 : t_n)$ and $(t_{n+1} : t_\infty)$. The cost of capital is expressed by the rate r, which equates the right part of the equation to P_0.

The period $(t_1 : t_n)$ can represent, for example, a typical business plan horizon (three to five years). Three-stage DDM can be used as well to feature a *transition period* in between the high-growth rate and long-term stable growth rate.

8.7.3 P/E Model

The formula examined in the previous point can be rearranged to express the cost of capital in terms of the well-known *price/earnings ratio* (*P/E*) multiple (we will discuss multiples in more detail later in the book):

$$K_{el}^* = \frac{Div_0 \times (1+g)}{P_0} + g$$

By replacing the term expressing dividends (Div_0) with the product of the earnings per share times the *payout ratio*[4] in the previous expression, we obtain:

$$K_{el}^* = \frac{payout \times EPS_0 \times (1+g)}{P_0} + g = \frac{payout \times (1+g)}{P_0/E_0} + g$$

The denominator P_0/E_0 is the firm's *price/earnings ratio* calculated from the profits of the last available balance sheet.

The main difference between the DDM and the *P/E model* is that the former is based on the growth of dividends while the latter focuses on the growth of earnings. If g is estimated on the basis of historical records of earnings or dividends, major differences may arise between the results of the two models.[5]

---

[4]As the *payout* is derived from *DPS/EPS*, it follows that *DPS/EPS* × *EPS* = *DPS* (where *DPS* = *Dividend per Share* = *Div*).

[5]In the *steady-growth* model analyzed in Paragraph 7.3 we assume that the growth rate of earnings and dividends is identical. This occurs because the model is based on the hypothesis that, in equilibrium, $g = ROE \times (1 - Payout)$.

8.8 MODELS BASED ON RETURNS' SENSITIVITY TO RISK FACTORS

The third approach used to estimate the opportunity cost of capital is based on identifying methods capable of measuring the impact of one or more risk factors on the value of a firm. The simplest solution is to assume that variations in asset values can be explained according to a model characterized by one reference index only.

The opportunity cost of capital is derived in this case according to the following model:

$$R_i = R_f + \beta_i \times (R_m - R_f) + \alpha_i + c_i$$

where:

R_i = return (opportunity cost of capital) of the asset i
R_f = return of the risk-free asset (generally the gross return of government bonds)
R_m = return of the reference market index
α_i = the specific return component (unexplainable by the market trend as a whole) of the single security
c_i = a random component with zero mean
β_i = an index of sensitivity of the returns of the i-security to the reference index (the market index).

According to the *capital asset pricing* model that will be discussed later on, the expected return on a stock (which can be linked to the opportunity cost of capital, K_e) is derived from the following simple expression:[6]

$$R_i = R_f + \beta_i \times (R_m - R_f)$$

This is true under the assumption that the specific and random risk components are neutralized, mostly through diversification. We will come back to this point later.

In other models (e.g., the *arbitrage pricing theory (APT)* model), risks and returns are explained by several factors, usually linked with financial parameters and macroeconomic variables. Although these models are often very convincing, they are very rarely used in practical applications due to issues regarding the estimation of the model parameters. For this reason,

---

[6]This relationship is true in expectation, so that the random risk components disappear as a consequence of diversification.

the authors decided to not discuss these models in this textbook;[7] we will nevertheless present an example of multi-factor model in the last chapter.

The estimates of the opportunity cost of capital obtained through the *capital asset pricing model* (CAPM) are based on a sensitivity index (*beta*) that is not a proper measure of risk. As a result, the derived values of K_e are acceptable only if we hold as true the assumption that the specific return component (α_i) can always be neutralized through diversification. This assumption is reasonable when we consider a financial investor spreading her available resources over a sufficiently large number of stocks. On the other hand, it is not acceptable in most situations involving the valuation of companies and acquisitions. As a matter of fact, the investment in the controlling stake of a company typically consists of a large chunk of the new owner's wealth, thus making a portfolio management framework less appropriate to assess the opportunity cost of capital. In case the new owner (or large shareholder) is a diversified investor (e.g., a large private equity fund), the diversification principle holds and CAPM can apply.

In case of strategic investors, namely business investors mostly interested in acquiring stakes in companies to develop synergies with them, the assessment of the cost of capital may be different as we are going to show in subsequent chapters.

8.9   THE CAPITAL ASSET PRICING MODEL

Given its simplicity and the wide availability of parameters necessary to apply its formula, the CAPM is the most commonly used model in the estimation of the cost of capital. It is used by *investment* and *merchant banks*, by consulting firms, and even by market authorities to fix tariffs in regulated industries.

The CAPM is based on the assumption that investors effectively diversify their portfolios, thereby neutralizing the part of the risk linked to the single *stand-alone* investments (the so-called *diversifiable risk*). Consequently, only the part of risk that cannot be eliminated by diversifying should be rewarded and should be featured in the estimation of K_{el}.

Assuming that the returns refer to stocks in indebted companies (in this case, $R_i = K_{el}^*$), the cost of capital can be defined as follows:

$$K_{el}^* = R_f + \beta_i \times (R_m - R_f)$$

---

[7]See S. Ross, "The Arbitrage Theory of Capital Asset Pricing," *Journal of Economic Theory*, 17 (December 1976): 341–360.

where:

K^*_{el} = opportunity cost of capital

R_f = return on risk-free securities

β_i = the measure of risk for CAPM that indicates the level of sensitivity of the returns of the ith asset to the market return

R_m = the return expected from a portfolio containing all the risky securities present on the market. Hence, $(R_m - R_f)$ represents the market risk premium (R_p)

8.9.1 CAPM with Taxes

When the CAPM is used to estimate the cost of capital, equation [8.2] should be re-expressed after taxes. Considering taxation at both company and individual level, it changes as follows:

$$K^*_{el} = \frac{1 - t_c}{1 - T} \times R_f + \beta_i \times \left(R_m - \frac{1 - t_c}{1 - T} \times R_f \right)$$

T indicates the comparative differential advantage from financing through debt. If $t_d = t_{pe}$, T becomes equal to t_c and the previous formula becomes:

$$K^*_{el} = R_f + \beta_i \times (R_m - R_f)$$

The *risk-free rate* (R_f) for the calculation of K_{el} is expressed gross of any withholding taxes.

In order to perform sound valuations, analysts should ensure both the consistency among parameters used in the formula and the consistency of the underlying hypotheses of the CAPM with the valuation profile.

We will analyze the criteria to estimate the model parameters in the following paragraphs. We will subsequently discuss the problem underlying the representativeness of the cost of capital obtained with the CAPM, also considering the role of the market for corporate control.

8.10 CALCULATING R_f

Interest rates are formed by two components. The first concerns the so-called *financial value of time* and is supposed to compensate for the *time value* of resources that are not used in the present and for the possible loss in purchasing power due to inflation. This component is usually defined as the *risk-free interest rate (R_f)*. The second element concerns the uncertainties and risks faced by lenders linked to the possibility of recovering only part of the amount originally lent. When estimating R_f, the following aspects should be considered.

The *nominal versus real risk-free rates* observed in the market (e.g., government bond returns) comprise three separate elements:

- Equilibrium interest rate in the long term (in real terms)
- A component representing the short- to medium-term deviations of the long-term interest rate (in real terms)
- Inflation expectations

Economists think that the long-term interest rate in equilibrium is determined by the interaction between supply and demand of "real" investments, and that it may change either because of major technological innovations that increase the productivity of the system or because of structural changes regarding the propensity of consumers to save or spend. The long-term real interest rate is typically very low, and any changes should be relatively slow.

Short- and medium-term deviations in the equilibrium rate mainly originate from economic cycles. For example, the real rate can fall below its level of equilibrium in periods of recession if investments and consumption experience a downturn. This can in turn lead to a temporary excess of money supply compared to demand and this situation translates into a lowering of rates. The opposite can occur when the economy is booming.

We do not observe directly real interest rates because market rates incorporate a premium to compensate for the expected depreciation of the purchasing power of money. The relationship between nominal rates (observable) and real rates (unobservable) can be expressed using the Fisher equation already presented.

The term structure of interest rates: The nominal interest rate is not expressed by a single value, but rather by a wide range of rates for different loan maturities. Various theories have been proposed to explain the "term structure" of interest rates.[8] According to the most popular theory (the so-called theory of expectations), long-term nominal risk-free rates can be higher or lower than short-term rates as a function of the expectations about the level of future short-term nominal rates. In other words, long-term risk-free rates are geometric means of the current short-term rates, the so-called spot rates, and of the expected short-term rates, the so-called

---

[8] A good review on the term structure of interest rates can be found in: C.R. Nelson in "The Term Structure of Interest Rates: Theories and Evidence," in J. L. Bicksler's, *Handbook of Financial Economics* (North-Holland Publishing Company, 1980).

forward rates. Thus, for example, if the five-year current rates are lower than the current short-term rates, the market expects that the annual rates will fall from t_2 to t_5.

Interest rates behavior has important implications for the valuation of investments and of businesses (and generally for all problems involving discounting). In principle, each cash flow obtained from a project (or a business) during the projected period of the estimate should be discounted at a rate consistent with its duration.

Rates R_1, R_2, ... R_n can be different especially as a function of expectations about inflation over time.

In ideal conditions, the interest rates trend should be consistent with the hypotheses on the inflation trend assumed in the cash flow projections.

The procedure based on rate differentiation depending on the maturity of the single cash flows is only a quick-and-dirty solution. The uncertainties and approximations that inevitably accompany the estimate of all valuation parameters do not justify such complications. In practice, flows are usually discounted by a rate corresponding to the maturity yield of those securities characterized by the same duration as the flow projections.

The problem is a little more complex if the valuation concerns a company or an acquisition. Indeed, the reference time frame in this case is very long or even unlimited if the perpetuity formulas and the growth models are applied.

In practical terms, the use of yields to maturity of long-term bonds— 10 years or more—is recommended in this case.

8.11 CALCULATING R_p

The market risk premium (MRP) or equity risk premium (ERP) is the excess return earned by the stock market in comparison with the return obtained by risk-free financial assets (usually government bonds). Such premium is therefore a measure of the compensation equity investors expect because of the relatively higher risk borne.

Although the notion of market risk premium is rather intuitive, no unanimous agreement has been reached in financial literature on either the methods used to measure the risk premium or its interpretation. In particular, two main approaches are used: the first one compares the historical returns obtained in the stock market with those of the bond market (the so-called *historical risk premium*); the second one values the excess return incorporated in stock quotes in the expectation of future earnings and interest rates (the so-called *expected risk premium* or *premium embedded in market prices*).

A large part of the literature deals with the analysis of historical risk premia, mainly focusing on the US market. There are two main problems that scholars have experienced in the analysis of historical risk premia (apart from the number of years analyzed) to be considered. The first is the approach to compute the average returns; the second is the type of bond chosen to be the proxy of a risk-free investment.[9] All these somehow subjective decisions may cause a quite significant variation in the final estimate of risk premia.

Historical returns can give a measure of what investors gained from the stock market in the past, but they do not seem to provide a clear indicator of the risk perceived by investors. In particular, empirical evidence suggests that the returns historically obtained in the markets are not necessarily (or rarely) an expression of the ex-ante average investors' expectations. Paradoxically, higher historical risk premia could indicate a decrease in the level of risk aversion rather than an increase. This occurs because a higher propensity to risk at aggregate level (which would imply a lower risk premium) usually translates into higher share prices and consequently into higher returns.

8.11.1 Historical Risk Premiums: Meaning and Calculation

The historical market risk premium is usually computed as the difference between the mean returns of stock returns and government bonds. In terms of duration of the bonds, there are three different horizons of the R_p: *short term, midterm,* and *long term.*

The stock returns are calculated by adopting the formulae presented at the beginning of this chapter while *risk-free* returns are calculated based only on the component representing the current return (*income return*). Variations in security prices are not considered since these are unanticipated elements of the *ex post total return.*

R_p is generally estimated with reference to a wide sample of traded stocks. The statistics must inevitably be tracked over a very long period

---

[9]R. Mehra and E. Prescott ("The Equity Premium: A Puzzle," *Journal of Monetary Economics,* Vol. 15, 1985, pages 145–161) were among the first to realize that an excess return of 6% obtained by investing in the S&P500 for several decades compared to Treasury bonds was too high if justified only by the need to compensate for the higher risk of holding stocks rather than bonds. On this point, see Siegel, *Stocks for the Long Run* (J. Irwin, 1988); E. Fama and K. French, "The Equity Premium," *Journal of Finance,* 57 (April 2000), pp. 637–659.

(usually more than 20 years) to neutralize the effect of fluctuations of returns in market cycles.

The main advantage associated with the calculation of risk premia based on historical records of stock returns lies in the apparent objectivity of the estimate. On the other hand, the weak points concern:

- The consideration that radical changes in the macroeconomic and macro-financial outlook can deprive past returns of their meaning.
- Past returns might not be a good proxy for expected returns.
- Returns might be biased. Many scholars pointed out that long-term returns are significantly affected by the so-called *survivorship bias*, that is the distortion caused by the *delisting* of companies that are bankrupt or in crisis.
- In less-developed countries, stock markets can be heavily influenced by a few stocks of large companies operating in the same industry: this would cause a strong bias of the computed historical returns.

An additional problem of using historical risk premia is the consistency of this parameter with the risk-free rate. This problem has two different aspects:

1. As noted, R_p is derived from the difference between stock returns and *risk-free* returns (which can be calculated based on the returns on short-, medium-, and long-term government bonds). Therefore, if R_f measures the return on long-term securities as the duration of the investment project under consideration is particularly long (15–20 years), R_p should also be calculated by subtracting the returns of long-term government bonds from the stock returns. By doing so, we neutralize the estimation error caused by the fact that long-term returns (and therefore, in our case, R_f) incorporate a liquidity premium, that is a premium for the risk of having inflation deviate from current expectations.
2. The second problem arises from the fact that R_p is generally estimated on the basis of historical records over very long time periods (50–70 years). Given that risk premia are obtained subtracting annual *risk-free* returns from annual stock returns, the historical *market risk premium* is (at least partly) influenced by the real long-term *risk-free* equilibrium rate.

When the real *risk-free* rate rises (due to a short- or medium-term shock that makes the rate deviate from the long-term equilibrium), the risk premium tends to decrease, because the returns on real assets are generally much stickier than interest rates.[10] The exact opposite occurs if the current

---

[10]J. J. Siegel, *Stocks for the Long Run* (New York: McGraw Hill, 2002).

risk-free rate remains below its long-term equilibrium level. As a result, R_f and R_p are consistent with each other if the current *risk-free* rates do not significantly differ from the long-term equilibrium returns based on which R_p was computed.

When these conditions are not met, the historical risk premium cannot be considered a reliable estimate of the expected R_p. As a matter of fact, in this case, the expectation of obtaining the same risk premium in the future as in the past is inconsistent with the current level of real *risk-free* rates.

8.11.2 From Historical Premia to Expected Risk Premia

The problems highlighted so far have led some experts and other important representatives of the financial community (large corporate banks, consulting firms, etc.) to conclude that historical returns should be abandoned in favor of prospective returns.

The calculation of prospective returns is usually based on consensus forecasts of profit growth for listed companies issued by sources such as Institutional Brokers Estimate System (IBES), Bloomberg, and so on, usually over a three-year period. For a longer time period between 10 and 15 years, a rate of growth *g* that is sustainable in the long-term is estimated. For the period that goes beyond the forecasting horizon, the market is assumed to grow at a rate similar to the nominal GDP growth rate.

The *ex-ante* expected market return is the rate that equates the discounted value of cash flows to the current value of the market index level at the reference date of the estimate.

The methodology is therefore basically the same as the one described when we introduced the *dividend discount model*, the only difference being that instead of a single stock the computation is done for the entire stock market. By subtracting from the prospective returns the expected *risk-free* rate, we obtain the *ex-ante risk premium* and use this parameter to estimate the cost of capital. A strong point in favor of the use of prospective returns lies in the fact that the previously discussed problem of consistency between R_p and R_f is more limited. As a matter of fact, *expected* R_p is generally derived from the difference between prospective return and expected *risk-free* rate. Therefore, in order to estimate the cost of capital, one must simply make sure that the *risk-free* rate used for the calculation of R_f does not considerably deviate from the base *risk-free* rate used in the calculation of the cost of capital based on the CAPM. However, this approach tends to lead to volatile estimates of the market risk premia and it should be used with caution.

8.12 ESTIMATING β

In the CAPM, the coefficient β refers to the component of risk in an investment that needs to be rewarded. In general, β is estimated by relating stock returns to market returns (with a simple regression technique).[11]

8.12.1 The Regression Parameters

The coefficient of the regression of stock returns (R_j) on market returns (R_m) represents the β of asset j:

$$R_j = \alpha + \beta_{jm} \times R_m$$

where:

α = the intercept of the regression and provides a measure of the actual performance in the period under consideration compared to the CAPM forecasts

β_{jm} = the slope of the regression line and it measures the risk of the stock; β_{jm} is equal to the ratio between the covariance between the returns on asset j and market returns and the variance of market returns:

$$\beta = \text{cov}\,(R_j,\ R_m)/\sigma^2 m$$

The R-squared (R^2) of the regression provides a measure of the regression line's ability to interpolate the data. From a financial point of view, this can be interpreted as part of the risk of a stock, represented by the variance attributable to the nondiversifiable market risk. Since the maximum value of R^2 is one, the difference $(1 - R^2)$ represents the share of the total risk attributable to diversifiable (specific) risk.[12]

8.12.2 Problems Arising Calculating Beta

Numerous sources and data providers (Bloomberg, Value Line, Standard & Poors, Risk Measurement Service by the London Business School, Morgan Stanley Beta Book, Merrill Lynch Beta Book, plus the major financial newspapers) regularly publish the β values for listed securities.

---

[11]In the APT and other multi-factorial models, β is calculated for each risk factor through the factorial analysis of stock returns.
[12]The problem of specific risk is dealt with in section 5.13.

Although the calculation method used by the different sources is the same (i.e., the regression technique), the results obtained can vary significantly according to the inputs used and the β estimation approach performed.

The major differences in terms of regression inputs include: (1) the duration of the estimate period for β; (2) the type and interval of the returns considered; (3) the market index used.

1. *Historical returns:* β is often calculated based on the last available five years. Other sources, including Bloomberg, consider by default only the last two years. The use of a longer time period has the advantage of considering a greater number of observations in the regression. On the other hand, longer time periods might be biased because it is more likely that they encompass structural changes in the firm/industry risk profile—such as changes in the financial structure that influence *levered β*. This is the main reason to support the use of a shorter period of historical records in the range between two and five years.

2. *Return type and interval:* Both stock returns and market returns should be calculated considering both the *capital gains* and the dividends received during the period under consideration. Some sources, including Bloomberg, calculate stock and market index returns only based on price changes without considering dividends.

   In theory, when deciding the time interval for the computation, annual, monthly, weekly, daily, or even infra-daily returns are all potential candidates. Some agencies, including Standard & Poors, use monthly returns. Bloomberg adopts by default weekly returns.

   Using daily returns has the advantage of increasing the number of observations in the regression. Nevertheless, such an approach exposes the estimation process to a significant bias in beta estimates caused by the lack of liquidity of certain stocks. For instance, the betas estimated for small firms, which are more likely to suffer from relatively infrequent trading, are biased downward when daily returns are used.

3. *The market index:* The choice of the market index to be used in the regression also affects the estimates of β.

   The beta of a stock is generally calculated with respect to the index of the market in which the stock is traded (the betas of US stocks are calculated with respect to the S&P 500, German ones are regressed on the DAX, etc.).

   Due to the emergence of more and more internationally diversified investors who allocate their assets in a number of different markets, it is becoming increasingly common to calculate betas with respect to international indices, such as the Morgan Stanley Capital Index.

Adjustment Techniques: Adjusted β   Some sources (e.g., Bloomberg) publish adjusted beta coefficients. These betas are adjusted to account for the fact that the value of β should tend toward 1 in the long term, meaning that excessively low or high values of observed betas in the market must, respectively, be increased or decreased.

To better understand this issue, let us consider the beta of a stock that has shown a bearish trend in a bullish market in recent years. For such a stock, the resulting beta estimate would be low regardless of the characteristics of the firm's risk profile. The opposite occurs in the case of securities that have persistently outperformed the market.

Nonetheless, not all sources use the same correction techniques.[13] For instance, Bloomberg calculates the *adjusted beta* as the weighted mean between the β of the simple regression (*raw beta*) and the β of the market, equal to 1, with fixed weights for all stocks, equal to two-thirds and one-third, respectively. Other sources do not use fixed weights but adopt different data according to the fundamentals of each company.

8.12.3   Industry-Level β

As already observed, errors in the estimation of the cost of capital can be limited using data that refer to a sample of comparable companies. In general, it is therefore preferable to use an average β calculated with respect to a sample of stocks from companies belonging to the same industry.

The aforementioned sources often also publish industry-level betas (also known as bottom-up betas), calculated as a weighted mean of the betas coming from the companies within a certain sector, each of them weighted by the ratio between the market capitalization of the single company and total sector capitalization.

The use of these data requires caution and careful consideration on the actual degree of comparability across the companies to be included in the

---

[13]The two most widespread correction methods are those suggested by Blume and by Vasicek. The first advocates the analysis of the level of autocorrelation of the betas over time. The second method makes corrections based on historical variances expressed by the beta in two different subperiods. For a more detailed analysis see: M. Blume, "On the Assessment of Risk," *Journal of Finance*, 1 (March 1971), pages 1–10; O. Vasicek, "A Note on Using Cross Sectional Information in Bayesian Estimate of Security Betas," *Journal of Finance*, VIII, 5 (1973): 1233–1239. Finally, some attempts to correct betas based on qualitative parameters concerning the company (e.g., the presence of strong or weak points, etc.) deserve to be mentioned. The models derived from this approach tend to explain the variability of security returns with respect to the market on the basis of a series of factors connected to the *fundamentals* of the company and the sector.

final sample from the point of view of business models, dimensions, and profitability.

In principle, the calculation of an average industry-level β involves the same procedure and the same devices necessary for the estimate of the average industry multiples, which will be discussed in subsequent chapters. In particular, the most used procedure is composed of the following steps:

- The choice of a comparable group of companies.
- The calculation of the betas for the firms included in the selected group.
- The calculation of *unlevered* betas. This phase can also cover the problem associated with the presence of excess liquidity compared to the level of financial debt (net positive financial position).
- The calculation of the average betas of the companies in the selected group.[14]

Selection of Comparable Companies As we will describe when addressing multiples, the comparability of the companies to be included in the sample must refer to their business sector, to the structure of the asset portfolio, and to the cost structure.

Comparable companies must be selected with the objective of finding a significant enough number of companies featuring substantial similarities with the firm to be valued.

A preliminary problem is that businesses often operate in more than one business area. Consequently, except for a few sectors, it is not always possible to calculate "pure" beta that refers to the specific area of interest. It's up to the analyst to evaluate to what extent the beta of a company operating in several businesses is biased.

Once the comparability of the businesses selected has been checked in terms of the main activities performed, other considerations can be made about the risk profile of the operating assets and of the managerial structure. In addition to typical sectorial elements, such as the level of vertical integration or the choices made in terms of productive outsourcing, more general terms also deserve consideration when determining companies' comparability, such as:

- The quality of the companies' management
- The organizational structure
- The size of the firm

If those specific risk factors are not taken into account satisfactorily, it may be necessary to include an *additional risk premium*.

---

[14]The average at this stage usually is either the aritmethic average or the mean. Some analysts prefer to use a weighted average where each beta is weighted on the basis of the total capitalization of the company it refers to.

Levered and Unlevered β $(\beta_L$ and $\beta_U)$ The values of the beta coefficients determined on the basis of market data are influenced by the company's operating and financial risk (i.e., they are *levered betas*).

If betas are applied in order to estimate the discount rate for the calculation of the value of an investment initiative, or for the valuation of a firm, the *leverage* effect on beta must be recalibrated as a function of the target financial structure considered in the valuation context.

This requires two adjustments:

- The neutralization of the leverage effect in the beta observed in the market (*unlevering*)
- The readjustment of the unlevered beta (*relevering*)[15]

The logic underlying the formula to calculate the *unlevered* betas can be understood by recalling the law of the preservation of value. The total amount of risk borne by stockholders and financial creditors corresponds to the operating risk of the venture being considered and, therefore, to the risk linked to the cash flows generated by invested capital.

Without Tax Benefits The above-mentioned principle can result in the following formula:

$$\beta_{assets} = \beta_{equityL} \times \frac{E}{E + D} + \beta_{debt} \times \frac{D}{E + D}$$

In this particular case with no tax benefits linked to indebtedness, β_{asset} will correspond to β_{equity} (*unlevered*). For practical purposes, it is often possible to assume that β_{debt} is very low. Consequently, the second element can be canceled, thereby obtaining:

$$\beta_{equityU} = \beta_{equityL} \times \frac{E}{E + D}$$

This equation can also be rewritten as follows:

$$\beta_{equityU} = \frac{\beta_{equityL}}{(1 + D/E)}$$

With Tax Benefits When the aforementioned equation is used to derive β_U from the data observed in the market, it is crucial to recall that in the presence of tax benefits, the value of market capitalization E should incorporate the current value of tax savings due to the tax deductibility of financial charges.

---

[15]The *relevering* phase is necessary to calculate K_{el}^* (in aggregated valuations for the estimate of the $WACC^*$ and in *equity-side* valuations). To calculate K_{eu} (in case of disaggregated valuations with the APV technique), it is necessary to consider the unlevered β.

Consequently, we need to adjust the estimated values to eliminate the effect of tax savings.

After some algebra, we can easily obtain a new formulation that is valid if and only if the actual debt advantage is measured at rate t_c:

$$\beta_{equityU} = \beta_{equityL} \times \frac{E}{E + D \times (1 - t_c)} + \beta_{debt} \times \frac{D}{E + D \times (1 - t_c)} \times (1 - t_c)$$

The expression above, assuming $\beta_{debt} = 0$, can be simplified as follows:

$$\beta_{equityU} = \beta_{equityL} \times \frac{E}{E + D \times (1 - t_c)}$$

This can be rewritten in the following more widely used formula:

$$\beta_{equityU} = \frac{\beta_{equityL}}{1 + (1 - t_c) \times D/E}$$

Such relationship can be used also for the calculation of relevered β_{equity} ($\beta_{equityR}$). When $\beta_{equityU}$ is known, $\beta_{equityRL}$ can be derived as a function of the financial structure of the venture to be evaluated, $(D/E)^*$:

$$\beta_{equityRL} = \beta_{equityU} \times [1 + (1 - t_c) \times (D/E)^*]^{16}$$

Net liquidity If a company exhibits net liquidity – meaning that its liquidity is higher than its financial debt - the beta calculated according to the approaches discussed so far will undervalue the true value of the beta. As a matter of fact, we can easily express the market capitalization of a company with net liquidity as:

$$C = (C{-}L) + L$$

where:

C = market capitalization
L = net liquidity
$(C - L)$ = market capitalization of the operations only.

The observed beta should then be equal to the weighted average of the levered beta and of the business beta (which corresponds to the "true" *unlevered beta*), i.e.

$$\beta_{equity} = \beta_{liquidity} \times \frac{L}{C} + \beta_U \times \frac{(C - L)}{C}$$

---

[16]In a growth scenario, the adjustments of the betas are affected by the limitations already discussed in relation to the formulae for the calculation of the opportunity cost of capital. The formulae should be adjusted according to the same criteria previously discussed.

where:

β_{equity} = observed beta
$\beta_{liquidity}$ = beta of the liquidity assets.

Since we can assume that the debt beta equals zero, this equation can be rewritten as:

$$\beta_{equity} = \beta_U \times \frac{(C - L)}{C}$$

Therefore, whenever a company is characterized by a positive net financial position, the unlevered beta is then calculated according to the following formula:

$$\beta_U = \beta_{equity} \times \frac{C}{(C - L)}.$$

8.13 DEALING WITH SPECIFIC RISKS

When the CAPM is adopted, only systematic risk factors should be considered to estimate the opportunity cost of capital. However, as discussed above, the variability of the cash flow of a business depends on total risk rather than on systematic risk only. Furthermore, the probability of a firm becoming insolvent is a function of the total risk.

Even from the point of view of financial investors who diversify their portfolio, overlooking specific risk factors could be dangerous.[17]

Exhibit 8.2 shows the different ways in which the problem related to risk assessment can arise when considering the perspective of a financial investor *vis-à-vis* a strategic investor.

Company A operates in the fashion sector and markets products with proprietary mark. Two scenarios are assumed with the same probability of occurrence. The mean result for both is 1,100.

Firm B markets products with both proprietary trademarks and licenses. The scenarios and the relevant probabilities are the same. However, there is

---

[17]See Van Horne, *Financial Management Policy* 12th ed. (Upper Saddle River: Prentice Hall 2001), p. 225: "The probability of a firm's becoming insolvent depends on its risk, not just on its systematic risk; hence, a case can be made for choosing projects in light of their effect on both the systematic and the total (systematic plus unsystematic) risk of the firm. Put another way, when insolvency or bankruptcy costs are significant, investors may well be served by the firm's paying attention to the total risk of the firm, not just to its systematic risk. Risky capital budgeting proposals can alter the total risk of the firm apart from their effect on its systematic risk. To the extent that unsystematic risk is a factor of at least some importance, total risk should be evaluated."

Exhibit 8.2 The licensee example

Company A—proprietary marks			Company B—proprietary marks and licensed marks		
Scenarios				Scenarios	
	Max	Min		Max	Min
Total result	1,200	1,000	Proprietary marks	600	500
Probability	0.5	0.5	Licenses	1,100	0
Mean result	1,100		Total result	1,700	500
			Probability	0.5	0.5
			Mean result	1,100	

the possibility of licenses not being renewed, with the consequent zeroing of the results concerning the products with licensed marks.

The probability of the licenses being renewed is 50 percent. The example is structured in such a way that the mean result of B is exactly the same as A.

If the valuation is carried out through the capitalization of the flow of the mean expected result at the rate calculated with the CAPM, the value of A is equal to the value of B. For instance, assuming a beta of the textile-fashion sector equal to 1.2, a 4 percent *risk-free* rate and a five-point market risk premium, both firms' K_{eu} would be:

$$K_{eu} = 0.04 + 0.05 \times 1.2 = 10\%$$

Thus, the values of A and B would be equivalent and equal to 11,000 (1,100/0.10).

We may wonder whether the estimated result is convincing. There is unfortunately no simple answer to this question. It depends on the point of view of who is making and using the valuation and on the efficiency of the underlying securities market.

In the case of a financial investor, the procedure is acceptable only if the opportunities of diversification available on the market are such to effectively neutralize the risk related to license renewal and if the operations of company B are not jeopardized in case of missed renewal of the licenses.

For instance, if the investor can put together a portfolio made up of a sufficient number of securities characterized by risk patterns similar to B, the valuation obtained "in a CAPM environment" would be correct as soon as it is reasonable to think that, *ex-post*, the results from an unfavorable scenario would be averaged with the results from a favorable scenario.

From the standpoint of a strategic investor interested in the acquisition of the entire capital of B, it is much more credible to believe that there will be a significantly higher risk.

The previous example gives us an idea of the possible practical considerations linked to the issues we discussed. Two alternatives are usually mentioned in valuation manuals to deal with and try to solve these problems:

1. The integration of the rate calculated in the CAPM setting with an additional risk premium as a compensation for the presence of specific risks
2. The use, for valuation purposes, of the rate obtained in the CAPM environment and the subsequent adjustment of the estimated value through a *discount*, depending on the type of specific risk considered[18]

The choice between the first and the second alternative is a function of the availability of reliable empirical information such as the level of *discount* granted in case of specific risk factors or the extent of rate adjustment. Information on the level of discount is generally very fragmentary. Therefore, in most circumstances the first alternative should be preferred.

In this case, the formula of the CAPM can be integrated as follows:

$$K_{el}^* = R_f + \beta_i \times (R_m - R_f) + ARP$$

where ARP represents the additional risk premium.

ARP, in general, should be a function of:

- Specific risk factors that stockholders are not assumed to neutralize through the diversification of their personal assets
- *Downsizing*, or the spread between the size of the business being evaluated and the average size of the companies listed on the stock exchange with respect to which the risk premium was statistically calculated

Data are usually available for an empirical estimate of the ARP. It refers to the (historically) highest returns obtained from investments in stocks of small-sized companies or in stocks characterized by special risk situations (e.g., the so-called *venture capital premium*, equal to the difference between the returns of *venture capital funds* and the returns of funds investing in stocks of public companies).

Another procedure used to calculate the discount rate in case of special situations of risk is to adjust the beta coefficient. This procedure allows for the estimation of the so-called *total betas*, where:

$$\text{Total beta} = (\text{Total variation/Systematic variation}) \times \beta = (1/\rho) \times \beta$$

where ρ is the correlation coefficient ($R^2 = \rho^2$).

---

[18] See, for example, S. Prat, *Business Valuation, Discounts and Premiums* (New York: Wiley & Sons, 2001).

We believe that this method of adjustment should be used with caution, as it discounts all the gaps and inaccuracies of the statistical records of data used and can lead to misleading results.[19]

Furthermore, the use of the *total beta* is based on the assumption that nonsystematic variability experienced in the past can reoccur in the future. There are no elements that can justify this assumption.

8.14 CONCLUSIONS ON THE ESTIMATION OF THE OPPORTUNITY COST OF CAPITAL

Some general guidelines can be drawn from the considerations discussed up to this point:

- If the valuation scenario is mainly characterized by exposure to market risk, the CAPM could be a reliable instrument for the extraction of sound data and information.
- If the scenario is characterized by uncertainty about the results of an innovative initiative/industry, the estimate of K_{eu} made in a CAPM setting should be integrated with an additional risk premium due to the high variability of the results typical of such initiatives.
- If idiosyncratic risk factors are detectable, the estimate of K_{eu} should be accompanied by a careful analysis of the choices made by experts in the estimation.
- We have already stressed the importance of making separate valuations of business areas characterized by different risk profiles and growth perspectives. This need becomes even stronger if some business areas are affected by specific risk factors.
- The estimate of the cost of capital is never obtained via a unique mathematical formula. It may be useful sometimes to verify the obtained estimates both by applying more than one method and by making a comparison with the estimates of K_{eu} concerning business activities characterized by risk profiles that are similar to those of the business being evaluated.
- Further analyses are advisable in case of major specific risks or in case of uncertainty about the significance of some parameters (such as the values taken by the index beta in abnormally volatile market conditions).

---

[19]The β of a security can significantly change depending on the number of observations on which the calculation is based. Obviously, the same problem holds when we discuss the specific risk of the security.

8.15   COST OF DEBT

The cost of debt (K_d) expresses the current cost of the firm's borrowed funds. For valuation purposes, K_d always refers to an estimate projected in the future and to businesses in situations of equilibrium that will not increase their net indebtedness. This can be better understood by mentioning that the value of a *steady-state* business is a function of the flows that the business is assumed to be able to generate. These flows must be discounted at the rate expressing the return investors expect from lending their money to the company for a particular length of time. Therefore, the cost of debt measures the current cost that the business must bear to finance new investment projects with debt, or in other words the cost that the firm would bear to refinance existing assets in line with its predetermined target financial structure.

8.15.1   Preliminary Questions

Now that K_d has been defined, other preliminary issues need to be clarified.

What Liabilities Should Be Included?   When referring to indebtedness, we always mean financial liabilities, that is, those liabilities bearing interest.[20] Other substitutive forms of debt include financing lease agreements and operating lease agreements.

Hybrid forms of capital such as convertible bonds are also considered to be financial liabilities.

Should the Time Horizon Be Short or Long?   Since the time horizon for flow projections is usually very long or even unlimited, K_d should be estimated over the long term. Such an approach allows for greater consistency with the hypotheses underlying the flow projections, in particular with respect to expected inflation when projections are developed in nominal terms.

This general rule is also valid if a business systematically finances itself by resorting to short-term funds. As a matter of fact, long-term rates usually convey sufficient information to estimate short-term rates as well.

8.15.2   Components of the Cost of Debt

K_d depends on two main factors:

- The current level of interest rates
- The possibility of the business not being able to fulfill its future obligations to pay interest and to repay the principal capital

---

[20]In some cases, commercial liabilities also bear financial interests. However, in general, these should not be treated as financial debt and, as a consequence, the passive interest associated with them should be included in the operating costs.

Thus, K_d is equal to the sum of the following quantities:

- A base rate expressing the current return on long-term risk-free investments
- A *spread* that increases parametrically with the risk of insolvency

We now look at these in more detail.

The Base Rate The choice of the risk-free base rate depends on the opportunity cost of the investors in the financial liabilities of the firm. For instance, in the case of bonds placed on the market, the return on government bonds (e.g., US Treasury bonds and German Bunds) should be a *benchmark* for potential investors.[21]

As far as bank loans are concerned, the base rate is usually represented by a financial parameter measuring the average rate applied in the bank's lending activities. This parameter includes a charge to cover the lender's financial costs. This parameter is not generally available over a long-term horizon. Hence, an acceptable solution to estimate the base rate is to sum the government bond yield and an average spread applied to the best customers (using the *prime rate* as a benchmark).

The Spread The *spread*, also known as risk premium, is usually estimated based on long-term *yields to maturity* (YTM) negotiated by businesses belonging to different risk classes.

The yields to maturity of listed corporate bonds can be obtained from the most widespread financial data providers. Such spreads can be cross-referenced with the bond *ratings* issued by the main agencies. Data therefore usually allow us to define a likely *spread* for each company given its industry, geographic location, and *rating*.

Such criteria can only be applied to companies that have a rating or that are comparable enough to other rated companies. Small and medium-sized companies are rarely rated by an independent rating agency, and their debt is usually not securitized and traded on the market. As a consequence, further approximations should be used when dealing with the estimation of the cost of debt of such companies.

For instance, some valuation textbooks suggest that K_d for small/medium firms should be estimated by *analogy* (i.e., by trying to determine

---

[21]Returns demanded by investors can be affected by possible differences in tax regimes. For example, if yields on government bonds are taxed at a subsidized rate, the base rate requested shall compensate for the tax disadvantage affecting those investors forgoing this form of investment.

the most suitable rating category for the business being evaluated). On the basis of the criteria disclosed by rating agencies, the analyst should try to determine what rating the company would be assigned if it had requested one. The following factors should typically be considered:

- The size of the firm
- The debt-to-equity ratio
- The coverage ratio (i.e., the number of times a company could sustain its interest payments with its earnings before interest and taxes)
- The return on invested capital

8.16   COST OF DIFFERENT TYPES OF DEBT

In the estimation of K_d, it is crucial to determine the mix of the main forms of indebtedness that the firm intends to use. In the case of investment projects supported by specific financing mix, K_d must be estimated with respect to those specific types of financing (e.g., projects supported by financial facilities or *project financing* operations).

On the other hand, if the financing is not predetermined, more general considerations can be made, since the cost of the different forms of financing tends to converge at least in the long term, as we will further discuss later.

8.16.1   Medium- to Long-Term Debt and Bonds

The cost of (medium and long-term) debt is the basic parameter used to estimate the cost of other forms of debt that are more complex and have special features. As already stated, the factors that determine the cost of long-term debt are:

- The yields to maturity of long-term risk free investments
- The *spread* as a function of the insolvency risk
- In general, for businesses that do not issue marketable securities, a charge that covers the costs borne by lenders (banks or other financial institutions)

The last two elements can generally be estimated through the analysis of the lending conditions reported in recent financing agreements.

8.16.2   Variable Rate Debt

The long-term rate is still the best estimate of K_d throughout the duration of the project under consideration, even for companies that use variable interest financing instruments.

8.16.3 Foreign Currency Debt

In principle, the cost of foreign currency debt can be translated in the cost of debt service measured adopting the national currency. K_d should be estimated considering the expected fluctuations in the exchange rate of the currencies being analyzed. The debt service flows should be converted into the national currency by applying forward exchange rates according to the relevant coupon/principal maturities. Alternatively, if the interest rate parity assumption is accepted,[22] it is possible to assume that the cost of exchange rate debt is quite similar to the long-term cost of debt in the national market.

8.16.4 Leasing

Since leasing agreements imply the obligation to pay regular predetermined amounts, they are equivalent to forms of financial debt.

If a company intends to systematically resort to financial leasing or operational leasing, the determination of the cost of debt becomes even more problematic. In practice, we can simply assume that the cost of the leasing service is equal to the cost of medium- to long-term debt for the company.[23]

8.16.5 Convertible Bonds

The estimation of the cost of raising capital through convertible bonds is not as straightforward as in the previous case. Convertible bonds are a hybrid form of financing as the debt can be transformed into risk capital by exercising the conversion right associated with the security.

To simplify the problem, let us switch the perspective of the analysis by looking at the point of view of investors in convertible bonds. What is the rate that those investors consider satisfactory? To better answer this question, we first have to precisely define the features of an investment in convertible bonds. Investors in convertible bonds actually hold a financial package made of two separate securities:

- A "pure" bond (i.e., a nonconvertible one).

---

[22]The interest rate parity theory in the international markets states that in a market without friction, any interest differential is compensated by an opposite change in the exchange rates. This produces a general market equilibrium situation (at least in the long term).

[23]Precisely, it must be observed that the financial profile of a lease can differ from the profile of other medium- to long-term forms of financing. Also, the risk for the investor can be affected by the nature of the agreement. However, this factor can be overlooked for the sake of simplicity.

- The right to transform the original investment into stocks based on a predetermined conversion price and on a set date (this right is an option similar to a *warrant*).

When estimating the cost of capital or performing a valuation, the appropriate way to deal with convertible bonds is to separate the total amount of capital raised through convertible bonds into the two components of these securities, namely the pure bonds and the *warrants*.

The problem can be easily solved by calculating the value of the instrument as a simple bond (so-called *bond value*). Such value can be determined by discounting the flow of the debt service schedule, composed of interest payments and capital repayment, at the yield to maturity (YTM) of comparable bonds with a similar duration and risk profile. At this stage, the component represented by the conversion right (*warrant*) can be simply obtained as the difference between the issue price and the *bond value*:

$$\text{Implicit warrant} = \text{Issue price} - \text{Bond value}$$

Based on the previous remarks, it is easy to conclude that financing through convertible bonds is actually a mixed financing with different costs of capital:

- The cost of debt linked to the bond component equal to the medium/long-term cost of debt for the firm (K_d)
- The cost associated with the sale of the conversion right (*warrant*), which could be linked to *equity* even if the implied cost capital is usually higher than K_{el}^*, since a *warrant* is a riskier instrument than the underlying stock (in fact, the return of a *warrant* "multiplies" the stock return)

Therefore:

- As far as the debt portion is considered, the convertible bond has a cost equal to the cost of medium- to long-term debt for the firm.
- As far as the *equity* portion is considered, the convertible bond has a cost higher than K_{el}^*.

Two equivalent solutions can now be proposed to estimate the cost of equity capital embedded in convertible bonds:

- Calculation of the mean cost of the "package" *warrant* + pure bond:

$$K_{\text{CB}} = K_d \times \frac{BV}{IP} + K_{\text{warr}} \times \frac{warr}{IP}$$

where:

K_{CB} = average cost of capital raised through the convertible bond issue
K_d = medium/long-term cost of debt
BV = bond value
K_{warr} = opportunity cost of capital for the warrant
warr = warrant value
IP = issue price of the convertible bond; inclusion of the bond component in the medium/long-term debt (with equal cost) and inclusion of the *warrant* component in the *equity* (with $K_{warr} > K_{el}^*$)

The cost of the capital raised through the sale of *warrants* can be estimated by adopting an approach based on option theory.[24]

APPENDIX 8.1: CAPM WITH PERSONAL TAXES

The CAPM describes the relationship between risk and expected return for financial assets and it can be used in the pricing of any risky securities. Hence, given the financial asset i, we have:

$$R_i = R_f + \beta_i \times (R_m - R_f)$$

It is worth highlighting that this relationship does not consider taxes. By introducing corporate and personal taxes, the equation should be adjusted in order to take into account the different forms of corporate, personal, and financial assets taxation. As a consequence, instead of a single risk-free rate before taxes, there will be a debt risk-free rate as well as an equity risk-free rate. Both of these will vary according to the proper taxation level applied to different securities' classes.

However, if the market is efficient, all financial assets characterized by the same level of risk must offer identical returns even net of taxes. Following this line of reasoning, the equation capturing the expected return (cost of capital) on an investment in shares, will be:

$$R_{equity} = R_{f\_equity} + \beta_i \times (R_m - R_{f\_equity})$$

In other terms, the proper risk-free rate expressing the equity cost of capital for company i must be equal to the return of risk-free shares. However,

---

[24] See the classic textbook by T. Copeland, J. Weston, *Financial Theory and Corporate Policy* (Reading, MA: Addison Wesley, 1992), p. 451.

this kind of return cannot be observed in practice, which means that such a rate can only be computed by adjusting observed data.

All financial assets bearing the same risk level must, by definition, grant an identical level of return net of taxes. On the basis of such assumption, we can state the following:

$$R_{f\_debt} \times (1 - t_d) = R_{f\_equity} \times (1 - t_e)$$

Rearranging the terms, we obtain:

$$R_{f\_equity} = R_{f\_debt} \frac{(1 - t_d)}{(1 - t_e)}$$

which is the equity risk-free rate as a function of both tax rates and debt risk-free rate. Such value can be directly obtained from market data.

Recalling a formula presented in this chapter, we have that:

$$T = 1 - \frac{(1 - t_c)(1 - t_e)}{(1 - t_d)}$$

This can be restated as:

$$\frac{1 - t_d}{1 - t_e} = \frac{1 - t_c}{1 - T}$$

This leads us to a new definition of R_{f_equity} as a function of T and t_c:

$$R_{f\_equity} = R_{f\_debt} \frac{(1 - t_c)}{(1 - T)}$$

Replacing this new definition of R_{f_equity} in the equation discussed above, we finally get:

$$R_{equity} = K_{el}^* = R_{f\_debt} \frac{1 - t_c}{1 - T} + \beta_i \times \left(R_m - R_{f\_debt} \times \frac{1 - t_c}{1 - T} \right)$$

## CHAPTER 9

Cash Flow Profiles and Valuation Procedures

9.1 FROM BUSINESS MODELS TO CASH FLOW MODELS

The aim of this chapter is to show that financial valuation methods produce reliable estimates if and only if a specific in-depth business analysis is performed. Such an analysis has to embrace not only strategic and competitive aspects, which are the basis for any valuation task, but also financial dynamics, including the debt profile over time. Such analyses allow the expert to define the most suitable cash flow valuation method to be applied in any specific case. In particular, the analyst has to decide whether to use the aggregated versus the disaggregated approach, and on the treatment of the tax advantages of debt.

Before starting the discussion, it is worth focusing on the analytical process that precedes the final stage of a valuation, that is, the application of a discounted cash flow formula. Exhibit 9.1 summarizes the different necessary steps to better understand the background of the company or project under consideration.

When valuing a company, a potential issue lies in the fact that standard plan horizons, usually around three to five years long or slightly longer, only explain a small portion of total firm's value. In fact, the bulk of the value is a function of the long-term results obtained beyond the standard plan horizons. It is therefore necessary to define a cash flow model that matches not only the financial dynamics of the medium-term (three to five years) forecasts, but also the assumptions made for the longer-term analysis.

Exhibit 9.1 Understanding the business model and choosing a valuation procedure

1. Understand the company's operations.

⇓

2. Understand the company's cash flow dynamics.

⇓

3. Compare the firm's operations with the typical ones found in its industry and competitors.

⇓

4. Evaluate the compatibility and the coherence of the assumptions made in the business plan with respect to:

   ▪ Business resources
   ▪ Sector trend
   ▪ Competitors' strategies

⇓

5. Define the assumptions necessary to forecast results beyond the plan's forecast horizon.

⇓

6. Define the company's operating cash flow profile and debt profile.

⇓

7. Select the most appropriate method to compute the DCF.

9.2 CASH FLOW PROFILES OF BUSINESS UNITS VERSUS WHOLE ENTITY

If at a multi-business company the business units are independent enough on an operational basis, it could be worthwhile to develop specific cash flow projections and specific assumptions beyond the standard plan horizon for each business area. This estimation process is often referred to by the international community as the *sum-of-parts (SOP) approach*.

It is important to note that an SOP valuation could sometimes prove to be meaningless. As a matter of fact, horizontal synergies between areas are often such an important element that a comprehensive analysis and valuation is necessary. For instance, when evaluating "multi-utility" companies, it is meaningless to try and assign the existing synergies across different services to a specific business area (i.e., energy, electricity, water). Therefore, in order to choose the most appropriate valuation process, we should follow these steps:

   ▪ Look for potential surplus assets or surplus businesses.
   ▪ Look for autonomously profitable business units.

Exhibit 9.2 Multi-business company valuation

+	Surplus assets
+	Specific business areas value (asset value)
+	Aggregated businesses value (asset value)
=	**Total asset value**
−	Financial (net) debt
=	**Equity value**

- Look for business activities that are best analyzed as a whole due to operations' synergies.
- Analyze the cash flows of the relevant units.

Therefore, the total company value when the company operates in more than one business is obtained as in Exhibit 9.2.

9.3 EXAMPLES OF CASH FLOW PROFILES

This section presents some typical cash flow profiles related to EBITDA and FCFO throughout the standard three to five years forecasted plan as well as in the phase beyond that. The choice between EBITDA and FCFO has already been addressed at the beginning of this book and it mainly resides in the level of investments in fixed assets and working capital (and in the related taxes).

Exhibits 9.3 and 9.4 present the cash flow profiles of two *public utility* companies: one in the natural gas distribution business (Exhibit 9.3) and the other in the hydroelectric generation business (Exhibit 9.4).

During the plan horizon, the cash flow of the energy company mirrors the consumption growth associated with new industrial and local client base. Beyond the plan horizon, the FCFO is significantly greater than the FCFO of the final year of the plan horizon (year 4). This is due to the lower long-term growth assumptions both for the expansion of current pipelines and for new acquisitions.

The development of the flow beyond the plan horizon is based on two major assumptions:

- A consumption growth rate in line with the GDP growth rate
- A price to customers that guarantees the full remuneration of invested capital

At this point, it is worth highlighting that the cash flows considered so far are expressed in nominal terms—that is, they include the expected increase in prices.

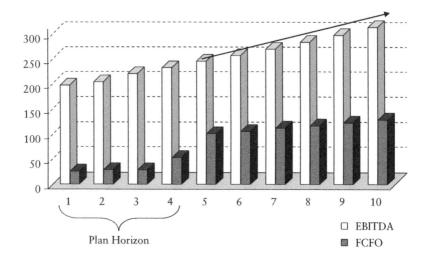

Exhibit 9.3 Cash flow examples: *public utility* (natural gas distribution)

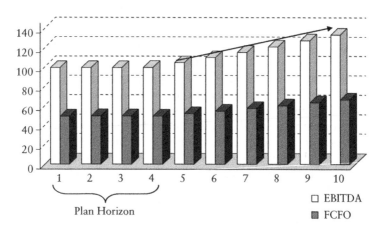

Exhibit 9.4 Cash flow examples: *public utility* (hydroelectric)

Exhibit 9.4 shows an even simpler case. It represents a company running a hydroelectric power plant. Some of the assumptions are that there is neither the need for extraordinary investments nor the necessity to expand the production capacity. Therefore, the cash flows beyond the plan horizon only grow due to an increase in (regulated) prices mirroring an increase in costs.

As previously stated, the EBITDA is systematically greater than the FCFO. This is due to the fact that the operating cash flow is computed by subtracting the amounts of maintenance investments and taxes from the EBITDA.

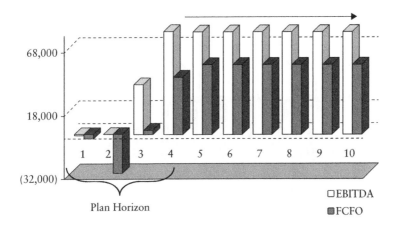

Exhibit 9.5   Cash flow examples: *print on demand*

Exhibit 9.5 refers to the launch of "print on demand" services for a company in the printing industry. The EBITDA and the FCFO trends during the plan horizon are similar to those of a typical start-up: negative financial results in the first years are followed by a development and expansion phase. In this case, the financial profile is a result of the necessary investments in fixed assets and promotional activities. At the end of the plan horizon, growth is assumed to stop due to the entry of new competitors in the same business area. The decrease in profit margins due to the increase in competition should nevertheless take into account the impact of inflation on cash flow.

Exhibit 9.6 shows the cash flow profiles of a company operating in the waste management industry—a landfill, to be precise. Differently from previous scenarios discussed, this venture has a limited life, as the landfill capacity is limited. The flow is simply determined by valuing the waste annually treated on the basis of average margins.

The financial representation (FCFO) highlights that, at the end of the investment's life, the flow is negative. This is due to the need for a new drainage system required to comply with safety regulations.

Exhibit 9.7 illustrates the cash flow projections in industries affected by cyclical dynamics (iron and steel industries). The dashed arrow represents the profile of the cycle projected on the basis of forecasts made by industry experts.

The specific problems for this valuation procedure are not related to the plan's forecast period but to the estimate of a standardized result of long-term cash flows that adequately incorporates the cycle dynamics.

A common solution used by financial analysts is to estimate the EBITDA and the FCFO values consistent with a standard scenario based on historical industry performance.

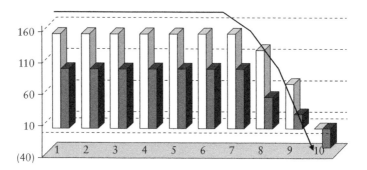

Exhibit 9.6 Cash flow profile examples: waste management company

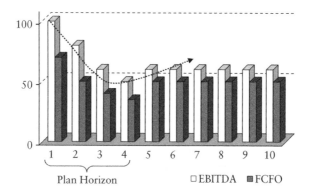

Exhibit 9.7 Cash flow profiles: cyclical sector

In this specific example, the plan horizon ends with the downturn phase of the cycle. The cash flows used to estimate the terminal value therefore hypothesize an average scenario where the highest results are balanced with the lowest ones. It is assumed afterward that the normalized flow can be projected onto an infinite horizon.

Finally, Exhibit 9.8 shows a bank's cash flow profile. The analysis is carried out in distinct business areas. In this specific case, in addition to the bank's lending activity, there are new businesses with growth perspectives, risk profiles, and capital commitments different from those of the traditional banking activity.

Historical data confirm the high correlation between GDP growth and the bank's traditional business growth. Thus, the traditional lending business is a mature business with a relatively "flat" cash flow profile.

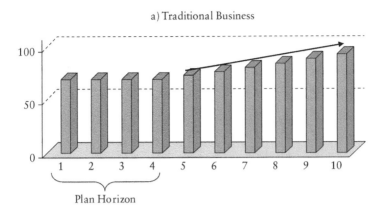

a) Traditional Business

Exhibit 9.8   Cash flow profiles: savings and loans (traditional business)

The portfolio management business has a higher growth potential in the short term. However, the growth pace is expected to slow down once the activity reaches a point of competitive equilibrium. As a consequence, the cash flow profiles will eventually grow at a slower pace, showing a high growth rate only for a limited number of years (as shown in Exhibit 9.9).

On the other end, in this specific example, the investment banking business has interesting growth potential in the medium term. The growth for this specific business has been limited to the plan horizon due to an expected high level of competition and to the cyclical evolution characterizing the investment banking business as a whole (see Exhibit 9.10).

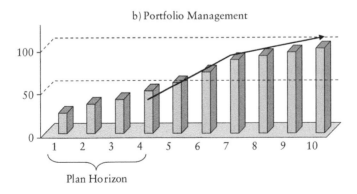

b) Portfolio Management

Exhibit 9.9   Cash flow profiles: savings and loans (portfolio management)

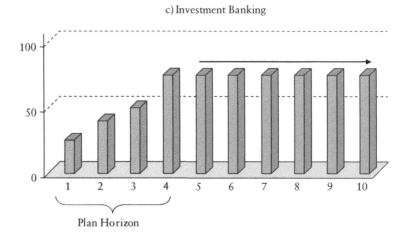

c) Investment Banking

Exhibit 9.10   Cash flow profiles: savings and loans (investment banking)

9.4   PROBLEMS WITH THE IDENTIFICATION OF CASH FLOW MODELS

We have highlighted that one of the key tasks in a valuation is the assessment of company's business model.

The business model credibility is also an important condition to sustain cash flow projections. There are at least two scenarios in which it is extremely difficult, or even impossible, to build a reliable cash flow model:

1. Companies lacking a distinctive competitive advantage in terms of strategic or operational resources.
2. *Captive* companies—that is, companies that are incapable of standing autonomously on the market because they heavily depend on one or a few clients.

If such conditions are met, the long-term cash flow profile tends to be highly unpredictable and a mere function of exogenous random factors.

Therefore, the stand-alone valuation of a captive company or of a company without distinctive characteristics should be based on the assumption that it is possible to gather the necessary resources to allow the company to stay and compete autonomously in the market.

9.5 CASH FLOW MODELS IN THE CASE OF RESTRUCTURING

All firms undergoing a restructuring process share two important characteristics:

1. *Throughout the plan horizon,* the company's financial dynamics mirror the restructuring process, which could lead to the divestment of surplus assets or of entire business units. Changes in the working capital can also significantly influence the cash flow profile.
2. *At the end of the plan,* the long-term cash flow profile is based on the likelihood of success of the restructuring as well as on the changes made to keep the key business resources.

Thus, the cash flow credibility depends on the credibility of the restructuring objectives. Due to the importance of future events, different assumptions are usually taken into consideration by using sensitivity analysis and by looking into alternative scenarios.

9.6 DEBT PROFILE ANALYSIS

Debt profile analysis has the following purposes:

- The identification of a realistic model for the pattern of the company's net financial debt
- The valuation of tax shields consistently with the debt profile used in the estimation process

To facilitate the discussion, we will split the problem into two parts, separating the debt profile held during the period covered by the business plan from the debt profile (or its projection) in the period beyond the plan.

9.6.1 Debt Profile in the Business Plan Horizon Forecast

The debt profile analysis during the plan horizon requires the availability of complete economic and financial projections. Therefore the plan should show the expected evolution of the equity capital and of the financial structure. This means that it will also be necessary to estimate the dividend distribution patterns since they impact the level of financial leverage.

The easiest and most transparent valuation process usually includes the independent estimation of tax shields. This is due to the fact that,

Exhibit 9.11 Relevant forecasts in evaluating W_{TS} (mln / €)

	t_1	t_2	t_3	t_4	t_5	t_6	t_7
Base scenario							
EBIT	40.2	47.4	55.1	61.2	67.9	73.4	78.3
FCFO	(5.8)	19.2	22.1	25	25.2	29.2	33.6
FINANCIAL DEBT(NET)	86.9	72.6	55.5	37.5	22.1	-	-
DIVIDENDS	9.1	9.9	12	13.8	16.2	18.5	20.8
INTEREST ($K_d = 7.4\%$)	6.4	5.4	4.1	2.8	1.6	-	-
TAX SAVINGS ($t_c = 36\%$)	2.3	1.9	1.5	1	0.6	-	-
Alternative Scenario							
FINANCIAL DEBT	86.9	72.6	60	60	60	60	60
INTEREST ($K_d = 7.4\%$)	6.4	5.4	4.4	4.4	4.4	4.4	4.4
TAX SAVINGS ($t_c = 36\%$)	2.3	1.9	1.6	1.6	1.6	1.6	1.6

during the plan horizon, debt follows dynamics determined by the cash flow generated by the business, the debt repayment plan, and the dividend policy. On the other hand, the use of the aggregated valuation method (discounting the FCFO at the WACC*) is questionable, as it gives approximate results.

Exhibit 9.11 highlights the results for a listed company as estimated by a major investment bank. The expert has integrated the four-year business plan with a three-year projection period in order to verify the debt dynamics and the tax benefits associated with leverage. The analyst concluded that, given the same dividend policy and with no buyback deals, the cash flow would allow the complete repayment of the existing debt.

Based on the aforementioned results, the analyst developed two scenarios for the valuation of tax benefits:

Scenario A: Consistently with the business cash flow generation and the current dividend policy, tax benefits are estimated based on the discounted tax savings throughout the debt repayment period.

Scenario B: A debt *floor* is defined (in this case: 60 million euro). A discussion with the management confirmed that the owners were in favor of taking advantage of moderate leverage. In addition, industry analysts would have favorably considered a leverage level of around 60 million euro (corresponding to a 0.5 debt/equity ratio).

Assuming these scenarios, the valuation of tax benefits during the plan horizon changes as follows:

Scenario A: W_{TS} = 6.2 million/€

Scenario B: W_{TS} = 9.4 million/€

The discounted value of tax savings has been determined using K_d in both scenarios.

9.7 DEBT PROFILE BEYOND THE PLAN HORIZON FORECAST

As mentioned, it is inevitable to use simplified assumptions for the cash flow trend beyond the plan horizon plan. In particular, we assume that:

- Perpetual cash flows are constant.
- Cash flows continue to grow in nominal terms.
- Cash flows continue to grow in real terms with articulated assumptions for the duration of real growth.

The credibility of the assumptions made obviously depends on the business category under consideration.

A similar reasoning can be followed for the cash flow profiles of the tax savings. Choices on tax shields can have a significant impact on the result of the valuation process.

9.8 THE VALUATION OF TAX ADVANTAGES: ALTERNATIVES

After having introduced an overview of the topic, this section discusses the different assumptions that experts consider in the estimation of W_{TS}.

ASSUMPTION 1: THE ABSOLUTE VALUE OF THE NET FINANCIAL DEBT AT THE END OF THE PLAN REMAINS CONSTANT.

W_{TS} can then be determined through the calculation of the present value of perpetual income, that is:

$$W_{TS} = \sum_{t=1}^{\infty} \frac{D_0 \times K_d \times t_c}{(1 + K_{TS})^t}$$

where D_0 = net financial debt at the end of the plan.

If we assume $K_{TS} = K_d$, the formula looks like the one reported in section 3.2:

$$W_{TS} = D_0 \times t_c$$

ASSUMPTION 2: THE AMOUNT OF NET FINANCIAL DEBT REMAINS CONSTANT IN REAL TERMS.

This scenario implies that debt increases with the inflation rate.

W_{TS} can be determined here using the formula of growing returns:

$$W_{TS} = \sum_{t=1}^{\infty} \frac{D_0 \times (1 + g_n)^{t-1} \times K_d \times t_c}{(1 + K_{TS})^t}$$

In a steady-state/no-inflation scenario—that is, with no cash flow growth in real or nominal terms—the assumption under consideration is consistent with the level of debt being constant.

As already noticed in section 4.1, the tax shields should logically be determined based on the average debt level in each period. To simplify, we can, however, use the debt level at either the beginning or the end of each period.

According to the first assumption, preferred by the authors, D_0 measures the amount of debt at the time of the valuation. When the goal is the calculation of the terminal value, it is better to use the net indebtedness existing at the end of the analytical cash flow projection—that is, the debt level at the end of the plan. As seen in section 4.1, the previous formula is then equal to:

$$W_{TS} = \frac{D_0 \times K_d \times t_c}{K_{TS} - g_n}$$

Exhibit 9.12 shows the debt patterns under the two assumptions we just considered.

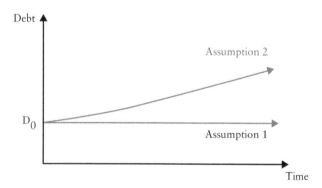

Exhibit 9.12 Debt patterns after the plan horizon forecast (assumptions 1 and 2)

ASSUMPTION 3: WITH REAL GROWTH, THE DEBT PROFILE IS EQUAL TO THE DEBT LEVEL ASSUMED IN THE CASH FLOW (FCFO) PROJECTION.

Under this assumption, debt conforms to the FCFO profile through different growth rates, which can be perpetual, differentiated according to the time period, or limited to a predefined period of time. Exhibit 9.13 graphically shows this concept.

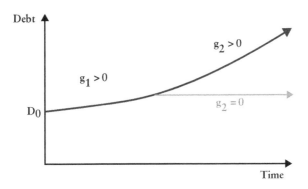

Exhibit 9.13 Debt pattern beyond the plan horizon forecast (assumption 3)

This assumption implies that the debt ratio stays constant over time. In particular, the growth in the value of the business (in nominal and real terms) corresponds to an equivalent increase in leverage.

It is important to remember that, whenever experts determine the terminal value using an aggregated method (i.e., by subtracting the growth rate from the WACC), they implicitly assume that the debt pattern mirrors one of the profiles shown in Exhibit 9.9.

The different relevant formulas are:

1. Constant Growth:

$$W_{\mathrm{TS}} = \sum_{t=1}^{\infty} \frac{D_0 \times (1+g)^{t-1} \times K_{\mathrm{d}} \times t_{\mathrm{c}}}{(1+K_{\mathrm{TS}})^t}$$

from which:

$$W_{\mathrm{TS}} = D_0 \times t_{\mathrm{c}} \times \left(\frac{K_{\mathrm{d}}}{K_{\mathrm{TS}} - g}\right)$$

In the previous formulas, g expresses the total *FCFO* growth rate, which incorporates both the "real" growth rate and inflation dynamics.

In a temporary growth scenario, it is assumed that debt does not even increase in nominal terms once the growth period ends. This assumption can obviously be relaxed if needed.

2. Limited Growth:

$$W_{TS} = \frac{D_0 \times K_d \times t_c \times \left(1 - \frac{(1+g_1)^T}{(1+K_{TS})^T}\right)}{K_{TS} - g_1} + \frac{D_T \times t_c \times K_d}{K_{TS} \times (1+K_{TS})^T}$$

3. Staged Growth:

$$W_{TS} = \frac{D_0 \times K_d \times t_c \times \left(1 - \frac{(1+g_1)^T}{(1+K_{TS})^T}\right)}{K_{TS} - g_1} + \frac{D_T \times t_c \times K_d}{(K_{TS} - g_2) \times (1+K_{TS})^T}$$

ASSUMPTION 4: LEVERAGE AT THE END OF THE PERIOD PROGRESSIVELY DECREASES TO ZERO OR TO A PREDEFINED FLOOR LEVEL.

Exhibit 9.14 graphically shows this assumption.

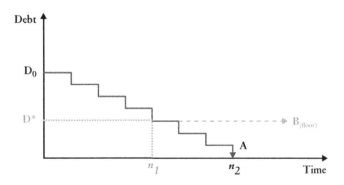

Exhibit 9.14 Debt pattern beyond the plan horizon (assumption 4)

In scenario A, we assume that debt is constantly repaid throughout the plan horizon defined by the analyst. In scenario B, once the desired debt level D^* is reached, debt is instead no longer repaid. The relevant formulas for the tax shields in these cases are the following:

Scenario A:[1]

$$W_{TS} = \sum_{t=1}^{n} \frac{D_0 \times t_c \times K_d \times \left(1 - \frac{(t-1)}{n}\right)}{(1 + K_{TS})^t}$$

Scenario B:

$$W_{TS} = \sum_{t=1}^{n} \frac{D_0 \times t_c \times K_d \times (1 - c \times t)}{(1 + K_{TS})^t} + \frac{D_0 \times (1 - c \times n) \times t_c \times K_d}{K_{TS} \times (1 + K_{TS})^n}$$

where:

- n refers to the number of years of the repayment period
- c refers to the debt repayment rate when there is a lower debt floor D^*:

$$c = \frac{D_0 - D^*}{n \times D_0}$$

Under the assumption that debt decreases to zero, it is possible to assume that first-year repayments are higher than end-of-period repayments. In this case, the analyst could use the discounted cash flow formula for a decreasing annuity:

$$W_{TS} = \frac{D_0 \times (1 - g) \times K_d \times t_c}{K_{TS} + g}$$

where g refers to the decreasing debt rate over an infinite horizon.

Exhibit 9.15 shows debt profiles assuming a constant repayment equal to 10 percent of the initial debt amount (A) and assuming decreasing repayment instalments based on a 10 percent yearly rate (B).

It is interesting to highlight that the W_{TS} values in the two scenarios do not differ significantly as long as we consider normal debt repayment periods (5 to 10 years).

---

[1]This formula is consistent with the assumption that interest is computed based on the level of debt at the beginning of the period. If interest is calculated at the end of the period, then the formula needs to be modified as follows:

$$W_{TS} = \sum_{t=1}^{n} \frac{D_0 \times t_c \times K_d \times \left(1 - \frac{t}{n}\right)}{(1 + K_{TS})^t}.$$

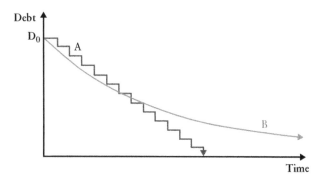

Exhibit 9.15 Debt profiles with constant repayment (A) and decreasing repayment (B)

Before discussing why we may want to relax the assumptions, we will verify their impact on tax benefits in Exhibit 9.16 under the valuation scenario described in section 9.6.

Exhibit 9.16 Valuation of tax benefits (plan horizon)

Assumptions	K_{TS}	W_{TS}	g
1) D constant	K_d	21.6	0
2) D constant in real terms	K_d	27.5	1.50%
3) D increasing at FCFO growth rate	K_d; K_{eu}	36.3	3%
4) D decreasing at 10%	K_d	9.2	−10%

It is necessary to point out that the analyst assumed a growth rate for the FCFO equal to 3 percent over an infinite time horizon in the estimation of the terminal value (this rate is the sum of the real growth rate and the inflation effect, estimated at 1.5 percent).

The alternative scenario assumes a lower debt limit of 60 million euros. W_{TS} is therefore computed based on a final year debt amount of 60 million euros.

W_{TS} has been determined using K_d in scenarios 1, 2, and 4. Two rates have instead been used in scenario 3: K_d for the tax savings of the original debt amount; K_{eu} for the incremental debt amount. If K_{eu} were the only rate used for all debt, we would have obtained a paradoxically lower W_{TS} than the one found in the no-growth scenario.

9.9   GUIDELINES FOR CHOOSING DEBT PATTERNS FOR DETERMINING VALUATIONS

Exhibit 9.16 shows how different choices for the estimate of tax benefits can significantly influence results.

It is important to find the most appropriate and realistic debt pattern to use in the valuation process. Three major guidelines can help experts:

1. *Business cash flows:* Businesses that generate cash flows are usually characterized by low leverage with the exception of abnormal growth periods. When a business generates cash, it is therefore reasonable to assume that debt decreases over, for example, a 10- to 20-year repayment plan.
2. *Book value of assets:* Debt dynamics should be analyzed based on the book value of the company's assets since it would be dangerous to assume that the ratio between debt and assets could exceed acceptable limits.
3. *Value creation role assumed by leverage in a specific industry:* It is useful to mention that leverage is considered an acceptable means of value creation for shareholders only in low risk (and relatively low but stable and visible profitability) industries. In these particular cases, it is then sensible to assume that the debt level increases over a long period or indefinitely.

Going back to one of the examples shown in this paragraph, the investment bank presented two different valuations of its tax benefits:

- In the first scenario, the analyst assumed debt to be repaid by t_5. Tax shields are therefore not considered beyond the plan horizon.
- In the second scenario, the 60 million euro floor is used to determine the *terminal value*. During a discussion with management, it became clear it would be advisable to keep a certain degree of leverage, and to rebalance the financial structure possibly via extraordinary dividend payments and buybacks in favor of shareholders.

Exhibit 9.17 summarizes the valuation of tax shields in both scenarios.

Exhibit 9.17   Valuation of tax shields (mln /€)

	SCENARIO A	SCENARIO B
W_{TS} plan horizon	6.2	9.4
W_{TS} BEYOND THE PLAN HORIZON	-	13.1
W_{TS} total	6.2	22.5

It should be noted that the tax savings for the period beyond the business plan horizon have been discounted at the same $K_{TS} = K_d$ used to determine W_{TS} in the business plan period.

9.10 SYNTHETIC AND ANALYTICAL PROCEDURES VALUATION

The financial model application will be analyzed in this chapter based on the distinction between synthetic and analytic procedure. These procedures will be discussed in further details in the next two chapters.

9.10.1 Synthetic Procedure

The synthetic procedure allows us to follow an easy estimation process over long periods of time. It is called *synthetic,* as it is based on the assumption of some parameters staying constant. In practice, the synthetic procedure can be considered a good method only when some conditions hold. In particular, it is valid under these conditions:

- The company or project under valuation is in an equilibrium situation and it is reasonable to assume that no deviations from equilibrium will happen (*steady state*).
- The company is in an equilibrium situation and we can reasonably assume that some relationships between variables (investments, revenue growth, and margin growth) hold. This produces a growth cash flow model over a long enough period of time (*steady growth*).

For instance, going back to the cash flow model introduced in section 9.2 and considering the case of the hydroelectric company, a synthetic valuation formula would be suitable since the long-term cash flow is very similar to a growing perpetuity in nominal terms. This is due to the regulated price mechanism allowing for a full recovery of inflationary effects.

On the other hand, the cash flow profile of an energy company discussed in this chapter could represent a typical example of long-term growth based on the gradual expansion of the distribution channel.

9.10.2 Analytical Procedure

By contrast, the analytical procedure requires specific cash flow projections over the company's plan horizon. In practice, these processes should be used when the company is not at full capacity due to expansions or contractions, new investments, or new restructuring processes.

Considering the limited length of analytical projections (usually not beyond 10 years), these processes require the need to estimate the company value at the end of the forecasted period. This value is usually known as the *terminal value* (TV).

According to the company's characteristics, the TV can assume two formulations:

1. The *company value in equilibrium*: In this case, the TV is determined following the formulas stemming from the synthetic procedure.
2. The *liquidation value* when the company's life is limited: This scenario can be used, for instance, in the case considered in Exhibit 9.5, regarding the cash flow profiles of a company in the *waste management* industry. Otherwise, it can be used for companies that are under licensing when their licenses will not be renewed.

9.11   THE STANDARD PROCEDURE

Financial analysts generally use a standard process:

- Analytical projections usually cover a period of 3 to 5 years, which can extend up to 7 to 10 years in some industries. They are based on the business plan built by management, while a potential further extension of the plan is added to take specific characteristics of the business into account (e.g., cyclicality).
- The terminal value is estimated based on the normalized cash flow from the last year of explicit forecast, or of the last 2–3 years especially in case of cyclical industry/companies. Hence, the typical cash flow structure is the one shown in Exhibit 9.18.

As an alternative to the process we just discussed—also known as the pure DCF method—the TV is also often estimated through multiples of a sample of listed companies with similar characteristics to the firm under consideration. This alternative will later be presented in detail while analyzing the multiples valuation technique.

As already mentioned, the analytical process horizon is often longer than the standard plan horizon. This fact goes back to the previously highlighted issue of cash flows constituting only a small portion of the company value. Analysts dislike this problem and try to extend the forecast period to partially solve it. While analyzing a valuation outcome, discussions often arise about the portion of the company value, respectively represented by the terminal value and by cash flow projections.

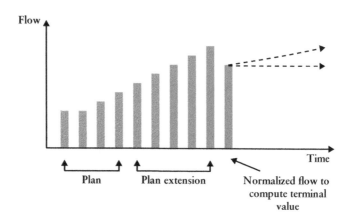

Exhibit 9.18 Typical cash flow projection in DCF valuations

In practice, the portion represented by the plan is relevant for two reasons:

1. It is a risk measure. As a matter of fact, if the flows over the following five to seven years represent a small portion of the company value (e.g., around 20 percent), the estimated outcomes are quite sensitive to the assumptions made in the terminal value determination.
2. If the cash flow plan represents a small portion of the company value, debt financing of an acquisition could be more complex.

Beside the aforementioned reasons, there are no other justifications why the TV should be above or below a specific percentage of the total estimated value.

## CHAPTER 10

A Steady State Cash Flow Model

10.1   VALUE AS A FUNCTION OF DISCOUNTED FUTURE RESULTS

In this chapter, we will discuss the three models based on the principle that corporate (and equity value) is a function of the discounted expected future results of a company:

- The first one is based on the formula of capitalization of normalized results. The crucial aspect of this model in the context of company valuation is the assumption that value is linearly dependent on long-term results.
- The second is a growth model in real terms. The crucial elements for the valuation are the factors on which growth is based—that is, the amount of investment necessary to sustain the company's growth and future profitability.
- Third, the multi-stage valuation model, which is based on the concept of limited periods of growth.

The discussion across this and the next chapter will follow this outline:

- Use of a methodology, the Adjusted Present Value (APV), that separately value the unlevered assets of a company and its tax shields distinct
- Proof of the equivalence of the first approach (APV) with the discounted FCFO model and the discounted FCFE model respectively

The equivalence of the results obtained through the different procedures will help us better understand the assumptions implied by the different models.

10.2 CAPITALIZATION OF A NORMALIZED MONETARY FLOW

Under the *steady-state* scenario, it is assumed that the company can sustain its average cash flow in the long-term through average yearly investments equal to the yearly depreciation. The absence of growth for the company implies that the working capital remains constant. The FCFO therefore coincides with the operating income net of taxes [EBIT $\times$ (1 − t_c)] while the FCFE is equal to the company's net income (NI).

Based on previous discussions, the valuation process is quite easy. The value could be determined by simply applying the capitalization formula to the average results projected by experts.

However, it is necessary to realize that capitalization formulas rely on many assumptions, including the fact that cash flows converge to the industry growth rate in the long run and the fact that the discount rate reflects expected price changes as well.

10.2.1 Steady-State Business under Inflationary Conditions

To analyze the issues linked to the use of capitalization formulas, it is necessary to clarify all the different critical aspects.

As previously seen, the assumption that the company needs to be in equilibrium (i.e., in a *steady state*) is fundamental for the use of synthetic valuation formulas. In particular, in a neutral inflation scenario, the most important assumptions implied by the model are:

The steady-state scenario without real terms growth implies:

- Constant revenues and costs
- New investment equal to yearly depreciation and absence of working capital changes
- A constant debt ratio

When all the aforementioned assumptions hold, cash flows are perpetual and net income is equal to the cash flow available for the shareholders (FCFE).

The neutral inflation scenario requires:

- Uniform price increases of products and services.
- Discount rates reflecting expected price changes.

- No increases in working capital needs; this is consistent with the assumption that current assets are balanced by current liabilities.
- No "paper profit". This implies that tax-deductible depreciation adjusts to match net investments and that inventory is valued with the LIFO method.

By combining the steady-state assumption with that of neutral inflation, we can define the following equilibrium state for a company:

- Revenues and costs increase linearly every year.
- Net operating cash flow (FCFO) increases proportionally to the inflation rate every year.
- Net financial debt increases every year proportionally to the inflation rate. As a matter of fact, if it did not, the debt ratio would decrease assuming that operating capital increases in nominal terms proportionally to the inflation rate. This would conflict with the steady-state assumption and it would require a different modeling of K_{el}^* and $WACC^*$.
- Due to the previous assumption, the FCFE is higher than net income by an amount equal to $(D \times p)$, which is equal to the increase in debt necessary to maintain the target leverage.

10.2.2   An Illustration of the Steady-State/Neutral Inflation Assumption

Exhibit 10.1 shows the cash flow dynamics of a company when the *steady-state* assumption is combined with a neutral inflation scenario. In particular, we assume that at time zero (T_0) prevailing expectation is a 10 percent annual inflation rate. Notice that this inflation rate is particularly high to emphasize its effects.

Column 2 in the table reports the basic data in a company's income statement in a no-inflation scenario $(g_n = 0)$. On the other hand, the other three columns show the results and cash flows for a neutral inflation scenario. The comparison between column 2 and the other three shows the effects of an inflation jump (from 0 to 10 percent).

The analysis of the last three columns allows us to understand the results and cash flow dynamics in a scenario with inflation (in other words, the analysis of the last three columns allows us to understand the dynamics of the results when inflation is stable at the 10 percent level).

Exhibit 10.1 Steady-state/neutral inflation scenario

Inflation rate	$p = 0$	$p = 10\%$		
	t_{-1}	t_0	t_1	t_2
Operating margin	3,000	3,300	3,630	3,993
Depreciation	(500)	(550)	(605)	(665.5)
Operating result	2,500	2,750	3,025	3,327.5
Interests	(200)	(620)	(682)	(750.2)
Taxes	(828)	(766.8)	(843.5)	(927.8)
Net income	1,472	1,363.2	1,499.5	1,649.5
Leverage at the end of period	4,000	4,400	4,840	5,324
FCFO	1,600	1,760	1,936	2,129.6
FCFE	1,472	1,763	1,939.5	2,133.5
W_{equity}	17,440	22,064	24,270	26,697
D/E	22.9%	19.9%	19.9%	19.9%

The Effects of an Inflation Jump By comparing columns 2 and 3 in Exhibit 10.1 we can observe the following:

- The operating income and the FCFO increase by the same percentage as the inflation rate.[1]
- Interest increases more than the inflation rate as interest rates include expected price changes based on the Fisher principle (see section 4.2). In our example, in the case of zero inflation, the interest rate is assumed to be equal to 5 percent. When the inflation rate is 10 percent, the interest rate becomes:

$$i_{nominal} = (1 + 0.10) \times (1 + 0.05) - 1 = 15.5\%$$

- The FCFE increases more than the inflation rate because net financial debt is supposed to grow proportionally to the inflation rate so that the debt ratio remains unchanged. In particular, the FCFE at T_0 is equal to

---

[1] For the sake of simplicity, we assume that the price change occurs at the beginning of every period.

the sum of the net income (which also measures cash flows based on previous assumptions) and the increase in debt in the same period (400).

- The tax impact on the FCFE decreases since nominal interest, which includes the portion necessary to maintain the real value of the borrowed capital unchanged, is fully deductible.[2]

At this point, we can conclude that, in a steady-state/neutral inflation scenario, the company value will have to increase proportionally to higher tax savings due to increased interest.

Even though the previous statement is theoretically correct, only a few companies take advantage of an inflation scenario in practice. Many others are in fact penalized. This is due to the fact that revenues and costs are not always linearly related and the company's working capital therefore needs adjustments. This case has not been considered in our analysis since we assume that current assets and current liabilities are balanced.

Cash Flow Dynamic in an Inflation Scenario The last three columns of Exhibit 10.1 show that the FCFO and the FCFE increase in nominal terms linearly to the inflation rate under a constant inflation rate. It is important to highlight that even interests increase linearly to the inflation rate. As a matter of fact, after the inflation jump, net debt increases annually in a linear fashion with respect to g_n. This adjustment is necessary to maintain the debt ratio constant.

Let us now verify how the company value can be determined. Let us assume the following parameters:

- Real K_{eu}: 8%
- Nominal K_{eu}: 18.8%
- Real K_d: 5%
- Nominal K_d: 15.5%
- t_c: 36%

Notice that the valuation takes place at the end of T_0.

---

[2]In case of neutral inflation, interest can be ideally divided into two parts: the first one represents the actual return on the borrowed capital; the second one, $(D \times p)$, represents a simple cash adjustment to keep the real value of the financing unchanged. Therefore, only the first part is a "cost" for the company. However, companies can fully deduct interests, including the second part, and take advantage, in the case of neutral inflation, of the tax system. This thesis was popular during the 1970s thanks to articles by F. Modigliani (F. Modigliani, R. Cohn, "Inflation, Rational Valuation and the Market," *Financial Analyst Journal* (March/April 1979), pp. 24–42).

Let us begin with the business valuation procedure carried out using the adjusted discount rate approach. Remember that:

Levered enterprise value = *Unlevered enterprise value* + *Tax shield*

$$W_L \quad = \quad W_U \quad + \quad W_{TS}$$

Estimating the Unlevered Value   The unlevered value of the company can be determined as the discount of a perpetuity that grows at the inflation rate (g_n):

$$W_U = \sum_{t=1}^{\infty} \frac{FCFO_0 \times (1 + g_n)^t}{(1 + K_{eu})^t}$$

$$W_U = \frac{FCFO_0 \times (1 + g_n)}{K_{eu} - g_n}$$

$$W_U = \frac{1,760 \times (1 + 0.1)}{0.188 - 0.10} = 22,000 \tag{10.1}$$

Using the Real Rate   The aforementioned formulas can be presented in another form. In particular, we could split K_{eu} into two elements: the real rate and the expected price change, that is:

$$1.188 = (1 + 0.10) \times (1 + 0.08)$$

We can rewrite [10.1] as:

$$W_U = \frac{FCFO_0 \times (1 + g_n)}{K_{eu\_real} + K_{eu\_real} \times g_n + g_n - g_n}$$

from which:

$$W_U = \frac{FCFO_0 \times (1 + g_n)}{K_{eu\_real} \times (1 + g_n)}$$

which can be simplified as:

$$W_U = \frac{FCFO_0}{K_{eu\_real}} \tag{10.2}$$

The new expression shows a well-known concept. As a matter of fact, in a neutral inflation scenario, the value of an asset generating cash flows and changing proportionally to the inflation rate can be determined by discounting the real cash flow by a real discount rate.

In the example shown in Exhibit 10.1, we obtain:

$$W_U = \frac{1,760}{0.08} = 22,000$$

Tax Shield Valuation   Assuming the steady-state/neutral inflation scenario, we know that the value of debt will have to be adjusted for inflation every year. The tax shield value will therefore be equal to:

$$W_{TS} = \sum_{t=1}^{\infty} \frac{D_0 \times (1+g_n)^{t-1} \times K_d \times t_c}{(1+K_{TS})^t}$$

$$W_{TS} = \frac{D_0 \times K_d \times t_c}{K_{TS} - g_n}$$

$$W_{TS} = D_0 \times \frac{K_d}{K_{TS} - g_n} \times t_c \qquad (10.3)^3$$

It is important to highlight that D_0 measures the level of debt at the beginning of the period used in estimations. The reason for this choice comes from the assumption that the first interest costs, and therefore the first tax shield, is determined based on the current debt level at the beginning of the

---

[3]It is interesting to note that as in the case of W_U, if we assume $K_{TS} = K_d$, [10.3] can be expressed with an alternate approach by decomposing K_d through the Fisher formula:

$$W_{TS} = \left[\frac{\frac{D_0 \times K_{d\_nom} \times t_c}{(1+g_n)}}{K_{d\_real}} \right]$$

As a matter of fact:

$$W_{TS} = \frac{4,400}{(1+0.1)} \times \frac{0.155}{0.05} \times 0.36 = 4,464$$

Note that in both [7.2] and [7.4], the FCFO and $(D_0 \times K_{d\_nom} \times t_c)$ are expressed net of price changes in T_1. It could seem paradoxical that the tax shield is greater than the debt itself, but the outcome is consistent with the fact that the business can deduct interest up to three times the "real" interest.

period. Interest should, however, be calculated based on the average level of debt for the period under consideration. This is dealt with using acceptable simplification.

In our example, assuming $K_{TS} = K_d$, we find:

$$W_{TS} = 4,400 \times \frac{0.155}{0.155 - 0.10} \times 0.36 = 4,464$$

Determining the Levered Value We can now determine the enterprise levered value as:

$$W_L = W_U + W_{TS}$$
$$W_L = 22,000 + 4,464 = 26,464$$

Note that both the unlevered value and W_{TS} increase in value every year due to inflation. As a matter of fact, also the amount of nominal debt increases linearly to g_n.

This confirms our conclusion that the unlevered and levered company values increase systematically proportionally to the inflation rate in a steady-state/neutral inflation scenario. Even more importantly, this means that both levered and unlevered companies keep their real value unchanged.

Once W_L is known, we can then determine the equity value:

$$W_{equity} = W_L - D$$
$$W_{equity} = 26,464 - 4,400 = 22,064$$

The amount of debt at the end of T_0 is subtracted from W_L to determine the value of equity. D is then the level of debt at the time of the valuation.

10.2.3 Discount Rate Adjustment Approach

We can now determine the value of the company using adjusted discount rate formulas. To do so, it is necessary to use the formulas presented in the previous chapters for a growth scenario. In particular, the proper formulation is the one consistent with the discount of tax benefits at the rate K_d.

Equity-Side Approach Let us begin with the *equity-side* approach:

$$W_{equity} = \frac{FCFE_0(1 + g_n)}{K_{el}^* - g_n}$$

K_{el}^* can be determined through the following formula introduced in previous chapters

$$K_{el}^* = K_{eu} + [K_{eu} - K_d] \times \left(1 - t_c \times \frac{K_d}{K_d - g_n}\right) \times \frac{D_0}{E}$$

In our case, we find that:

$$K_{el}^* = 0.188 + (0.188 - 0.155) \times \left(1 - 0.36 \times \frac{0.155}{0.155 - 0.1}\right) \times \frac{4{,}400}{22{,}064}$$

$$K_{el}^* = 0.187904$$

$$W_{equity} = \frac{FCFE_0(1 + g_n)}{K_{el}^* - g_n} = \frac{1{,}939.5}{0.1879 - 0.1} = 22{,}064$$

Interestingly, K_{el}^* is paradoxically lower than K_{eu}, even if by a small amount. This seems illogical since the risk taken by shareholders is higher when the company is levered. However, we have to go back to the previous results to understand how this result is in fact correct. As we discussed then, the opportunity cost of capital will increase less when tax benefits are present than when they are not. This emphasizes the incremental flow for shareholders coming from tax shields. In our example, tax benefits are so high that $(1 - t_c \times \frac{K_d}{K_d - g_n})$ becomes negative. The tax shield value to shareholders is then greater than the loss of value caused by the worsened risk profile caused by higher leverage.

Asset Side Approach   We can now consider the asset side approach:

$$W_{assets} = \frac{FCFO_0(1 + g_n)}{WACC^* - g_n}$$

Based on our example, we can determine that:

$$WACC^* = 0.1879 \times \frac{22{,}064}{26{,}464} + 0.155 \times (1 - 0.36) \times \frac{4{,}400}{26{,}464}$$

$$WACC^* = 17.315\%$$

And the value is:

$$W_{assets} = \frac{1{,}760 \times 1.1}{0.17315 - 0.1} = 26{,}464$$

Some Concluding Remarks Our previous discussion introduced all the assumptions and valuation formulas in a steady-state/neutral inflation scenario. It also highlighted the links between the asset-side and equity-side methods.

Nevertheless, the criteria used for the calculation of the company value are particularly aggressive[4] for the following reasons:

1. As previously mentioned, the neutral inflation hypothesis cannot be accepted for all companies. There are many reasons why this assumption might not hold:
   a. In some industries, revenues do not readily adjust to costs and replacement costs increase by more than the inflation rate.
   b. The tax system does not allow for the revaluation of depreciation (except in those countries where inflation is very high and where the technique of inflation accounting is admitted).
   c. The assumption that inflation does not cause an increase in working capital is not realistic.
2. The previously developed method implies that the business maintains a constant leverage in real terms. Being inconsistent with this assumption may cause severe bias in the valuation output.
3. If tax benefits from debt are estimated including personal taxes, it is possible that the benefits coming from the deductibility of nominal interest would disappear. As a matter of fact, if nominal interest on business debt is taxed this way, the underwriters of the debt will experience a zero-sum game between their taxes and the benefit obtained by the business.

All this considered, when inflation was a big problem, financial economists concluded that the tax benefit from nominal interest could have offset the disadvantage of not being able to adjust depreciation. On the other hand, the tax benefit could have very rarely created shareholder value (with respect to the scenario with no inflation) contrary to what our previous discussions showed.

---

[4]The adjective *aggressive* is used to indicate a superficial use of valuation formulas. The expression is borrowed by T. Copeland, T. Koller, and J. Murrin, *Valuation: Measuring and Managing the Value of Companies* (New York: John Wiley & Sons, 1994), p. 283.

10.2.4 Summary of Valuation Formulas Consistent with a Steady-State/Neutral Inflation Scenario

Exhibit 10.2 presents a summary of valuation formulas consistent with the steady-state/neutral inflation hypothesis:

Exhibit 10.2 Valuation formulas in steady-state/neutral inflation scenario

ASSETS SIDE	APV APPROACH	$$W_{assets} = \frac{FCFO_1}{K_{eu} - g_n} + D_0 \times t_c \times \frac{K_d}{K_d - g_n}$$
	STANDARD APPROACH	$$W_{assets} = \frac{FCFO_1}{WACC * - g_n}$$
EQUITY SIDE	STANDARD APPROACH	$$W_{equity} = \frac{FCFE_1}{K_{el}^* - g_n}$$

To simplify, let us quickly review the meaning of the above symbols:

- W_{assets}: value of the operating capital (asset value)
- FCFO: operating cash flow

- *WACC**: weighted average cost of capital when tax shields are present as determined by using [d.1]
- W_{equity}: equity value
- FCFE: cash flow available to shareholders
- K^*_{el}: cost of equity, when tax shields are present as determined by using [d]
- K_{eu}: cost of equity of an unlevered company
- g_n: expected inflation rate

At this point, it is important to highlight some important considerations for the application of the above formulas:

- The APV approach has two advantages: transparency and flexibility. Those who perform the valuation appreciate the value component given by W_{TS} and the assumptions behind this scenario—that is, the linear relationship between debt and the inflation rate and the presence of tax shields based on the tax rate t_c.
- However, these assumptions are not always credible. For instance, if the company generates cash, it is more realistic to think that the debt amount will decrease. Under these conditions, the APV approach would work better as it allows us to adjust the tax shield value (W_{TS}) to a debt profile consistent with the business plan, the long-term cash flow, and the leverage policy that the management intends to adopt. These specific aspects will be discussed in detail in the following paragraph when analyzing the "Hydroelectric Co." example.
- On the other hand, adjusted discount rate formulas face another well-known problem. As a matter of fact, as we previously discussed, the debt ratio used to determine K^*_{el} and the $WACC^*$ should be computed on the basis of the economic value of the business, which, in this case, should include the tax benefits linked to the increase in debt.

Therefore, we can conclude that the process of adjusting discount rates is often used in an approximate way and without a thorough analysis of the underlying assumptions. These assumptions, however, are the key to a correct application of the formulas.

10.2.5 Valuing Hydroelectric Co.

The business in this example operates in the electric generation industry.
Assumptions for the valuation:

- The company manages a hydroelectric plant. No expansion of the plant is possible.

- Depreciation is equal, on average, to the investment necessary for the maintenance of the current capacity.
- Management thinks that the current leverage can be maintained in the long term.
- It is assumed that tariffs adjust to costs.
- Current assets and current liabilities tend to balance.

Exhibit 10.3 shows the balance sheet, income statement, FCFO, and FCFE of Hydroelectric Co. at the time of the estimate.

Exhibit 10.3 Hydroelectric Co. financial statements

BALANCE SHEET

ACCOUNTS RECEIVABLE	28,000	ACCOUNTS PAYABLE	30,000
INVENTORY	2,000	FINANCIAL DEBT	100,000
NET FIXED ASSETS	300,000	SHAREHOLDER EQUITY [*]	200,000
	330,000		330,000

[*] Net of income.

INCOME STATEMENT

REVENUES	90,000
OPERATING COSTS	−37,000
OPERATING MARGIN	53,000
DEPRECIATION	−14,000
EBIT	39,000
FINANCIAL INTERESTS	−7,000
TAXES	−14,800
NET INCOME	17,200

	FCFO	FCFE
OPERATING MARGIN	53,000	53,000
INVESTMENTS	−14,000	−14,000
CHANGE IN WORKING CAPITAL	–	–
TAXES	−17,400	−14,800
FINANCIAL INTERESTS	–	−7,000
ADJUSTMENTS OF NOMINAL FINANCIAL DEBT [*]	–	1,961
	21,600	19,161

*Determined as 2% of the financial debt outstanding at the beginning of the period ($98,039 \times 1.02 = 100,000$).

The other important assumptions for the valuation are:

- K_{eu} for the hydroelectric industry (in nominal terms)   8%
- K_d 6.5%
- Expected inflation rate   2%
- t_c 37%

Hydroelectric Co. Valuation: Steady-State/Neutral Inflation Scenario In order to verify the different results obtained following numerous assumptions, we will use the APV approach to value Hydroelectric Co. It implies, as we know, that:

$$W_L = W_U + W_{TS}$$

In this specific case, W_U can be determined as follows:

$$W_U = \frac{FCFO_1}{Keu - g_n}$$

$$W_U \frac{21,600 \times (1.02)}{0.08 - 0.02} = 367,200$$

W_{TS} can be calculated with the following expressions:

$$W_{TS} = D_0 \times t_c \times \frac{K_d}{K_d - g_n}$$

$$W_{TS} = 100,000 \times 0.37 \times \frac{0.065}{0.065 - 0.02} = 53,444$$

From which:

$$W_L = 367,200 + 53,444 = 420,644$$

With the available data, we can finally determine the equity value by subtracting the value of net financial debt from W_{asset} (Exhibit 10.3):

$$W_{equity} = 420,644 - 100,000 = 320,644$$

Alternative Debt Profiles It is now possible to check the sensitivity of the value just computed to various debt profiles.

For instance, by observing that the business model of Hydroelectric Co. constantly generates cash flow, it is logical to believe that the debt level will tend to decrease or to at least stay constant.

Under the assumption of decreasing debt and assuming a 10-year debt repayment plan, the value of tax shields will change as shown in Exhibit 10.4.

Exhibit 10.4 Debt profile

t_1	$100,000 \times 0.065 \times 0.37 = 2,405$
t_2	$90,000 \times 0.065 \times 0.37 = 2,164$
t_3	$80,000 \times 0.065 \times 0.37 = 1,924$
t_4	$70,000 \times 0.065 \times 0.37 = 1,683$
t_5	$60,000 \times 0.065 \times 0.37 = 1,443$
t_6	$50,000 \times 0.065 \times 0.37 = 1,202$
t_7	$40,000 \times 0.065 \times 0.37 = 962$
t_8	$30,000 \times 0.065 \times 0.37 = 721$
t_9	$20,000 \times 0.065 \times 0.37 = 481$
t_{10}	$10,000 \times 0.065 \times 0.37 = 240$

The discounted value of the tax shield series using a discount rate $K_d = 6.5\%$ is 10.4 million. This amount is 80 percent lower than the result given in an increasing debt scenario (53.4 million).

If we consider the assumption that debt stays constant, the tax shields would become:

$$W_{TS} = D_0 \times t_c$$

$$W_{TS} = 100,000 \times 0.37 = 37,000$$

Hydroelectric Co. Valuation: The Adjusted Discount Rate Process It can be interesting to verify our results of the valuation of Hydroelectric Co. with the quick-and-dirty adjusted discount rate process, which is similar to the approaches frequently used in practice.

We calculate the $WACC^*$ on the basis of the book value debt ratio:

$$K_{el}^* = 0.08 + (0.08 - 0.065) \times (1 - 0.37) \times \frac{1}{2}$$

$$K_{el}^* = 8.47\%$$

$$WACC^* = 0.0847 \times 0.66 + 0.065 \times (1 - 0.37) \times 0.33 = 6.94\%$$

Applying the synthetic approach, we find:

$$W_{asset} = \frac{FCFO_1}{WACC* - g_n}$$

$$W_{asset} = \frac{21,600 \times (1 + 0.02)}{0.0694 - 0.02} = 445,992$$

It is interesting to notice that, in a perpetual nominal growth scenario, the value computed under this approach is 25 million greater than the value found through the APV method. Such a result is explained by the use of the book value of debt in the formula, which is higher than the effective one. In fact, economic—and not book—values are supposed to be considered in these formulas. In this specific case, the economic value of equity is significantly higher than the book one, leading to this impressive difference in results.[5]

10.3 THE PERPETUAL GROWTH FORMULA

We analyzed the impact of nominal growth on value in the previous paragraph.

We now consider the scenario of perpetual growth in real terms. To simplify the analysis, we will refer to a no-inflation scenario.

Growth models are presented in every finance book and wherever valuation and securities analysis are discussed because they allow for the simplification of many problems. They are also the basis to analyze more complex models that will be presented later. Growth formulas are also used in other chapters, where we discuss opportunity cost of capital estimates based on current stock prices and theory of multiples.

The perpetual growth model can be useful to value a business when the business model and the industrial context are such to believe that the cash flow will grow in the long term (at least 20 to 30 years). Therefore, it is better to apply this method to industries that grow in line with the whole economy (e.g. utility companies). Alternatively, it is better to use models based on limited growth assumptions.

10.3.1 Perpetual Growth Model for Unlevered Companies

The perpetual growth model applied to unlevered businesses, that is, to companies with no debt, is known as the *Gordon model*, named after Myron Gordon, the person who spread its use in the United States of America during the 1950s and 1960s.[6]

---

[5]The difference between the two estimates (€421 million and 446 million) depends on two factors pushing in opposite directions: (1) the book leverage level (our case), which increases the value of tax shields; (2) the use of the *WACC**, which implies lower tax shields.

[6]M. Gordon and E. Shapiro, "Capital Equipment Analysis: The Required Rate of Profit," *Management Science* (October 3, 1956): 102–110.

The formula to compute the value of an unlevered company can be presented as follows (notice that when there is no debt, the FCFO and the FCFE coincide):

$$W_{equity} = \frac{FCFE_1}{K_{eu} - g_r} \tag{10.5}$$

Let us use an example to better discuss its meaning. Assume that the income statement of a company is:

- EBIT   2,500
- Interests   0
- Taxes (37%)   (925)
- Net income   1,575

The cash flow dynamic is shown in Exhibit 10.5. The dashed line parallel to the horizontal axis shows the net cash flow of the business available to shareholders (FCFE) in a steady-state scenario. The flow is equal to 1,575 from T_0 to infinity since there are no new investments except renewals, which are equivalent to depreciation in a steady-state scenario.

What happens when the company invests 20 percent of its cash flow in new investments for each period? The rate of return for these new investments net of taxes is expected to be 12 percent.

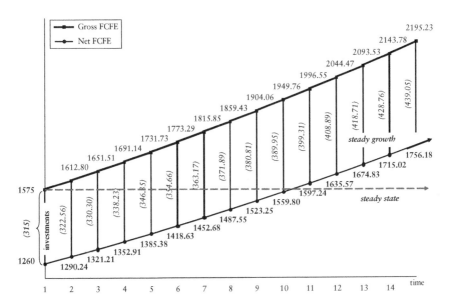

Exhibit 10.5 Cash flow dynamic in a constant-growth scenario

The FCFE at time T_1 is equal to 1,260 (20 percent less than the flow in the steady-state scenario). Furthermore, notice that from T_2 onward, the cash flow is no longer equal to 1,575, but to 1,612.8 since the reinvestment of 315 in T_1 increases the future flow by 37.8 from T_1 to infinity. It is important to mention that the 12 percent rate of return is determined by dividing the reinvested equity amount by the incremental amount net of depreciation. We also assume that depreciation contributes to the systematic renewal of the reinvestment in T_1.[7]

In T_2, the business reinvests 20 percent of its cash flow in the same period (1,612.8). Consequently, the gross cash flow is equal to 1,651.5 (i.e., the sum of the flow in T_2 and the incremental flow of the new investment) from T_3 to infinity. The growth process is limited to a few periods in the table. Nevertheless, we can imagine a scenario in which this recurs for an unlimited period of time.

Characteristics of the Gordon Model We can now finally introduce some of the major characteristics of this model and its implications:

1. The net cash flow distributable as shareholder dividends grows at a constant rate (g_r) equal to 2.4 percent:

1,260	1,290.24	1,321.2	1,352.9	. . . . ∞
T_1	T_2	T_3	T_4	. . . . ∞

2. The flow before new investments and reinvestments grows at the same rate g_r.
3. The rate gr is equal to the rate of return expected from new investments multiplied by the cash reinvestment ratio:

$$g_r = \frac{\text{incremental net income}}{\text{reinvestment}} \times \frac{\text{reinvested flow}}{\text{generated flow}}$$

In our example:

$$g_r = 0.12 \times 0.20 = 2.4\%$$

1. The company value grows yearly based on the same rate g_r. As a matter of fact, based on equation [10.5]:

$$W_{0\_equity} = \frac{FCFE_1}{K_{eu} - g_r} \quad W_{1\_equity} = \frac{FCFE_2}{K_{eu} - g_r}$$

---

[7] In fact: 37.8/315 = 12%.

Assuming K_{eu} is equal to 10 percent, then:

- In T_0: $W_{0\ equity} = \dfrac{1.60}{0.10 - 0.024} = 16{,}578.9$

- In T_1: $W_{1\ equity} = \dfrac{1{,}290.24}{0.10 - 0.024} = 16{,}976.8$

It is easy to see that $W_{1\ equity}$ is equal to $W_{0\ equity} \times (1 + g_r)$. As a matter of fact:

$$16{,}578.9 \times (1 + 0.024) = 16{,}976.8$$

1. The value of the business, in a growth scenario, is equal to the sum of the base value calculated in a no-growth scenario (i.e., in the steady-state scenario) and the net present value of the growth opportunities (NPVGO):

$$W \text{ of a growth business} = W_{base} + NPVGO$$

In our example, the base value can be computed by discounting the steady-state scenario FCFE:

$$W_{base} = \frac{FCFE\ steady\ state}{K_{eu}}$$

$$W_{base} = \frac{1{,}575}{0.10} = 15{,}750$$

On the other hand, NPVGO is equal to the net present value of reinvestments. To be precise, in T_1, we will have:

$$NPVGO_1 = (315) + \frac{37.8}{0.10} = 63$$

In T_2:

$$NPVGO_2 = (322.56) + \frac{38.71}{0.10} = 64.51$$

This calculation could be replicated in T_2 and so on, as long as the firm continues to grow. The cumulate NPVGO of all those reinvestments can be expressed as:

$$NPVGO = \frac{63}{(1 + 0.10)} + \frac{64.51}{(1 + 0.10)^2} + \ldots\ldots \ldots\ldots + \infty$$

The above calculation, in a perpetual growth scenario, has an infinite number of factors. However, it can be simplified if we consider that the reinvested sums grow at a constant rate gr and the return on new investments stays constant. Hence, the net present value (NPV) will also grow at a constant rate g_r. The previous expression then becomes:

$$\frac{63}{(1.10)} + \frac{63 \times (1 + 0.024)}{(1.10)^2} + \frac{63 \times (1 + 0.024)^2}{(1.10)^3} + \dots\dots + \infty$$

It represents a growing perpetuity at a constant rate, the value of which can be computed using the following formula:[8]

$$NPVGO = \frac{63}{(0.10 - 0.024)} = 828.9$$

At this point we can verify how the value of a business is formed. Remember that:

- Value of a company in a growth scenario $= W_{base} + NPVGO$

Hence:

- Value of a company in a growth scenario $= \dfrac{1{,}575}{0.10} + \dfrac{63}{(0.10 - 0.024)} = 16{,}578.9$

The value we just computed is equal to the one we found using the Gordon model in period T_0. As a matter of fact:

$$W_{equity} = \frac{FCFE_1}{K_{eu} - g_r}$$

$$W_{equity} = \frac{1{,}260}{(0.10 - 0.024)} = 16{,}578.9$$

The business valuation model in a growth scenario can be used to verify some well-known principles from which valuation rules derive. In our previous example, we assumed that the return on new investment (12 percent) was greater than the cost of capital (10 percent). Intuitively, we can then state that the growth process creates value in this case. Let us now check what happens if ROE $= K_e = 10$ percent by modifying Exhibit 10.5.

---

[8]This formula is used to compute the net present value of a perpetual yield that grows at a constant rate.

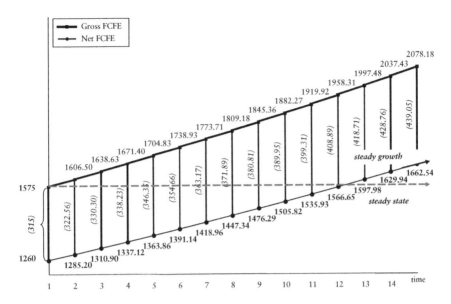

Exhibit 10.6 Flow dynamic in constant growth scenario (ROE = K_e)

In Exhibit 10.6, g_r is equal to 2 percent. As a matter of fact:

$$g_r = \text{ROE} \times \text{Flow reinvestment rate}$$
$$g_r = 0.10 \times 0.20 = 0.02$$

Let us now determine the value of the company by using both the steady-state approach and the Gordon model:

- Steady-state approach: $W_{\text{equity}} = \dfrac{1,575}{0.10} = 15,750$

- Gordon model: $W_{\text{equity}} = \dfrac{1,260}{0.10 - 0.02} = 15,750$

We can now state the following:

1. The base value of the business under consideration is exactly equal to the one computed using the Gordon model. This conclusion can be surprising once we observe that the business's cash flow and dividends increase

every year. At the same time, we can observe that the net present value of growth opportunities is systematically null. As a matter of fact:

$$\text{NPVGO}\, T_1 = (315) + \frac{31.5}{0.10} = 0$$

The company then increases in size (due to the increase in investments and cash flow), but not in value.

2. When the return on new investment equals the cost of capital, the value of the company can be computed by applying the perpetuity formula, that is, by simply discounting the steady-state cash flow. This does not mean that the size of the company or its corresponding cash flows will not grow, but it simply implies that there is no corresponding value creation.

3. The value of the company grows in time simply as a reflection of the reinvested sums:

$$W_0 = \frac{1,260}{(0.10 - 0.02)} = 15,750$$

$$W_1 = \frac{1,285.2}{(0.10 - 0.02)} = 16,065$$

From T_0 to T_1, the value of the company has grown by 315, which is equal to the amount of money not distributed to shareholders and reinvested into the company.

1. If ROE $< K_e$, the growth process destroys value because the NPVGO is negative. We can see this discussing our previous example and assuming that the new investment rate of return is equal to 8 percent. In this case, assuming that the reinvestment is equal to 20 percent of the flow, g_r equals:

$$g_r = 0.08 \times 0.2 = 1.6\%$$

Consequently, the value computed with the Gordon model is:

$$W_{\text{equity}} = \frac{1,260}{(0.10 - 0.016)} = 15,000$$

By comparing these results with the base value with no investments, we can easily see that the company has destroyed shareholder value by an amount equal to 750.

10.3.2   Constant Growth Model for Levered Companies (APV Approach)

We have shown that the value of the company increases proportionally to the g_r rate when cash flows grow, conditionally to the new investment rate being equal to or greater than the opportunity cost of capital. Assuming that the level of leverage remains constant, the growth process implies that net financial debt will grow year-by-year based on gr. In fact, if this were not the case, the market value of leverage would tend to decrease.

Let us now analyze the problems linked with the application of growth formulas to levered companies. We will start with the APV approach.

Refer back to our previous example and assume that:

- The operating cash flow (FCFO) reinvestment rate is equal to 20 percent.
- The new investment rate of return on the operating capital is 12 percent.

Also assume the following:

- Net financial debt: 5000
- Interest rate (K_d): 5%

Based on these new assumptions, the company's income statement now reports the following results:

Operating result	2,500
Interests	(250)
Net income before taxes	**2,250**
Taxes (37%)	(832.5)
Net income (FCFE)	**1,417.5**

As we know, the levered value of the company is equal to the sum of its unlevered value and the value of the net tax shield:

- Unlevered value of the company in a growth scenario:

$$W_U = \frac{FCFO_1}{K_{eu} - g_r} = \frac{1,575 - 315}{0.10 - 0.024} = 16,578.9$$

This value is equal to the one derived in the preceding paragraph.

- Tax shield (when $K_{TS} = K_d$):

$$W_{TS} = \frac{D_0 \times K_d \times t_c}{K_d - g_r} = \frac{5,000 \times 0.05 \times 0.37}{0.05 - 0.024} = 3,557.7$$

It is important to highlight that D_0 is equal to 5,000 because it is assumed that the company will make its first investment at the end of T_1 and it will take on debt at the same time. Therefore, the first tax shield refers to current debt (=5000)

■ Levered company value:

$$W_L = 16,578.9 + 3,557.7 = 20,136.6$$

As in the example discussed in the previous paragraph, the computed value can be divided into two parts: the base value and the net present value of growth opportunities. Using the data from the previous example, we have the following:

■ Unlevered NPVGO: $-315 + \dfrac{37.8}{0.10} = 63$

■ Tax shield value: $120 \times 0.37 = 44.4$

The unlevered NPVGO is equal to the difference between the total investment in T_1 and the net present value of the incremental flow (FCFO). The tax shield from the investment in T_1 is equal to the debt undertaken to finance the investment multiplied by the tax rate. This tax rate expresses the savings linked to the tax shield (in the case of a perpetuity: $W_{TS} = D \times t_c$).

The expected value of all growth opportunities is:

■ *Unlevered NPVGO* $= \dfrac{63}{0.10 - 0.024} = 828.9$

■ *Tax shield* $= \dfrac{44.4}{0.05 - 0.024} = 1,707.7$

To summarize, we can break up and reaggregate the components of the value of the company as determined by the APV approach:

Unlevered base value[9]	15,750.0
Unlevered NPVGO	828.9
Unlevered value in growth scenario	16,578.9
Base value of tax shields	1,850.0
Value of incremental tax shields	1,707.7
Unlevered company value in growth scenario	20,136.6

Our previous discussion highlights a very important conclusion: the creation of value in a growth scenario is mostly due to the incremental tax shield

---

[9]The 15,750.0 is the value we found in the previous section.

linked to the increase (based on g_r) in debt. This is another crucial point to bear in mind when using the constant growth models. As a matter of fact:

- The rate leading to the exact value of the tax shield can be less than t_c.
- It is not certain that the company can systematically use tax shields related to its interest payments.
- The hypothesis of using K_d in order to discount the incremental tax shields is not at all prudent. In our previous example, if W_{TS} were to be determined using K_{eu}, the tax shield value would consistently decrease from 1707.7 to 291.1. As a matter of fact:
- The tax shield value from the first reinvestment is:

$$W_{TS1} = \frac{(5,000 \times 0.024 \times 0.05 \times 0.37)}{0.10} = 22.2$$

- The net present value of all tax shields instead equals:

$$W_{TS} = \frac{(5,000 \times 0.024 \times 0.05 \times 0.37)}{0.10 - 0.024} = 291.1$$

10.3.3 Discount Rate Adjustment Methods

In the perpetual growth scenario, the use of the adjusted discount rate formulas requires the same caution as the nominal growth approach discussed in the previous subsection. Specifically:

- We should use the same formulas consistent with the tax shield discount rate chosen by the expert to determine K_{el}^* and the WACC*.
- The debt ratio should be expressed based on the economic equity value, which should include the net present value of the incremental tax shields.

Going back to the value of equity computed through the APV method, it is possible to verify the use of the adjusted discount rate formulas when discounting the tax shields at K_d:

$$W_{equity} = W_{assets} - D$$
$$W_{equity} = 20,136.6 - 5,000 = 15,136.6$$

$$K_{el}^* = 0.10 + (0.10 - 0.05) \times \left(1 - 0.37 \times \frac{0.05}{0.05 - 0.024}\right) \times \frac{5,000}{15,136.6}$$

$$K_{el}^* = 0.1047$$

Once K_{el}^* is computed, we can determine W_{equity} with the usual adjusted discount rate process:

$$W_{\text{equity}} = \frac{FCFE_1}{K^*_{el} - g_r}$$

$$W_{\text{equity}} = \frac{1,222.5^{10}}{0.1047 - 0.024} = 15,136.6$$

The value determined above corresponds to the one computed through the APV process. The same result can be obtained starting from the asset-side perspective by using the $WACC^*$ and the $FCFO_1$.

10.3.4   Steady-Growth Scenario: A Wrap-up

Exhibit 10.7 shows a summary of the valuation formulas consistent with a constant growth scenario.

They are similar to those previously examined at the beginning of this chapter. However, the application of these formulae is more complex. To be precise, there could be issues linked to real growth scenarios as well as to the use of K_d in the computation of the net present value of tax shields.

It is also necessary to check the methods used in the computation of the FCFO and the FCFE. In the case of real growth, they should be computed consistently with the reinvestment needed to sustain growth in real terms.

For convenience, we will recall the meaning of the above symbols:

- W_{asset} = operating capital value (asset value)
- W_{equity} = equity value
- $FCFO_1$ = expected operating cash flow at time 1
- $FCFE_1$ = expected equity cash flow at time 1
- $WACC*$ = weighted average cost of capital when tax benefits are present, as determined by using the appropriate formulas and the chosen tax rate
- K^*_{el} = equity cost of capital when there are tax benefits, as determined by the appropriate formulas and the chosen rate
- K_{eu} = equity cost of capital for an unlevered company
- g_r = cash flow growth rate in real terms
- t_c = tax rate
- D_0 = net financial debt at the beginning of the period
- K_d = cost of debt
- K_{TS} = tax benefit discount rate

---

[10]The $FCFE_1$ is obtained by subtracting the value of reinvestments (315) from the $FCFE_0$ (1417.5) and adding the increase in indebtedness (120): 1417.5 − 315 + 120 = 1222.5.

Exhibit 10.7 Valuation formulas in a perpetual growth scenario

ASSETS SIDE	APV APPROACH	$$W_{asset} = \frac{FCFO_1}{K_{eu} - g_r} + D_0 \times t_c \times \frac{K_d}{K_{TS} - g_r}$$
	STANDARD APPROACH	$$W_{asset} = \frac{FCFO_1}{WACC^* - g_r}$$
EQUITY SIDE	STANDARD APPROACH	$$W_{equity} = \frac{FCFE_1}{K_{el}^* - g_r}$$

The formulas are the same as those in Exhibit 10.2 in which we assume, however, that the tax benefits are discounted using K_d. This hypothesis can be modified even if we are in a steady-state scenario.

10.4 FORMULAS FOR LIMITED AND VARIABLE (MULTI-STAGE) GROWTH

In the previous section we observed that the perpetual constant growth formula implies an "aggressive" valuation approach. The main issue linked to this method is that we can rarely prove a relationship between unlimited real-term growth of an industry and macroeconomic variables. This assumption mostly holds for companies such as the utility ones.

Apart from these exceptions, it is preferable to assume that growth is limited. As a matter of fact, once the expansion period is over, a company is then characterized by an equilibrium phase (steady state). In such a case, perpetual growth formulas are substituted by limited growth formulas, which are represented as follows:

Exhibit 10.8 Valuation formulas: limited growth

ASSETS SIDE	APV APPROACH	$$W_{asset} = \frac{FCFO_1 \times \left[1 - \frac{(1+g)^T}{(1+K_{eu})^T}\right]}{K_{eu} - g} + \frac{FCFO_{T+1}}{K_{eu} \times (1 + K_{eu})^T}$$ $$+ \frac{D_0 \times K_d \times t_c \times \left[1 - \frac{(1+g)^T}{(1+K_{TS})^T}\right]}{K_{TS} - g} + \frac{D_0 \times K_d \times t_c \times (1 + g)^T}{K_{TS} \times (1 + K_{TS})^T}$$
ASSETS SIDE	STANDARD APPROACH	$$W_{asset} = \frac{FCFO_1 \times \left[1 - \frac{(1+g)^T}{(1+WACC^*)^T}\right]}{WACC^* - g} + \frac{FCFO_{T+1}}{WACC^* \times (1 + WACC^*)^T}$$
EQUITY SIDE	STANDARD APPROACH	$$W_{equity} = \frac{FCFE_1 \times \left[1 - \frac{(1+g)^T}{(1+K_{el}^*)^T}\right]}{K_{el}^* - g} + \frac{FCFE_{T+1}}{K_{el}^* \times (1 + K_{el}^*)^T}$$

It is crucial to highlight that rates are expressed in nominal terms. This means that, once the growth period is over, the FCFO and the tax shields do not increase proportionally to inflation. If such an assumption cannot be proven to hold, the expert should use variable-growth formulas. Assume a value equal to the expected inflation rate for g_2. For simplicity, we will once again remind the reader of the meaning of the above symbols:

- W_{asset} = operating capital value (asset value)
- W_{equity} = equity value
- $FCFO_1$ = expected operating cash flow at time 1
- $FCFE_1$ = expected equity cash flow at time 1
- $WACC^*$ = weighted average cost of capital when tax benefits are present, as determined by using the appropriate formulas and the chosen tax rate
- K_{el}^* = equity cost of capital when there are tax benefits, as determined by the appropriate formulas and the chosen rate
- K_{eu} = equity cost of capital for an unlevered company
- g = (limited) growth rate for cash flows
- t_c = tax rate
- D_0 = net financial debt at the beginning of the period
- K_d = cost of debt
- K_{TS} = discount rate for tax shields

Variable-growth formulas are useful when the valuation assumptions require consideration of different growth rates for different time periods. For instance, they would require a strong growth period for the first few years and then a more moderate growth rate once the exceptional growth is over. Some finance textbooks present what is referred to as a *three-stage formula*. However, for practical purposes, they tend to be a useless complication.

Exhibit 10.9 demonstrates variable-growth formulas, where:

W_{asset} = operating capital value (asset value)
W_{equity} = equity value
$FCFO_1$ = expected operating cash flow at time 1
$FCFE_1$ = expected equity cash flow at time 1
$WACC^*$ = weighted average cost of capital when tax shields are present, as determined by using the appropriate formulas and the chosen tax rate
K_{el}^* = equity cost of capital when there are tax shields, as determined by the appropriate formulas and the chosen rate

K_{eu} = equity cost of capital for an unlevered company
g_1 = cash flow growth rate in the $[1,T]$ period
g_2 = cash flow growth rate from $T+1$
t_c = tax rate
D_0 = net financial debt at the beginning of the period
K_d = cost of debt
K_{TS} = discount rate for tax shields

The above formulas express a two-stage estimate approach. As a matter of fact, it is assumed that the business valuation is based on the hypothesis that cash flows grow at a rate equal to g_1 up to T, and at g_2 from then on.

Exhibit 10.9 Valuation formulas in a variable-growth scenario

ASSETS SIDE	APV APPROACH	$W_{asset} = \dfrac{FCFO_1 \times \left[1 - \frac{(1+g_1)^T}{(1+K_{eu})^T}\right]}{K_{eu} - g_1} + \dfrac{\frac{FCFO_{T+1}}{(K_{eu}-g_2)}}{(1 + K_{eu})^T}$ $+ \dfrac{D_0 \times K_d \times t_c \times \left[1 - \frac{(1+g_1)^T}{(1+K_{TS})^T}\right]}{K_{TS} - g_1} + \dfrac{\frac{D_0 \times t_c \times K_d \times (1+g_1)^T}{(K_{TS}-g_2)}}{(1 + K_{TS})^T}$
	STANDARD APPROACH	$W_{asset} = \dfrac{FCFO_1 \times \left[1 - \frac{(1+g_1)^T}{(1+WACC^*)^T}\right]}{WACC^* - g_1} + \dfrac{\frac{FCFO_{T+1}}{(WACC^*-g_2)}}{(1 + WACC^*)^T}$
EQUITY SIDE	STANDARD APPROACH	$W_{equity} = \dfrac{FCFE_1 \times \left[1 - \frac{(1+g_1)^T}{(1+K_{el}^*)^T}\right]}{K_{el}^* - g_1} + \dfrac{\frac{FCFE_{T+1}}{(K_{el}^*-g_2)}}{(1 + K_{el}^*)^T}$

10.5 CONCLUSIONS

Limited- and variable-growth formulas do not require to be analyzed in more depth. The possible application problems and distortions have already been covered in the previous two paragraphs when discussing the formula for the capitalization of expected cash flows and the perpetual constant growth formula.

Generally, limited- and variable-growth formulas are used to make estimates of company values with relatively small g_1 and g_2. Alternatively, it would make more sense to use an analytical valuation process inclusive of a terminal value. As a matter of fact, in these cases, strong growth periods are characterized by changing cash flows, which should be represented explicitly.

In practical applications, g_2 is frequently equal to the expected long-run growth rates of macroeconomic variables such as GDP or the consumption rate. Such an assumption is valid only if it can be proven that there exists a strong correlation between the industry growth rate and GDP. This usually happens, as we have previously mentioned, in public utilities and banking/insurance sectors.

If there is no correlation, g_2 is purely a subjective choice.

Finally, it is important to mention that g_1 and g_2 also incorporate the nominal growth, which is linked to the expected price variation.

It is worth mentioning that, in case of temporary or variable growth, the value obtained by applying the APV approach does not necessarily match the one derived from the procedure based on the standard DCF approach. As already noted, such equivalence holds only when $K_{TS} = K_{eu}$.

## CHAPTER 11

Discounting Cash Flows and Terminal Value

The discount of explicit cash flows year by year and of the terminal value is the most popular technique used by analysts in the international financial community.

When using this approach, two common issues should typically be dealt with:

1. The identification of the time horizon for the explicit projections of cash flow;
2. The appropriate methods used to estimate the terminal value.

11.1   EXPLICIT PROJECTIONS

The *time horizon* of cash flow projections should satisfy various requirements, and in particular:

- Show the cash flow dynamics linked to time periods characterized by financial restructuring of business concerns.
- Show the cash flow dynamics linked to extraordinary investment cycles.
- Analyze growth phases because of competitive imbalances.
- Describe performance dynamics in industries characterized by cyclical trends.

Finally, when the project's duration is tied to the availability of irreplaceable resources, renewals, or concession contracts, the time horizon can correspond to the exhaustion of these resources or the maturity of concession contracts.

We reported that, according to international practice, the length of the explicit projection period varies from 7 to 10 years in low-capital-intensive sectors and extends up to 10 to 15 years in industries whose specific assets tend to have an extremely long economic and technical life (e.g., hydroelectric, petrochemical and steel plants, etc.).

Therefore, analysts usually begin with a business plan that does not exceed three to five years; the plan can then be further extended to cover three to five years more.

As mentioned, the plan extension needs to fulfill a double requirement:

- The entire length of the business cycle should be covered.
- The overall portion of value obtained by discounting the cash flows of the explicit annual projections should be reasonable as compared to the discounted value of the terminal value. This share generally changes according to the business area under consideration (5 to 7 years in low-capital-intensive industries; 10 years and longer in industries with a long economic and technical life of their tangible assets).

11.2 ESTIMATION OF THE TERMINAL VALUE

As previously discussed, a company's terminal value can assume two meanings:

1. The company breakup value
2. The equilibrium value of the company

The first assumption rarely occurs, and it may concern valuation of companies operating with contracts or concessions with a low possibility of renewal as well as projects destined to exhaust their life cycle in a limited time horizon, which can be defined in advance.

The second assumption usually represents the common case under consideration, since the time horizon of a business cannot be defined in advance in most cases.

Therefore, in case of a basic DCF,[1] terminal value can be obtained through one the following procedures:

- Calculation of the net present value of fixed income with a limited or unlimited duration
- Calculation of the net present value of growing income with an unlimited duration
- Calculation of the net present value of income with a limited or variable growth

---

[1] As we will see in Chapters 12 and 13 the terminal value can also be estimated using the multiples method.

In order to elaborate on the formulas used to estimate terminal value, we refer to the discussions presented in previous chapters.

Recall that the two approaches analyzed during the discussion of analytical methods, that is, the adjusting discount rate and adjusting unlevered value approaches, could also be used in the estimation of terminal value.

Exhibit 11.1 illustrates the two alternative methods. To be concise, we represent the calculation of a perpetual constant flow.

Exhibit 11.1   Basic DCF: alternative methods

BASIC DCF—APV APPROACH

		EXPLICIT PROJECTIONS	TERMINAL VALUE
W_{asset}	$W_{UNLEVERED}$:	$\displaystyle\sum_{t=1}^{T}\frac{FCFO_t}{(1+K_{eu})^t}$	$+\dfrac{TV_{unlevered}}{(1+K_{eu})^T}$
	W_{TS}:	$\displaystyle\sum_{t=1}^{T}\frac{D_t \times K_d \times t_c}{(1+K_{TS})^t}$	$+\dfrac{TV_{TS}}{(1+K_{TS})^T}$

BASIC DCF—STANDARD APPROACH

	EXPLICIT PROJECTIONS	TERMINAL VALUE
W_{asset}	$\displaystyle\sum_{t=1}^{T}\frac{FCFO_t}{(1+WACC^*)^t}$	$+\dfrac{TV_{levered}}{(1+WACC^*)^T}$
W_{equity}	$\displaystyle\sum_{t=1}^{T}\frac{FCFE_t}{(1+K_{el}^*)^t}$	$+\dfrac{TV_{levered}}{(1+K_{el}^*)^T}$

Where:

W_{asset}	*operating capital value*
$W_{unlevered}$	*unlevered value*
W_{equity}	*equity value*
WACC*	*weighted average cost of capital*
K^*_{el}	*equity cost of capital*
K_{eu}	*equity cost for an unlevered firm*
FCFO	*free cash flow from operations*
FCFE	*free cash flow to equity*
K_{TS}	*discount rate from tax benefits*
t_c	*company tax rate*
TV unlevered	*terminal value net of tax benefits*
TV levered	*terminal value inclusive of tax benefits*

11.3 EVALUATION OF GAS SUPPLY CO.

We present the valuation case of Gas Supply Co., a utility operating in the distribution of natural gas. The valuation was carried out with the prospect of a public offering.

Considering the trends assumed by analysts, the cash flow profile then looks as in Exhibit 11.2, which we will discuss later.

Looking at Exhibit 11.2, we can conclude that the valuation procedure, consistent with the cash flow profile, is the one that we defined as "explicit with terminal value." Moreover, in this case, the terminal value can be obtained using the formula for the calculation of the net present value of income with a limited or variable growth.

11.3.1 Main Assumptions Concerning the Industry

- The assumptions concerning the evolution of the market of natural gas distribution in cubic meters are expressed in Exhibit 11.3.

It is assumed, moreover, that governmental deregulation of the industry should have led to:

- A gradual adjustment of the tariffs to the industry average since the new calculation procedure will also take qualitative standards such as quality of service and safety into account.
- New competitive dynamics, following the separation of distribution activities from selling activities, which will kick in in two to three years.
- A higher differentiation of the residential market from the industrial market, with the latter characterized by larger quantities and lower margins.

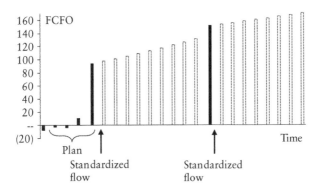

Exhibit 11.2 Gas Supply Co.—profile of free cash flow from operations net of taxes (FCFO) assumed for the evaluation

Exhibit 11.3   Expected consumption of natural gas in Italy

Cubic meters	t0	t1	var %	t2	var %	t3	var %
Residential use	26	26.5	1.90%	27	1.90%	27.5	1.90%
Industrial use	24	24.5	2.10%	25	2%	25.5	2%
Thermoelectric use	21	21.5–22.5	2.4%–7.1%	22–24.5	2.3%–8.9%	23–28	4.5%–14.3%
Overall	71	72.5–73.5	2.1%–3.5%	74–76.5	2.1%–4.1%	76–81	2.7%–5.9%

Climatic conditions are expected to be constant and in line with those recorded in t-1 over the plan horizon, whereas the consumption for residential use could slightly decrease due to a higher efficiency of heating systems.

11.3.2   Company's Strategies

■ *Selective growth* through the acquisition of concessions and of small-to-average size distribution or retail firms able to guarantee wide efficiency recovery margins and distribution synergies. Priority is given to those geographical areas where the firms are already present.
■ *Acquisition of new "large" customers*[2] through targeted offers able to exploit the competitive presence and ability of the group, giving priority to the geographical areas where the group is already present.

On the basis of the aforementioned assumptions and of an accurate analysis of the evolution of revenues and costs element by element, the management has built the budget for Gas Supply Co. over the plan horizon (from t_1 to t_4).

Exhibits 11.4 and 11.5, respectively, show the values of Gas Supply Co.'s assets and liabilities at the date of the evaluation and a summary of its income statement. It is useful to highlight that the high leverage is mainly due to recent important acquisitions in the core business. Exhibit 11.6 shows the cash flows dynamics obtained from the budget prepared by the company's management.

---

[2] "Large" customers are defined here as the users characterized by an annual gas consumption higher than 200,000 m³ who, according to Italian law, can request to buy gas from transporters different from the one that made the connection to the gas network.

Exhibit 11.4 Gas Supply Co.: asset and liability statement (in mln €)

Asset and liability statement 31/12/1999

Receivables	705.9	Payables	218.1
Inventories	9.6	Other operating liabilities	210.6
Net tangible assets	269.2	Retirement indemnity	28.7
Other operating assets	18.7	Financial debts	356
		Equity	190
	1,003.4		1,003.4

Exhibit 11.5 Gas Supply Co.: income statement (in million €)

Income statement 31/12/1999

Revenues	727.2
EBITDA	167.6
EBIT	61.9
Financial charges	21.3
Income before taxes	40.6
Taxes	14.2
Net income	26.4

Exhibit 11.6 Gas Supply Co. cash flow statement (FCFO) (in million €)

	2000	2001	2002	2003
Net operating profit	84,6	79,2	87,6	107,2
Intangible amortizations	7,8	10,3	13,3	16,5
Tangible amortizations	104	112,4	117,3	108,1
Provisions and depreciations	2	2	2,1	2,2
EBITDA	198,4	203,9	220,3	234
Taxes on operating profit	−33,8	−31,7	−35	−42,9
Variations in working capital	10,9	12,6	21,8	19,7
Investments	−187,35	−173,9	−200,5	−191,3
(intangibles)	−32,3	−25	−30	−35
(tangibles)	−155,1	−148,9	−170,5	−156,3
Other variations in tangible assets	5,3	−12,5	−12,8	−13,5
Variations in retirement indemnity and provisions	−1	−0,5	−0,1	4,8
FCFO	−7,55	−2,1	−6,3	10,8

11.3.3 Net Present Value of Cash Flow over the Plan Horizon

Since the valuation is performed using the APV approach, the appropriate cost of capital is K_{eu}, estimated on the basis of the capital asset pricing model discussed in Chapter 8

$$K_{eu} = R_f \; (nominal) + RP \times \beta_u,$$

in which:

- R_f *(nominal)* is the rate of return of a ten-year treasury bond before tax deduction, equal to 5 percent.
- *RP* is the expected *Risk Premium*, estimated at 3.5 percent.
- β_u is equal to 0.6 and corresponds to the average beta of a sample of gas distribution companies listed on European stock exchanges.

On the basis of the identified parameters, K_{eu} has been estimated to be equal to 7.2 percent:

$$K_{eu} = 0.05 + 0.035 \times 0.6 = 7.2\%$$

Present Value of Cash Flow of the Plan   Thus, the net present value of the company's cash flow during the period is shown in Exhibit 11.7.

$$NPV = \sum_{t=1}^{4} a_t \times b_t = (5.8)$$

It is worth it to mention that the net present value is negative due to the relevant investments, which are expected to be made over the plan horizon. We will come back to this point later.

Exhibit 11.7   Discounted cash flows

t	a. FLOW	b. DISCOUNT RATE
1	(7.55)	$(1.072)^{-1}$
2	(2.1)	$(1.072)^{-2}$
3	(6.3)	$(1.072)^{-3}$
4	10.8	$(1.072)^{-4}$

11.3.4   Assumptions to Determine Terminal Value

In the estimation of the terminal value (TV), we will assume that growth, whether internal growth or a growth driven by acquisitions, will gradually decrease.

We can reasonably assume that Gas Supply Co.'s position in the market allows it to continue to pursue an external growth strategy through the acquisition of small competitors.

Nevertheless, taking into account that the competition is expected to increase as a consequence of governmental deregulation of the industry, we prudently assume that Gas Supply Co. can increase the number of users only by 300,000 units over a 10-year period.

With reference to the following period, we will simply assume a growth rate equal to the increase in long-term prices (1.5 percent per year).

On the basis of such a scenario, analysts have described the procedure for the calculation of TV as follows:

Normalization of the FCFO at the End of the Plan   In this specific situation, the process of normalization seeks to estimate the FCFO at the end of the plan in a steady-state context in order to proceed to the estimate of the investment in support of the acquisition campaign of 300,000 new customers in 10 years.

The analysis points out that the amortization allocated for t_4 overvalues the maintenance investment by about €49 million. Thus, there is no growth in this scenario.

Therefore, the normalized FCFO can be calculated as:

EBIT	107.2
Tax (40%)	−42.9
Overestimation of the maintenance investments	40.0
Normalized FCFO	104.3

It is useful to point out that analysts normally adopt this simplified procedure, assuming that variations in working capital and in other minor items are equal to zero in a steady-state context.

Investment in Support of Growth   Investment in support of growth in the number of users is estimated at 10 percent of standardized earnings before interest and taxes (EBIT) and is equal to €10.4 million in t_5. This sum also includes the variation in net working capital.

Estimating g_1 Rate Using this available information, we can estimate the growth rate of the FCFO during the period from t_5 to t_{14}. We need to observe that g_1 is composed of three components:

1. The growth due to the increase in consumption per user, estimated by the analysts to be 1 percent annually.
2. The growth referable to the new investment: the analyst estimates an increase in earnings net of taxes equal to €1.2 million and a level of investments equal to €10.4 million, derived from the expected growth (both organic and by acquisitions of new customers). This leads to a FCFO growth rate equal to 1.15 percent:

$$g = \frac{1.2}{10.4} \times \frac{10.4}{104.4} = 1.15\%$$

Rate of return × Rate of reinvestment

3. The "nominal" growth due to the recovery of cost increases, estimated at about 1.5 percent yearly.

So, the FCFO growth rate during the period from t_5 to t_{14} is estimated by adding up the three preceding elements:

$$"real"g_1 = 1\% + 1.15\% = 2.15\%$$

$$"nominal"g_1 = (1 + 0.0215) \times (1 + 0.015) - 1 = 3.7\%$$

The valuation analysis of Gas Supply Co. underlines that the use of steady-growth models always implies some distortions of corporate reality. As a matter of fact, the growth process will not, in practice, follow the scheme provided by the model: investments will not be distributed uniformly during the period from t_5 to t_{14}.

Nevertheless, the use of the variable growth model for the case we are dealing with can be considered as an acceptable simplification.

Estimating g_2 Rate In the case of Gas Supply Co., the analyst assumes that the FCFO growth—in real terms—ends in the period following t_{14}. Consequently, g_2 simply corresponds to the nominal growth rate (1.5 percent per annually) equal to the expected variation in prices.

11.3.5 Calculating the TV

First Period (t_5–t_{14}) After defining the inputs, the TV can be computed using the familiar formula:

$$TV_1 = \frac{FCFO^* \times \left[1 - \frac{\left(1 + g_1\right)^{10}}{(1 + K_{eu})^{10}} \right]}{K_{eu} - g_1}$$

in which:

FCFO* = the standardized free cash flow, net of the expected reinvestment for t_5: $104.3 - 10.4 = 93.9$

g_1 = the nominal growth rate, equal to 3.7%

K_{eu} = the opportunity cost of unlevered capital, already estimated as 7.2%

Thus, we can apply the previous formula and obtain:[3]

$$TV_1 = \frac{93.9 \times (1 + 0.015) \times \left(1 - \dfrac{1.438}{2.004}\right)}{0.072 - 0.037} = 769.1$$

Second Period (after t_{14}) The portion of the TV referring to the second period could be obtained by applying the following formula:

$$TV_2 = \frac{FCFO^*}{(K_{eu} - g_2) \times (1 + K_{eu})^{10}}$$

The FCFO* represents the free cash flow in t_{15}, gross of implicit reinvestment of the same year, since we assume that from t_{15} forward the company will not face situations of "real" growth, which involve the necessity of reinvesting a portion of the FCFO.

Thus, the FCFO* can be easily obtained calculating the amount of the standardized FCFO, already determined with respect to t_{14}:

$$FCFO^* = 104.3 \times (1 + 0.037)^{10} = 150$$

Applying the previous formula:

$$TV_2 = \frac{150 \times (1 + 0.015)}{(0.072 - 0.015) \times (1 + 0.072)^{10}} = 1{,}332.7$$

The Overall TV Summing up the two components of the terminal value, we obtain:

$$TV = 769.1 + 1{,}332.7 = 2{,}101.8$$

The value of the TV we just calculated refers to the end of the plan horizon. Thus, it needs to be discounted back to the valuation date.

---

[3]The normalized free cash flow net of reinvestment must be multiplied by one plus the inflation rate, since 93.9 expresses a flow at t_5 prices.

11.3.6 Overall Evaluation of Gas Supply Co. from an Unlevered Perspective

On the basis of the calculations developed in the previous points, we can easily see that the value of Gas Supply Co. is essentially represented by its terminal value.

As we have previously mentioned, some analysts are perplexed when the company value obtained through the DCF model is disproportionately over-represented by its terminal value. As a result, analysts tend to lengthen the plan horizon in order to increase the weight taken on by the net present value of cash flow in the explicit period of estimation. Otherwise, they tend to streamline the investment program, thereby increasing the size of the FCFO in the short term.

We already mentioned that there exists no rational justification for these adjustments. On the contrary, when the net present value of the cash flow produced in the explicit estimation period is a relevant share of the value of the estimate, operations have a short payback period. This could be considered as protection against risk, but it does not constitute an indicator of high quality of the value obtained.

We have to recognize that the previous conclusion tends to mainly hold in industries characterized by a high level of predictability of future cash flows, such as the utilities sector. In industries with high risk, by contrast, the imbalance of value in favor of the terminal value can sometimes represent a legitimate source of concern.

Summing up, in the case of Gas Supply Co., the existing imbalance between the present value of cash flows in the explicit period and the TV is simply connected to the company's implementation of an investment program that is meant to strengthen company's positioning advantage before the competition intensifies as a consequence of market deregulation.

11.3.7 Estimating Present Value of Tax Shields

As for the debt profile during over the plan horizon, if we consider the investment program during the period going from t_1 to t_4, net borrowing increases from €356 million to €462 million. This increase is also due to dividend distribution, expected to increase from 15 to 30 million throughout the plan horizon.

Exhibit 11.8 shows the trend of financial charges and their corresponding tax shields, calculated on the basis of a tax rate equal to 36 percent.

Assuming that K_{TS} is equivalent to the cost of debt (= 6%), the present value of the tax shields is then equal to €30.26 million.

At the end of the plan horizon, Gas Supply Company's net borrowing is equal to €462 million. The problem is then the estimation of the trend of debt in the period following the end of the explicit forecast period.

Exhibit 11.8 Gas Supply Co.: debt, interest payments, and tax shield from t_1 to t_4 (in million €)

	1999	2000	2001	2002	2003
DEBT	356,0	396,0	415,0	442,0	462,0
FINANCIAL CHARGES		22,1	23,9	25,1	26,6
TAX SHIELD		7,9	8,6	9,0	9,6

In general, analysts can picture three different scenarios:

- Scenario a: At the end of the plan, debt grows together with the FCFO.
- Scenario b: At the end of the plan, debt remains stable in absolute value.
- Scenario c: At the end of the plan, debt gradually decreases (we assume that the decrease happens at the rate of 5 percent per year).

We can now proceed with the calculation of W_{TS} in each of the outlined scenarios.

Scenario a: First Period ($t_5 - t_{14}$) The value of W_{TS} can be calculated following the procedure we have already outlined to calculate the TV. That is:

$$W_{TS_1} = \frac{D_4 \times K_d \times t_c \times \left[1 - \frac{(1 + g_1)^{10}}{(1 + K_{TS})^{10}}\right]}{K_{TS} - g_1}$$

D_4 indicates the amount of expected debt at the end of the plan, equal to €462 million (refer to Exhibit 8.6).

Assuming $K_{TS} = K_{eu}$, the previous expression can be rewritten as follows:

$$W_{TS_1} = \frac{462 \times 0.06 \times 0.36 \times \left(1 - \frac{1.438}{2.004}\right)}{0.072 - 0.037}$$

$$W_{TS_1} = 80.5$$

Scenario a: Second Period (after t_{14}) Following the outline we have already sketched out, we can write:

$$W_{TS_2} = \frac{D^* \times K_d \times t_c}{(K_{TS} - g) \times (1 + K_{TS})^{10}}$$

D^* indicates the amount of debt at the end of the first period and it can be obtained calculating the amount of debt at the end of the plan horizon assuming a growth rate $g_1 = 3.7\%$. Therefore:

$$D^* = 462 \times (1 + 0.037)^{10} = 664.4$$

Applying the previous formula:

$$W_{TS_2} = \frac{664.4 \times 0.06 \times 0.36}{(0.072 - 0.015) \times (1 + 0.072)^{10}} = 125.6$$

We can then obtain the overall value of W_{TS} by adding up its two components at the end of the plan:

$$W_{TS} = 206.1$$

Scenario b   In scenario b, we assume that debt at the end of the plan remains constant. As we have already seen in the previous chapter, the net present value of tax shields can be determined on the basis of the K_d rate in a steady-state context, since we can assume a homogeneous level of risk associated with the current (which equals the future) debt service and its corresponding tax benefits.

Thus, W_{TS} can be easily calculated in the following way:

$$W_{TS} = D_n \times t_c$$
$$W_{TS} = 462 \times 0.36 = 166.3$$

Scenario c   To simplify, we assume that the current debt at the end of the plan decreases at an annual rate equal to 5 percent. Thus, we obtain:

$$W_{TS} = \frac{D_4 \times K_d \times t_c}{K_{TS} + g}$$

From which:

$$W_{TS} = \frac{462 \times 0.06 \times 0.36}{0.06 + 0.05}$$
$$W_{TS} = 90.7$$

We assume that K_{TS}, the discount rate of tax shields, is equal to K_d in this case as well, since the risk associated with gradually decreasing benefits can be absorbed by the risk referable to the current debt service.

Thus, the value of tax shields in the three outlined scenarios is equal to:

VALUE AT THE END OF THE PLAN (t_4)	
SCENARIO a (growing tax shields)	206.1
SCENARIO b (stable tax shields)	166.3
SCENARIO c (decreasing tax shields)	90.7

We need to make some observations and take important factors into account to choose the most realistic approach to the estimation of W_{TS} in our specific example. In particular:

- Considering the remarkable reduction in the amount of investment in the period going from t_5 to t_{14}, Gas Supply Co. begins again to generate substantial cash flows.
- Moreover, once the company complete its initial public offering, it shall increase the return on equity in order to fulfill investors' expectations. If we assume that its equity value will equal about €1.5 billion after its placement on the stock market, the company will most likely distribute dividends in the amount of about 45 to 40 million to reach a similar dividend yield to the average one offered in the utilities sector.
- Considering the low return on invested capital and the restrictions imposed by the tariffs system, the existing shareholders of Gas Supply Co. will most likely use the information gathered during the premarketing phase and determine accordingly what profitability level should be attained—also using financial leverage—in order to meet investors' expectations.

We can draw a conclusion from the previous observations: Gas Supply Co.'s net borrowing will slowly tend to decrease. Thus, the analyst in charge of the company valuation determines that Scenario c is the most realistic one in this case because of the significantly lower than average leverage in the industry.

If the assumption of a gradual reduction of debt holds, the net present value of tax shields expected in the period beyond the explicit yearly forecast is equal to €71.8 million at the date of valuation.

11.3.8   Estimating Gas Supply Co.'s Overall Value

Gas Supply Co.'s value is composed of its unlevered value plus the value of its tax shields calculated in the previous paragraph:

W ASSET-UNLEVERED	**1,585.7**
w_{TS} *during the plan*	30.26
w_{TS} *after the plan*	71.8
W ASSET-LEVERED	**1,687.76**
DEBT *(at the date of valuation)*	(356)
W EQUITY	**1,337.76**

It is useful to mention that if we were to use the weighted average cost of capital (*WACC*) widespread approach, the tax shields value, assumed to be in line with the company's free cash flow,[4] would even be higher than the previously rejected result obtained in Scenario a.[5]

In a scenario with growth, the assumptions implicit in the currently used valuation procedures can turn out to be particularly optimistic, leading to unreasonable estimates.

The example we proposed outlines the clear superiority of the APV approach, which allows for the adjustment of the profile of tax shields.

---

[4]The commonly used formulas imply the assumption that the debt ratio stays constant and that the debt profile is therefore aligned with the development of the company value.

[5]By adopting the *WACC* technique, the tax benefits are discounted at different rates, in particular:

- The tax benefits of debt existing at the date of the valuation are assumed to be discounted at the rate K_d (cost of debt).
- The tax benefits linked to the increase in indebtedness caused by the company's growth are discounted using a "mixed" procedure based on two rates, K_d and K_{eu} (opportunity cost of the equity of a company without debt).

## CHAPTER 12

Multiples: An Overview

12.1 PRELIMINARY REMARKS

12.1.1 Multiples and Discounted Cash Flow

The multiples method enables us to define the equity and/or enterprise value of a company using negotiated prices of stocks of similar firms.

The multiples method seeks to develop a relationship between the actual price of shares of comparable listed companies and an accounting metric (such as net income, cash flows, revenues, etc.). This relationship, that is, the multiple, is then applied to the firm's internal metric in order to determine the value of the company through a simple multiplication.

A valuation performed with multiples is based on two assumptions:

1. The company's value changes proportionally to the internal variables chosen as a measure of performance;
2. The growth rates of both cash flows and the risk level are constant.

If both these hypotheses are verified, the multiples method gives a more "neutral" measure than the one based on the firm's cash flow (DCF), as it takes into account the market expectations on both the growth rate and the discount rate.

In reality, companies rarely satisfy these two hypotheses: cash flows might have different growth rates and the risk level could vary. Moreover, the best measure of performance to be used to compare different companies is not easily identifiable.

On the other hand, financial methods are usually based on expected cash flows, which relate directly to the company being evaluated, and on the discount rate derived from the risk of the business and of the sector it belongs to. This method, in order to be successful, depends on an accurate estimation of cash flows and of the risk measure as well as on reliable hypotheses assumed to calculate the cost of capital.[1]

To summarize:

- The financial method requires assumptions on future results and the translation of these hypotheses into cash flow projections. It requires the analysis of the company's risk profile and the consequent estimation of the opportunity cost of capital.
- The multiples method avoids these estimations and takes the expected growth rate and risk appreciation directly from market data through the use of multiples.

Nevertheless, the issue concerning the presence of subjectivity in the estimation process is not completely solved. The valuator selects the group of companies which are most similar to the one under consideration. The extent of comparability across companies is always limited for several reasons: the type of activity performed by the company, its size, its risk profile, and its different leverage ratios.

An Obvious Problem The previous considerations involve an obvious problem: the core of the multiples method lies in entrusting the market with the correct estimation of growth prospects and risk profiles. Nevertheless, limited comparability across businesses requires some verification of their similarity with the business being evaluated. Such verification assumes that the person calculating these estimates has formed their own judgment about the business prospects. It is easy to fall into a paradox: if the one carrying out the estimation adjusts multiples according to their own expectations, the market approach will inevitably tend to replicate the results obtained with a subjective valuation, leading to a useless duplication.

This obstacle can be easily overcome by analyzing the differences among multiples of the chosen comparable companies based on objective elements. This step is always recommended except in cases when the market approach displays an ideal situation of comparability across businesses, such as industries characterized by uniform technologies, non-substitutable products/services, and similar growth prospects.

---

[1]For a discussion on the comparative effectiveness of the multiples method and DCF, see S. N. Kaplan, "The Market Pricing of Cash Flow Forecasts: Discounted Cash Flow vs. The Method of 'Comparables,'" *Journal of Applied Corporate Finance*, 4 (1996).

12.1.2 Stock Market and Deal Multiples

Multiples can refer to values taken from two different market contexts:

- The stock market
- The market for corporate control

In the former case, they are called stock market multiples. In the latter one, they refer to transactions carried out by comparable businesses and they are called deal multiples.

These two types of multiples usually lead to the estimation of different values. In normal situations, that is, when we face neither speculative phenomena nor a transfer of control, stock multiples express stand-alone values, whereas deal multiples refer to expected market prices.

Therefore, stock multiples cannot provide sufficient information to estimate the market price attached to the entire firm, whereas deal multiples cannot provide reliable stand-alone values.

Analysts usually try to overcome the problem of expected market prices through the adjustment of the valuation estimate obtained through stock market multiples with the so-called *acquisition premium* in the following way.

As already observed, the procedure associated to this adjustment is quite easy (see Exhibit 12.1). The negotiated price in the case of an acquisition is usually higher than the stock market price because acquisition

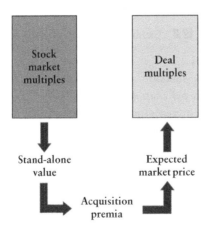

Exhibit 12.1 Stock market and deal multiples

prices incorporate benefits that buyers expect. On the other hand, in a normal situation, stock prices should mirror stand-alone values.

The previous concerns and issues linked to the estimation of the acquisition price will be further discussed in Chapters 14 and 15.

12.1.3 Financial and Business Multiples

Another important distinction is between financial multiples and business multiples. In the former case, multiples seek to identify the connection between a company's equity market price and some important measures such as cash flows, net income, or EBITDA. In the latter case, the company's equity market price is linked to specific elements which are relevant for the business model typical of the sector the company is in. Exhibit 12.2 reports examples of business multiples according to some sectorial grouping of businesses.

Financial multiples can be easily interpreted using simple economic rules that enable us to identify their dimension in terms of returns, growth, and risk expectations.

Business multiples, on the other hand, give us a picture of the performance or the position of the company within a specific group with respect to specific drivers.

Therefore, the rationality of business multiples is conditioned on the fact that the identified value drivers for a specific business model effectively capture the sources of value generation for a certain company or industry.

Exhibit 12.2 Examples of business multiples

Utilities

Gas distribution

■ *Value per consumer*

Electricity generation

■ *Value per megawatt installed*

Publishing (newspapers)

■ *Value per copy*

Internet (web portals)

■ *Value per single access*

Rental companies

■ *Value per single rented item (e.g., car rental)*

Oil companies

■ *Value per barrels of oil equivalent*

12.2   THEORY OF MULTIPLES: BASIC ELEMENTS

To better understand the topic that will be discussed in this paragraph and to underline the limitations of its assumptions, it is necessary to specify that:

1. The discussions reported here will only refer to financial multiples.
2. The analysis of multiples is based on the equations discussed in Chapter 7 while addressing analytical methods. As we will see, the choice of a particular type of multiple (P/E, EV/EBIT, and so on) changes the perspective taken by the valuator and the analysis that has to be performed while the factors responsible for the generation of value remain the same.
3. Growth, which is the most important element for a good understanding of multiples, is assumed to happen at a rate consistent with a steady growth model.

Several assumptions will therefore be made. Among these, two are the most relevant:

1. The return on a new investment opportunity does not change over time.
2. The growth rate is constant and is equal to the yield achieved through the systematic reinvestment of a part of the cash flow generated by the company.

12.2.1   Different Types of Multiples

Exhibit 12.3 shows the multiples that are normally used in the valuation of nonfinancial companies. Only some of those multiples—namely the equity-side ones—can be applied to banks and other financial companies as well.[2]

Two types of multiples can be identified in Exhibit 12.3: multiples calculated only with respect to the market value of equity (P) and multiples calculated with respect to the total value of the company (EV—enterprise value). In this latter case, the numerator of the formula consists of the sum of the value of equity and of net financial debt (to be precise, the market value of debt should be used).

Multiples of the former type allow us to reach an estimate of the value of equity in a direct way. On the other hand, the use of multiples linked to the whole enterprise value leads to an indirect estimation of the value of equity by subtracting the market value of financial debt from the company value.

---

[2] See M. Massari et al., *The Valuation of Financial Companies* (Hoboken, NJ: Wiley, 2014).

Exhibit 12.3 The most frequently used multiples and their formulas

Enterprise value	Equity value
■ **EV/EBIT** *(Enterprise Value/Earnings before Interest and Taxes)* $$\frac{Market\ capitalization + Debts\ value}{EBIT}$$	■ **P/E** *(Price/Earning Ratio)* $$\frac{Market\ capitalization}{Net\ profit}$$
■ **EV/EBITDA** *(Enterprise Value/Earnings before Interest, Taxes, Depreciation and Amortization)* $$\frac{Market\ capitalization + Debts\ value}{EBITDA}$$	■ **P/CE** *(Price/Cash Earnings)* $$\frac{Market\ capitalization}{\left(\begin{array}{c}Net\ profit + amortizations \\ + depreciations\end{array}\right)}$$
■ **EV/Sales** $$\frac{Market\ capitalization + Debts\ value}{Sales}$$	■ **P/BV** *(Price/Book Value)* $$\frac{Market\ capitalization}{Equity}$$

Exhibit 12.4 shows the relationship between the different balance sheet sections and the multiples which refer to them.

In Exhibit 12.5, multiples are divided into two sections: "direct" multiples and "indirect" multiples.

While direct multiples form the relationship between either P or EV and quantities representing economic results, indirect multiples express the

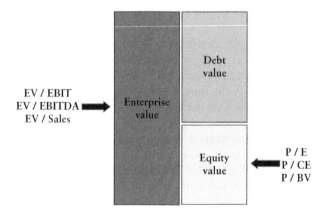

Exhibit 12.4 Balance sheet expressed in market values and its corresponding multiples

Exhibit 12.5 Direct and indirect multiples

Direct Multiples	Indirect Multiples
P/E (Price/Earnings ratio)	*P/BV (Price/Book value)*
EV/EBIT (Enterprise value/Earnings before interest and taxes)	*EV/Sales (Enterprise value/Sales)*
EV/EBITDA (Enterprise value/ Earnings before interest, taxes, depreciation and amortization)	
P/CE (Price/Cash earnings)	

relationship between P or EV and quantities which do not directly express how much value the company is able to generate. The book value of equity (BV) or sales actually generate value only if the firm reaches adequate levels of return. If there are differences between the returns of comparable firms and the returns of the firm under consideration, indirect multiples can only be used after making adjustments to take into account the observed differences in terms of returns.

In a scenario with growth, not even direct multiples can provide reliable estimations if the growth rates of the peer companies and of the company under consideration are remarkably different. The following paragraphs will analyze the relationship between multiples and the growth rate in detail.

12.2.2 Current, Trailing, and Leading Multiples

The first concern regards the choice of the period to be used for the estimation of multiples. Analysts usually make this distinction:

- Current multiples are obtained by comparing stock prices and the values of the last available balance sheet.
- Trailing multiples are calculated by comparing stock prices and the results obtained 12 months before the date chosen to calculate the index. The results of the previous 12 months refer to the last four quarterly reports or the last two semiannual reports provided by the companies.
- Leading multiples are obtained by comparing stock prices and the results expected in the following year(s). Expectations are usually based on the consensus forecasts published by financial analysts associations.

The following scheme shows how multiples are structured:[3]

Current multiple	Trailing multiple	Leading multiple
$\dfrac{P_0}{E_{T0}}$	$\dfrac{P_0}{E_{LTM}}$	$\dfrac{P_0}{E_{T1}}$

where:

E_{LTM} = earnings per share referring to the last 12 months

E_{T1} = earnings per share expected in the next year

E_{T0} = earnings per share generated in the last year

If budget results are taken as reference to compute multiples for companies in the sample, leading multiples will be chosen as the best representative estimation. In other words, there is a need for consistency between the variables (profit, EBIT, sales) used to calculate the multiples of the group of comparable firms and the corresponding variables of the firm to which the multiples will be applied.

This problem can be better understood through the following example of a firm involved in the gas distribution industry, in which results are highly influenced by climate changes. Business A, which must to be evaluated with multiples, performs according to the industry trend. Earnings per share for A are:

	T_0	T_1
Earning per share	190	240

The current and leading P/E ratios of the industry are:

$$\frac{P_0}{E0} = 19 \qquad\qquad\qquad \frac{P_0}{E1} = 16$$

In T_0, both the results of the industry and of A are negatively influenced by an unfavorable climate trend. Analysts were not fooled by the decrease of earnings per share, understanding that it was only temporary. Therefore, the current P/E is increased since quotations have minimally suffered from

---

[3] Other terms than those reported here are used in the literature to identify these three kinds of multiples.

the current profit decrease. There are two alternatives to calculate the value of *A*, which are both correct:

(a) $\dfrac{P_0}{E_0} \times E_0(A)$ $19 \times 190 = 3{,}610$

(b) $\dfrac{P_0}{E_1} \times E_1(A)$ $16 \times 240 = 3{,}840$

Methods (c) and (d) would not be accepted because they lead to estimations of value, which are too far from the previous calculations.

(c) $\dfrac{P_0}{E_1} \times E_0(A)$ $16 \times 190 = 3{,}040$

(d) $\dfrac{P_0}{E_0} \times E_1(A)$ $19 \times 240 = 4{,}560$

The choice of leading multiples over current or trailing ones is usually caused by anomalies in current results. Current or trailing multiples usually lose their reliability in the presence of a temporary crisis, restructuring, and so on in the company.

12.3 PRICE/EARNINGS RATIO (P/E)

12.3.1 P/E with No Growth

The P/E multiples can be obtained using the formulas of the financial method. In particular, it is useful to refer to the capitalization formula of standardized free cash flows outlined in Chapter 7.

The model starts with the assumption that buying a share implies receiving an unlimited flow of dividends:

$$P_0 = \sum_{t=1}^{\infty} \frac{DIV_t}{(1+r)^t}$$

where:

P_0 = market price of the stock at the time 0
DIV_t = dividends distributed in time *t*
R = discount rate for the dividend flow (In case of a levered firm, this is equal to K_{el}^*.)

If there is no growth, *DIV* will be constant and it will be equal to earnings per share. At the same time, in a steady-state context, earnings per share will be equal to the cash flow to shareholders. This is why we can consider as valid the assumptions that amortization exactly covers reinvestment requirements and that net working capital is constant. The formula can then be expressed as follows:

$$P_0 = \frac{E_0}{K^*_{el}}$$

from which we obtain:

$$\frac{P_0}{E_0} = \frac{1}{K^*_{el}}$$

In the absence of growth, the P/E multiple will be equal to the reciprocal of the levered cost of capital of the firm. Consequently, variation across different P/E values of firms can be traced back to:

- Differences in the risk profiles of the selected firms, which should be reflected in the discount rate K_{eu}.
- Differences in the financial leverage of firms: K^*_{el} tends to increase (and the multiples to decrease) whenever debt rises.

12.3.2 P/E in a Growth Context

If there are growth opportunities, the formulas cannot be based on total profits, since part of these profits will be used to sustain the investment needed to support the firm's growth. This requires the leverage ratio to remain constant over time. The part of profits that is not used to sustain the company's growth can be distributed to shareholders as dividends.

Transferring part of the earned profit from one year to the next makes the new profit higher. As a matter of fact, as seen in section 7.3, this is due to the fact that the growth rate is obtained by multiplying the part of the profit reinvested by the rate of return.

$$g = (1 - Payout) \times ROE$$

where:

g = growth rate
$Payout$ = earnings distribution ratio
ROE = return on equity for the new investment

If the growth trend is constant over time, the following formula can be used:

$$P_0 = \sum_{t=1}^{\infty} \frac{DIV_0 \times (1+g)^t}{(1+K^*_{el})^t}$$

and:
$$P_0 = \frac{DIV_0 \times (1+g)}{K_{el}^* - g}$$

Some analysts still believe that valuation can be based on profits rather than payable dividends even in a growth scenario. To be convinced of the contrary, it is useful to recall that financial formulas always require the value to be determined with respect to the cash flow available to shareholders. Therefore, if profits were to be partially distributed, the new investment should be proportionally financed by raising new capital in order to keep the leverage ratio constant. In this case, the cash flow to shareholders, that is to say, payable dividends, would equal the value of net income decreased by the amount of capital raised, keeping the target capital structure fixed.

Since dividends are equal to net income multiplied by the payout ratio, we can also write:
$$P_0 = \frac{E_0 \times Payout \times (1+g)}{K_{el}^* - g}$$

From that formula, we can easily obtain the P/E ratio:
$$\frac{P_0}{E_0} = \frac{Payout \times (1+g)}{K_{el}^* - g}$$

Finally, dividing by $E_0 \times (1+g)$, we get
$$\frac{P_0}{E_1} = \frac{Payout}{K_{el}^* - g}$$

which is equal to the leading multiple instead of the current one. As a matter of fact, we can assume that $E_0 \times (1+g) = E_1$ in a steady growth context.

Previous formulas show that differences in the P/E values among companies can be related not only to the factors seen in the steady state context, but also to the expected growth in profits and dividends.

We notice that the last formula is based on the idea of steady growth rate; with temporary growth, the P/E ratio is also linked to the duration of growth.

12.3.3 Deepening the Analysis

We must make an important observation at this point. Since the payout factor is in the numerator of the previous formulae, saying that the P/E ratio depends on the growth factor g is not entirely accurate. The P/E ratio actually depends on the value generated by growth—that is, on the return on investment realized by reinvested profit with respect to the opportunity cost of capital.

This concept was discussed in Chapter 7 while addressing the Gordon model and can be shown by slightly modifying the previous formula expressing the P/E ratio in a steady growth context:

$$\frac{P_0}{E_1} = \frac{Payout}{K^*_{el} - g} \tag{12.1}$$

We can rewrite this as:

$$\frac{P_0}{E_1} = \frac{1}{K^*_{el}} + \frac{ROE - K^*_{el}}{K^*_{el}} \times \frac{1 - Payout}{K^*_{el} - ROE \times (1 - Payout)}$$

where:

$\dfrac{1}{K^*_{el}}$ = the "basic" P/E; i.e., the P/E ratio of the firm in the absence of growth

$\dfrac{ROE - K^*_{el}}{K^*_{el}}$ = the "excess return" with respect to the opportunity cost of capital, that is, a standardized index of value generation

$\dfrac{1 - Payout}{K^*_{el} - ROE \times (1 - Payout)}$ = the index of the present value of reinvestments as a whole. To be precise, the numerator expresses the annual rate of reinvestments, while the denominator is a discount factor. Since the relationship has been developed from the Gordon model, the addend $ROE \times (1 - Payout)$ expresses the growth rate of annual reinvestments.[4]

The P/E ratio can now be interpreted as the sum of two addends:

1. The P/E ratio with no growth
2. The present value of growth compared to E (obtained multiplying the two items of the second addend together)

---

[4]To better understand this point, it is useful to observe that if we multiply this

$$\frac{(1 - Payout)}{(K^*_{el} - ROE \times (1 - Payout))}$$

The relationships can be summarized as follows:

Exhibit 12.6 Factors that influence the P/E multiple

Factor	Relationship to P/E Ratio
■ Operating risk	Inverse
■ Leverage ratio	Inverse
■ Payout (growth rate being equal)	Direct
■ ROE (growth rate being equal)	Direct
■ Growth rate (payout being equal)	Direct
■ Growth duration	Direct

12.4 THE EV/EBIT AND EV/EBITDA MULTIPLES

12.4.1 EV/EBIT with No Growth

As in the previous case, the EV/EBIT multiple can be obtained by further developing the formulas seen in Chapter 7. The enterprise value (EV) can be calculated by discounting the free cash flow from operations using the WACC*. In the particular case of no growth, the EBIT measures the free cash flow from operations, assuming that amortization is equal to the level of investments and that there are no variations in net working capital. Therefore:

$$EV_0 = \frac{EBIT_0 \times (1 - t_c)}{WACC_*}$$

by E_1 we obtain:

$$E_1 \times \frac{(1 - Payout)}{(K_{el}^* - ROE \times (1 - Payout))} = \frac{(1 - Payout) \times E_1}{(K_{el}^* - ROE \times (1 - Payout))}$$

$$= \frac{\dfrac{I_0}{E_0} \times E_0 \times (1 + g)}{(K_{el}^* - ROE \times (1 - Payout))}$$

which, after some simplifications, leads to:

$$\frac{I_0 \times (1 + g)}{(K_{el}^* - g)}$$

which equals the present value of future reinvestments.

Dividing both terms by the EBIT, we obtain:

$$\frac{EV_0}{EBIT_0} = \frac{1 - t_c}{WACC^*}$$

This relationship shows that, holding the tax rate equal and constant across companies, the values assumed by the EV/EBIT multiple in a peer group only depend on the weighted average cost of capital.

Multiples calculated in comparable companies have to be interpreted assessing two factors very carefully:

- Mismatches in their risk profiles, despite the fact that, as we already know, comparability between companies is always imperfect
- Mismatches in their financial structures

With respect to the second factor, if the rate expressing the tax advantage of debt is sufficiently low (because of alternative tax shields or because of the effect of personal taxes as discussed), the EV/EBIT ratio is not influenced by the company's financial structure (while the P/E ratio is always influenced by it).[5]

Otherwise, the EV/EBIT ratio is a growing function of the leverage ratio, as long as the degree of leverage does not cause substantial financial distress.

12.4.2 The EV/EBIT Ratio in a Growth Scenario

Assuming a scenario of steady growth, part of the EBIT will be used for new investments while working capital will increase. For this reason, the preceding valuation equation will change as follows:[6]

$$EV_0 = \frac{(EBIT_0 \times (1 - t_c) - I_0 - \Delta WC_0) \times (1 + g)}{WACC^* - g}$$

where:

I = expenditures for new investment (assuming renewal investments are equal to amortization)

ΔWC: variation in the net working capital

---

[5]This is a particular strength of the EV/EBIT ratio, usually highlighted by US financial analysts. More generally, Anglo-Saxon analysts support the idea that if one considers the impact of personal taxes, the differential debt benefit significantly decreases.
[6]In the development of the valuation equation one assumes that the process of growth is already in progress at t_0.

The EV/EBIT multiple, as with the P/E multiple, can be rearranged in a different way as well. The previous formula can be rewritten as follows. In particular, we can notice that:

$$(I_0 + \Delta WC_0)/EBIT_0 = b \times (1 - t_c)$$

where:

b = reinvestment rate of the free cash flow from operations net of taxes[7]

Replacing what we obtained above and including the term $(1 - t_c)$ in the numerator, we obtain:[8]

$$\frac{EV_0}{EBIT_1} = \frac{(1 - t_c) \times (1 - b)}{WACC^* - g}$$

Since the algebraic complement to the reinvestment rate $(1 - b)$ is equal to the flow effectively available to remunerate financial capital, we can say that $(1 - b)$ corresponds to the payout from the asset-side perspective:

$$\frac{EV_0}{EBIT_1} = \frac{(1 - t_c) \times Payout}{wacc^* - g} \qquad (12.2)$$

The comparison between equations [12.2] and [12.1] clearly shows how the EV/EBIT multiple is equivalent to the P/E ratio from an asset-side perspective. All the considerations discussed for the P/E ratio are then equivalent to the EV/EBIT case.

In particular, the EV/EBIT ratio can be broken down as follows:[9]

$$\frac{EV_0}{EBIT_1} = \left(\frac{(1 - t_c)}{WACC^*} + \frac{ROI - WACC^*}{WACC^*} \times \left[\frac{(1 - Payout) \times (1 - t_c)}{(WACC^* - ROI \times (1 - Payout))} \right] \right)$$

In the same way we discussed the P/E ratio, the factors explaining the EV/EBIT values are:

- The basic multiple (i.e., the value assumed by the multiple in a no-growth context)

---

[7] The rate of reinvestment of the free cash flow from operations after taxes is actually equal to $\dfrac{I_0 + \Delta WC_0}{EBIT_0 \times (1 - t_c)}$; so $b \times (1 - t_c) = \dfrac{I_0 + \Delta WC_0}{EBIT_0}$.

[8] $\dfrac{EV0}{EBIT1} = \dfrac{(1 - t_c) - b \times (1 - t_c)}{WACC^* - g} = \dfrac{(1 - t_c) \times (1 - b)}{WACC^* - g}$.

[9] The proof is the same as the one reported in footnote 3. We must specify that the ROI appearing in the formula is net of taxes.

- An index of the generation of value, represented by the excess return with respect to the cost of capital
- An index of the present value of reinvestment

EV/EBITDA   In the discussion of the EV/EBIT multiple, we always assumed that renewal investments are equal to the level of amortization in a no-growth scenario. On the other hand, the level of amortization reported in the balance sheet is usually significantly different from the economic-technical amortization. This is why analysts prefer the EV/EBITDA multiple. In this way, the analysis is based on the free cash flow from operations (EBITDA) and on its reinvested part. The multiple can be broken down as follows:[10]

$$\frac{EV_0}{EBITDA_0} = \frac{1}{WACC^*} - \frac{T_0/EBITDA_0}{WACC^*} - \frac{I_0/EBITDA_0}{WACC^*}$$

where:

T_0 = tax on earnings before interest and taxes; so $T_0 = EBIT_0 \times (1 - t_c)$
I_0 = overall investment needed to sustain the company's competitive position and its production capacity

The first term, as in the EV/EBIT ratio, indicates that the multiple is a function of the risk profile and the leverage ratio. The second term identifies the impact of taxation on EBITDA. Finally, the third term looks at the real impact of the investments required to maintain the company's operating capacity and its market position.

Analysts have a strong preference for the EV/EBITDA multiple because it represents the value of the gross cash flow of the company.

Therefore, since there is generally a certain margin of flexibility in the company's level of investment, the EV/EBITDA multiple constitutes a sort of payback index of the price paid for an acquisition.

This multiple is particularly interesting and useful in capital intensive industries where there are significant differences between the EBIT and the EBITDA and when the peer companies have different levels of vertical integration.

The EV/EBITDA ratio is frequently used in cases of depreciation of particular relevant intangible assets (copyrights, licenses, patents, goodwill), since they are not usually linked with a substantial financial meaning.

All the considerations discussed for the EV/EBITDA ratio still hold in a growth scenario.

---

[10]Developing an evaluation equation, we assume that the growth process is already in progress at t_0.

12.5 OTHER MULTIPLES

12.5.1 EV/Sales

The EV/Sales multiple can also be obtained from the implicit financial valuation formulas.

Since the value of a firm in steady-state context is:

$$EV_0 = \frac{EBIT_0 \times (1 - t_c)}{WACC^*}$$

Rewriting the EBIT as the product between the revenues from sales and the return on sales (Sales × ROS), we obtain:

$$EV_0 = \frac{Sales_0 \times ROS_0 \times (1 - t_c)}{WACC^*}$$

Dividing both terms by the return of sales, we arrive at the multiple we are interested in:

$$\frac{EV_0}{Sales_0} = \frac{ROS_0 \times (1 - t_c)}{WACC^*}$$

Keeping the weighted average cost of capital constant, this relationship shows that the EV/Sales multiple depends on the ROS, which is one of the most effective indicators of a company's performance.

To be concise, we will skip the breakdown of the factors responsible for the values assumed by the EV/Sales ratio in a growth scenario.

Intuitively, we can conclude that, holding the rate of growth equal for all firms, companies that are characterized by higher rates of investments should be characterized by lower EV/Sales values. In the data, we can see that the EV/Sales multiple is actually lower in capital-intensive industries.

Price/Book Value (P/BV) The book value is the difference between the net book value of a company's assets and the net book value of its liabilities. The book value of some assets is usually influenced by the principles used to create the balance sheet, such as the principles used in the calculation of the level of amortization and the accounting methods applied to other items (such as inventory, intangibles assets, goodwill, etc.).

Assuming that the accounting principles adopted by the selected companies are similar, the values of the P/BV multiple can be interpreted using synthetic financial formulas.

Starting from the equation for the valuation of a company in a steady-state condition:

$$E_0 = \frac{E_0}{K^*_{el}}$$

We can then express the net profit (E) as the product between equity and the return on equity (ROE):

$$P_0 = \frac{ROE \times BV_0}{K^*_{el}}$$

We then divide both terms by BV_0:

$$\frac{P_0}{BV_0} = \frac{ROE}{K^*_{el}}$$

The formula shows that the P/BV multiple is explained by the relationship between the return on equity and the opportunity cost of equity. This relationship is the basic principle of the *theory of generation of value*. When $ROE = K^*_{el}$, the value of the company's equity must equal its book value, since the investment in the equity of the company yields a return equal to the rate accepted by the market. Under these circumstances, neither value creation nor value destruction occurs.

When we see that $ROE > K^*_{el}$, the management is instead creating wealth and the company's equity market value is consequently higher than its corresponding book value. If $ROE < K^*_{el}$, the return on equity is lower than the minimum rate accepted by shareholders: in this case, the equity market value is lower than the company's book value.

Many analyses carried out in different sectors confirm that the market capitalization of companies characterized by significant return ratios is higher than their equity book value while the opposite happens for firms that are not particularly profitable.

There is a direct relationship between the value of the P/BV multiple and the company's growth rate. As in the aforementioned cases, P/BV is mainly determined by the firm's growth pattern. In particular, holding the growth rate equal across firms, companies with a higher expected return will be characterized by higher multiples values (as growth will be sustained by a lower level of investment).

12.6   MULTIPLES AND LEVERAGE

12.6.1   P/E and the Financial Leverage

We have outlined that the financial leverage ratio influences the value of the company's multiples in the previous paragraph. We will now further discuss this topic.

For the sake of simplicity, we will run our analyses in a steady-state scenario characterized by no growth. In this case, as we have already shown, multiples are a function of K^*_{el} and the $WACC^*$: in particular, the P/E multiple is a function of K^*_{el} while the EV/EBIT and the EV/EBITDA ratios are a function of the $WACC^*$.

We will also assume that the implicit cost of debt represented by the effects of potential financial crises is negligible for levels of leverage that will be considered in our discussion.

From a practical point of view, the analysis presented in this paragraph, based on a rather restrictive hypothesis, can provide only a general description of the relationship between multiples and financial leverage. In other words, this relationship can explain differences in values of multiples calculated for similar firms characterized by different financial structures. Exhibit 12.7 shows the theoretical relationship between the P/E ratio and leverage.

This relationship becomes clear in a steady-state scenario. Holding the level of operating capital constant, variations in the financial structure are obtained by replacing debt with equity and vice versa. Therefore an increase of debt implies shares buyback and, consequently, an increasing level of earnings per share (assuming that the ROI is higher than the cost of debt).

Therefore, by the *law of conservation of value,* discussed in Chapter 3, the increase in earnings per share must be balanced by a decrease in the

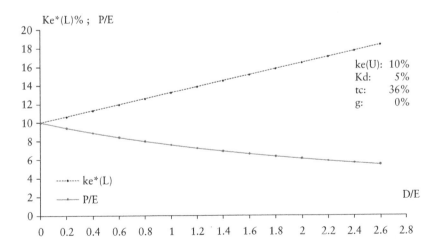

Exhibit 12.7   The relationship between P/E and leverage

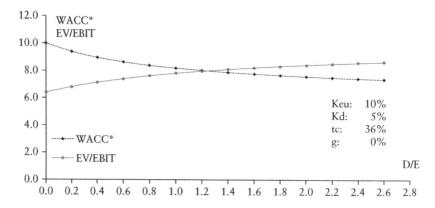

Exhibit 12.8 Theoretical relationship between the EV/EBIT ratio and leverage

P/E ratio. This relationship mirrors the balance between an increase in the return rate caused by higher leverage and the rate of return required by the market.

12.6.2 The EV/EBIT Ratio and Financial Leverage

Exhibit 12.8 shows the existing relationship between leverage and the EV/EBIT multiple. This particular multiple is a growing function of leverage. When leverage increases, the enterprise value (EV) progressively increases as a function of increasing tax shields (W_{TS}).

The same conclusions are valid for the EV/EBITDA ratio.

It is important to observe that the theoretical relationship between the EV/EBIT ratio and financial leverage shown in Exhibit 12.4 is based on the approach chosen for the valuation of tax shields (in particular, W_{TS} represents here the present value of a constant perpetuity of tax savings, discounted at the K_d rate).

12.6.3 The P/BV Ratio and Financial Leverage

In Exhibit 12.9, the P/BV ratio's growth depends on two factors:

- As a consequence of the steady-state assumption, an increase in leverage implies a corresponding reduction in equity.
- The positive leverage effect ($ROI > K_d$) justifies the increase in the value of tax benefits due to leverage.

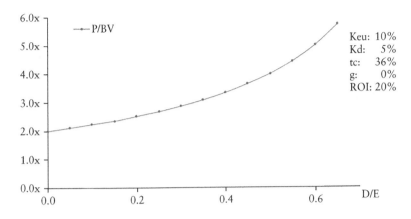

Exhibit 12.9 Figure theoretical relationship between the P/BV ratio and leverage

The previous assumptions can be verified with an example. Assume that company A is characterized by the following parameters:

$$FCFO = EBIT \times (1 - t_c) \qquad 100$$
$$K_{eu} \qquad\qquad 10\%$$
$$K_d \qquad\qquad 5\%$$
$$t_c \qquad\qquad 50\%$$
$$\text{Invested capital (book value)} \qquad 500$$
$$ROI \text{ (after tax):} \qquad 20\%$$

Exhibit 12.10 shows how the P/BV values for company A change with changes in the financial leverage (D/E). As seen in the previous examples, it is assumed that the increase in financial leverage is not accompanied by a financial crisis that would in turn justify an increase in the value of bankruptcy costs.

The P/BV multiple, assuming no leverage, is equal to the ratio between the after-tax ROI and the cost of capital (K_{eu}), as shown in section 12.5.

Exhibit 12.10 Trend of the P/BV multiple with different leverage levels

D	0	100	200	300	400
EV^{12}	1000	1050	1100	1150	1200
$E = EV - D$	1000	950	900	850	800
D/E	0	0.1052	0.222	0.353	0.5
$PN = CI - D$	500	400	300	200	100
P/BV	2	2.375	3	4.25	8

12.7 UNLEVERED MULTIPLES

Since multiples are used to make a valuation "by analogy," it is important to look for the best conditions of comparability. If the financial structures of the selected companies are different and are not easily comparable to the financial structure of the firm being evaluated, it could be useful to adjust multiples accordingly to artificially obtain the same financial structure. To accomplish this, it is necessary to calculate unlevered multiples characterized by being free of any leverage effect.

Financial textbooks suggest many methods to adjust the P/E ratio based on the relationship between K_{el}^* and K_{eu} introduced in equation [3.6].

Starting from the relationship discussed before:

$$\frac{P_0}{E_0} = \frac{1}{K_{el}^*}$$

we obtain K_{el}^*:

$$K_{el}^* = \frac{1}{P_0/E_0}$$

Recalling equation [3.6], which expresses the relationship between K_{el}^* and K_{eu}:

$$K_{el}^* = K_{eu} + (K_{eu} - K_d) \times (1 - t_c) \times \frac{D}{E}$$

We can then replace K_{el}^* and K_{eu} with their corresponding expressions in terms of price–earnings ratios:

$$\frac{1}{P/E_L} = \frac{1}{P/E_U} + \left(\frac{1}{P/E_U} - K_d \right) \times (1 - t_c) \times \frac{D}{E} \qquad (12.3)$$

and we can then solve for the unknown quantity: $\frac{1}{P/E_U}$:

$$\frac{1}{P/E_U} = \frac{1}{P/E_L} \times \frac{E}{E + D \times (1 - t_c)} + K_d \times (1 - t_c) \times \frac{D}{E + D \times (1 - t_c)}$$
$$(12.4)$$

Exhibit 12.11 shows an application of the adjustment of levered P/E.

We can then apply equation [12.4] on the basis of the data in Exhibit 12.11.

Exhibit 12.11 Adjustment of P/E

	Levered Firm
Income	100
Financial charges	(6)
Earnings before taxes	94
Taxes (tax rate = 50%)	(47)
Net profit (E)	47
Enterprise value(EV)	550
Net borrowing (D)	100
Market capitalization (S)	450
Price/Earnings ratio(P/E)	9.57

Assuming that K_d is equal to the company's cost of debt $(6/100 = 6\%)$ and inserting the values of Exhibit 12.11 in the previous formula, we obtain:

$$\frac{1}{P/E_U} = \frac{1}{9.57} \times \frac{450}{450 + 100 \times (1 - 0.5)} + 0.06 \times (1 - 0.5)$$
$$\times \frac{100}{450 + 100 \times (1 - 0.5)}$$
$$\frac{1}{P/E_U} = 0.10$$

from which:

$$P/E_U = \frac{1}{0.10} = 10$$

We do not comment on other methods for the calculation of the unlevered P/E ratio. All alternatives are based on the *law of conservation of value* and are not very different from the classical procedure we just discussed.[11]

---

[11]It is worth it to mention an alternative method for the adjustment of the Price/Earnings ratio using company's data. This is based on the following equation, which defines the relationship between the P/E ratio of a levered firm and the P/E ratio that the same firm could have if it were totally financed by equity (the unlevered P/E ratio): $\frac{P}{E}\text{levered} = \frac{P}{E}\text{unlevered} \times \frac{S}{RO - Ip} \times \frac{RO}{EV - t_c \times D}$

S = stock capitalization of the unlevered firm
D = debt value
RO = income
I_p = interest expense

The previous equation enables us to calculate the P/E ratio without considering the effect of the financial structure of comparable firms—that is, the corresponding theoretical P/E ratio in case of no leverage.

The unlevered P/E ratio must be modified according to the leverage of the evaluated firm. This can be easily proven using the equation in 12.3.

12.7.1 Limitations of This Method

Not all experts agree on multiples adjustment. Four factors force us to consider the obtained results with caution:

1. Beyond a certain leverage ratio, the tax advantages of debt are balanced by the costs of financial crises in unfavorable scenarios (bankruptcy costs).
2. We do not have empirical evidence to verify what level of the leverage ratio is linked to high enough bankruptcy costs to the point that they become relevant for the market.
3. We do not have sufficient empirical evidence to believe whether the market evaluates W_{TS} on the basis of K_d or K_{eu} discount rates or of other intermediate parameters. We also do not know for how long the market will take tax shields into consideration.
4. In a growth scenario, we do not know how the market will determine W_{TS} (the level of assumed discount rates, the horizon considered, etc.). We refer you back to Chapter 4 for a discussion on this topic.

EV = enterprise value

t_c = tax rate

$t_c \times D$ = debt tax shields

We then proceed from the previous equation to calculate the unlevered P/E ratio:

$$(P/E)\ \text{unlevered} = \frac{(P/E)\ \text{levered}}{\dfrac{S}{EBIT - Ip} \times \dfrac{EBIT}{EV1 - t_c \times D}}$$

Using 9.5, we get to:

$$(P/E)\ \text{unlevered} = \frac{9.57}{\dfrac{450}{94} \times \dfrac{100}{500}} = \frac{9.57}{0.957} = 10$$

This adjustment (and other similar ones) apparently eludes the problem of the estimation of the cost of capital parameters. As we know, the critical aspect is related to the appreciation of the present value of tax shields. In the methodology shown, as in other textbook formulas, we assume that W_{TS} equals $T_c \times D$.

Therefore, we can conclude that although the suggested adjustments are irreproachable from a theoretical perspective, they are not always reliable from a practical point of view.

12.7.2   A More Transparent Procedure

We will now proceed with a discussion on a practical procedure to understand if and in what measure the degree of leverage influences the multiples of a selected group of companies. After calculating the parameters for the multiples, we calculate the estimates of W_{TS} for all the companies of the selected group based on the principles discussed in Chapter 4. Their unlevered EV/EBIT ratio can then be calculated by subtracting W_{TS} from the EV.

As a matter of fact, the unlevered multiple can be obtained based on the following relationship:

$$EV = \frac{EBIT \times (1 - t_c)}{K_{eu}} + W_{TS}$$

We can divide by the EBIT we obtain:

$$\frac{EV}{EBIT} = \frac{(1 - t_c)}{K_{eu}} + \frac{W_{TS}}{EBIT}$$

We can then move the W_{TS} / EBIT ratio to the left-hand side:

$$\frac{EV - W_{TS}}{EBIT} = \frac{(1 - t_c)}{K_{eu}} \qquad (12.5)$$

This procedure can highlight the importance of the parameters of the model and of W_{TS} in particular. It is otherwise meaningless when the aforementioned adjusted formulas are used.

If the considered companies are from countries characterized by different tax regimes (and, consequently, by different tax rates), this procedure allows us to neutralize their different tax effects. As a matter of fact, starting from [12.5], we can write:

$$\frac{EV - W_{TS}}{EBIT \times (1 - t_c)} = \frac{1}{K_{eu}}$$

Therefore, by considering the value of the EBIT after taxes in the denominator, we can obtain the value of the EV/EBIT ratio net of the effect of leverage and tax factors.

12.8   MULTIPLES AND GROWTH

We have highlighted in the previous paragraphs that the growth rate is the most important factor for the explanation of the market value of the multiples of a group of selected companies belonging to the same business area.

We will now further the discussion on the relationship between multiples and the growth rate. The objective is to provide instruments to explain differences between multiples of the companies within the selected group. In particular, several elements will be introduced:

- An important limitation of the Gordon model consists of its simplification of reality. This is particularly true in the case of start-up companies and in the case of firms that have not reached an economic equilibrium yet. As a matter of fact, the growth process can be sustained in these cases only through new capital coming either from the shareholders or from debt holders, which would in turn lead to an increase in the leverage ratio. The Gordon model, however, requires a constant level of leverage instead. It is then obvious how the Gordon model would be inconsistent in these cases.
- In general, the model that we will examine is inadequate not only for the valuation of start-up firms but also for those phenomena of growth driven by mergers and acquisitions.
- Moreover, we will assume that the company under consideration has no debt. The objective is to better describe the relationship between growth and multiples. We have already shown in Chapter 4 how different methods used to evaluate tax benefits with an increase in leverage can significantly modify the final value. Furthermore, we also lack any empirical evidence suggesting how the market would behave in this case.

An effective method to show how growth can influence multiples consists of the analysis of the theoretical trend of some multipliers with respect to two different industries' risk, return, and cash flow profiles. These sectors are:

- The "pure" public utilities sector (e.g., natural gas and electricity generation and transportation companies)
- Hi-tech companies

These two industries have been selected because their respective risk profiles, market performance, and duration of growth are very different. As a matter of fact, while the public utilities sector is characterized by unlimited moderate growth, high-tech companies are driven by high limited growth.

The following adjustments could be applied to many other sectors according to their risk profile, market return, and growth.

12.8.1 Public Utilities Multiples

We can generally assume that "pure" public utilities have the following characteristics:

- A limited risk level and, consequently, a low opportunity cost of capital (K_{eu} is estimated at 7 percent in the following example).
- A moderate rate of return, usually established by the governmental body in charge of the supervision of these industries.
- A long-term growth period which follows the GDP trend.
- A low-profit reinvestment rate. This is due to the lack of growth opportunities in the sector and to the fact that shares characterized by a low risk-performance profile should usually guarantee a reasonable dividend repayment.
- Exhibit 12.12 illustrates the theoretical trend of the P/E multiple for "pure" public utilities.

Exhibit 12.12 is built on the basis of parameter values commonly accepted by financial analysts:

- $K_{eu} = 7\%$ (in nominal terms)
- *Payout* = 70%
- Duration of growth: unlimited

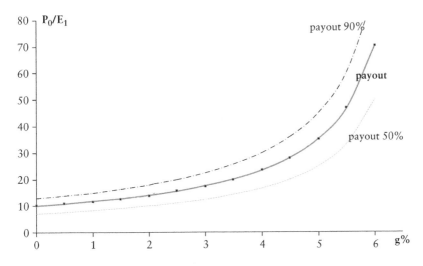

Exhibit 12.12 P/E trend with respect to the growth rate

In Exhibit 12.12, the graph showing the P_0/E_1 trend (the $EV_0/EBIT_1$ ratio and the $EV_0/EBITDA_1$ ratio have the same profile in a no-leverage scenario) is obtained on the basis of the relationship reported in section 12.3:

$$\frac{P_0}{E_1} = \frac{Payout}{K_{eu} - g}$$

To be precise, the bolded line refers to the dividend payout ratio, which is considered normal in the industry (70 percent). Its profile mirrors the reinvestment rate of return: holding the payout ratio constant (equal to 1 − Share of reinvested earnings), the trend of the growth rate only depends on the rate of return. Using the Gordon model, we know that the growth rate is equal to the product of the ROE times the rate of reinvestment of profit:

$$g = ROE \times b$$

where:

g = growth rate
b = reinvestment rate (1 − Payout ratio)
ROE = return on equity

These simple considerations allow us to project point B on the curve in Exhibit 12.12. B has an interesting meaning, as it is identified by the growth rate g^*, for which the rate of return is equal to the opportunity cost of capital. Assuming a payout ratio equal to 70 percent (and a corresponding reinvestment rate equal to 30 percent) and a ROE of 7 percent (equal to the value of K_{eu} in the example), we get to:

$$g^* = 0.07 \times 0.3 = 2.1\%$$

Holding the assumption that $ROE = K_{eu}$ at point B, growth neither creates nor destroys value. The multiple obtained by projecting B onto the vertical axis, valued at 14.28, is equal to the price–earnings ratio in a steady-state scenario with no reinvestment. If profits were fully distributed, the multiple would become:[12]

$$\frac{P_0}{E_1} = \frac{1}{K_{eu}} = 14.28$$

---

[12]It is interesting to observe that if we had calculated the current P/E ratio instead of the leading P_0/E_0 multiple, our results would have been as follows:

P_0/E_0 with no growth $= \dfrac{1}{Keu} = \dfrac{1}{0.07} = 14.28$

P_0/E_0 with growth $= \dfrac{Payout \times (1+g)}{Keu - g} = \dfrac{0.7 \times 1.021}{0.70.021} = 14.58$

By increasing or decreasing the payout ratio, the graph shifts upward and downward, respectively.

In particular, considering the previous comments, we can choose different values for the payout ratio and identify the corresponding points g_1, g_2, ..., g_n that equal the value of growth when the return on new investments is equal to the cost of capital.

$$Payout: 90\% \; g_1 = 0.1 \times 0.07 = 0.7\%$$

$$Payout: 70\% \; g^* = 0.3 \times 0.07 = 2.1\%$$

$$Payout: 50\% \; g_2 = 0.5 \times 0.07 = 3.5\%$$

Also, projecting g_1, g_2, ..., g_n on the lines corresponding to the different payout ratios leads to the points B_1, B_2, ..., B_n, which lie on the same straight line corresponding to a multiple equal to 14.28. This is a consequence of what has already been discussed: when the return on new investment is equal to the cost of capital, the P/E multiple is a function of a unique variable, K_{eu}.

Finally, the 14.28 multiple identifies, regardless of the payout ratio, a line of separation between companies that create value and those that destroy value through the reinvestment of part of their profits. These considerations are valid only for firms that belong to the same risk class (i.e., K_{eu} is held constant) and that are characterized by the same perpetual growth model.

12.8.2 Multiples in the Technology Sector

Exhibit 12.13 has been created using parameters that usually describe industries with a higher-than-average risk profile. In particular, the graph refers to the trend between the P/E ratio and growth in technology companies.

Commonly assumed parameters are:

$$K_{eu} = 12\%$$

$$Payout\ ratio = 30\%$$

$$Duration\ of\ growth = 10\ years$$

In this case, even if the return on new investment is equal to the cost of capital, the base multiple does not correspond to the multiple for a growing company (as it instead happens for the P_0/E_1 ratio). This is due to the fact that the price at t_0 (P_0) in the Gordon model incorporates the yearly reinvestment rate ($1 - Payout$), which would instead be paid out to shareholders in a no-growth scenario:

P_0/E_0 with "zero value growth" $= \dfrac{1}{Keu} + (1 - Payout) = \dfrac{1}{0.07} + \dfrac{I_0}{E_0} = 14.28 + 0.3 = 14.58$.

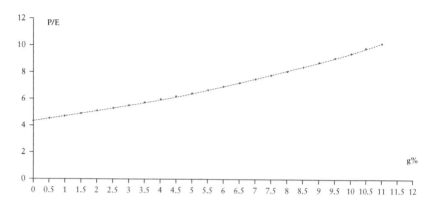

Exhibit 12.13 Trend of the P/E ratio with respect to the growth rate

In comparison to Exhibit 12.12, the scale of growth is much greater. The companies under consideration can exploit development opportunities. The growth period, in this case, must be limited according to the size of the market and the level of competition. In Exhibit 12.13, the multiples have been calculated using the temporary growth model. In particular, the growth (g) period is assumed to end after 10 years and to be followed by a 10-year-long steady-state world ($g_2 = 0$).

Comparing Exhibits 12.12 and 12.13, we can easily notice that the effect of growth on the value of the multiple is much more limited in the high-tech sector. This is due to two factors:

- Growth is assumed to be perpetual in the utilities sector, while it is limited to a 10-year period in the technological sector.
- Using the same hypothesis in the utilities sector, every percentage point of growth generates value. Since the risk in utilities is lower, K_{eu} is lower, too.

This example allows us to draw some conclusions on the analysis of multiples in industries impacted by relevant innovations.

Since in this industry business plans usually present a high growth rate (and historical results, which are the basis for the calculation of growth, are often modest), the most important element in the valuation becomes the appreciation of the expected cash flow profile.

In these cases, the two-stage growth models discussed in Chapter 7 are not sufficient to deal with the phenomenon. It is instead better to use three-stage growth models:

- The first stage, limited to the first 5 years, represents the extension of the business plan.

- The second stage, limited to 10 years, refers to the depletion of the development cycle of the business area.
- The third stage is characterized by a growth rate not higher than the long-term GDP growth rate.

We have to say that the growth of cash flow, which is the correct parameter to calculate the company's value and to analyze its multiples, is sometimes confused with the market growth rate. This must be avoided, as it assumes that there is no competition and that all the companies in the industry are faced with the same opportunities. Some analysis on the value taken by multiples in developing industries in the speculative market phases show that common mistakes in valuations are due to analysts' superficial behavior, who often consider market forecasts as the basis to calculate the company's growth rate.

12.9 RELATIONSHIP BETWEEN MULTIPLES AND GROWTH

The relationship between growth and multiples helps to interpret differences in the values of multiples for the selected firms. The relationships explored in Exhibits 12.12 and 12.13 between multiples and growth forecasts are reliable if and only if these conditions take place:

- The duration of growth is uniform. This means that the same growth model is adopted for all the selected companies.
- The risk level is uniform. In other words, even if the selected companies operate in the same business area, there are no relevant differences in the business model, quality of management, competitive position, and so on.
- Companies use their undistributed profits in projects characterized by equivalent expected returns.

Since not all of these conditions always hold, analysts cannot simply accept the relationship between multiples and growth expectations shown in the previous two examples.

A procedure that can help enhance the analysis between multiples and analysts' growth forecasts of a selected sample of companies is to map the relationship in a graph. Exhibit 12.14 is an example of this.

This map represents the characteristics of the selected companies; it can be done with respect to:

- Elements that can differentiate the companies with respect to their risk profile

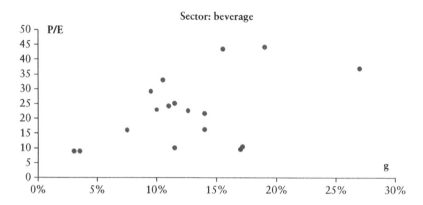

Exhibit 12.14 Map of multiples with respect to growth

- Duration of growth
- Strategies and objectives disclosed by management in terms of returns in the short and long term
- Consistency between the firms' growth forecasts and their resources

If the comparable companies can be positioned on the map on the basis of the aforementioned factors, the map becomes a useful instrument to also position the company under valuation.

Mapping multiples represents a qualitative approach, which could eventually help analysts with the identification of the most appropriate criteria to be used in the company's valuation. In particular, mapping is useful to:

- Assess whether the calculation of multiples is a rational and sensible decision for the firm's valuation.
- Segment the selected group of companies to improve the comparability with respect to the company under valuation.
- Use procedures to calculate multiples based on the use of a regression or extrapolation.

12.10   PEG RATIO

Portfolio managers often compare the PE multiple to the analysts' growth forecast in order to find under- or overvalued stocks. The PE/g (PEG) ratio is generally used as a useful measure that is standardized with respect to growth.

In fact, the PEG index is rarely used in business valuations. The procedure is based on multiples adjusted with respect to growth according to the following relationship:

$$adjusted\_multiple = \frac{mc}{(1 + g')} \times (1 + g'')$$

- mc = current multiple (with respect to 200x results) of comparable firms
- g' = growth rate expected for the comparable firms for the period between 200x and 200y
- g'' = growth rate for the company being valued for the period between 200x and 200y

This procedure has been used to evaluate Internet companies and it has usually been applied to sales multiples (EV/Sales). Analysts used this method because the growth prospects of Internet companies were significantly different from country to country. Since the most comparable companies were listed in the United States, multiples calculated with respect to US companies could be modified to be applied to other Internet companies located in different countries.

With this approach, adjusted multiples would represent an estimation of the values we would have obtained if the selected companies' expected growth rate had been equal to the one of the valuated firm. Even if the adjusted method is useful, it is unfortunately characterized by some theoretical approximations and pitfalls. The adjustment of the multiple is simply based on the assumption that the risk profiles of both the comparable companies and the company under consideration are not influenced by the expected growth rate.[13]

12.11   VALUE MAPS

Building on the analysis of multiples' fundamentals, an alternative approach to relative valuation (especially popular for financial companies) consists in regressing a multiple such as the P/BV against a measure of profitability like the ROE for a panel of comparable companies. Usually, a simple linear regression is performed; if the regression line fits reasonably well to the set of data—the coefficient of determination (R-squared) is assumed as an

---

[13]For a broader discussion on the PEG ratios, see A. Damodaran, *Damodaran on Valuation* (Hoboken, NJ: John Wiley & Sons, 2006).

indicative measure of the fitting[14]—the regression line itself can become a valuation or investment selection tool. The basic intuition of this approach is that the profitability is the major driver of market value of companies; therefore, a certain level of profitability should affect (in a linear and/or nonliner manner) the multiple. The regression is usually presented through graphs called *value maps*. Exhibit 12.15 shows, for example, a least squares regression for 44 comparable companies in the financial sector. The first regression is linear and the second is quadratic. They both seem to have a good fit for the data: the R^2 is 0.48 for the linear model and 0.54 for the quadratic one. The coefficients indicate that the quadratic curve fits the data better than the linear one, so it's the regression to prefer (we do not discuss here the theory and procedures for curve fitting, but most spreadsheet packages currently in circulation include functions and algorithms to perform regressions and best-fitting analyses).

From an investor's point of view, the value map can be a useful tool to make investment decisions. Companies below (and significantly distant from) the regression line (or curve) can be considered, all the rest being equal, as undervalued and therefore as investment opportunities. Symmetrically, firms above the regression line appear to be overvalued and are therefore potential divestment or shorting candidates. Finally, the companies positioned on the line or close to that, emerge as fairly valued by the market and they appear to deserve a "neutral" investment recommendation. Of course, value maps just offer a partial view of the value determinants and they overlook other potential factors impacting the multiple. In the previous example, the evidence is that ROE is an important element for multiples but definitely not the only one. Statistically, half of the variance of the data remains unexplained or, to be more precise, could be explained by factors different from ROE.

Other than a tool for portfolio decisions, value maps can be used as an equity valuation technique. For example, assume that the 44 companies examined before are all adequately comparable for a target we would like to evaluate. The regression equation expressing the quadratic curve for the comparables is:

$$\frac{P_0}{BV_0} = 3.412 - 0.218\,ROE + 0.008\,ROE^2$$

---

[14]For valuation purposes the R-squared coefficient could be sufficient as a rough indication of the regression or curve fitting. But for more accurate analyses, more advanced econometrics tools are required. A good starting reference is A. H. Studenmund, *Using Econometrics: A Practical Guide* (New York: Pearson, 2011).

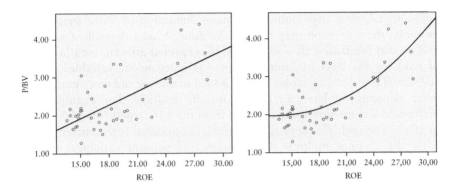

Exhibit 12.15   Value maps for a sample of financial companies

Knowing that the companies we aim to value have an ROE = 14.54 percent, by using such input in the equation we get a *P/BV* of 1.93. Considering then that the current book value of the equity for the company is €3,924 million, we conclude that a fair valuation for the equity would be €7,587 million.

When valuing a company the regression of the P/BV multiple against ROE is a very popular pick, but other combinations of variables may perform equally or even better. In terms of multiples, the P/E ratio is usually an alternative good candidate while in terms of profitability measures possible choices are: the return on average equity (ROAE) that is the return over the mean of the current and expected equity book value, and the return on assets (ROA) that is the ratio between the operating income and the total assets.

Some warnings have to be cast about the preparation of value maps. The actual comparability of the companies included in the regression is key as usual. A trade-off between the number of comparables and the strictness of the comparability criteria does apply and has to be managed by the valuator. As shown in the previous example, a linear regression is not always the best approach: the goodness of fit of nonlinear solutions should be explored in order to catch more precisely the nature of the relation between multiple and fundamentals. Finally, as for ROE and other profitability measures, the use of expected values rather than current ones is recommended. In fact, expected values do incorporate the growth element as well and so they add to the explanatory power of the regression. Actually, in case the industry analysis shows that the companies are expected to experience different growth patterns, the regression of the multiples may be run against the growth rate itself (*g*).

If the panel of comparables is rather large, an alternative valuation strategy is to perform a regression of the multiples against more than one fundamental, thus overcoming the major limitation of value maps. For example, the regression may include the multiple as a dependent variable and several fundamentals—such as ROE, expected growth, beta (a proxy of risk), or the level of capitalization—as independent variables. Other additional firm-level variables may be added to understand more granularly what elements do have an impact on the multiple. For example, we performed a regression using the data from the 136 largest listed US banks in 2012. The multiple (dependent variable) considered is the current P/BV while the assumed multiple determinants (independent variables) are the long-term growth rate (g_s) forecasted by analysts, the level of capitalization (TR), the stock beta, and the return on the average book value of equity (ROAE). By running the regression, we obtain:

$$P/BV = 123.27 + 0.27 \text{ Growth} + 1.06 \text{ TR} - 54.00 \text{ Beta}$$

$$+2.94 \text{ ROAE}[7.36] [0.74] [1.37] [-5.28] [6.84]$$

The R^2 of the regression is 49.60 percent, and the t-test statistics are shown under the independent variables. The signs of the determinants are coherent with predictions: growth, level of capitalization, and profitability contribute positively to the P/BV ratio while the level of risk (reflected in the beta) has a negative impact. From a statistically point of view, the variables Growth and TR do not appear to be significant.[15] Actually, if we rerun the regression using only the last two variables, we obtain a result with R^2 of 48.71 percent, not far from the previous result, but in this case we have a more parsimonious estimation model.

This sort of augmented regression can be used in two ways, depending on the valuation purpose. On the one hand, it allows the identification of apparently undervalued or overvalued companies, thus suggesting possible investment (long or short) opportunities. On the other hand, the coefficient of the regression may be applied to firm fundamentals to compute the multiple and thus estimate the equity value.

APPENDIX 12.1: P/E WITH GROWTH

$$\frac{P_0}{E_1} = \frac{Payout}{K_{el}^* - g}$$

---

[15]The evidence that the level of capitalization (Tier 1 ratio) is not a statistically significant variable should not come as a surprise considering that, as we already mentioned, the level of leverage doesn't play an overwhelming role in defining the level of risk of banks.

multiplying and dividing by K^*_{el};

$$\frac{P_0}{E_1} = \frac{Payout}{K^*_{el} - g} \times \frac{K^*_{el}}{K^*_{el}} = \frac{Payout \times K^*_{el}}{(K^*_{el} - g) \times K^*_{el}}$$

adding and subtracting $[ROE \times (1 - Payout) - K^*_{el}]$,

$$\frac{P_0}{E_1} = \frac{Payout \times K^*_{el} + ROE \times (1 - Payout) + K^*_{el} - ROE \times (1 - Payout) - K^*_{el}}{(K^*_{el} - g) \times K^*_{el}}$$

$$\frac{P_0}{E_1} = \frac{K^*_{el} - ROE \times (1 - Payout)}{(K^*_{el} - g) \times K^*_{el}} + \frac{Payout \times K^*_{el} + ROE \times (1 - Payout) - K^*_{el}}{(K^*_{el} - g) \times K^*_{el}}$$

since $g = ROE \times (1 - Payout)$, the following expression can be rewritten as:

$$\frac{P_0}{E_1} = \frac{K^*_{el} - ROE \times (1 - Payout)}{[K^*_{el} - ROE \times (1 - Payout)] \times K^*_{el}}$$
$$+ \frac{Payout \times K^*_{el} + ROE \times (1 - Payout) - K^*_{el}}{[K^*_{el} - ROE \times (1 - Payout)] \times K^*_{el}}$$

simplifying the first term $[K^*_{el} - ROE \times (1 - Payout)]$ and collecting $(-K^*_{el})$ in the second term:

$$\frac{P_0}{E_1} = \frac{1}{K^*_{el}} + \frac{ROE \times (1 - Payout) - K^*_{el} \times (1 - Payout)}{[K^*_{el} - ROE \times (1 - Payout)] \times K^*_{el}}$$

collecting $(1 - Payout)$ in the second term:

$$\frac{P_0}{E_1} = \frac{1}{K^*_{el}} + \frac{(ROE - K^*_{el}) \times (1 - Payout)}{[K^*_{el} - ROE \times (1 - Payout)] \times K^*_{el}}$$
$$= \frac{1}{K^*_{el}} + \frac{ROE - K^*_{el}}{K^*_{el}} \times \frac{(1 - Payout)}{K^*_{el} - ROE \times (1 - Payout)} \quad ^{16}$$

---

[16] An alternative procedure is presented in M. L. Leibowitz and S. Kogelman, "Inside the P/E Ratio: The Franchise Factor," *Financial Analyst Journal* (Nov.–Dec, 1990): 17–35.

CHAPTER 13

Multiples in Practice

13.1 A FRAMEWORK FOR THE USE OF STOCK MARKET MULTIPLES

The practical considerations about of market multiples presented in this chapter are based on the principles discussed in Chapter 12. We aim at providing the key tools to apply the relative valuation via multiples, and to critically assess relative valuations carried out by third parties. Our discussion is organized in the following way:

- How to build the sample of comparable companies in the industry under consideration.
- How to define a short list of companies comparable to the one being studied.
- How to "clean" the sample.
- How to assess the validity and actual comparability of multiples.
- How to cross-check the consistency of different multiples, business models, and value drivers.
- How to choose the proper multiples for the valuation.

13.1.1 Building the Panel of Comparables

The sample of comparable companies can be selected using the main international databases (i.e., Bloomberg and Datastream are the most popular), which include information about the industry they belong to, the kind of activity they perform, their degree of diversification, as well as all the economic and financial information required to calculate their multiples.

The first step of the analysis consists of the identification of the industry the company works in. The direct competitors of the company—when available—are usually good candidates in terms of comparability. Bear in mind that geographical markets of reference and countries where shares are listed are not necessarily the same, as in the case of a European company listed in a non-European stock market.

Once the comparable companies are identified, their data are downloaded for every selected company to calculate their respective multiples and test their significance. Such data should include stock-market capitalization, the number of shares outstanding, balance sheet items, and information about the companies' degree of diversification (revenue by business area).

13.1.2 Making a Short List of Comparable Companies

Usually, not all the companies selected in the first round of analysis are valid comparables or can express meaningful multiples. The reasons why this happen are two:

1. *The industry classifications adopted by the data providers are not always correct or consistent.* For instance, companies that manage only trade activities are not distinguished from those that carry out manufacturing activities. This problem often emerges when the industry comprises a limited number of companies.
2. *Companies are classified according to their main activity.* However, the company may run other businesses even completely unrelated to the main one. This situation may significantly bias the multiple expressed by the potential comparable.

Presence of Other Businesses When the comparable company run also unrelated business, the decision to be made is whether that company is an appropriate comparable or not.

The main principle that drive the selection of the valid comparable companies is the relevance of the activities unrelated to the core business. Such relevance should be evaluated at both sales level and operating margin level.

As a rule of thumb, a company is a potentially sound comparable if the main business has a weight of at least about 70% on the total revenues or operating margin. If the core business has a lower weight, it is generally appropriate to exclude this company from the sample.

However, when the other businesses instead represent complementary activities to the core one, the company's exclusion from the sample is not always recommended. An example can prove useful.

Many European public utilities companies made in recent years relevant investments in the telecommunication and financial services businesses in order to exploit existing commercial relationships with clients and existing distribution networks. These choices implied a change in their strategy, which initially was been rewarded by the market in terms of share prices.

In such a case, it was generally correct not to exclude from the sample the public utilities that underwent a diversification strategy. By keeping the diversified utilities in the sample even if the company to be valued was a "pure" player, the computed multiples were able to embed the value associated with a potential expansion of the business model.

13.1.3 Cleaning the Sample

Cleaning the sample aims at eliminating meaningless multiples, which would be likely to bias the average multiple value.

These multiples lack economic meaning when the company is not in a balanced and sustainable situation. When the current or expected results are too low or even negative the multiples based on net income, the EBIT, or the EBITDA are not meaningful.

A simple rule for discovering anomalies in the multiples is to compute both the values of "direct" multiples (P/E, EV/EBIT, EV/EBITDA) and of "indirect" multiples (EV/Sales, P/BV). If the two categories of multiples are inconsistent, the analyst should explore in depth the reasons for such situation and possibly discard the companies that show inconsistent values.

13.1.4 Checking the Validity of the Multiples

Once the sample has passed the first cleaning phase, further checks have to be run and adjustments have to be made in order to get meaningful and reliable valuations.

The main circumstances that require further analysis and adjustments are summarized in list below.

A. In depth analyses regarding the validity of multiples in cases where:
   - Results are influenced by significant positive or negative extraordinary items.
   - Current taxes are balanced by tax credits.
   - The net financial position is negative (i.e., there is net liquidity);
   - Within groups, minorities hold important stakes in the consolidated companies.
   - The company has issued convertible bonds and warrants.
   - Changes in capital have occurred recently.

B. Further analyses regarding multiples' comparability:
   - Companies adopt different and inconsistent accounting principles.
   - Companies are subject to different tax systems.
   - Companies have significantly different financial structures.

Each of the points above will be discussed briefly in the following paragraphs.

13.2   THE SIGNIFICANCE OF MULTIPLES

13.2.1   Extraordinary Items

The need to calculate P/E multiples excluding results from extraordinary items is rather straightforward and does not need additional comments.

It is worth mentioning that measures such as the EBIT and the EBITDA can also contain extraordinary components that are not always highlighted in the notes reported in financial statements. For instance, in industrial and commercial companies, income derived from an extraordinary disposal of goods (i.e., the fire sale of inventory) can influence operating results in a significant way. The same can occur with exchange rate gains or losses due to extraordinary commercial transactions, and so on.

13.2.2   Tax Credits

Another frequent cause of distortion that needs to be corrected is the existence of tax credits (previous tax-deductible losses, reductions in tax rates or of the taxable income derived from temporary facilitating laws, etc.).

The results from which multiples are calculated should usually be expressed net of the normalized tax liability calculated using the marginal tax rate. This is due to the fact that tax benefits are usually just temporary. It has to be mentioned that in normal market efficiency conditions, market capitalization should include the present value of the expected tax benefits.

For these reasons, analysts generally perform a double adjustment: the first is a normalization of the tax burden while the second concerns market capitalization. The example shown in Exhibit 13.1 can clarify this procedure.

We assume that companies A and B are completely similar in the following table; B can, however, exploit tax credits with a present value equal to 2,000. Therefore, its market capitalization turns out to be higher than A's. The adjustments reported in the table allow us to obtain identical P/E values for the two companies.

13.2.3   Positive Net Financial Position

With a significant positive net financial position, multiples can turn out to be distorted. As a matter of fact, we can assume that market capitalization is equal to the sum of the company's base-value, represented by its core activity, and its liquidity surplus.

Consequently, analysts generally subtract the value of net liquidity from the company's capitalization and the financial revenues to which it refers net of the respective tax effects from net income.

However, the such procedure is not always appropriate. If liquidity is created through an increase in capital, particularly through an initial public

Exhibit 13.1 The relevance of tax credits

	Company A	Company B
Earnings Before Taxes	1,000	1,000
Corporate Taxes (37%)	370	0
Other Taxes	100	100
Net Income	530	900
Equity Value	7,950	9,950
Unadjusted P/E	15	11
Adjusted Result (Tax rate = 37%)	530	530
P/E with Adjusted Net Income	15	18.7
Present Value of Tax Credits	–	2,000
P/E with Adjusted Equity Value and Adjusted Net Income	15	15*

*(9950 – 2000)/530

offering, and is planned to finance an investment program, it is possible that the valuation of the project reflected in market capitalization assumes that the liquidity will be used for the program development.

Consequently, in this case, the capitalization adjustment according to liquidity can yield biased results.

The market capitalization adjustment according to liquidity should therefore be based on the assumption that liquidity forms a surplus asset in every sense.

13.2.4 Group Structures

The majority of difficulties that are going to be discussed hereafter do not apply if a holding company owns 100 percent of the capital of its sub-sidiaries. As a matter of fact, group results are entirely referable to the shareholders of the holding company.

However, if there are minority shareholders in the subsidiaries, part of the group results belongs to them.

The consolidated financial statement allows us to find what belongs to third parties by referring only to the last line of the income statement: the net income respectively of the parent company's shareholders and of the minority shareholders in the subsidiaries. Nevertheless, this is not possible for intermediate results (such as the EBITDA, the EBIT, cash flows).

As a consequence, there is no consistency between the market value of the listed parent company and intermediate results which reflect the performance of the entire group (thus including third parties interests).

The only multiples for which the homogeneity prerequisite is respected are the Price/Earnings ratio calculated without net income adjustments and the Price/Book value ratio.

This distortion is unavoidable as it is not clear whether and how the market value of a holding company also "captures" a part of the value referable to third parties. Among the different methods that aim at limiting this distortion, the procedure based on adjusting the holding company's market capitalization is widely appreciated.[1] Two different options are possible:

1. The addition of the book value of the minority shareholders' equity to the capitalization of the holding company;
2. The addition of the estimated value of the minority shareholders' equity to the capitalization of the holding company.

Analysts generally prefer the former option for the sake of simplicity. By doing so, third parties' equity is perceived as financial debt.

13.2.5 Capital Increases

When an increase in equity occurs close to the period in which the multiples are calculated, it is necessary to verify that the consistency between market prices and the company values used in the multiples still exists.

This issue arises because a capital increase leads to an immediate effect on the market capitalization of the company due to the capital increase and on the unit price of the stock. Nevertheless, the effect on the results is deferred.

In the case of right issues, the intensity of the effects produced by the capital increase depends also on the methods used in its implementation and, particularly, on the gap between the price of the new shares issued and the market price in the period prior to the transaction.

This statement can be better explained by precisely showing the effects of a capital increase on market capitalization and on a listed company's share prices.

Market Capitalization It can be assumed that a company's market capitalization after a capital increase changes in the following way:

$$\begin{array}{l} \text{Capitalization } \textit{after} \\ \text{the capital increase} \end{array} = \begin{array}{l} \text{Capitalization } \textit{before} \\ \text{the capital increase} \end{array} + \text{Money raised}$$

---

[1] A possible alternative, generally less convincing, consists of the hypothesis that the relationship between the net income of the holding companies and the net income of third parties is also valid for the other results in the income statement, such as EBIT, EBITDA, etc.

Share Prices   The price after the transaction (P_1) should correspond to the weighted average of the price of the old shares and the subscription price of the new ones. The following equation expresses this concept:

$$P_1 = TERP = (P_0 \times N + P_e \times M)/(N + M)$$

where:

$TERP$ = Theoretical Ex-Rights Price; that is, the market price after the exercise of the right to subscribe new shares
P_0 = market price before the exercise of the right
P_e = price of the new shares issued
N = number of old shares
M = number of new shares issued

The effect on the unit share price is called the *dilution effect* in financial jargon. It depends on the gap between P_0 and P_e: the transaction would not impact P_0 if and only if the issue happened at a price equal to the market price $(P_0 = P_e)$. If the issue price is instead significantly lower than the market price, the dilution effect can be very relevant. In the case of a free shares distributed to shareholders $(P_e = 0)$, we can observe the maximum dilution effect.[2]

13.2.6   Convertible Bonds, Warrants, and Stock Options

If convertible bonds have been issued, the company has acquired financial resources that have been invested and have contributed to the generation of results. When the conversion right is exercised, the same results will have to be divided among a greater number of shares.

Accepting the assumption of efficient markets, investors should take this possibility into account and make informed long-term choices based on "diluted" earnings per share, cash flows, EBIT.

Consequently, multiples should also be calculated with respect to the updated value of earnings per share after the conversion of any shares and not the current EPS. Diluted earnings per share are usually calculated and reported by the main databases.

We should highlight that the calculation of diluted earnings per share is not always easy: as a matter of fact, it is often impossible to predict whether subscribers will exercise their conversion rights. For example, if the

---

[2]For an example, refer to Appendix 13.1 at the end of this chapter.

conversion price is higher than the current market price of the stock, it will be more advantageous to not exercise the conversion rights and wait instead for the repayment of the bonds.

If warrants exist, the problem becomes more complex. Contrarily to the case of convertible bonds, financial resources will flow into the company only in the future, at the moment of subscription of the new shares to which the rights refer. The issuance of warrants leads to the same adjustment issues we discussed with regard to an increase in capital even though the capital increases are only "potential" in this case.

Stock option plans can create dilution effects that are completely equivalent to those discussed in the previous cases. This depends on the subscription conditions foreseen in the plans.

13.3   THE COMPARABILITY OF MULTIPLES

13.3.1   Accounting Principles

The comparability problem is more serious when the sample is composed of companies from countries that have different accounting principles. For example, the European accounting principles are still substantially different from those used in Anglo-Saxon countries, as well as from those adopted in the Far East.

Even if all the selected companies are in the same country, the results of some business areas are often significantly influenced by the choices carried out in the financial statement. For example, it is usually necessary to adjust the income statements of the companies in the sample using uniform criteria to calculate the provisions for risks, and to value their financial investments.

13.3.2   Different Tax Systems

The tax rate—which expresses the impact of taxes on the company's income—measures that part of the income taken from the company and transferred to the public administration. Therefore, holding EBT constant, different tax rates lead to different equity values and therefore different market capitalizations.

This problem has particular relevance when multiples like the EV/EBIT, the EV/EBITDA, and the P/BV are compared. As a matter of fact, the denominators in these ratios are all gross of the tax burden. In the P/E ratio, however, the denominator is an item net of taxes and the *tax system* bias is therefore generally neutralized.

13.3.3   Different Degree of Leverage

The problems of comparability with respect to companies in the sample that are more levered than others or are characterized by a significantly different average financial position from the one of the company under consideration, have been widely discussed in previous chapters.

The use of adjustment formulas that are technically correct is not always appropriate because of the uncertainty surrounding the real possibility of exploitation of tax shields linked to the deductibility of interest.

Nevertheless, leverage adjustments can help explain differences in the values of multiples in some specific instances. As already explained, these adjustments are particularly useful in the following cases:

- In industries where future results are highly predictable and stable over time, therefore leading to a high level of credibility surrounding the effective use of tax benefits
- When the tax benefits are particularly high

13.3.4   Searching for Significant Relationships between Multiples, Business Models, and Value Drivers

Once the sample has been selected correctly and the adjustments discussed in the last two paragraphs have been carried out, the observable differences in the multiples can be finally analyzed from a pure business perspective.

The reasons why some companies belonging to the same sample are valued more by the market have to be understood. As a matter of fact, the differences in valuation that are observed must mirror beliefs on the companies' ability to enhance their earnings per share. The key point is then to understand what value drivers are used by the market to evaluate this capability and how the selected companies are positioned with respect to the most relevant value drivers.

The final goal is to rank the sample companies and the company being valued according to the validity of the business model itself and the deployment of differential resources/advantages with respect to competitors.

This kind of analysis requires a deep knowledge of the industry. This is also a reason why the big investment firms tend to build teams of specialized analysts that cover only one or few industries.

13.4   MULTIPLES CHOICE IN VALUATION PROCESSES

The process that has been explained so far concludes with the definition of a handful of multiples that will have to be applied to the firm that is being valued.

This choice represents the summary of the analysis that has been accomplished in the previous stages and requires the solution to the following problems:

- *The definition of a reference period for the calculation of the market price of comparable companies:* Analysts often prepare spreadsheets where the multiples are calculated both based on the last available price and on the average price of the previous periods. The choice of the reference period generally occurs in the last stages of the analysis. As a matter of fact, the information collected can give useful hints for the interpretation of the behavior of the market for the stocks of the companies in the sample.
- *The selection of the multiples for the company's valuation:* Analysts generally use programs that calculate all the multiples that have been discussed in the previous chapter. However, for the purpose of the valuation, the least meaningful multiples are rejected.
- The calculation of the value synthesizing the information derived from the selected multiples.

13.4.1 Time Horizon

The logic of the market approach would require the market prices used in the multiples calculations to be taken from time periods close to the reference date of the valuation. It is, however, often preferable to calculate multiples based on the two months, half year, or even annual average of prices prior to the valuation date.

Such a choice is motivated by the concern that market prices are affected by anomalies or manipulations. By extending the observation period, the anomalous values will instead tend to balance themselves out.

It does not make sense to create a single rule on this topic. This choice has to be made on a case-by-case basis depending on the level of trading volumes, which are considered an indicator of the representativeness of the prices present in the market.

13.4.2 Selection of Multiples

Financial analysts usually perform valuation processes using a grid formed by two to four multiples.

For the valuation of industrial companies, the most widely used multiples are:

- EV/EBIT
- EV/EBITDA
- EV/Sales

The reasons for this choice are most likely due to the fact that the P/BV multiple is less meaningful in manufacturing sectors, while the P/E ratio is generally more sensitive to the criteria used in the preparation of the company's financial statements.

Nonetheless, it is crucial to mention that there are relevant exceptions to this rule.

In the valuation of banks and insurance companies, multiples of the book value and multiples of specific economic value drivers representing the performance of the companies that belong to that particular industry (i.e., the net interest income, net fees and commissions, net trading revenues, etc.) are used more frequently.

In the search for the most suitable multiples, it can be useful to carry out an empirical comparison that shows the ability of different multiples to explain the value of the target company. As a matter of fact, it is possible to assess if the market implicitly attributes the ability to estimate the price of a company to a particular variable. The best way to do this is to run an analysis on the correlation between the multiples and the particular variable under consideration for the companies in the sample. The greater the correlation, the more the multiple is able to capture the company's market price.[3]

13.4.3 Synthetic Value of the Selected Multiples

The problem consists in summarizing the various values of the multiples of the sample companies into a unique value.

There are different ways to do so. We list a few methods, based on their frequency of use:

- *Computation of the multiple average and median.* The median can generally be considered as a satisfactory choice for those industries where companies have substantially uniform business models. In this case, the differences observed between multiples can be traced back to the sample companies' growth perspectives and their capability to generate superior performances. A further condition is that the company that is being valued is an average player in the market with respect to the aforementioned factors.

---

[3]It is important to highlight that such analyses, in order to prove useful, should be based on samples made up of an adequate number of comparable companies and should be subject to a test of statistical significance.

■ *Segmentation of the sample in homogeneous subcategories.* A technique that is frequently used by financial analysts is the regrouping of the sample companies into two or three subcategories to enhance the firms' comparability with the company that is being valued. The segmentation should occur based on objective criteria, such as size, international presence, ownership of particularly important brands and technologies, etc. Analysts should then understand to what subcategory the company under consideration belongs. The value of the benchmark multiple is finally obtained calculating the arithmetic average of the multiples of the companies that belong to this subcategory.

■ *Procedures based on extrapolation.* In some cases, the analysis of sample multiples allows us to find relevant relationships between the values of the indices and the specific value drivers. The procedures described in the previous points might not be entirely convincing in cases when, for example, the positioning of the valued company is very different from the one of the other sample companies. In these situations, analysts sometimes use techniques that are based on the interpolation or the extrapolation of the multiples observable in the sample.

Finally, the estimated value of the company is obtained by calculating the simple average of the values derived from the use of each multiple as applied to the company to be valued. If the analysts thinks that some multiples are more relevant than others, weighted averages might be used instead.

13.5 ESTIMATION OF "EXIT" MULTIPLES

The problem of estimating exit multiples is relevant in two instances:

■ For the *terminal value* estimate, which is the value of the company at the end of the analytical projection period of the cash flows (t_n) in the valuation methods based on analytic DCF models.
■ For the estimate of the divestiture value in acquisitions with short time horizons (t_n), typically realized by private equity funds.

In both cases, analysts have to form forecasts on the evolution over the time of the multiples calculated on the basis of the actual stock prices.

In order to face this problem rationally, it is convenient to split it up into two parts:

■ The estimate of the average industry multiples at t_n
■ The estimates of the multiples of the different companies belonging to the industry at t_n

13.5.1   Industry Multiples at t_n

The predictable level of the average multiples in the industry depends on two different factors:

- The attractiveness of the market in which the companies belonging to the specific industry operate with respect to the future period t_n
- The long-term evolution of the average multiples with respect to the entire stock market, which depends on the trend of interest rates and on the attractiveness of risky investments compared to risk-free ones

Some analysts maintain that the value of multiples must necessarily converge to the average value of the multiples calculated over a sufficiently long period (the last 10–15 years). Alternatively, one can calculate the theoretical multiple in the absence of growth that can be obtained as a function of the estimate of the opportunity cost of capital of the sector.

13.5.2   Differentiation Level

After the average multiple of the industry has been calculated, one can move on to the second stage of the analysis that aims at verifying whether the average multiple needs to be adjusted according to elements that differentiate the company that is being valued from the other companies in the same industry.

Such an adjustment is justified if the analyst is able to make credible projections on the cash flow profile for the period following t_n and therefore for divestiture periods that last no more than three to five years.

The basic idea is the following: given that the average multiple is an appropriate valuation index for companies that are characterized by results profiles that are similar to the industry average, the companies that are able to sustain higher growth rates than the competitors' should be valued with higher multiples, and vice versa.

The level of correlation of exit multiples can be evaluated through the analysis of the same factors that explain the dispersion of current multiples.

Alternatively, analysts can use the practical insights derived from the theoretical relationship between multiples and expected growth rates.

13.6   AN ANALYSIS OF DEAL MULTIPLES

The analysis of multiples linked to comparable transactions allows us to obtain significant information regarding a company's *likely market price*. This concept has already been introduced where we discussed the different informational content of stock market and deal multiples.

A main difference between deal multiples and stock market multiples consists of the reasons that can explain the volatility of the values in the group of selected transactions.

For stock market multiples, the volatility is, at least theoretically, the consequence of investors' consideration of the strengths and weaknesses of the companies that belong to the sample from a stand-alone perspective.

On the other hand, the value of deal multiples also depends on the context and specificities of the transaction.

As we will explain better later, the divestiture price is influenced by two types of factors:

1. Market factors, such as the competition level between willing buyers and the acquisition values estimated by each of them
2. Transaction factors, such as the percentage of acquired capital, payment methods (cash or acquirer's stock), the contractual terms regarding the guarantees given by the seller, mechanisms that tie part of the price to future results (earnouts), the existence of surplus assets that can allow the acquirer to make levered transactions, and so on

Therefore, the analysis of deal multiples requires the collection and interpretation of a certain amount of information regarding transactions that can significantly influence the negotiated price and the value of multiples consequently. We are going to focus on a few elements that are particularly crucial in this analysis.

13.6.1 Percentage of Acquired Capital

Deal multiples have greater significance when the transaction involves the company's entire capital. As a matter of fact, if the control stake is acquired, it is possible that the negotiated price also includes a control premium in addition to the proportional value of the acquired capital.

The possible existence of the premium does *not* allow for the calculation of the value of the entire capital through a simple proportion as in the following example. Therefore, if the price paid for 60 percent of the capital is 1,200, the value of 100 percent of the company is not $1,200 \times (100/60) = 2,000$.

This problem is not easy to solve because analysts are not able to objectively evaluate the existence and size of the premium; the information provided represents only a guideline to perform this kind of analysis.

When the transaction concerns the acquisition of a qualified minority stake, other problems arise. As a matter of fact, the acquisition of a minority stake can represent a simple financial investment, as in the case of a fund investing in a company with the objective of subsequently divesting from it through an IPO. The minority acquisition could also simply be linked to production or commercial agreements, as in the case of an acquirer who is an industrial operator. Finally, the acquisition of a minority stake is sometimes part of a transaction to acquire control in multiple stages.

In these cases, the significance of the price can change radically. For instance, if the acquisition of the minority interest is part of a broader program of transfer of control, acquirer and seller could have agreed on a price for the entire capital and have split it nonproportionally between the first installment and the following ones for the sake of convenience.

13.6.2   Characteristics of the Acquirer

Deal multiples relative to sale transactions to industrial counterparts are generally higher than multiples of transactions carried out with financial investors.

As a matter of fact, the acquisition prices should include a part of the value expected to be derived from the so-called *merger synergies.*

We should also highlight that this indicator is disavowed in some cases: As a matter of fact, some private equity funds follow an active entrepreneurial approach, for example, focusing on the creation of value through the aggregation of small and medium-sized firms with the goal of obtaining operating synergies or gaining significant market shares in the industries in which the companies operate.

Using the previously explained investment strategies, these funds can pay higher prices than the stand-alone value of the acquired companies. Consequently, the significance of deal multiples in these cases could be similar to the one of multiples of industrial transactions.

In conclusion, the analysis of deal multiples heavily depends on the characteristics of the acquirer with differences between:

- "Strategic" buyers
- Investment funds with an active/entrepreneurial approach that follow an entrepreneurial approach
- Investment funds that engage in transactions mainly of a (passive) financial nature.

13.6.3   Existence of Surplus Assets

A typical problem that exists when dealing with deal multiples is the existence of surplus assets. As a matter of fact, the total acquisition value is estimated by adding the value of the surplus assets to the acquisition value of the core business.

Consequently, deal multiples will have to be adjusted by subtracting the value of the disposal of the assets that are not functional to the core business from the price paid by the acquirer. It is easy to observe that the same problem can also exist with stock market multiples. However, holding all other factors constant, the need for such an adjustment is lower in this case because the stock market tends to undervalue surplus assets, especially if they are not crucial for cash flow generation.

It is possible, however, that in the case of a transfer of control, the acquirer also considers the money that will be recovered through the disposal of nonstrategic assets.

13.6.4 Payment Methods

Deal multiples are more significant in valuation processes when the acquisition is paid in cash. In many transactions the acquisition occurs instead through the transfer of the acquirer's shares or in a mixed form (shares plus cash).

If the payment method is the transfer of shares, a problem of relative valuation arises: the transaction could have taken place by inflating value of both the target's and the acquirer's shares.

This problem is particularly serious when either the acquirer's or the target company's shares are not listed and therefore no objective benchmark exists.

13.6.5 Earnouts

Another essential element in this discussion is the effective payment terms, which can be fragmented in multiple stages or include earnouts.

As mentioned before, an earnout provision implies that part of the price to be paid depends on the future achievement of the business plan objectives defined during the negotiations.

The price therefore cannot be determined ex-ante. This is a particularly thorny problem in the construction and interpretation of deal multiples. As a matter of fact, the presence of earnouts means that the price paid can vary depending on the results, even if the contracts usually include upper and lower price limits.

Earnout agreements are also usually not disclosed by parties, which makes the adjustment of multiples even more difficult.

13.6.6 Trend of Deal Multiples over Time

The trend of deal multiples over time mirrors the conditions that are created in the control market, which provides either sellers or buyers with a more favorable environment. The model of price formation in that market represents a useful logical tool for the interpretation of the levels reached by deal multiples.

The key factors are the level of competition among willing buyers and the size of merger synergies.

The analysis of the trend of deal multiples over time allows us to reconstruct the historical price paid within specific industries. However, only a true understanding of the current trend can provide a more reliable estimate of deal prices.

Exhibit 13.2 shows the trend of the Price/Book Value multiple with respect to a sample of transactions that took place in the Italian banking industry between 1995 and 2001.

The data shown in the figure allow us to see a significant increase in the multiples over the years 2000 and 2001 with respect to the average over the entire period. Therefore, the simple average over the whole period of time is a misleading indicator of the likely market price for transactions with transfer of control that could be realized in the more recent period.

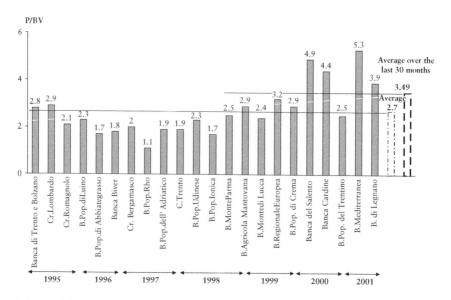

Exhibit 13.2 Trend of the Price/Book value multiple in a sample of transactions in the banking industry

13.7   THE COMPARABLE APPROACH: THE CASE OF WINE CO.

The discussion of the case presented in this paragraph has the goal of showing a valuation procedure based on multiples and to show the unavoidable approximations and problems that analysts run into in real-life cases.

This valuation example refers to an acquisition transaction of part of the capital of a winery carried out by a private equity fund.

13.7.1   The Logic of the Transaction

The wine market went through some important changes over last decade. High-quality wine has become a status symbol and a product that is therefore subject to a similar treatment as consumer goods. This has stimulated a growing interest in the industry among financial investors, favoring, therefore, a significant increase in the market value of companies holding well-known and historical brands.

The transaction we will discuss here is the acquisition of a 40 percent stake in the capital of a winery that owns important and well-known wine brands. The goal of the investment is to further strengthen the fund's presence in the high-quality products segment also through the acquisition of new wine estates.

The divestiture will occur in about three to five years through the sale in the stock market of the shares acquired by the fund.

The business plan prepared by the management assumes that the new acquisitions will absorb a relevant part of the cash flow and that the new investments will start generating cash flows in about five to seven years, considering the time that is necessary to start production in new vineyards and the waiting period for the ageing of the product.

The net flow that can be distributed through dividends (FCFE) over the plan horizon is therefore relatively low and the investment return is mainly created by the difference between the acquisition price and the offer price in the market for Wine Co.'s shares.

13.7.2   Relevant Information for the Valuation

In the picture we have described, the most relevant information for the fund's investment decision can be summarized with:

- Current multiples (stock market and deal multiples), according to which a bid for the target is formulated
- The value of the multiples of comparable companies estimated considering the expected divestiture period (the exit multiples)

Given the exit mechanism assumed by the fund management (an IPO), only stock-market multiples will be analyzed for the estimation of exit multiples.

13.7.3   The Selection of Comparable Companies

The group of listed comparable companies has been found through research in the Bloomberg database.

Two samples of wineries have been selected: the first one includes only European companies while the second one contains only non-European companies (Australia, United States, Chile, and Canada).

The analyst in charge of the valuation has decided to focus the analysis only on the first sample, considering that the European market is more meaningful for the calculation both of the likely market price of Wine Co. and of the estimate of the amount that can be gained through the sale of the stake that is expected to take place through a public offering in a European stock market.

Exhibit 13.3 shows the characteristics of both the sample of European companies and the target company in terms of sales, number of hectares of vineyards owned, and profitability. Moreover, we can also see the sales breakdown with respect to quality, type of product (white and red wines), and export shares.

A first look at Exhibit 13.3 suggests that the last two selected companies have to be excluded from the group of comparable companies because they are mainly commercial companies. The residual sample is composed of five Spanish companies with a production that mainly includes medium–high quality red wines.

Therefore, Wine Co. and the selected companies are sufficiently similar to justify a comparative valuation. Despite their similarity, some differing elements still exist that call for further analyses. They include the following facts:

▪ Wine Co.'s number of vineyard hectares and sales are lower than the selected companies'. As a matter of fact, Wine Co.'s land properties are owned directly by the family that controls the company. Therefore, Wine Co.'s book value is unbalanced with respect to the sample companies. However, this is not considered particularly important for the valuation for many different reasons. First, the business plan anticipates the acquisition of some agricultural properties that will allow Wine Co. to go to the market with an important vineyard property. Second, the company controls the management of the vineyards through 20-year rental agreements and is therefore able to assure standards of quality over a prolonged time horizon.

Exhibit 13.3 Characteristics of comparable companies (sample of European companies)

Firm	Nationality	Currency	Hectares owned	Current data (€m)			EBITDA (% sales)	EBIT (% sales)
				Sales	*EBITDA*	*EBIT*		
Comp. 1	Spain	Euro	1,016	202.5	28.1	21.6	13.88%	10.67%
Comp. 2	Spain	Euro	200	13.3	5.5	4.5	41.35%	33.83%
Comp. 3	Spain	Euro	120	57.6	23.0	26.9	41.11%	32.61%
Comp. 4	Spain	Euro	500	30.5	11.6	9.9	38.03%	32.46%
Comp. 5	Spain	Euro	150	43.2	5.4	3.2	12.50%	7.41%
Comp. 6	Germany	Euro	n.a.	232.4	12.8	8.7	5.51%	3.74%
Comp. 7	Germany	Euro	n.a.	251.2	24.4	10.1	9.71%	4.02%
Target firm	Italy	Euro	30	55.0	17.0	15.0	30.20%	27.10%

Firm	Breakdown sales for quality of produced wine			Breakdown sales for geographical area	Kinds of wine produced
	High quality	*Average quality*	*Low quality*		
Comp. 1	68%	30%	2%	Spain: 64.0%, other: 36.0%	Red wines
Comp. 2	47%	37%	16%	Spain: 82.9%, other: 17.1%	Red wines
Comp. 3		88%	12%	Spain: 29.5%, other: 70.5%	Red wines
Comp. 4		70%	30%	Spain: 84.9%, other: 15.1%	Red wines
Comp. 5		70%	30%	Spain: 86.1%, other: 13.9%	Red wines
Comp. 6		n.a.		Germany: 100.0%	Wines and sparkling wines
Comp. 7		n.a.		Germany: 57.6%, France: 22.0%, East Europe: 20.4%	Sparkling wines
Target firm	60.0%	20.0%	20.0%	Italy: 40.0%, USA: 60.0%	Red wines

- The sales breakdown according to geographical areas shows a high degree of concentration in the US market. This can be seen as a positive fact considering the US market's higher growth rates compared to the European one, but it can also be a peculiar risk factor in comparison with the selected comparable companies. As a matter of fact, some analysts believe that the US market will be characterized by increasing competition driven by national producers (i.e., Californian wines) and by Australian and Chilean producers.

13.7.4 Analysis of Value Multiples

The data on the value multiples of the selected companies is shown in Exhibit 13.4. The "price" columns show the most recent market price, the average price in the previous semester, the minimum and maximum price in the last six months. The column *market capitalization,* whose values have

Exhibit 13.4 European companies multiples

Firm	Currency	Current price	Price Average 6 months	Price Minimum 6 months	Price Maximum 6 months	Stock number (m)	Average market cap	Floating shares (m)	Net debt	TEV
Comp. 1	Euro	15.70	14.68	10.80	16.30	17.8	261.1	10.8	57.4	318.5
Comp. 2	Euro	8.40	8.88	8.40	9.50	5.4	48.3	n.a.	17.9	66.2
Comp. 3	Euro	27.19	24.04	19.50	28.50	7.7	185.8	4.8	39.3	225.1
Comp. 4	Euro	13.35	13.57	13.00	15.00	14.3	193.4	3.2	17.9	211.3
Comp. 5	Euro	6.19	6.30	5.90	6.94	6.1	38.7	1.7	46.0	84.7

Firm	Sales multiples			EBITDA multiples			EBIT multiples			RN multiples			PN
	LTM	Ex. t0	Ex. t+1	LTM	Ex. t0	Ex. t+1	LTM	Ex. t0	Ex. t+1	LTM	Ex. t0	Ex. t+1	LTM
Comp. 1	1.6x	1.4x	1.3x	11.3x	9.4x	8.7x	14.7x	13.1x	11.9x	17.4x	16.2x	14.6x	2.0x
Comp. 2	5.0x	4.0x	3.6x	12.0x	9.7x	10.1x	14.7x	13.1x	11.6x	21.0x	21.6x	17.8x	2.4x
Comp. 3	4.4x	3.9x	3.7x	10.8x	9.8x	8.4x	13.6x	12.0x	10.4x	12.4x	11.0x	10.5x	2.0x
Comp. 4	6.5x	5.2x	5.4x	18.2x	14.0x	13.9x	21.3x	15.7x	21.5x	21.2x	19.9x	19.3x	3.4x
Comp. 5	2.0x	1.8x	1.9x	15.7x	12.2x	11.1x	26.5x	53.7x	43.1x	43.0x	10.7x	12.7x	0.7x

been used in the multiple calculations, is based on the average prices of the last semester.

The multiples are respectively calculated on the last available financial statement data (LTM), on the closing forecasts for the current accounting period (Ex. t0), and on the analyst's forecasts regarding the following accounting period (Ex. t+1).

The "floating" column shows the number of shares available in the market. This value can be considered as an indicator of the liquidity of the stock, and consequently, of the significance of stock prices.

A first analysis of the multiples suggests the exclusion of company no. 5 from the sample, as it is not aligned with the other selected companies either in terms of profitability or of financial structure. The financial statements of company no. 5 highlight elevated wine inventory costs that are not easily recovered through products pricing.

The multiples of company no. 5 show the typical asymmetry discussed earlier: the EBIT and EBITDA multiples for this company are very high and out of measure compared to the sample, whereas the sales and book value multiples are very low. This causes us to describe the EBIT and EBITDA multiples as "fake multiples" void of any economic significance.

A further important element that concerns some of the selected companies is the modest gap between the values of the EBIT and the P/E multiples. This fact calls for a check of the effective size of the tax effects. The results of the analysis are summarized in Exhibit 13.5. They show that with a marginal tax rate of 35 percent, two companies face an effective tax rate of 3 percent and 6 percent.

In these particular cases, the size of the current tax levy is mainly explained by the advantages coming from investments and by the company's level of exports.

13.7.5 Tax Rate Adjustments for Multiples

We explained that multiples can turn out to be meaningless when the effective tax rates are significantly different with respect to both the analyzed sample and the target company.

In order to neutralize this effect, the analyst valuing Wine Co. has made the following adjustments:

- The present value of the lower tax rate has been estimated for a five-year period, which is the expected length of the tax concessions. This value has then been subtracted from the company's market capitalization.
- The net result has been recalculated using the full tax rate equal to 35 percent.

Exhibit 13.5 Estimates of the fiscal effects

Firm	Calculation tax rate t-3				Calculation tax rate t-2			
	EBT	Tax	Net income	Tax rate (real)	EBT	Tax	Net income	Tax rate (real)
Comp. 1	16.74	5.68	11.06	33.9%	19.29	6.75	12.54	35.0%
Comp. 2	4.92	1.72	3.20	35.0%	3.70	1.40	2.30	37.8%
Comp. 3	12.30	0.71	11.59	5.8%	14.64	1.32	13.32	9.0%
Comp. 4	8.99	2.30	6.69	25.6%	10.49	1.20	9.29	11.4%

Firm	Calculation tax rate t-3				
	EBT	Tax	Net income	Tax rate (real)	Theoretical tax rate
Comp. 1	20.52	6.29	15.04	30.7%	35.0%
Comp. 2	3.70	1.40	2.30	37.8%	35.0%
Comp. 3	15.89	0.93	14.96	5.9%	35.0%
Comp. 4	9.40	0.30	9.10	3.2%	35.0%

Exhibit 13.6 Calculation of the present value of the tax benefits linked to tax concessions

Firm	EBT	Theoretical tax rate	Theoretical taxes	Real taxes	Theoretical - real	Discount rate[*]	RF present value
Comp. 1	20.52	35.0%	7.18	6.29	0.90	4.33	3.88
Comp. 2	3.70	35.0%	1.30	1.40	−0.11	4.33	−0.45
Comp. 3	15.89	35.0%	5.56	0.93	4.63	4.33	20.05
Comp. 4	9.40	35.0%	3.29	0.30	2.99	4.33	12.94

The estimate of the adjustments has been highlighted in Exhibit 13.6. The table shows the calculation of the tax benefits deriving from tax concessions of the selected companies. It can be observed that these benefits have a significant size in two cases (Comparable 3 and Comparable 4).

Finally, Exhibit 13.7 shows the multiples adjusted with respect to these tax benefits. It is important to highlight that the P/E multiple now has a more coherent trend with respect to the EV/EBIT and the EV/EBITDA multiples.

As already mentioned, the adjustments have been made by subtracting the present value of the tax benefits from the market capitalization, and in the P/E ratio case, by "normalizing" the tax burden applying a marginal tax rate equal to 35 percent.

13.7.6 Valuation of Wine Co. Based on Multiples

For the valuation of Wine Co., the analyst used the following procedure:

- He selected the following multiples: EV/Sales; EV/EBITDA; EV/EBIT and used the results obtained in t0 as the reference values. Recall that the following analysis was performed at the beginning of t+1 and the analyst therefore decided to use the data referred to t0, even though they were just provisional, instead of using the last available financial statement.
- He calculated the value of "Wine" based on the selected multiples as shown in the following table (the multiples refer to Exhibit 13.7), shown in Exhibit 13.8.

The average value of €187 million that he obtained refers to the assets of Wine Co. The value of equity can then be calculated by subtracting the net financial position at the date of the estimate, equal to €18 million, from W_{asset}:

$$W_{equity} = 187 - 18 = €169 \text{ million}$$

Finally, the stock market multiples have been compared with the implicit multiples of some recent transactions. Expectedly, the EV/EBIT and the EV/EBITDA multiples turned out to be higher than those obtained from the market multiples. This is understandable, considering that these transactions were carried out by "strategic" acquirers. Therefore, the price paid includes the expected synergies coming from the integration of the companies' commercial networks.

Based on the information collected, the benchmark price to use in the negotiations with the target company's shareholders has been determined to be around €180 million (value for 100 percent of assets).

13.7.7 The Exit Multiples Estimate

The average value of multiples at the investment date shows that the degree of attractiveness of the industry is high and an analysis made in the last

Exhibit 13.7 Adjusted multiples of European companies

Firm	Price				Stock number (m)	Average market cap	Adjusted average market cap	Net debt	TEV	Adjusted TEV
	Current	Average 6 months	Minimum 6 months	Maximum 6 months						
Comp. 1	15.70	14.68	10.80	16.00	17.8	261.1	257.2	57.4	318.5	314.6
Comp. 2	8.40	8.88	8.40	9.50	5.4	48.3	48.8	17.9	66.2	66.7
Comp. 3	27.19	24.04	19.50	28.50	7.7	185.8	165.7	39.3	225.1	205.0
Comp. 4	13.35	13.57	13.00	15.00	14.3	193.4	180.4	17.9	211.3	198.3

Firm	Sales multiples			EBITDA multiples			EBIT multiples			RN multiples			PN
	LTM	Ex. t0	Ex. t+1	LTM	Ex. t0	Ex. t+1	LTM	Ex. t0	Ex. t+1	LTM	Ex. t0	Ex. t+1	LTM
Comp. 1	1.6x	1.4x	1.2x	11.2x	9.3x	8.6x	14.6x	12.9x	11.8x	19.3x	17.0x	15.4x	2.0x
Comp. 2	5.0x	4.1x	3.6x	12.1x	9.8x	10.1x	14.8x	13.2x	11.7x	20.3x	20.6x	17.0x	2.5x
Comp. 3	4.1x	3.6x	3.4x	9.9x	8.9x	7.6x	12.4x	11.0x	9.5x	16.0x	14.2x	13.6x	1.7x
Comp. 4	6.5x	4.9x	5.1x	17.1x	13.1x	13.1x	20.0x	14.7x	20.1x	29.5x	27.7x	26.8x	3.2x

Exhibit 13.8 Value of "Wine" through multiples

EV/Sales	$3.5 \times 55.0 = 192.5$
EV/EBITDA	$10.4 \times 17.0 = 175.1$
EV/EBIT	$12.9 \times 15.0 = 193.5$
Average Value	*187.0*

four years (Exhibit 13.9) shows that the average value of the multiples grew over time.

Based on the aforementioned framework, the analyst went through the following steps:

- He chose the EV/EBIT ratio as the proper exit multiple, also considering the impact of depreciating assets on the meaning of the EV/EBITDA ratio for the selected companies.
- The average of the multiples forecasted in t+1 was chosen as a benchmark for the EV/EBIT ratio, based on the hypothesis of lowering growth expectations in the market.
- Finally, considering that the divestiture will occur through an IPO, the value of the multiple has been prudently reduced by 15 percent. This is in line with the inclusion of an "IPO discount" with respect to the expected multiples at the starting date of the offer. The exit multiple has therefore been determined in the following way (Exhibit 10.6):

$$EV/EBIT_{t+1} \times 0.85 = 13.3 \times 0.85 = 11.3$$

Considering that the exit multiple is 23 percent lower than the implicit multiple,[4] the transaction can allow a fair remuneration of the capital invested in the project if two conditions occur:

1. The objectives of the plan will be respected, so that the EBIT growth will balance the gap between the exit multiple and the multiple implicit in the acquisition price.
2. The acquisition is financed with significant leverage in order to increase the internal rate of return (IRR) from the fund's perspective.

---

[4]The implicit multiple can be calculated by dividing the estimated asset value of Wine Co. (€187 million) by the current EBIT. It is therefore equal to 187/15 = 12.5.

Exhibit 13.9 Multiples trend in the last four years

	Comp. 1	Comp. 2	Comp. 3	Comp. 4	Average
EV/Sales					
t-3	0.8x	3.9x	4.9x	3.3x	3.2x
t-2	1.0x	4.5x	5.6x	4.7x	4.0x
t-1	1.1x	3.7x	4.6x	5.7x	3.8x
t0	1.0x	5.1x	3.5x	7.0x	4.2x
EV/EBITDA					
t-3	7.9x	10.2x	11.6x	9.4x	9.8x
t-2	9.7x	11.6x	13.1x	13.0x	11.8x
t-1	9.4x	9.0x	11.1x	16.4x	11.5x
t0	7.5x	12.1x	8.5x	18.4x	11.6x
EV/EBIT					
t-3	12.0x	11.3x	14.1x	11.7x	12.2x
t-2	13.7x	13.1x	15.7x	14.9x	14.4x
t-1	12.3x	10.2x	13.5x	18.1x	13.5x
t0	9.7x	14.8x	10.8x	21.6x	14.2x
P/E					
t-3	17.2x	17.0x	20.9x	16.3x	17.9x
t-2	18.4x	19.2x	23.4x	23.0x	21.0x
t-1	13.0x	21.5x	18.6x	26.9x	20.0x
t0	11.5x	20.5x	13.0x	32.1x	19.3x
P/BV					
t-3	1.4x	3.3x	3.5x	1.8x	2.5x
t-2	1.7x	3.8x	3.9x	3.0x	3.1x
t-1	1.3x	2.7x	2.8x	3.7x	2.6x
t0	1.2x	2.5x	1.7x	3.5x	2.2x

APPENDIX 13.1: CAPITAL INCREASES AND THE P/E RATIO

The following graph can help you better understand the problem regarding the calculation of current multiples—that is, the multiples calculated using the data reported in the last available balance sheet.

On April 1, 201X + 1 (point A) a capital increase occurs (the timeline of the transaction is shown in Exhibit 13.10). The data of the transaction are the following:

Net Income in 201X: €12 million

Number of Shares: 12 million

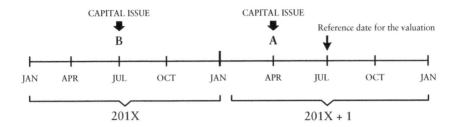

Exhibit 13.10 Multiple estimation during the period of a capital increase

Earnings per Share: €1

Market Price: €15

Market Capitalization: €15 × 12,000,000 = €180 million

P/E:15

Number of New Shares: 6 million

Subscription Price: €10

The market capitalization after the transaction will be €240 million, equal to the sum between the previous capitalization and the capital that has just been raised.

The unit price of the shares after the transaction will instead equal:

$$P_1 = TERP = (180 \text{ million} + 60 \text{ million})/18 \text{ million shares} = €13.33$$

And the dilution coefficient is:

$$c = 15/13.33 = 1.125$$

If we divide the market price following the transaction by the "old" earnings per share, we obtain:

$$P_1/EPS_0 = 13.33/1 = 13.33$$

However, if we calculate the earnings per share considering the number of new issued shares as well, we obtain:

$$\text{Diluted earnings per share} = 12,000,000/18,000 = €0.66$$

$$\text{From which:} \quad P_1/EPS_{0 \text{ dil}} = 13.33/0.66 = 20$$

In fact, both of the multiples we just calculated are not correct since the quantities placed at the numerator and denominator are not homogeneous. In the first case, the price dilution is not reflected in the earnings per share;

in the second, the earnings per share do not consider the income linked to the new capital raised.

In order to avoid the problems just pointed out, we can use the dilution coefficient c in order to adjust the market prices following the transaction (or alternatively the earnings per share). Using the data of the previous example, we have:

$$\text{Adjusted price} = P_1 \times c$$

$$13.33 \times 1.125 = 15$$

We then obtain the P/E multiple:

$$P/E = P_{1 \text{ adjusted}}/EPS_0 = 15/1 = 15$$

If we instead want to adjust the earnings per share:

Adjusted earnings per share = Earnings per share before the transaction/c

$$EPS_{0 \text{ adjusted}} = 1/c = 0.88$$

from which

$$P/E = P_1/EPS_{0 \text{ adjusted}} = 13.33/0.88 = 15$$

However, if the transaction occurs at point B (i.e., in June 201X), the following effects take place:

- The market prices following the transaction turn out to be "diluted" in the way that has been explained previously.
- The 201X result will include the income coming from the newly raised capital for one semester.

If these conditions occur, it is possible to calculate the company's multiples using the following procedure:

- Adjust prices using the coefficient c.
- Subtract the income derived from the capital increase (or the lower negative interests if the raised capital has been used to repay debt) from the 201X result.

Using this procedure, the multiples turn out to be net of the effects due to the increase in capital.

## CHAPTER 14

The Acquisition Value

In this chapter, after introducing the principal definitions of value, we will discuss some models useful in the assessment of acquisition value (with reference to either the entire capital of a company or a controlling stake of the company) within transactions aimed at integrating companies such as mergers and acquisitions (M&A) and joint ventures.

We will see how the *acquisition value*, to a great extent, determines the prices in the market for corporate control[1] and, consequently, the *fair market value* of companies in every sector.

To present the concepts to be illustrated in the following chapter, we will discuss the mechanisms and the forces responsible for the formation of the prices negotiated between buyers and sellers in the market for corporate control. The indications that can be inferred from the models presented will eventually be linked to the procedure for calculating premiums and discounts in the context of business valuation.

14.1   DEFINITIONS OF VALUE: AN OVERVIEW

In this section, we introduce three definitions of value that assume particular relevance in the area of interest for financial analysts and experts specialized in business valuations.

The proposed definitions are based on the model of determining value that will shortly be made more precise; they explain concepts of value that are clearly differentiated, in relation to specific purposes.

Also in the legal and accounting fields, specific definitions of value (i.e., standard of value) are often used. However, such standards are frequently described in general terms and refer to professional practice and techniques.

---

[1]The expression *market for corporate control* was coined in the early 1960s by finance scholars to describe the market for the buying/selling of businesses, as opposed to the market for goods and services.

For these reasons, the definitions of value used in this book will, as far as possible, be linked with the definitions in use in other fields, with the objective of providing a general methodological framework for the problems of valuation that need to be tackled by jurists and accountants.

Stand-alone Value Stand-alone value is the value estimated on the basis of the results obtained by the management and the opportunities for growth that the company could reasonably expect, relying upon the technological, marketing, and managerial resources that are available to it.[2]

Our definition of stand-alone value refers to the *controlling-interest level,* namely the value calculated from the perspective of current existing shareholders (or of the management that runs the company).

Assuming this perspective, the basis for calculating value is the business plan realized by the management (or by an external analyst), without taking into account any interventions that could be made by a potential (strategic) buyer in case a transfer of control takes place.

Acquisition Value (Investment Value) This is the value of a company determined from the point of view of a specific acquiring company. Therefore, the investment value includes the benefits related to merger synergies that the buyer expects to obtain as a result of the integration of the activities of the target company and the company that carries out the acquisition.

The following elements constitute the acquisition value:

- The stand-alone value of the target company.
- The value of merger synergies that generate incremental cash flow in the target company.

---

[2] Should a loss-making enterprise be assigned a positive stand-alone value? To answer the question one needs to understand the nature and cause of the losses. If the negative results could be reversed, contingent upon the market situations that are susceptible to change, then the firm could receive a positive stand-alone value as the prospects of the income in normal operating conditions exceed the sustained losses. The same conclusion holds in cases where the losses were caused by errors made by management, but there exists a credible plan for revival and the business has the resources to achieve it. If, on the other hand, the losses are not transitory, and the management is not in a situation to formulate credible interventions to confront them, one must conclude that the stand-alone value tends inexorably to zero, ending up being negative. This does not mean, however, that the capital of a company losing money could not receive a market price that is positive, with potential buyers effectively interested in the same business, or a positive liquidation value.

■ The value of merger synergies that could be obtained in other businesses led by the controlling shareholders as well as any other private benefits accruing to controlling shareholders. These issues will be treated in the next chapter.

The notion of the acquisition value is related to the more general concept of investment value used in the legal and accounting literature. We could define the acquisition value as the investment value estimated by a specific buyer within an acquisition. Such notions of value will be further discussed in this chapter.

Fair Market Value The likely market price implies a concept of *exchange value*.

It indicates the value that can be attributed to a business considering the valuations that, presumably, would be formulated by the *generic* potential buyers that are interested in acquiring the business.

It is, therefore, a sort of consensus value that can be assigned in a company by a group of potential buyers, as a function of the nature and the dimensions of the merger synergies expected in the scope of a particular area of business.

If the expert performs the valuation using the DCF method, the basis for calculating the *likely market price* is the business plan of the target company modified by the merger synergies that can be shared in relation to the characteristics and the motivations of the group of potential buyers. This theme will be examined in greater depth later while the notion of fair market value will be discussed further in the next chapter.

Fair Value and Intrinsic Value In the Anglo-Saxon setting, the notion of fair value was originally developed in the legal field, in order to define a standard of value to protect the interests of minority shareholders.

Furthermore, the rules imposed by the adoption of the IAS by listed European companies require, in some cases, that the financial interests be valued at their respective fair values. Also, for periodic assessment of the value of intangibles, accountants ought to refer in most instances to the fair value of same.

According to the prevalent interpretation, this notion of fair value is similar to that, already discussed, of fair market value. Therefore, this definition of fair value by identifying a use value ought to incorporate also the value of the synergies with respect to a specific strategic investor.

In conclusion, the expression *intrinsic value*, often used by financial analysts, indicates a generic definition of value obtained by the generally accepted techniques of fundamental analysis. The research on listed securities issued by merchant and investment banks often compares such intrinsic value with the market value of a company in order to find evidence of its under- or overvaluation.

14.2 VALUE CREATED BY AN ACQUISITION

The value created by an acquisition is equivalent to the difference between the present value of the flow expected by the acquirer following the transaction and the price paid for the capital of the target company.

The present value of the flow expected by the acquirer is normally defined by the term *acquisition value*.

Therefore:

$$NPV_{acq} = W_{acq} - P$$

where:

NPV_{acq} = net present value of an acquisition transaction
W_{acq} = value of acquisition of the capital of the target firm
P = price paid by the acquirer for the capital of the target firm

The measure of the difference between P and W_{acq} depends, as will be shown in the following chapter, on the bargaining power between buyers interested in concluding the transaction, which in turn depends on the level of competition that characterizes the market for corporate control. It is clear, therefore, that the acquisition value also identifies the maximum price that the buyer would be willing to pay. This constitutes one of the key elements to be considered in negotiating with the selling party.

14.2.1 Differential Approach

An acquisition, like any other investment, must be interpreted and evaluated considering the effects that it would produce within the business model in which it takes place. Each new transaction of significant size not only gives rise to consequences in quantitative terms—that is, in terms of the direct financial results—but also tends to change the various relationships within the organizational structure of the company, as well as the relationships between the business itself and its economic environment.

To identify and appreciate, in quantitative terms, the effects of an acquisition, business economists often apply a scheme of analysis which is based on the comparison between a base-scenario referable to the business in absence of the scheduled acquisition or investment, and an innovative-scenario represented by the business as is expected to evolve if the acquisition takes place.

The principles exposed in the first chapters, which are at the base of the financial valuations, permit the formulation of an analysis focused on three value drivers, which synthesize the multiple effects of integrating the companies involved in the transaction.

Following this approach, the major consequence produced by an acquisition can be brought back to three fundamental effects:

1. A quantitative differential effect, in terms of the incremental cash flows that are produced in the acquiring entity following the transaction
2. A qualitative differential effect, in terms of the risk profile of the acquirer
3. A differential effect on the company's creditworthiness, which takes place when the entity resulting from the merger of the companies carrying out the transaction could increase its leverage

Therefore, following this systemic logic, the value of acquisition of the target company can be represented as follows:

$$W_{acq(B)} = W_{A+B} - W_A$$

where:

$W_{acq(B)}$ = acquisition value of the target firm
W_{A+B} = value of the new entity created through the integration of the operations of A and B
W_A = value of the buyer in absence of the transaction

In order to evaluate W_{A+B} we will analyze in greater detail the effects of these differential factors.

Differential Effects on Cash Flow   Following an acquisition, the flow referable to the acquiring company increases as a result of the flow generated by the target company, in addition to the incremental flow that results from the process of integration that the acquirer intends to realize after having acquired control. The flow so qualified measures the phenomena that, in general, come to be characterized as merger synergies and economies.

For simplicity, this flow can be classified according to the following scheme:

- Incremental cash flow related to collusive policies; this concerns the benefits related to the consolidation of the market share of the acquirer along with the consequences on pricing policy and on the costs of marketing. These benefits, which often represent the true motivations of an acquisition, are rarely measurable *ex ante* in objective terms.

■ Incremental flow related to improvements in operations efficiency; as shown in numerous case histories, this concerns the benefits that often could be quantified by an acceptable approximation since the estimates can be based on reliable data. The uncertainty relates to the effectiveness of the organizational interventions enabling the pursuit of economic benefits. For example, evidences suggest that many acquisitions initially claimed to be particularly beneficial actually turn out to be dramatically unsuccessful because of the difficulty in merging diverse organizational cultures.

■ Incremental flow referable to exploitation of elements of an intangible nature (i.e., marketing, technology, and human capital resources and capabilities).

Differential Effects on the Risk Profile Acquisition transaction can modify appreciably the risk profile, both with reference to the systematic risk factors as well as to the idiosyncratic risks.

We already mentioned that when valuing a company, lower specific risk factors could have a significant impact on the value as the players in the market for corporate control do not necessarily base their decisions on the principle of portfolio diversification suggested by the classical financial theory.

For example, an acquisition could determine a significant increase in size, improving, as a consequence, the organizational structure. Increasing a company's size could also consolidate its market and bargaining power with respect to clients and suppliers.

Merger transactions taking place at the industry upstream level are often motivated by the need to control the quality and availability of strategic factors or resources. Therefore, they tend to reduce the overall company risk profile.

On the contrary, other acquisitions can negatively affect the risk profile: for example, in the case of vertical integrations, the gain from operating leverage can give rise to a major unfavorable variability in results as a function of fluctuations in the market.

Therefore, acquisitions can produce various positive or negative effects in terms of risk, which could be offset entirely or in part by a deterioration of the systematic risk.

Differential Effect on the Capacity to Obtain Credit As pointed out earlier, the improvement in risk profile generally allows the company a greater use of financial leverage, given the same level of financial costs.

If the debt is increased in such situations, the tax benefits related to the deductibility of interest from taxable income could give rise to an increase in value due to tax savings.

14.2.2　Potential Benefits

Acquisition transactions are also motivated by objectives that are not directly translatable into incremental monetary flow. For example, certain acquisitions represent just a first move, set by the management, in order to be able to catch future potential business opportunities. Many acquisitions of companies located in foreign countries, which are expected to show future high rates of growth, often have the implicit purpose of timely entering a certain geographical market in order to benefit from the opportunities it will bear.

Considering these potential benefits, we can conclude that the acquisition value is formed by three elements:

$$W_{acq} = W_{base} + W_S + W_O$$

where:

　W_{base} = stand-alone value of the target firm
　W_S = economies/synergies consequent to the acquisition
　W_O = value of the opportunities created by the acquisition itself

The open models of valuation discussed earlier constitute the logical tool that allows the estimation of opportunities of value creation through the development of new areas of business and the opening of new markets.

14.3　VALUE-COMPONENTS MODEL

In valuing acquisitions, the three phenomena briefly outlined (effects of quantity, quality, financial structure) can be valued synthetically or can be separately the object of specific estimates. We favor the second alternative for two main reasons.

First, the analytical estimations of the sources of value of an acquisition help to better understand the assumptions that form the basis of the validity of the transaction. Second, this type of analysis helps to identify the specific areas of risk in the acquisition itself.

We call this type of analysis *model of the stratification of value*. We will introduce it from a methodological point of view, and then we will point out the opportunity of adopting an abridged procedure, which gives

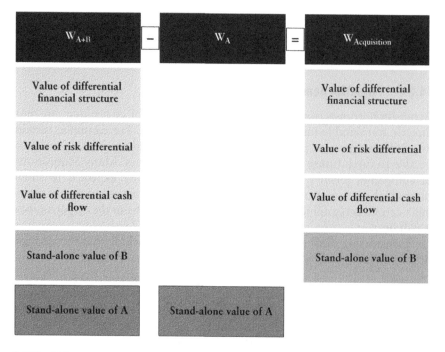

Exhibit 14.1 Value-components model

satisfactory results in the majority of cases. The process of estimating the acquisition value according to this approach could be divided into different phases, each of which focuses on a particular layer of value. These concepts are summarized in Exhibit 14.1.

The proposed approach works better if the analyst utilizes the disaggregated method of valuation starting with the estimate of unlevered value and valuing separately the tax shields.

In the following example, it is assumed, for the sake of simplicity, that the flow is rendered in perpetuity and that the level of existing debt at the time of reference remains constant.

1. Determination of stand-alone value of A and B (equity value)

$$W_{\text{STAND-ALONE}} = \frac{FCFO_A}{K_{\text{eu\_A}}} + D_A \times t_c + \frac{FCFO_B}{K_{\text{eu\_B}}} + D_B \times t_c - D_A - D_B$$

where:

$FCFO$ = operating cash flow net of taxes produced from A and B when they operate separately

K_{eu} = discount rates appropriate for firm A and firm B in absence of debt

D = net financial debt

t_c = tax rate

2. Determination of the value of risk differential

$$W_{RISK\_DIFF.} = \frac{FCFO_{(A+B)}}{K_{eu\_m}} - \frac{FCFO_A}{K_{eu\_A}} - \frac{FCFO_B}{K_{eu\_B}}$$

where:

K_{eu_m} = discount rate modified to account for the attenuation of risk factors

It is worth noting that K_{eu_m} can be estimated from the average of the rates K_{eu_A} and K_{eu_B}, weighted by the present values of the flow generated by A and B. In other words, the average rate is a function of the value of A and B. Then, the average rate so obtained can be further adjusted taking into account the lowering of specific elements of risk.

3. Determination of the value of incremental flow due to synergies

$$W_{FLOW\_DIFF.} = \frac{\Delta FCFO_{(A+B)}}{K_{eu\_m}}$$

where:

$\Delta FCFO_{(A+B)}$ = incremental cash flow due to the process of integration of activities of A and B

4. Determination of value related to differential of financial structure

$$W_{FIN\_STRUCTURE\_DIFF.} = \Delta D_{(A+B)} \times tc$$

where:

$\Delta D_{(A+B)}$ = net incremental debt bearable by the new business entity created integrating the activities of A and B

Exhibit 14.2   Company A and B financials

	Buying Company (A)	Target Company (B)
Operating cash flow net of taxes (*FCFO*)	4,000	3,000
Unlevered cost of capital: (K_{eu})	20%	15%
Unlevered value: $W_u = (a/b)$	20,000	20,000
Net financial debt: (D)	10,000	8,000
Tax rate*	37%	37%
Levered value $W_1 = (c + d \times e)$	23,700	22,960
Value of equity: W_e	13,700	14,960

*That is the tax rate applied to corporate income which indicated also the tax benefits derived from the deductibility of financial charges.

14.3.1   Application of the Model

The procedure for estimating the acquisition value described in the previous sections may be illustrated through a simplified example (the cash flow is every time rendered in perpetuity). The relevant financial data of company A and B—respectively buyer and target—are presented in Exhibit 14.2.

Following the integration of activities of A and B, the expected differential effects are:

- Savings due to the improvement in efficiency of business operations that give rise to major operating cash flow net of taxes in the amount of 1,000 per annum ($\Delta FCFO = 1,000$).
- Attenuation of specific risk factors, considering the new overall risk profile of the activities performed jointly by A and B. The new rate K_{eu_m} was estimated to be 16 percent (note that this estimate is referred to the rate appropriate to discount the flow produced by A and B as a merged entity, thus including $\Delta FCFO$; note as well that it is slightly smaller than the average of the rates, previously adopted in order to evaluate the buying company and the target company, weighted by the respective asset values).
- Increase in debt capacity of 6,000 (for which $\Delta D = 6,000$). On the basis of the preceding data we can easily determine the layers of value related to the differentials of flow, of risk, and of financial structure.
- Flow differential

$$W_{FLOW\_DIFF.} = \frac{\Delta FCFO}{K_{eu\_m}}$$

$$W_{FLOW\_DIFF.} = \frac{1,000}{0.16} = 6,250$$

■ Risk differential

$$W_{\text{RISK\_DIFF.}} = \frac{FCFO_A + FCFO_B}{K_{\text{eu\_m}}} - \frac{FCFO_A}{K_{\text{eu\_A}}} - \frac{FCFO_B}{K_{\text{eu\_B}}}$$

$$W_{\text{RISK\_DIFF.}} = \frac{4,000 + 3,000}{0.16} - \frac{4,000}{0.15} - \frac{3,000}{0.20}$$

$$W_{\text{RISK\_DIFF.}} = 3,750$$

■ Financial structure differential

$$W_{\text{FIN\_STRUCTURE\_DIFF.}} = \Delta D \times t_c$$

$$W_{\text{FIN\_STRUCTURE\_DIFF.}} = 6,000 \times 0.37 = 2,220$$

On the basis of the preceding calculations, we can now represent the acquisition value as follows (Exhibit 14.3).

It is worth noting that, although the investment value includes the tax benefits relative to the new debt of 6,000, the debt will not be deducted from the asset value in order to calculate the equity value.

In fact, it must be assumed that the funds raised from the financing are invested in new assets, with a value not less than that of the original debt.

In the specific case, since the example refers to a steady-state scenario, it can also be considered that the funds originating from the new debt were

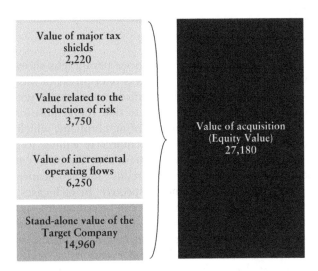

Exhibit 14.3 Elements (layers) that form the value of acquisition

directed to the repayment of capital at least equal to the stake of the shareholders of the acquiring a company.

Simplified Version of the Model The model of value stratification constitutes a valuable logical tool. It allows an orderly analysis of the factors that enter in the creation of value. In general, however, it may be useful to adopt a simplified version, which does not include the pricing of the segments of value related to the differentials of risk and financial structure. The two fundamental sources of value that remain are represented by:

- Base value of the target company
- Net present value of the flow related to the economies/synergies following the merging of the activities of the target company and the acquiring company

This simplification complies with the caution principle. The estimation of the differential for risk and financial structure often requires valuations based exclusively on elements that heavily rely, in general, on subjective estimates. Often, therefore, these estimates tend to be aggressive.

In the preceding example, the aggressive estimate of the value of acquisition for B is 27,180 while a more cautious estimate would be 20,674.

14.4 FURTHER CONSIDERATIONS IN VALUING ACQUISITIONS

14.4.1 The Analysis Standpoint

The considerations developed in the previous paragraphs show that in the case of the valuation of acquisitions, what is relevant is not the value of the target company in itself but what the acquirer intends to do with it.

In more rigorous terms, one can state that the acquisition value is a function of the flow accruing to the acquiring company, which reflects the consequences of the interventions the acquirer is willing to perform on the target company. This means, very often, that the interventions of the acquirer take on greater importance and reduce the significance of the flow projections made from a stand-alone perspective. In such cases, the flow—on the basis of which the acquisition value can be estimated—is the result of innovative projections that take into account strategic moves, management choices, divestment of assets or significant new investments, and so on. In other cases, the planned post-acquisition interventions are relatively modest and can be translated into the plan of estimation of flow with a simple adjustment and integration of the flow estimated under the hypothesis of autonomy of operations of the target company.

14.4.2 Estimating the Cash Flow

As mentioned, for various reasons, the flow relevant to the estimation of the acquisition value is different from that achieved in a stand-alone scenario. These principally include:

- Carrying out of strategic moves with the consequent modification of the objectives of the target company in terms of growth and market share. These measures can require significant investments in fixed assets and working capital and modification of the profitability patterns.
- Carrying out of interventions aimed at reducing operating costs. This might involve eliminating duplicate business activities or departments.
- Economies of scale in the operations, organizational, and commercial areas.
- Economies of scale as a consequence of the rationalization/completion of product lines/portfolios.
- Abandoning of some areas of business with consequent divesture. At times, this includes charges associated with ending certain businesses.
- Synergies in the area of technology, marketing, and exploitation of the distribution network.

A deeper and more complete analysis of the above-mentioned factors lies beyond the scope of this book. In terms of value, the benefits achieved by the integration of activities between the target company and the buyer (the acquirer) are expected to come from the ability of the post-merger entity to become more efficient and/or effective. However, two factors are relevant:

- First, benefits from the integration of activities tend to be overestimated, or, from a symmetric perspective, the charges, which are to be sustained in order to concretize the benefits, are overlooked. This is amply supported by an extensive literature on M&A consequences: the analyses confirm that in many transactions there are greater advantages for the shareholders of the merged or acquired company than for the acquiring company.
- Second, at times, it is necessary to undertake severe reorganizations, which take longer than originally prospected. This means that certain other specific risk factors can arise from the actual attainability of the incremental flows resulting from the integration of two nonhomogeneous business entities.

If these elements of uncertainty are effectively identifiable, it is advisable to proceed with the specific valuation of the flow related to the economies/synergies attained, as foreseen from the value-stratification model by correcting, as required, the discount rate of the flow related to these synergies/economies considering the specific risk elements they imply.

14.4.3 Time Horizon of Explicit Cash Flow Projections

In general, when estimating the value of acquisition the use of synthetic financial methods is not practical nor advisable. In fact, the value created by acquisition is in large part due to the interventions taken by the acquiring company with respect to the target company: such interventions determine instability in the cash flow that should be captured by financial projections usually at least of three years.

Therefore the number of years for the projection of the cash flow is a function not only of the broader industry and firm characteristics but also of the time horizon along which the merger would produce its effects.

14.4.4 The Debt Profile

Post-acquisition interventions often affect the debt profile dynamically. Therefore, the current debt profile could differ considerably from the level it is expected to reach when the post-merger company achieves a situation of stability.

Context is important: in particular, when estimating the acquisition value of a company targeted for merger into the acquirer, the dynamic of the leverage of the target firm in the period following the acquisition tends to lose relevance. As seen earlier, we must understand the amount by which the acquisition changes the debt profile of the acquirer and whether these changes will generate tax benefits.

14.4.5 Asset-Side versus Equity-Side Valuation

In general terms, the equity-side approach is advisable if there are obligations that could limit the possibilities for shareholders to draw on the cash flow generated by a new initiative: similar conclusions also apply to the estimate of the value of acquisitions.

It is worth underlining that if the flow is not easily available, FCFE should be modified as a function of the cash flow actually—not just potentially—available to shareholders through the distribution of dividends, or in other forms (e.g., buybacks).

The modification of the method that forecasts the discounting of the cash flow available to shareholders is useful, for example, when it is required to evaluate acquisitions realized in countries enforcing limitations on financial resources transfers in favor of foreign shareholders.

14.5   ACQUISITION VALUE OF PLASTIC MATERIALS CO.

14.5.1   Assumptions for Estimating Stand-Alone Value

The firm Plastic Materials Co. holds a healthy competitive position in the market for PVC-based products, and it has recently focused on more specialized products. After completing the transaction, the acquirer intends to merge with Plastic Materials Co. The business plan covers a period of six years. After the sixth year, it is assumed that the activities of the company would reach the full functionality. The terminal value would be calculated on the basis of a multiple of five times the EBIT, estimated by using comparable listed companies. It is assumed, furthermore, that the acquisition could produce benefits in terms of operations and commercial activities. Prudently, it is expected that these benefits would cease after the forecasted six-year plan.

Exhibit 14.4 shows the trend of monetary flow from operations, in the absence of measures taken by the acquirer, and the results of the estimation (we refer to the unlevered value of Plastic Materials).

It is worth noting that in the first year of the plan, it is expected that the working capital will increase significantly, mainly due to the extension of the terms of payment to the suppliers, which are not in line with the common industry practice.

14.5.2   Estimating the Value of Synergies

It has been forecasted that the merger of the two companies will generate both commercial and organizational synergies. These benefits are estimated in terms of operating cash flow net of charges, of investments, and of changes on working capital. The results of the estimates are represented in Exhibit 14.5. As stated earlier, the flow is estimated prudently for a period of six years (and therefore has no impact on the terminal value) and is discounted by K_{eu}.

14.5.3   Acquisition Value of Plastic Materials Co.

The acquisition value of Plastic Materials Co. can be determined by using the value-components model:

€/000

Unlevered stand-alone value of Plastic Materials Co.	121,839
Present value of the flow related to the synergies emerging from the acquisition	19,436
Acquisition value (unlevered)	**141,275**

Exhibit 14.4 Plastic Materials Co.: stand-alone cash flow

Plastic Materials Co.	LCm					
Stand-alone operating cash-flowa	t_1	t_2	t_3	t_4	t_5	t_6
a) EBITDA	28,835	30,172	31,760	33,789	37,185	38,889
b) D&A	(5,076)	(6,178)	(6,582)	(7,424)	(8,292)	(7,286)
c) Taxes	(14,255)	(14,396)	(15,107)	(15,819)	(17,336)	(18,962)
d) Operating profit after taxes	9,504	9,598	10,071	10,546	11,557	12,641
e) Capex	(8,945)	(9,181)	(8,389)	(7,021)	(7,231)	(7,448)
f) WC	(8,625)	(2,280)	(2,203)	(2,000)	(2,160)	(1,761)
Cash flows (d + b + e + f)	(2,990)	4,315	6,061	8,949	10,458	10,718
Final value						158,015

Valuation results

BP cash flows = 25,528   Terminal value = 96,321   Unlevered value = 121,839

$K_{cu} = 8.6\%$

Exhibit 14.5 The case of Plastic Materials Co.

Plastic Materials Co. Cash-flows from synergies	LCm					
	t_1	t_2	t_3	t_4	t_5	t_6
a) Production and logistics optimization	800	824	848	872	900	927
b) Raw materials efficiencies	1,200	1,236	1,273	1,311	1,350	1,391
c) Sales force rationalization	750	773	795	820	844	870
d) Increased size purchasing power	1,250	1,287	1,326	1,366	1,407	1,449
e) Cash flows (a + b + c + d)	4,000	4,120	4,242	4,369	4,501	4,637
Discounted final value						19,436
Discounting rate = 8.6%						

To value Plastic Materials Co., we have adopted the *simplified value stratification method,* which excludes the pricing of the possible differential effects of the transaction on risk profile and leverage.

14.6 ACQUISITION VALUE OF CONTROLLING INTERESTS

14.6.1 Private Benefits and Benefits Shared among All Shareholders

A problem that has attracted the attention of scholars and practitioners regards the value to be attributed to a company's controlling stake, which represents not the entire equity but also a stake granting a significant level of control over the choice of management. The interest in this theme derives from the fact that, in general, the value of such stakes is higher in proportion than value of the shares of the capital they represent.

To introduce this discourse, we can start from the simplified version of the model of value stratification. This sheds light on the essential elements that contribute to determining the acquisition value of a company:

- Base value of the target company ($W_{\text{stand-alone}}$)
- Net present value of the flow related to the expected benefits arising from the integration of the two merged companies ($W_{\text{diff. flows}}$)

Note that the resulting flow that prices $W_{\text{diff. flows}}$ can be classified by distinguishing:

1. Flow produced by the target company and that therefore accrues to earnings, which can be distributed to all the shareholders
2. Flow obtained directly only by the acquirer or by other businesses under its control

The first case could involve, for example, the incremental earnings related to a more efficient choice in terms of managerial structure or operations. In the latter case, the return is in terms of incremental income from royalties charged by the acquirer to the acquired firm; or incomes generated from the transfer of materials or other goods, allocation of the services to the acquired company, for example.

Since, as we shall see shortly, among the benefits derived from the improved management of the target company, we can also classify the nonmonetary ones (e.g., psychological benefits) and other private benefits specifically accruing to the controlling shareholder. In order to avoid misunderstandings, we shall henceforth adopt the following definitions:

- We will call divisible benefits (or flow) those that contribute to the formation of earnings in the target company and that can be divided among the all the shareholders of the target company in proportion to the shares held.
- We will call the indivisible benefits (or flow) those that are found outside the target company and go entirely and solely to the person (or entity) controlling the merged companies; therefore these benefits are defined indivisible because they are not assigned according to the quota of shares held in the target company.

Financial economists generally refer to the benefits that we have termed indivisible, using the expression private benefits of control.[3]

14.6.2 Determining the Acquisition Value

When an acquisition does not concern the entire capital, but a fractional part of it, which is anyway sufficient to guarantee the control over the company,

---

[3] See, for example, A. Dyck and L. Zingales, "Private Benefits of Control: An International Comparison," *Journal of Finance* (April 2004); the authors underline that the common feature .... is that some value, whatever the source, is not shared among all the shareholders in proportion of the shares owned, but is enjoyed exclusively by the part in control. Hence, the name *private benefits of control*.

the price limit that the acquirer could pay for the block of shares would be calculated using the following expression:

$$W_x = (W_{base} + W_{div}) \times x + W_{ind}$$

where:

W_x = acquisition value of the block of shares
W_{base} = stand-alone value of the target firm
W_{div} = value of the divisible benefits relating to the synergies and opportunities
W_{ind} = value of the indivisible benefits that relate to the synergies and opportunities
x = percentage of the capital to which the shares refer[4]

For the reasons abovementioned, W_{base} and W_{div} are weighted for the valuation of the share in proportion to x. Hence, the quantity $(W_{base} + W_{div}) \times x$ could be defined as the proportional value of the controlling interest. The third component (W_{ind}) is, on the other hand, a constant. Developing the synergies and seizing the external opportunities is therefore possible if and only if control is attained.

14.6.3 Application of the Model

The following example demonstrates that the relationship between the acquisition value of a majority share (W_x) and the value of the fraction of the capital that it refers to tends to grow as the size of the share shrinks, to the extent that it guarantees control.

In the case at hand, the stand-alone value of the business which is the object of the acquisition, was estimated in €180 million. These estimates, which refer to the entire share capital of the firm constituting 100 million shares of common stock, appeared fair and consistent with the company's financial results. Besides the possibility of acquiring 100 percent of the capital, an acquisition of 75 percent or only 51 percent was hypothesized. On the basis of the data, it is required to identify the price limits corresponding to the various sizes of the blocks of shares acquired. Management considered this information useful to conduct negotiations with the seller.

The acquiring group considered it possible to shrink certain operative costs of the entity formed, as well as a modest restructuring of production; the incremental value of these changes to the business was estimated to be

---

[4]The percentage x is assumed guaranteeing the control of the company.

about €20 million. The rationale of the transaction was also the exploitation of the commercial network of the target company, as well as the deployment of its well-known brand for marketing the products in three of the firms controlled by the acquirer. This was expected to increase the net margins of the three subsidiaries up to €65 million in present value.

On the basis of the data, the acquisition value of 100 percent of the capital (W_{acq}) is equal to €265 million. This amount is obtained by adding the stand-alone value of the target company (W_{base}), which is equal to €180 million, the incremental value due to the change in management, W_{div} of €20 million, as well as the value of the flows generated by the three subsidiaries (W_{ind}) equal to €65 million. It is now a matter of estimating W_x, in the various cases, depending on the size of the block of shares considered.

This is easily done by using equation 14. For example, the acquisition value of a 60 percent stake will be:

$$W_{base} \times 0.6 + W_{div} \times 0.6 + W_{ind} \times 1$$
$$180 \times 0.6 + 20 \times 0.6 + 65 \times 1 = 185$$

And the unit acquisition value for the shares will be:

$$W_x = \frac{185 \text{ bn}}{(N \times x)}$$

where:

W_x = unit acquisition value of the shares
N = overall number of outstanding shares
x = fractional share of the total equity capital

Exhibit 14.6 shows the increasing acquisition value of the shares (W_x) according to the varying size of the block. This is due to the fact that the component of value W_{ind} does not depend on the size of the stake, as long as control is guaranteed. After passing the threshold of 50 percent, the unit acquisition value falls, since the possibilities of attaining the prospected business synergies decrease as well as the acquirers' ability to make rationalizing changes.

In the example, the unit acquisition value of the shares in the case of the acquisition of the entire capital is €2.65. If 75 percent of the capital is acquired, the unit value becomes €2.867, and it is equal to €3.275 in case the fraction of capital is 51 percent.

Exhibit 14.6 shows the changes of W_x in more complex cases. We assume that the share ownership in the company is widely spread among the

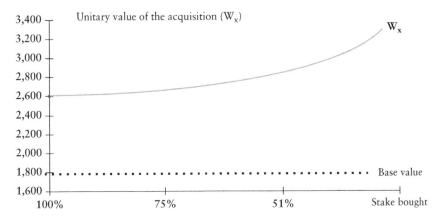

Exhibit 14.6 Trend of the unit acquisition value of shares as a function of the capital fraction acquired

public, and that this allows a less than 51 percent stake to be required for a *de facto* control of the business. In the other case, it is assumed that a block of shares below the threshold, which assures a majority in an extraordinary shareholders meeting (in the example, assumed equal to 66.7 percent), does not guarantee the full value extraction from W_{ind}.

With these conditions, in order to calculate W_x, W_{ind} needs to be appropriately modified with a coefficient of adjustment, estimated as a function of the risk due to not being able to realize the desired synergies. Below a certain level of control, it is also prudent to correct the quantity W_{ind} since the actions of management could be disturbed by the presence of other relevant shareholders. Therefore, W_x can be obtained using the following new expression:

$$W_x^* = (W_{base} + W_{div} \times a_1) \times x + W_{ind} \times a_2$$

where:

a_1 = coefficient of adjustment for the risk of not realizing the planned changes

a_2 = coefficient of adjustment for the risk of not realizing the desired group synergies

In the example, the coefficients a_1 and a_2 are equal, respectively, to 1, and to 0.8 in the case of a 66.7 percent threshold. Exhibit 14.7 shows that after the jump corresponding to 66.7 percent of the capital, W_x continues to grow in the closed interval until 51 percent. Beyond this point, the adjusted value of W_{ind} is maintained at a new constant: above the 51 percent

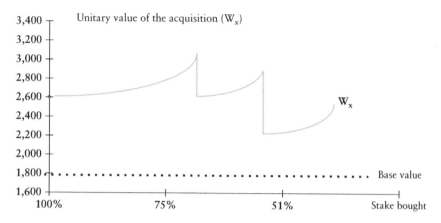

Exhibit 14.7 Trend of the unit acquisition value of the shares as a function of the risk of not obtaining the desired synergies

threshold, the adjustment coefficients grow progressively in relation to the risks that those with lesser shareholdings could gather forming a new competing majority. Below the 35 percent threshold, the risks of the loss of control are so high that W_{div} and W_{ind} tend to fade. In other words, an investment holding of less than 35 percent would, in the given situation, be of a purely financial nature.

14.7   OTHER DETERMINANTS OF CONTROL PREMIUM

The analyses developed in the previous paragraphs show the type of relationship existing between the present value of divisible benefits and the bargaining price for the acquisition of the controlling stake in a company.

If we assume that the market for acquisitions is competitive and that this limits the bargaining power of the acquirers, the model could also explain the size of the control premium effectively paid in concrete negotiations.

As we shall see in the next chapter, even if the argument is considered of great interest, the research until now has not been extensive and the results obtained have not always been convincing. In fact, it is a difficult issue to deal with, because of both the difficult construction of an appropriate database, and the isolation of the other motivations, identified by the financial literature, as plausible sources of the value of control. To frame the question, it is helpful to start with a classification of the benefits related to control.

As pointed out earlier, in general, these benefits, which are called private, can be subdivided into nonmonetary benefits (not referable to earnings to the controlling shareholder) and monetary ones (Exhibit 14.8).

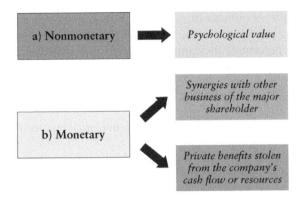

Exhibit 14.8 Private benefits related to control

Theoretical literature often attributes a simply psychological value to control, therefore independent of the potential benefits that can be extracted from the position of control.[5] Undoubtedly, it is a relevant factor that cannot explain, however, the high levels of premiums paid in many transactions.

Consequently, the control premiums are more often related to the present value of monetary benefits.

We can include within this class of benefits the opportunities that the position of control makes possible to exploit such as the starting of new ventures exclusively by the controlling shareholder, or the exploitation of external synergies, those that make use of the intangible assets of the controlled firm in order to benefit other businesses that are subsidiary to the controlling shareholder. The exploitation of the distribution network of the controlled firm, as in the case illustrated earlier, is a typical example.

Another class of private benefits for the controlling shareholder is the possibility of draining (or tunneling) a part of the flow of the business for its own purposes. Examples of this are the above-market-level compensations for executives (who are also controlling shareholders), transactions unfavorable for the minority shareholders, and the private use of goods that are owned by the business.

These phenomena are at the basis of indivisible benefits: thus their presence gives rise to dynamics of acquisition value that are similar to those illustrated in Exhibit 14.8.

According to some studies, practitioners tend to attribute an extra value to control for reasons other than those discussed up to now.

---

[5]M. Harris and A. Raviv, "Corporate Governance. Voting Rights and Majority Rules," *Journal of Financial Economics* (1988), pp. 203–235.

For example, in transactions in which the counterpart is a private equity fund, often the price given to the seller is higher when the acquired stake is more than 50 percent of the capital. Thus, a value is attributed to control, independent of incremental flow, related to synergies with the other ventures invested by the acquirer.

The reasons are various; for example:

- The buyer could be willing to pay a higher price just for the possibility itself of carrying out the transaction.
- The buyer could be willing to pay a higher price when a subsequent divestiture of the controlling interest is more feasible because different ways out are available.
- The buyer could consider acquiring afterward the residual share of capital under more favorable conditions.

14.8 ACQUISITION VALUE IN A MANDATORY TENDER OFFER

Depending on the jurisdiction and on the national takeover laws, the transfer of control issue represents, usually for listed companies, a further complication in the model of the formation of the acquisition value of the controlling interest discussed in the previous section. The complication derives from the obligation to offer the same price for the shares that do not form part of the controlling interest, and this results, typically, in the transfer of part of the value of control to minority shareholders.

It is possible to identify the price limit for the acquisition of the controlling interest given the obligation to launch a public offer (which would nullify the NPV of the transaction) through the following expression, in which the proposed offer price is the average of the market price and the price paid for the controlling block:

$$P_{pc} \times a + \left[\frac{(P_{pc} + P_m)}{2} \right] \times (1 - a) \leq w_{acq}$$

where

P_{pc} = price per share of the shares bought off-market
a = percentage of capital represented by the block
P_m = average market price in the 12 months prior to the offer
w_{acq} = unit acquisition value of shares

The equation expresses a very simple concept: the weighted price paid for 100 percent of the capital of the target company must be less than or equal to the total acquisition value of the shares.

The price limit can be derived by putting the first term equal to w_{acq} and resolving for P_{pc}. Thus, we obtain:

$$P_{pc} = \frac{2w_{acq} - P_m \times (1 - a)}{(1 + a)}$$

Recalling the example discussed in the previous section, suppose that the controlling interest is equal to 40 percent of the capital (formed by 100 million of shares) and the remaining shares are spread among the public.

We know that the unit value of acquisition is €2.650. Assume also that the average market price in the preceding 12 months is €1.800. On the basis of this data, we have:

$$P_{pc} = \frac{2 \times 2.65 - 1.80 \times (1 - 0.4)}{(1 + 0.4)} = 3.0143$$

From the value of P_{pc} we can now deduce the price proposed for the public offer. For simplicity, we will assume a price equal to the average of the price of acquisition of the controlling share and the market price:

$$P(\text{Offer}) = \frac{3.014 + 1.800}{2} = 2.4071$$

Total cost of acquiring 100 percent of the capital is:

Controlling interest: 3.0143×40 million shares $= 120.573$ million
Public offer: 2.4071×60 million shares $= \underline{144.427 \text{ million}}$
Total cost: 265.000 million

Therefore, a transaction drafted in this way has a total cost of €265 million, which is equal to the acquisition value. It is clear that an acquirer would not want to carry out a transaction with a net present value of zero. Thus, in the preceding equation, a value of w_{acq} less than €2.650 is required.

It is worth noting that when the analysts consider the launch of the public offer, the market prices tend immediately to converge toward the offer price that presumably would be proposed to the market. Furthermore, since an increase in the quantity traded is generally registered in these situations, the more recent prices tend to weigh when the weighted averages of the prices themselves are calculated.

As a consequence, one must take into account the phenomenon that was pointed out by modifying the parameter P_m in the formula discussed earlier.

14.9 MAXIMUM AND MINIMUM EXCHANGE RATIOS IN MERGERS

In economic terms, a merger can be considered a reciprocal investment transaction made by the companies involved in it. If they are independent, the exchange ratio, which means the number of shares of the surviving company obtained for each share of the merged company, constitutes, *de facto*, a price negotiated between the parties.

For the sake of transparency and fairness, the exchange ratio (ER) falls within the interval defined as follows:

■ The maximum value of ER is the one that has a neutral impact on the value of the shares of the buyer company (Company A).
■ The minimum value of ER consists of the value with neutral effect from the perspective of the target company's shareholders (Company B).

Therefore, the maximum and minimum exchange rates indicate the limits beyond which a merger would assume a negative net present value, respectively, for the shareholders of the buyer company and for those of the target company.

Referring to the analyses to the unit value of the shares of A and B, the maximum value of ER should satisfy the following equation:

$$w(A)_{A+B} = w(A)$$

$w(A)_{A+B}$ indicates the unit value of the surviving company after the merger and $w(A)$ the value of the shares of A if the merger does not take place. Hence, the quantity $w(A)_{A+B}$ also reflects the value of benefits derived from the merger. Therefore:

$$w(A)_{A+B} = \frac{W(A) + W(B) + W_{\text{FLOW\_DIFF.}}}{N_A + N_B \times ER}$$

where:

$W(A)$ = value of the buyer company in the absence of the transaction

$W(B)$ = value of the target company in the absence of the transaction

$W_{\text{FLOW\_DIFF.}}$ = present value of the earnings flow related to synergies expected after the transaction

N_A and N_B = number of shares that form the equity capital of the two companies

ER = exchange ratio

Therefore, we obtain the value of ER that satisfies the equation $w(A)_{A+B} = w(A)$:

$$ER_{max} = \frac{W(A) + W(B) + W_{FLOW\_DIFF.}}{w(A) \times N_B} - \frac{N_A}{N_B}$$

From the perspective of the buyer company's shareholders, the merger is advantageous, or at least neutral if the following condition holds:

$$w(B) \times 1/ER \leq w(A)_{A+B}$$

where:

$$w(B) = \text{unit share value of B}$$

This means that the value of the shares of A received in exchange of those of B, taking into account the benefits of the merger, should be greater than—or equal to—the value sacrificed in the transaction. Therefore, by combining the equations above, we get:

$$ER_{min} = \frac{w(B) \times N_A}{W(A) + W_{FLOW\_DIFF.}}$$

Exhibit 14.9 shows the area of possible exchange ratios in relation to a growing value of benefits expected by the transaction.

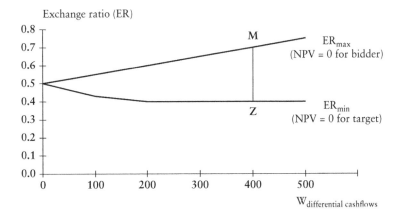

Exhibit 14.9 Possible exchange ratios in relation to the size of the benefits expected in the merger

In the example, the base value of the buyer company is double that of the target company (2,000 compared to 1,000). Moreover, to simplify, A and B have the same number of shares and, therefore, the exchange ratio is 0.5 in the case of the absence of any benefits from the merger.

Exhibit 14.9 illustrates how, with relevant synergies, the exchange ratio negotiated could diverge appreciably from the stand-alone values of the buyer and target companies when synergies are not actually factored. Given a certain present value of the benefits expected from the merger (e.g., 400), the position of ER on the segment MZ depends on the intensity of the competition between companies potentially interested in the transaction and the bargaining power of the parties that take part in the negotiations.

14.9.1 Structuring Ratios in Mergers

Exhibit 14.10 shows how, with indivisible benefits coming from the merger, the movement of the exchange ratio could vary with respect to the case previously presented in Exhibit 14.9.

If the flows arising from the merger are indivisible, then the lower limit of the possible exchange ratios is defined by the dotted line a. That is because the shareholders of the merged company tend to value the suitability of the transaction exclusively with regard to the stand-alone flow (and therefore to $W_{base}(A)$ and $W_{base}(B)$).

From the perspective of the buyer company, on the other hand, if the benefits are indivisible, the upper limit of ER (within which the transaction gives rise to a net benefit) tends to climb when the value created by the transaction is not also shared by the former shareholders of B (dotted line b).

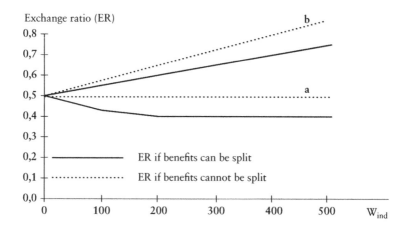

Exhibit 14.10 Movement in exchange ratio in presence of indivisible benefits

These conclusions are based on the assumption that the shareholders of B are not involved in the management of the new business entity resulting from the merger. Alternatively, the transaction could give rise to indivisible benefits in their favor as well. As a consequence, the movement of the lower limit of ER could be different from the one represented in Exhibit 14.10.

The presence of indivisible benefits favoring both parties involved in the transaction typically occurs in the case of joint ventures based on the establishment of a Newco, transactions similar to pure mergers.

14.10 EXCHANGE RATIO AND THIRD-PARTY PROTECTION

The model of the formation of exchange ratios discussed in the previous paragraph points out the limits within which the merger creates value, or determines at least neutral results, from the perspective of the shareholders involved in the transaction.

The critical aspect in the model is the pricing of merger synergies. In fact, in case of overvaluation of the benefits expected by the integration of the business entities to be merged, the shareholders of the surviving or the merged companies could be penalized by the transaction's terms, as could also be the creditors of both the companies.

This risk occurs if, in order to determine the exchange ratio, the valuation of the benefits achieved following the merger goes exclusively in favor of one of the two parties.

The problem is even more delicate when the merger is accomplished by the incorporation of a company whose capital is controlled, but not entirely owned by the surviving company. In this case, in the absence of a free negotiation between the parties, the minority shareholders of the merged company could be penalized by an exchange ratio favorable to the surviving company.

The financial/economic and legal literature have pointed out, in this regard, the need of valuation criteria as uniform as possible to be used to determine the exchange ratio.

In practice, the problem of estimating the exchange ratio can be resolved by adopting two approaches:

1. Estimation of the value sacrificed in the merger by the shareholders in the surviving and merged companies.
2. Estimation of the value brought by the merger. This involves an approach that is more correct in theory, but not always easily applicable.

In the first case, the exchange ratio could be determined on the basis of fair market value of the companies involved in the merger, estimated with homogeneous criteria.[6]

In the second case, as pointed out earlier, the problem of estimation is more complex, and it requires the estimate of the contribution of both the companies to the realization of the expected merger synergies.

It is interesting to note that when the exchange ratio is determined on stand-alone values, implicitly the value of the merger synergies is attributed to the companies involved in the transaction in proportion to their stand-alone values.

APPENDIX 14.1: OTHER VALUE DEFINITIONS

Value to the Seller

The value to the seller is equal to the discounted value of the earnings the business produces to whoever currently controls it. Therefore, the value to the seller of a company identifies the price with respect to which the transaction assumes a zero net present value to the seller. The interest in this notion or value is evident: it indicates the minimum price at which the transaction could take place.

It is worth considering that often, the estimation of the value to the seller also requires the valuation of the so-called private benefits of control.

For small businesses it concerns, for example, the use of the assets belonging to the company, and the services and compensation to the entrepreneur and his relatives at more favorable terms than the market ones. In the case of companies belonging to an industrial group, in order to estimate this value, there should be considered also the earnings that are obtained by other companies of the group—for example, through the intercompany transfer of goods and services, and use of the distribution network of the company being transferred, and so on.

If the private benefits that derive from control are limited, the value to the seller tends to correspond to the value of the company estimated

---

[6]On the subject of the choice of most appropriate notion of value, in order to determine the exchange ratio, many diverse opinions have been expressed. According to some scholars, it should be the fair market value; according to others, the stand-alone value. On one point there is no doubt: the same definition of value should be used for both companies interested in the transaction. The problem pointed out here is more complex when only one of the companies is listed. The notion of value expressed by market prices, which provide important information, is not in fact always clearly identifiable.

autonomously (stand-alone value), thus ignoring the earnings due to the expected managerial decisions and interventions realized by the potential buyers.

Anyway, the preceding considerations do not mean that the potential sellers would be willing to lose the control of the firm at a price corresponding to the value to the seller. Indeed, the analysis developed omits two factors of relevance:

- Very often, psychological factors come into play; they are related to sentimental bonds with the business or to personal image advantages, or simply to the fact that the entrepreneur does not wish to stop being an entrepreneur. In these cases, the value to the seller should also incorporate the valuation of these further elements. Given that, in practice, these are difficult to be valued objectively, the problem is resolved in the context of the negotiations, for example, by giving up some of the enterprise assets or leaving the entrepreneur with a certain corporate exposition role after the transfer of control.
- The value to the seller represents that price level that leaves the wealth of the seller unaltered (remembering that when the price equals the value to the seller, the net present value of the transaction is zero). It is reasonable to infer that the seller would want instead to have a transaction that has a positive present value, and therefore tends to systematically overprice the value, claiming that this refers to the most likely market price.

In fact, the discrepancies observed between the prices and value to the seller depend on—in addition to psychological elements—the general business environment and on the effervescence that cyclically pervades the market for corporate control.

Public Offers Price

The share price to be determined in public offerings (initial public offering, or IPO) deals with the need of estimating the price target in the context of listing the company, as well as in the case of seasoned equity offerings or private placements to professional investors. This kind of price is a function of the expectations of the market makers about the ability of the company to reach its earnings potential. In practical terms, this valuation depends on both industry-level factors, reflected in the market multiples of comparable companies, and more idiosyncratic elements such as the trends in the profitability of the company itself.

The price fixed within the offer is only, at first blush, the fruit of a valuation made by the sponsor and financial advisors assisting the company in the offer. Subsequently, these estimates come to be adjusted through a series of contacts with institutional investors for the placement of the securities. This process involves, therefore, a sort of negotiation between multiple parties.

Liquidation Value

The liquidation value indicates the present value of the sums that can be obtained through the alienation of the assets of the firm in the most appropriate way, net of the sums set aside for the repayment of the debts and for the termination of legal obligations, and net of the tax charges related to the transaction and the costs of the process of liquidation itself.

It is clear that the liquidation value—which is an estimate of the corporate assets value in case of liquidation—is not a focus of this book. It is, however, worth highlighting that, in the case of a distressed company, the liquidation value conveys relevant information as it is typically the lower bound of the valuation range.

## CHAPTER 15

Value and Prices in the Market for Corporate Control

15.1 PRICE FORMATION IN THE MARKET FOR CONTROL

From a business valuation point of view, the functioning of the market for corporate acquisitions assumes importance for numerous reasons. The level of competition existing in the market of control in every industry depends on:

- Contribution of the market to the restructuring of the offer of products and services, granting the efficient allocation of assets within and among industries
- The degree to which the transactions involving a transfer of control benefit the buyer company's shareholders rather than the target company's, considering, therefore, the legal regime provisions aimed at protecting the minority shareholders of both the companies involved in the transaction
- The policies aimed at increasing the overall functionality of the market itself—for example, the possibility of carrying out leveraged buyout deals, and the presence of rules allowing or facilitating the execution of mergers and acquisitions, thus improving the dynamism of the market for control
- Lifting the ban on bids for some categories of firms (i.e., state-owned companies)

The analysis of how the market for corporate control works is shedding light on many topics we cover in the book.

For example, some problems in interpreting deal multiples mentioned in previous chapters can be understood more clearly using the model of price formation in the market for corporate control. Furthermore, the concept of *fair market value*, which is the cornerstone of that market, is of particular relevance in valuation, also from the legal and accounting point of view. For this reason, we devote this chapter to framing detailed discussion of such topic.

15.1.1 Competitive Market for Acquisitions

The definition of *competitive market for acquisitions* relies on the idea of a rivalry between potential acquirers. In other words, the market becomes competitive if the firms tend to exploit all the opportunities to realize value-creating acquisitions. The market for acquisitions is not competitive if, on the other hand, a significant number of firms is not interested in external growth opportunities. The motivations for such attitude are various, but the consequence is a weakening of the competition among potential acquirers.

High levels of transparency form the main prerequisite to the effective competitiveness in the market for control. In this sense, the activism of merchant bankers and consultants specialized in scouting possible targets as well as prospective buyers significantly contributes to the functioning of the market.

Another source of transparency for the market is the systematic monitoring for target firms performed by the finance units of large companies. The teams put in charge of this task develop a sound and often thorough understanding not only about targets' characteristics but also of the nature of the benefits that the other potential buyers can derive from a certain acquisition.

On the other hand, some conditions can hinder the formation of a well-developed market for acquisitions. For example, until the 1990s in Italy, the lack of financing channels and providers focused on backing M&A transactions negatively affected the development of the market for corporate control.

There can also be normative barriers (e.g., antitrust regulations) that limit the number of potential acquirers. Finally, collusive activities can emerge between potential buyers, or some buyers can be excluded for other reasons, curbing the participation in the market.

The intensity of the competition in the market for control tends to vary widely from country to country and, especially, from industry to industry. It also tends to follow a cyclical pattern, where the bigger players in a certain industry tend to initiate M&A waves that also affect other competitors, thus reshaping the industry composition.

15.1.2 Mechanism of Price Formation

How are prices in the market for corporate control formed? The answer relies on some basic principles of microeconomics theory, which apply also to this kind of market.

In equilibrium, the estimated values of target firms should be identical for every potential buyer.[1] In this case, the competitive mechanism would establish the following equality:

$$P = W_{acq}$$

where:

P = negotiated price
W_{acq} = value of the target firm estimated from the viewpoint of any potential acquirer

As already observed in section 11.3, if $P = W_{acq}$, the net present value of the deal is zero, eliminating any possible excess profit (or, if one prefers, any creation of value) for the buyer. This equilibrium is rarely found in practice, since any business (buyer or target) has its own peculiarities that make the transaction more or less attractive from a subjective point of view. It is, thus, reasonable to expect that the value of acquisition will differ from buyer to buyer.

Only in certain cases is it possible that a certain number of competitors formulate fairly similar strategies, valuing the target firm in a substantially equivalent manner. If, more realistically, W_{acq} is appreciably diverse for each acquirer, under conditions of sufficient competition, P is located within the following interval:

$$W_{acq}y < P \leq W_{acq}x$$

where $W_{acq} x$ expresses the value of the target firm estimated by acquirer x, which succeeds in the acquisition, and $W_{acq} y$ the value estimate related to the potential buyer y, the last one to exit the competition. $W_{acq} y$ is, therefore, the highest estimate among the participants in the acquisition contest, clearly apart from x.

This relation implies that the competitive mechanisms taking place among the potential acquirers will increase P up to the point that the economic benefits expected from the transaction are rendered negative for each unsuccessful acquirer.

---

[1]The following conditions need to be met:

- The presence of a sufficient number of potential buyers and a certain number of target firms
- The motivations (value drivers) of the acquisition need to be the same for all the potential buyers
- The expectations about the scenario need to be uniform

The position of P within the interval depends on the number of candidates that have substitute characteristics, in the sense that they could be acceptable alternatives from the point of view of the buyer. If there exists more than one substitute, it is fair to expect that P will be only slightly higher than $W_{acq}x$. In fact, in this case the negotiating power of the target firm, which lacks the characteristics of *uniqueness,* is more limited.

It is worth noting other cases where the above mentioned market for acquisitions is not able to function properly:

1. When there is only one buyer and a certain number of potential candidates. The buyer enjoys a monopolistic position—thus, in this case and P should be set close to the stand-alone value of the target firm. In practice, the negotiating skills of the vendor or the need by the acquirer of closing the deal quickly can increase the level of P.
2. When there exists only one potential acquirer and one candidate. In this case, there exists a situation of *bilateral monopoly.* Thus, P is substantially indeterminate, and its dimensions reflect the negotiating skills of the two parties involved in the transaction.

15.2   BENEFITS ARISING FROM ACQUISITIONS

In the scheme illustrated earlier, we identified two stages in the formation of prices:

1. The phase of competition, setting the P up to the point where the buyers expecting the lesser benefits from the acquisition must quit the contest
2. The phase of *bilateral monopoly,* where P is indeterminate because it depends on the ability and contractual power of the parties

We have already noted that in certain cases, only the second stage is present, or else in others the acquirer holds a monopolistic position.

To apply to the scheme presented, a further effort is to be accomplished: it regards locating the economic, business, and industrial context in which both stages or monopolistic situations are found. The problem that is presented, at least conceptually, is very simple: it would be sufficient in fact to ascertain the number of potential acquirers and how much they would value the target firm.

Practically, however, estimates in this sense are as a rule extremely difficult. It is fair to assume, though, that:

1. The number of potential acquirers is a function of the achievability of certain types of benefits following the acquisition.

2. The estimated benefits achieved by the potential acquirers tend to converge to the same order of magnitude, depending on the level of uniformity of the economic effects of the processes of integration between the acquirers and the candidates for acquisition.[2]

In this case, one could turn usefully to a classification of the post-acquisition benefits proposed by common strategic studies. This is based on the assumption that, in certain cases, the benefits achieved by an acquisition can be due to a considerably higher number of acquirers, or, on the other hand, only when certain preconditions are met, for example, specific industry-level characteristics. With all the limitations of any classification, it is possible to distinguish three types of benefits in relation to their area of potential realization:

1. Benefits related to an elevated number of potential acquirers
2. Benefits based on technological or business model affinity with firms belonging to the same sector
3. Benefits related to particular instances of mergers or to advantages not perceived by other firms

15.2.1 Benefits Related to an Elevated Number of Potential Acquirers

These characteristics rise from the fact that the considered benefits can also follow in the absence of interrelations of an operative or market-related character. Here are some typical examples:

- The possibility of exploiting the tax advantages offered by the acquired firm
- The elimination of easily recognizable management deficiencies (of personnel utilization, organization of productive processes, distribution channels, and so on)

Among the benefits being examined—for the sake of simplicity, synergies of a general nature—the creation of value due to the liabilities restructuring is also included.

In fact, if the market for control is competitive, and if the willing buyers tend to realize levered transactions, the values of acquisition should

---

[2]The size aspect can lose relevance in the case where the value drivers of the acquisitions are made of intangibles: indeed, intangibles do not have physical limitations for being exploited.

incorporate the present value net of the benefits linked to tax deductibility of interest charges related to the portion of the transaction financed using debt.

Such an approach—when widespread in a certain market—tends to increase the prices of acquisition of target firms characterized by low debt ratios (in fact, with reference to these businesses the exploitation of leverage could be more consistent).

15.2.2   Benefits Based on Affinities with Other Firms

In this category are firms, possibly in the same sector, with technological or business affinity. It also includes the advantages related to vertical and horizontal integration: cost savings due to economies of scale, better use of fixed and intangible resources, improved pricing policies due to an increased market share, and so on. These advantages are also called *endemic synergies*, bringing to notice the fact that they are typically developed within a specific sector.

15.2.3   Benefits Related to Mergers or Advantages Not Perceived by Other Firms

The benefits classified in this last category can be regarded as business synergies, that for complementarity exist between the target firm and a specific acquirer, assuming significant relevance; they also include "unique" benefits due, for example, to the localization of the activities of the target firm with respect to those of the acquirer. For instance, the processes of horizontal concentration, which have found favor with some types of utilities (in particular with the local distribution of gas), have primarily involved enterprises present in the same geographical area, in order to reduce distribution costs for servicing consumers present in close areas.

15.2.4   Elements in Each Benefit That Influence Prices

The classification of merger synergies so far presented allows some theoretical deductions with regard to the formation of prices in the market for control:

1. With reference to the synergies classified in the first benefit type, competition must exist to attain an elevated bargaining power. It can be observed that some of the benefits of this type tend to be priced not only in the more restricted area of strategic buyers, but also among investors specialized in private equity, which tends to be a competitive approach.
2. With reference to synergies based on affinities with other firms, as already observed, the level of bargaining power depends on the presence of a

group of willing buyers effectively interested in realizing mergers for similar reasons. In this case, the group of willing buyers come to form a specific segment of the market for control, and the price level of business capital is correlated to the size of the benefits achieved following the merger.

3. With reference to the synergies classified by unperceived advantages, it is not possible to draw general conclusions, as these can be easily collocated in a bilateral monopoly-negotiating context.

The preceding theoretical deductions seem to be confirmed by observations of the prices negotiated by clusters of deals taking place in various industries.

The analysis of the processes of concentration, which have interested some sectors (in particular, the food and utility sectors), shows that the principal competitors have followed similar strategic directives, and these have driven them to value target firms on the basis of similar parameters. For example, in the utilities sector, the scenario changes because of the processes of privatization and liberalization: such processes have significantly favored industry concentration through M&A. Some emerging players have assumed the pivotal role in aggregation and have been inspired by a similar business model, drawn by the greater control of resources (e.g., the supply of gas and electrical energy) and to a consolidation of competitive advantages.

These actions have increased the contractual power of target firms, fostering, as a consequence, the increase in the prices of companies.

15.3   FROM THE PRICING MODEL TO THE FAIR MARKET VALUE

The considerations in the previous sections show that the fair market value can ideally take place between two extremes having precise economic significance.

In the absence of a group of active potential strategic buyers, where by *active* we mean a group that is motivated by exploiting the opportunities to realize the acquisition, the fair market value tends to converge to the stand-alone value.

If, on the other hand, we assume that a willing buyer looking for business synergies does exist, the fair market value of the company should include the extra value related to the control. Apart from the control value, the present value of a portion of the synergies themselves should be included because they determine the bargaining power of the target company. Such bargaining power depends also on the level of competition between potential acquirers. Exhibit 15.1 illustrates this concept.

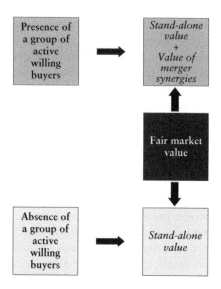

Exhibit 15.1 Positioning of fair market value

Exhibit 15.1 showing the links between fair market value, business strategies, and competitive behavior of the willing buyers is also popular among US experts. Of particular importance are the following considerations by S. Pratt:[3] "It is important to note that the buyer and seller are hypothetical, as opposed to any one specific, identified buyer or seller. This is intended to eliminate the influence of one buyer or seller's specific motivations. However, if there is an active group of competing buyers or sellers with a common set of motivations, this group could constitute the market in which the 'hypothetical' buyer and seller might meet to transact, and thus the price that the group would find acceptable could constitute fair market value."

15.3.1 Estimation Methods for Practitioners

Practitioners usually adopt three different methods of estimating the fair market value:

1. The analysis of the multiples referred to transactions where the control stake or the entire equity of comparable companies has been sold (deal multiples).

---

[3] S. Pratt, *Business Valuation. Discount and Premiums* (New York: John Wiley & Sons, 2001), page 13.

2. The analysis of the market multiples of comparable companies (stock market multiples). In this case, in general the values obtained are modified taking into account *premium of acquisition* in order to reduce the difference between the market prices (similar to the values estimated from the perspective of financial investors) and strategic values, estimated from the perspective of acquirers that are motivated by an entrepreneurial logic (the theme of premium of acquisition will be treated below).
3. The development of empirical valuation methods that establish a relation between business size (value drivers) and value. These methods are based on parameters observed during negotiation for the transfer of control stakes, or of the entire equity, in specific industries (e.g., the value per consumer in the case of utilities).

The problem arising from those three methods consists in verifying that the data on the deals analyzed are representative of the consensus prices in the period in which the estimation takes place. The main conditions that allow us to assume that the historical prices are also likely prices for new transactions can be listed as follows:

- The willing buyers participating in the segment of market where the deal takes place are still active; this implies that in the specific sector there exists recognizable strategic motivation for external growth.
- The current level of expectations should not change significantly in comparison with the past.
- The strategic importance of the company to be valued should be similar to the one recognized in deals concluded in the past.

15.4 FAIR MARKET VALUE ESTIMATED ADJUSTING STAND-ALONE CASH FLOWS

In the following pages, we will discuss an approach to estimating the probable market price that is not based directly on empirical indicators but on the attempt of replicating the reasoning behind the acquisition-price formation mechanism. In order to simplify the discussion, we will present some estimates of the probable market price based on changes and modifications of the earnings flow of the target firm from a stand-alone perspective.

Working directly on the cash flow can provide useful information to be used for the valuation:

- The procedure clarifies the factors that can assume relevance in the estimate of the value of acquisition determined by willing buyers and its impact on the differential cash flow expected from the acquisition.

- The indications so obtained can be easily compared with the valuation obtained from the multiples of similar transactions.
- Finally, if sufficient data regarding similar transactions are not available, the correction of stand-alone flows often constitutes the only available alternative for the determination of the fair market value of the firm.

15.4.1   Endemic Synergies: Cutting Fixed Costs

The shareholders that control Alpha, a pharmaceutical company, have mandated a merchant bank to search for a buyer. Alpha's specialty products are reputed to have an interesting market positioning. The main Alpha financial data are shown in Exhibit 15.2. The financials have been appropriately adjusted and represent a situation of normal functioning.

The stand-alone value of Alpha can be easily estimated using the formula in absence of growth described earlier:

$$W_{\text{unlevered}} = \frac{FCFO}{K_{\text{eu}}}$$

Assuming that in normal conditions FCFO is equal to EBIT net of taxes and that K_{eu} can be estimated to be 9 percent in real terms, we get the following valuation:

$$W_{\text{unlevered}} = \frac{18,600}{0.09} = 206,667$$

The seller considers the valuation so obtained quite far from the fair market value of Alpha. In fact:

- Pharmaceutical companies not controlled by large groups and still available on the market are quite few. Therefore, there are limited potential acquirers interested in external growth transactions.
- The potential acquirers are mainly interested in leveraging their portfolio of products.

Exhibit 15.2   Alpha's financials €/000

Revenues	271,000
Fixed costs	(100,000)
Variable costs	(140,000)
EBIT	31,000
Taxes (40%)	(12,400)
EBIT net of taxes	18,600

Assuming these conditions, it is reasonable to hold that the potential buyers would value Alpha considering that, after the merger, relevant cost-cutting actions could be enforced. This implies, obviously, that the willing buyers should be able to deploy their own resources and managerial capabilities in order to carry out the downsizing of Alpha operations.

Analyzing the operative structures of the willing buyers, it emerges that the fixed costs of Alpha could be reduced by about 15 percent. As a consequence, the flow becomes as shown in Exhibit 15.3.

Based on the modified operating results, we could calculate the new value of Alpha as follows:

$$W_{\text{unlevered}} = \frac{27,600}{0.09} = 306,666$$

Another aspect that could increase the value of acquisition of Alpha is the possibility of making a subsequent spinoff, thus deducting the depreciation of the value of intangibles in the product portfolio.

It is interesting to observe that, especially in the pharmaceutical industry, companies often estimate value of a product's portfolio by discounting the related flow gross of taxes, because of the gross compensation of the fiscal benefits related to the amortization of the price of the portfolio.

15.4.2 Estimating the Break-Up Value

Break-up value indicates the value that can be realized by breaking up a company's assets and then selling them separately. The basic idea is the following: in case of the separate alienation of the branch of a firm, it is often possible to get a higher value than if the firm is sold entirely; this is because, in this way, it could be more profitable to negotiate the selling with potential acquirers interested only in specific assets.

In other words, through a break-up, it is possible to increase the level of competition between willing buyers; the level of competition could, on the other hand, be more limited by offering the entire company's equity either because of the larger size of the transaction or because willing buyers may not be interested in some of the assets making up the company portfolio.

Exhibit 15.3   Revised Alpha's financials (€/000)

EBIT of Alpha	31,000
Lesser structural cost	15,000
Taxes	(18,400)
Adjusted income	27,600

The concept of break-up value has become fashionable in the United States during the 1980s: in that period, there were many hostile takeovers of listed companies to be later broken up and then sold, often with huge profits for the raiders.

The break-up value can be so determined:

$$\text{Break-up value} = \frac{\text{Sum of values of the}}{\text{company's assets}} - \frac{\text{Charges for realizing}}{\text{the break-up}}$$

The values of the individual assets can be determined through the most appropriate methodology. In general, the most widely used technique is that based on multiples of comparable companies and, to a lesser extent, the DCF method.

The break-up logic is typical of the financial actors in the market for control (private-equity funds, raiders, etc.). This implies that reasoning in terms of break-up value is often used to understand how a firm can be valued from the perspective of this category of actors and can offer insightful indications in order to estimate the fair market value of a multi-business firm.

Break-up Value of Delta   Delta is present in two areas of business: cardboard and matches. Exhibit 15.4 shows the projection of the cash flow developed from a stand-alone perspective.

In order to estimate the stand-alone value of the company, the financial advisor involved in the transaction has estimated a cost of capital (K_{eu}) equal to 10.2 percent. The terminal value was estimated assuming that the flow at the end of the period (€14.2 billion) increases at the rate of inflation of 2 percent ($g_n = 2\%$).

Therefore, the terminal value (TV) can be calculated using the following expression:

$$TV = \frac{FCFO_{T5} \times (1 + 0.02)}{K_{eu} - g_n}$$

Exhibit 15.4   Delta: cash flow projection (€/billion)

	T1	T2	T3	T4	T5
GROSS OPERATING MARGIN	23.2	25.4	27.0	28.0	30.1
Δ WORKING CAPITAL	(2.1)	(1.2)	(1.2)	(1.0)	(1.7)
Investment	(9.2)	(9.7)	(6.3)	(6.5)	(8.0)
TAXES	(5.2)	(5.6)	(5.8)	(6.1)	(6.2)
FCFO	6.7	8.9	13.7	14.4	14.2

Exhibit 15.5 Stand-alone value for Delta

Present value of flow in the plan period	42.15
Present value of TV	108.8
Unlevered value	150.9

Then, we get:

$$TV = \frac{14.2 \times (1 + 0.02)}{0.10 - 0.02} = 176.8$$

The stand-alone value of Delta can be obtained (€/ML) as shown in Exhibit 15.5.

An analysis of the situation of the market for acquisition in the two sectors where Delta is present allows the conclusion that there can be a more advantageous deal based on the separate selling of the cardboard business and the matches one. The flow for each business is represented in Exhibit 15.6.

In Exhibit 15.6, in order to calculate the gross operating margin, the general fixed costs are allocated to the two business units on the basis of the revenues. It is assumed that the willing buyers interested in the cardboard business, which has unexploited production capacity, can limit these costs by 40 percent.

As for the matches business, the willing buyers seem, on the basis of research, able to limit structural costs to the extent of 60 percent and to obtain a 20 percent cost reduction for the direct costs related to the purchase of raw materials. This information is summarized in Exhibit 15.7.

Exhibit 15.6 Delta: businesses' cash flow (€/bln)

	T1		T2		T3		T4		T5	
	Cardboard	Matches	Cardboard	Matches	Cardboard	Matches	Cardboard	Matches	Cardboard	Matches
Gross operating margin	13.9	9.3	15.2	10.2	16.2	10.8	16.8	11.2	18.0	12.1
Δ Working capital	(1.1)	(1.0)	(0.7)	(0.5)	(0.6)	(0.6)	(0.6)	(0.4)	(0.9)	(0.8)
Investment	(6.0)	(3.2)	(6.0)	(3.7)	(3.0)	(3.3)	(3.0)	(3.5)	(5.0)	(3.0)
Taxes	(2.2)	(3.0)	(2.0)	(3.6)	(2.2)	(3.6)	(3.0)	(3.1)	(3.1)	(3.1)
FCFO	*4.6*	*2.1*	*6.5*	*2.4*	*10.4*	*3.3*	*10.2*	*4.2*	*9.0*	*5.2*

Exhibit 15.7   Delta: modified cash flow (€/billion)

	T1		T2		T3		T4		T5	
	Cardboard	Matches	Cardboard	Matches	Cardboard	Matches	Cardboard	Matches	Cardboard	Matches
FCFO	4.6	2.1	6.5	2.4	10.4	3.3	10.2	4.2	9.0	5.2
Modified fixed costs	6.0	4.0	6.0	4.0	7.0	5.0	7.0	5.0	7.0	5.0
Savings in raw materials costs	–	2.0	–	2.0	–	2.0	–	2.0	–	2.0
New taxes	(3.0)	(3.0)	(3.0)	(3.0)	(3.5)	(3.5)	(3.5)	(3.5)	(3.5)	(3.5)
MODIFIED FLOW	*7.6*	*5.1*	*9.5*	*5.4*	*13.9*	*6.8*	*13.7*	*7.7*	*12.5*	*8.7*

K_{eu} for the two businesses 10.0% for Cardboard and 10.3% for Matches respectively.

The terminal values are determined by means of the same formula already used, assuming also the same parameters of growth in nominal terms.

The costs for realizing the breaking up of Delta's businesses have been estimated in present value terms to be €27 billion.

It is now possible to determine the break-up value of Delta (€/billion) as shown in Exhibit 15.8.

In this case, the break-up value is greater by 35 percent than the value estimated from a stand-alone perspective.

15.4.3 Endemic Synergies: Exploiting the Commercial Network

Beta, a dairy products company, is characterized by widespread distribution network spanning almost nationwide, which is a key strength for the company's competitive success.

Exhibit 15.8   Break-up valuation for Delta

Cardboard business value	141.3
Matches business value	90.2
Break-up charges	(27.0)
Break-up value of Delta	204.5

Exhibit 15.9 Beta: cash flow projection (€/billion)

	T1	T2	T3	T4	T5
Gross operating margins	47.0	49.0	50.0	51.3	53.0
Δ Working capital	(3.2)	(2.1)	(1.9)	(1.9)	(2.0)
Investment	(13.1)	(12.2)	(12.0)	(10.0)	(12.0)
Taxes	(16.0)	(17.2)	(18.7)	(19.0)	(20.0)
FCFO	*14.7*	*17.5*	*17.4*	*20.4*	*19.0*

Exhibit 15.9 shows a projection of the flows from the stand-alone perspective.

The stand-alone value of Beta can be obtained using the following parameters:

$$K_{eu} = 10.7\%$$

Terminal value = Calculated on the basis of €19 billion cash flow and a growth in nominal terms equal to the inflation rates (2%)

Therefore, using the same equation of the preceding case, the terminal value can be obtained as follows:

$$TV = \frac{FCFO_{T5} \times (1 + 0.02)}{K_{eu} - g_n}$$

and then:

$$TV = \frac{19.4}{0.107 - 0.02} = € \ 222.8 \ bln$$

It is possible, now, to obtain the unlevered value of Beta (€/bln), as shown in Exhibit 15.10.

Beta represents the ideal target firm for some international groups in the sector. Apart from the brand, which is of considerable importance in the Italian markets, the asset of interest is represented by the commercial organization, which could be used by willing buyers for the distribution of their own products.

Exhibit 15.10 Stand-alone valuation for Beta

Present value of the flow in the plan	65.4
Present value of the terminal value	134.0
Unlevered value of Beta	199.4

Exhibit 15.11 Beta: modified cash flow (€/bln)

	T1	T2	T3	T4	T5
Operating cash flow	14.7	17.5	17.4	20.4	19.0
Flow related to the commercialization of new products	8.0	8.0	8.0	8.0	6.0
Total cash flow	*22.7*	*23.5*	*25.0*	*28.4*	*25.0*

A merchant bank interested in promoting the transaction has estimated that through distribution network of Beta, the three potential acquirers that have the more fitting complementarities with Beta could distribute a huge quantity of their products. The cash flow from operations (FCFO) related to the incremental sales could reach €18 billion per year, and €6 billion in T5 considering the prospective need for new investment and modernization of the distribution network.

Taking into account the contributions of the potential acquirers, the cash flow reported in Exhibit 15.11 can be modified as follows.

Adopting the same parameters for both the discount rates and the calculation of terminal value, Beta can be valued at €268 billion. Such value can be assumed to be an approximation of the probable market value of Beta, considering the fact that, on the basis of the assumptions, the acquisition is considered "strategic" by more than one of the willing buyers.

15.5 PREMIUMS AND DISCOUNTS IN VALUATION

Up to this point, we have discussed three main topics:

1. The criteria for determination of value of an acquisition (investment value) of the entire equity or for a control stake
2. The logic of the price formation for stakes in the market for control
3. Based on the conclusions derived from the preceding points, the problem of estimating fair market value

The given arguments are connected to a theme of particular interest in the area of valuations: the estimation of premiums and discounts. The purpose of premiums and discounts is to make adjustments to a certain base value, for two purposes:

1. Reconciling the differences among the characteristics of the target firm of the valuation and the characteristics of the sample of comparable firms selected in order to perform the estimates.

2. Reconciling the differences between the different notions of value. For example, as observed earlier, if the valuation is made through market multiples and the objective of the estimation is the determination of fair market value, the application of a premium could transform the base valuation obtained in the notion of value searched for.

Indeed, the observable differences with respect to the base value are always due either to the risk profile or to the size or profile of cash flow. Therefore, the calculation of a premium or a discount can be considered equivalent to a rectification of the discount rate, or to an adjustment of the flow, or to both of them.

Reasoning in terms of premiums and discounts rather than of adjustment of the discount rate/cash flow is simply a matter of the accepted conventions among experts in valuation that often are justified for the following reasons:

- The adjustment of rates or flow results in a less convincing choice for the demonstrability of the parameters on the basis of which the rates and flow are modified.
- The approach for calculating the base value does not allow other choices. For example, if the base value is determined through multiples, the calculation of a premium or a discount is the most effective alternative for adjusting the base value as a function of the difference between the characteristics of the firm to be valued and the characteristics of the firms that form the sample of comparables, or a function of the notion of value which the multiples themselves express.

15.5.1 A Practical Check

As the application of a premium or discount can modify substantially the result of the estimate, it can be useful to verify the measure of the equivalent correction in terms of rates or flow. An example will clarify the concept.

The stand-alone valuation performed using the DCF method has the following results:

Normalized flow	10,000
Discount rate	10%
Time period	20 years
Stand-alone value	= 85,135

$$\sum_{1}^{20} \frac{10,000}{(1 + 10\%)^t}$$

The analyst has to determine the value of a 20 percent shareholding, not related to control. If, on the basis of available information, a discount of

30 percent is applied on the proportional value, the value of the shareholding is equal to:

$$85,135 \times 0.2 \times 0.7 = 11,919$$

The discount of 30 percent is, alternatively, equal to:

- An adjustment of the stand-alone flow always at 30 percent
- An adjustment of the discount rate, which from 10 percent must increase to about 15.75 percent

In fact, if we reduce the whole base-value using the discount, we will get:

$$85,135 \times 0.7 = 59,594$$

We can now deduce the rate that allows us to obtain the same result:

$$59,594 = \sum_1^{20} \frac{10,000}{(1+x)^t}$$

$$x = 15.75\%$$

Therefore, a discount of 30 percent is equal to an increment in the rate from 10 percent to approximately 15.75 percent in function of the risks associated with the absence of control. If the flow is a perpetual annuity, a discount of s implies an increase of $\left(\frac{1}{1-s} - 1\right)$ of the rate.

15.6 THE MOST COMMON PREMIUMS AND DISCOUNTS

In the most recent studies in finance, the premium for control is, in general, derived from the presence of private benefits favoring the shareholders involved in the firm's business. As already mentioned, these benefits consist directly in monetary flows, or otherwise regard the *general attributes* of control, which means the power to decide the strategic directives, the financing policies, and the power as well to request the quotation on the stock market or to sell the entire capital or a majority shareholding in the market for control.

In the professional literature on valuation, the definition of the control premium is much more evanescent: sometimes the term is used as a synonym of *majority premium* or of *acquisition premium*.

In this book, we will follow the more restrictive definition attributed to private benefits of control, because this allows us to discuss the significance of the empirical analyses performed more effectively, and to be in accord with the levels of value we have already discussed.

The acquisition premium, in general, is placed in relation to the valuations made by strategic investors in the market of control. This can be measured from the perspective of one specific acquirer or of a plurality of generic potential acquirers.

In business valuation, the premium always refers to generic potential acquirers, as this notion of the premium is coherent with the principles adopted in forming the estimates of fair market value.

Be reminded that the assumption that fair market value incorporates a part of the strategic value relating to the development of merger synergies is based on the hypothesis that there exists a group of willing buyers interested in concluding the acquisition. This circumstance allows us also to assume the presence of a segment of the market that functions according to the criteria previously described.

15.6.1 Discounts at the Shareholder Level

The discounts due to the controlling arrangements and to the size of the shareholdings to be valued represent the issues most frequently discussed in the literature and in the professional praxis. For the sake of simplicity, the discounts in question are collectively defined as *minority discount*.[4]

Many scholars suggest that the lesser value of a minority shareholding can be due to two distinct factors:

1. Impossibility of deciding strategic directives and participating in the selection of management; these are in general defined as *discounts due to a lack of control*.
2. Difficulty in trading the shares' blocks of lesser relevance to the control; in this case, the label generally applied is *discounts due to a lack of liquidity*.

The logic underlying the *discount for the lack of control* relies on the poor protection granted to the holders of smaller blocks of shares. For example, in the presence of good earnings results, the majority shareholder could be reluctant in assuring a congruent remuneration flow in the form of dividends. Or else, minority shareholders could be penalized by extraordinary transactions, like mergers or increases in capital with an exclusion of the right of choice; the control could be transferred to new and unwelcome

---

[4]In the literature on financial management, when the acquisition premium is referred to minority stockholdings, relevant for a firm's governance, it is named *majority premium*. If we assume this meaning, then the acquisition premium is defined as the value of control depending on the ratio of shares, which the stockholding refers to.

shareholders; assets of particular importance could be transferred at terms not equally shared with minority participants, and so on.

In conclusion, minority shareholders could be penalized by the fact that the controlling shareholders succeed in draining some of the business flows to their own advantage.

The *discount for lack of liquidity*, on the other hand, regards the difficulty in trading in the minority shares at an equitable price, and reasonable time period, or the lesser grade reserved for the minority holdings in the presence of the need of giving guarantees for obtaining finance.

Also if, logically speaking, the proposed distinction can be shared, in practical terms the lack of control and of liquidity are two sides of the same coin. In fact, shares that represent a limited fraction of the equity are, in general, more difficult to be sold. Those that even potentially have an influence on control, on the other hand, tend to assume a strategic importance and, therefore can be more easily traded.

These deductions are coherent with the observations based on experience and the indications arising from the general practice: the "discounts" applied—and, in general, reported in the valuation manuals—are inversely proportional to the fraction of the capital that they refer to.

It is useful to note that the preceding reflections are uniquely aimed at introducing the problem from a conceptual perspective. In practice, the opportunity of applying a minority discount must always be appreciated in the context of the specific valuation and, in particular, analyzing the structure and composition of the ownership structure, the model of corporate governance, and the presence of specific clauses/agreements in the company statutes.

Discounts for the Lack of Control The estimate for the discount for the lack of control, as we have already mentioned, should be done case-by-case.

In particular, it is worth highlighting that, if the minority is protected by contractual or statutory clauses, the calculation of the discount could turn out to be meaningless. These clauses could regard, for example:

- The right, in case of a transfer of control, to sell the minority shareholding at the terms agreed upon for the cession of the majority (tag-along right)
- The requirement of a favorable vote of the minority shareholders for any non-ordinary managerial decision (e.g., capital increase, disposal of relevant assets, etc.)

These are agreements typically included in the selling contracts of minority interests to private equity funds and merchant banks, aimed at guaranteeing the exit from investments at the same conditions obtained by the controlling shareholder(s).

If, on the other hand, the minority interests are not protected by specific agreements, the discount for the lack of control depends on the general protections enacted by company norms and statutes. The literature on valuation distinguishes between different types of minorities as a function of the possibility of influencing or blocking certain types of decisions.

Liquidity Discounts　As already mentioned, this category of discounts is logically connected to the preceding category. The agreements that give the minority an equal treatment with that of the majority determine an upgrading of the share, which allows it to reenter the market for control. Thus, for the reasons already discussed in section 12.6.2, in this case the estimate of the level of liquidity is not required.

If those agreements do not exist, or do exist for a limited period, the charge of a minority discount as a function of the level of liquidity is justifiable.

Basis for Calculation of the Discounts　In the context of the valuation process, in general, a control stake is evaluated without considering its level of liquidity. This is because the assessment on its relevance in terms of control affects the size of the liquidity discount and the way it is estimated.

It needs to be observed that the measurement of the discount cannot be set aside from the criteria adopted by the analyst in the context of the estimation of the base value of the firm.

In fact, the analyst could appreciate the lower value relating to the lack of the power to control, in the context of the cash flow estimate. For example, if the valuation is realized on the basis of dividends that the analyst expects will be likely distributed, the application of a discount to the value estimate could be a duplication.

Analogous considerations hold for the discount for the lack of liquidity. In fact, some analysts increase the discount rate for the flows as a function of liquidity factors, and thus they implicitly obtain the effect of lowering the value of the estimate. Also, in this case, the risk of duplication is evident.

The choice of the basis of calculation of the discounts is not as obvious as it would seem at first sight. If, by definition, the minority shareholding cannot be given a strategic value, the base value should simply be represented by the stand-alone value. Nevertheless, the choice in this sense could seriously penalize the minority shareholders in the case that the fair market value results much higher than the stand-alone value.

On the other hand, the acquirer (even if this relates to the majority shareholder) may not be willing to negotiate transaction prices above the stand-alone value level, when the fair market values are by nature volatile and therefore there exists the possibility that they may not be recovered in the subsequent transactions.

The problem mentioned does not present a straight technical solution, as it regards a question of fairness. We may conclude that the stand-alone value constitutes the minimum base value of reference to be assumed for the application of the discount.

15.6.2 Discounts at Company Level

The business valuation literature admits the possibility of applying a discount with respect to the base value of the entire equity, because of two factors:

- The presence of specific risk elements such as the dependence of the business on a strategic supplier, high levels of clients' portfolio concentration, or deficiencies in the organizational structure
- The lower liquidity typical of the market for control in comparison with that of the stock markets

As for the first point, it is useful to note that the opportunity of the discount is evaluated as a function of the method adopted by the analyst.

If specific risk factors of the transaction are already treated at the cash flow estimate level or at the discount rate level, the application of such discounts is not required; Otherwise, one would obtain a duplication, and the value of the estimate might be improperly penalized.

Referring, on the other hand, to the second point, the valuation literature does not have a precise position on the opportunity, in the case of the valuation of entire equity of an unlisted company, of applying a discount motivated by lack of liquidity with respect to listed companies. The doubts arise from the fact that the parameters of valuation (in particular the opportunity cost of capital) are often gained from the stock markets, and therefore refer to investments characterized by high liquidity standards.

In our opinion, the discount should not be applied when, logically, it is at least debatable to assume the stock market as a benchmark, simply because the market for control is characterized by motives that have nothing to do with those typical of financial investors.

Holding Discounts The *holding discount* is sometimes included in the class of company-level discounts. It deals with the undervaluation of listed holding companies in comparison with the sum of the market values of the shareholding held in other listed companies. The discount may be motivated by the fact that a holding could be seen as a non-optimal shareholdings portfolio, which is of little interest from the perspective of a generic buyer.

Another motive often purported to be responsible for the holding companies' undervaluation is based on tax inefficiencies considerations (e.g., the generation of taxable capital gains in the case of the alienation of the securities).

It should be outlined that when the holding company has a proprietary managerial staff, the present value of the costs at the holding company level, not relatable to the controlled companies, should be deducted from the corporate value of the holding companies. This may, as well, be a possible explanation for the holding discount.

15.7   VALUE LEVELS AND VALUE EXPRESSED BY STOCK PRICES

The premiums and discounts should be coherent with the base of calculations. Thus, to discuss the issue one needs to start from the (base) levels of value.

The valuation literature in general advances the following classification:

- Strategic value (synergistic or strategic control base); this is the value related to the strategic acquirers willing to realize post-merger changes that can give rise to cost savings and synergies.[5]
- Stand-alone value (controlling interest base); this is the value of the business determined as a function of the plans of the management or of the shareholders involved in the management of the company. We have already said that the stand-alone value is a "full" value, obtained after removing the effects on the cash flow of factors related to the possible presence of private benefits.
- Marketable minority shareholding value (marketable minority interest base); this is the value related to the minority shareholdings (the ones excluded from control) that could be sold in stock markets. The characterization of the notion of value expressed by market prices is a crucial argument; in fact, market prices represent the benchmark for the estimate of possible premiums and discounts.
- The value of nonmarketable minority shareholdings (nonmarketable minority interest base); this is the value related to stakes excluded from control and difficult to be sold. Mainly, this is equal to the present value

---

[5]The value of acquisition, defined also as investment value, already discussed in Chapter 11.

of the cash flow expected to accrue to the holder of the stake, taking into account the firm performance and the mechanisms protecting the minority shareholders.

15.7.1 The Notion of Value Expressed through Market Prices

In estimating premiums and discounts, the most serious problem from both a theoretical and methodological point of view is the uncertainty in the level of value expressed through market prices.

The question is relevant for two reasons:

1. As we know, the method of market multiples represents one of the most fundamental approaches to the valuation of companies; therefore, it is very important to have a clear idea of the meaning of the values expressed by the multiples.
2. As we will see, data relating to control and takeover premiums are calculated assuming the stock-market prices of the companies whose control is being transferred as a benchmark.

Focusing on the financial literature on the topic, the main proposed approaches are the following:

- *The market prices of shares having right to vote are a function of the divisible cash flow.* In presence of norms that offer a sufficient protection to minority shareholders, preventing, in particular, the controlling shareholders from stealing a significant share of the profits, and assuming that the firms are well managed, the market prices should, indeed, approximate the stand-alone value.[6]
- *The market prices of shares having the right to vote also incorporate fraction of the present value of the private benefits related to control.* This is due to the probability that following a hostile takeover, the minority shareholdings form a part of the controlling interest, and assuming that the contending management for obtaining control are willing to surrender a part of the private benefits by offering a price higher than the

---

[6]This approach is also accepted in the practitioners' literature concerning the definitions of value applied to the procedures of impairment testing; see Mercer Capital, *Valuation for Impairment Testing* (Peabody Publishing, 2002), p. 17: "If a public company's earnings are optimised, suggesting that there are few, if any changes to be made to improve them absent business synergies, there is a growing understanding that this company's public stock multiples may yield a controlling interest value."

one that is expected after the transfer of control. On the basis of these assumptions, as we will see, some scholars interpret the observed differences between the price of voting shares and the price of shares with partial or no voting rights as a measure of the private benefits of control.

■ *The market prices of voting shares incorporate also a fraction of the value estimated from the perspective of strategic buyers.* This implies that the prices are a function of stand-alone cash flow, of a fraction of the divisible flow related to the development of synergies that favor all the shareholders, and, in conclusion, of a fraction of the private benefits. If such hypothesis is met, then multiples, takeover premiums, control premium have uncertain significance. In fact, the multiples refer to an undefined notion of value positioned between stand-alone value and fair market value; takeover premiums are a biased measure of merger synergies; finally, the prices of shares characterized by different voting rights do not explain the valuation of the private benefits related to control, but a mix of elements related to the strategic value of the business.

Any of these hypotheses could be credible in relation to the financial environment and to the market cycle. In fact, in presence of speculative phenomena, the market prices can presumably explain the potential acquisition values. This is verified, for example, when in some industries, the market for control is particularly favorable to the sellers and, as a consequence, the market participants assume that the listed companies related to that industry could become targets for acquisitions.

On the other hand, during bearish phases of the market cycle, the prices could be appreciably lower than the stand-alone value of the listed companies. In general, the market is interested, in these conditions, by public offerings aimed at delistings motivated by the fact that the repurchase of the shares grants a positive net present value transaction.

In spite of the previous caveats, the thesis that market prices in the long term converge to stand-alone values can be shared and in fact is coherent with the practice of valuation generally followed by practitioners and analysts in carrying out research on listed securities and in preliminary valuations on securities of new companies that are entering the market (initial public offerings).

15.8   ESTIMATING CONTROL PREMIUMS

As already said, the international financial literature shares the idea that the control premium has a reason to exist if, and only if, the control of a business allows one to extract private benefits.

We have already specified that these benefits can mainly assume three forms as discussed previously in this chapter:

1. Benefits of a psychological nature.
2. Monetary benefits that the controlling shareholder can extract from the business and that correspond to an equivalent curtailment of divisible benefits.
3. Benefits that refer to the control of the assets of the firm, which translate into monetary benefits that are developed outside the firm itself. As a consequence, *external synergies* do not affect divisible flows and therefore do not necessarily damage the minority shareholders.

In the studies on this issue available to date, two different methodologies have been introduced to estimate the benefits of control:

■ *The comparison of the price of sold controlling stakes and the market prices following the announcement of the transaction.* The procedure is based on the hypothesis that the market prices following the transfer of control incorporate the divisible benefits attained after the change in management. Thus, the differential between the price paid for the controlling block and the market price following the transaction announcement should represent the measure of the private benefits attained by the acquirer.[7]

■ *The comparison between the prices of shares having different voting rights;*[8] for example, in Italy the shares without voting rights usually trade at a discount in respect to voting shares. According to scholarly analyses, the discount to which these are quoted can be otherwise interpreted as the premium to which the ordinary shares are quoted, where this premium is given for the right to vote that characterizes only the ordinary shares.

This kind of approach to the measurement of the value of control is based on the premise that the shares traded in the market, though not belonging to the controlling share, incorporate part of the private benefit. It is useful to point out that this assumption can be accepted, assuming that the minority

---

[7]See M. Barklay and C. Holderness, "Private Benefits of Control of Public Corporation," *Journal of Financial Economics* (1989): 25, pp. 371–395; and A. Dick and L. Zingales, "Private Benefits of Control: An International Comparison," *Journal of Finance 59* (2004).
[8]See T. Nenova, "The Value of Corporate Votes and Control Benefits: A Cross-Country Analysis," *Journal of Financial Economics* 68(3) (2003).

shareholders enter "to form a part of the controlling interest during a hostile takeover, if the contending management, just to obtain control, is disposed to surrender part of the private benefits by offering a higher price to those who have shares under the new management."[9]

The research available in general confirms certain theoretical observations:

- The size of the observable private benefits in different countries can be explained by some main factors such as:
  - Level of shareholders protection
  - Quality of the laws relating to transfer of control
  - Quality of the laws' enforcement system
- The share of the benefits reflected in the prices that are negotiated for the controlling stakes depends on the competition existing in the market for control of businesses.

15.8.1 Role of Premiums in Valuation

From the insights derived from empirical studies focused on specific national markets, as well as on the cross-country analysis, we can infer some conclusion, which can be useful in businesses valuation, namely:

- The research performed, as already noted, confirms some theoretical hypotheses regarding the effect of some environmental and industry-specific factors on the size of the premium for control.
- In particular, the private benefits of control and, consequently, the negotiated premiums, are lower in Anglo-Saxon countries (i.e., the United States and the United Kingdom).
- The research shows, on the contrary, that control premiums are particularly high in some countries, including Italy. For example, the value of control estimated by Dick and Zingales[10] for Italy is 37 percent of the market capitalization while it is, on average, 16 percent and 1 percent in the United States and United Kingdom, respectively.

The presence of a pyramidal control structure in some countries[11] could justify the particularly large size of the premium. Indeed, some scholars

---

[9]M. Bigelli, p. 95, "Under these premises the value of voting rights depends on the amount of the private benefits extractable and the probability that a minority share will result pivotal in winning the contest for the control."

[10]See A. Dick, L. Zingales.

[11]See G. Nicodano, "Corporate Groups, Dual Class Shares and the Value of Voting Rights," *Journal of Banking and Finance*, 22 (1998).

suggest that, the higher the degree of separation between ownership and control (obtained by means of non-voting shares, pyramids, and cross-ownership structures), the higher the premiums.

Accepting this thesis, the size of the control premium observed with reference to Italy could be explained as the result of transactions in which the counterparties have a pyramidal company structure while it would overestimate the value attributable to control with respect to negotiations between counterparties not listed on market.

For the specific need of valuation, in general, the studies miss a point: considering the limitations of the available data, the sizes of the private benefit are not controlled at industry level. In theory, the possibility of extracting private benefits and the intensity of competition in the market for corporate control are presumably affected by the industries' characteristics, thus determining the size of premiums.

15.8.2 Some Conclusions

We can conclude that the available empirical researches support the existence of private benefits of control and back the approach of practitioners who include in their calculations the control premiums.

The size of private benefits compared with the value of the equity should be performed by analyzing the following elements:

- Environmental factors (the studies show that the premiums change across countries, depending on the different legal systems, enforcement effectiveness, and business ethics features)
- The effects of leverage due to pyramidal structures
- Industry-specific characteristics affecting the size of private benefits
- Level of competition in the market for control and consequent bargaining power of the sellers

The extent of private benefits actually rebated to the sellers is a function of those mentioned factors. In business valuation, the fair market value of control does not depend, therefore, merely on the value of the private benefits registered at industry level, but also on the fact that willing buyers are compelled to transfer a part of those benefits to sellers.

15.9 ESTIMATING ACQUISITION PREMIUMS

The calculation of acquisition premium within business valuations is based on the assumption that, in the area of the market for control specifically analyzed, stakes' prices include the portion of merger synergies expected to be attained by the management.

The most common technique for estimating premiums of acquisition consists in the calculation of *takeover premiums,* which are the difference between the company's shares price in the stock market before the acquisition is announced[12] and the price (per share) offered by the bidder.

The observable premiums of acquisition in a given deal's sample also incorporate the premium of control discussed in the previous section (especially when the market conditions allow the extraction of significant private benefits).

In fact, as pointed out before, merger synergies could refer to two distinct elements:

- Divisible benefits derived from better managerial capabilities as well as from the development of new effective strategies
- Private benefits, which accrue only to the controlling shareholder(s)

Data regarding takeover premiums are easily available. Consequently, in general, those data tend to be more reliable than those presented in academic researches on the control premium topic (the takeover premiums are systematically collected in specialized data banks and by merchant and investment banks while researches are targeted to academic circles).

Among the most common sources, Mergerstat, which systematically collect deals data for the US market, deserves a particular mention, as well as Zephyr, which mainly covers the European market.

The findings derived from the large database regarding the US market support certain theoretical hypotheses, namely:

- The size of takeover premiums shows a cyclical pattern.
- There exists a connection between the size of premiums and deal characteristics (payment in cash, in stocks, etc.).
- The paid premiums change appreciably from industry to industry.
- The paid premiums change appreciably in relation to the purchased percentage of capital. This confirms the hypothesis of the existence of a leverage effect of control premiums incorporated in takeover premiums, as we have already discussed in the previous section.
- The premiums are higher when the target firms are distressed, thus, the benefits expected from a prospective restructuring could be significant.
- Though the empirical research confirms that in the United States the value of private benefits of control is significantly greater than in other countries, one is not allowed to conclude that the takeover premiums

---

[12]For example, Mergerstat, a data provider, measures premiums in comparison to the market price of shares in the preceding periods (one day, one week, one month . . .).

measured in the United States represent a more reliable measure of the "strategic value" granted by target companies.

Takeover premiums for the estimate of the fair market value could be used when the following conditions are met:

- The data must refer to the specific target company's industry.
- The motivations for the observed transactions should be similar, at least in part, to the ones showed by the willing buyers of the target company.
- The size of the deals considered should be similar to that of the target firm.
- The deals considered to calculate the premium should refer to the entire equity or to a large stake, and, preferably, should be made in cash.

Even if the number of the deals analyzed is reasonably high, it is clear that the conditions of comparability can rarely be satisfied. This implies that, in order to estimate the premium, the analyst should perform a series of checks and assessments to adjust the raw data.

A particularly sensitive aspect regards the application, in the distinct phases of the valuation process, of both acquisition and control premiums. This is due to the risk of duplications or deficiencies in the estimate. This issue will be further discussed in the following section.

15.10   ACQUISITION AND CONTROL PREMIUMS IN A PERFECT WORLD

The following simulation shows the relationships between acquisition and control premiums calculated using the procedures described in the previous paragraphs.

The simulation assumes an (ideal) situation where:

- The market prices express stand-alone values and, following transfers of control, incorporate the value of divisible merger synergies.
- Private benefits will be entirely rebated to sellers.

Exhibit 15.12 shows the meaning of the previous assumptions: In a transaction involving a transfer of control, it is assumed that the market prices increase until they incorporate the whole value of the expected divisible merger synergies, following the transaction. If the entire value of the

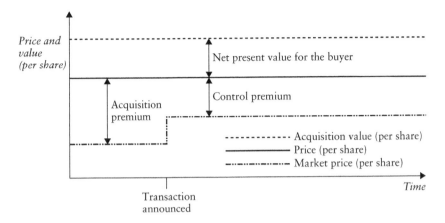

Exhibit 15.12 Acquisition and control premium

private benefits is not returned to the market, the observable control premium would measure exclusively a fraction of the actual control value.

Exhibit 15.13 shows the data referred to a hypothetical sample made of five transactions where there is a transfer of control.

Exhibit 15.13 shows the quantities e, f, g, and h, which are directly observable from the market data.

The quantities a, b, c, and d, which are not known by external analysts, explain the formation of quantity f from the perspective of the five acquirers.

The quantities i, l, m, and n can be determined from the quantities e, f, g, and h, which, as mentioned, are directly observable.

The adjusted fair market values can be determined by modifying the raw premiums data, as shown in Exhibit 15.13.

The fair market value of the entire equity of the firm is obtained simply from the following relationship:

$$W_{\text{stand alone}} \times (1 + n) \times (1 + m)$$

The fair market value of a control stake is obtained by:

$$W_{\text{stand alone}} \times e \times (1 + n) \times (1 + m/e)$$

The simulation allows the discussion within a rational framework of the limits of the available data on premiums and the estimate approximations commonly adopted.

In particular, it is easy to observe that the data on acquisition premiums can be misleading when they refer to transactions involving limited

Exhibit 15.13 Simulation of the acquisition and control premiums

	Formula	A	B	C	D	E	Average
a) W stand-alone		1,000	2,000	1,500	3,000	3,200	
b) Divisible merger synergies		200	300	400	900	900	
c) Private benefits		50	70	100	–	300	
d) W_{acq} (100%)	$a + b + c$	1,250	2,370	2,000	3,900	4,400	
e) Control stake in %		60%	80%	35%	52%	65%	
f) Takeover price (per share)	$[(a + b)*e + c]/(o*e)$	1.283	2.388	2.186	3.900	4.562	
g) Market price before the announcement (per share)		1.0	2.0	1.5	3.0	3.2	
h) Market price after the announcement (per share)	$(a + b)/o$	1.2	2.3	1.9	3.9	4.1	
i) Acquisition premium	$(f - g)/g$	28.33%	19.38%	45.71%	30.00%	42.55%	33.19%
l) Control premium	$(f - h)/h$	6.94%	3.80%	15.04%	0.00%	11.26%	7.41%
m) (Control value)/(equity) ratio	$l*e$	4.17%	3.04%	5.26%	0.00%	7.32%	3.96%
n) Acquisition premium net of control premium	$i - [(f - h)/g]$	20.00%	15.00%	26.67%	30.00%	28.13%	23.96%
o) # shares		1,000	1,000	1,000	1,000	1,000	

Exhibit 15.14 Premium as a function of the acquired fraction of capital

	Formula	A	B	C	D	E	F
a) W stand-alone		1,000	1,000	1,000	1,000	1,000	1,000
b) Divisible merger synergies		200	200	200	200	200	200
c) Private benefits		100	100	100	100	100	100
d) W_{acq} (100%)	a + b + c	1,300	1,300	1,300	1,300	1,300	1,300
e) Control stake in %		30%	40%	50%	60%	70%	80%
f) Takeover price (per share)	$[(a + b)*e + c]/(o*e)$	1.533	1.450	1.400	1.367	1.343	1.325
g) Market price before the announcement (per share)		1.0	1.0	1.0	1.0	1.0	1.0
h) Market price after the announcement (per share)	$(a + b)/o$	1.2	1.2	1.2	1.2	1.2	1.2
i) Acquisition premium	$(f - g)/g$	53.33%	45.00%	40.00%	36.67%	34.29%	32.50%
l) Control premium	$(f - h)/h$	27.78%	20.83%	16.67%	13.89%	11.90%	10.42%
m) (Control value)/(equity) ratio	$l*e$	8.33%	8.33%	8.33%	8.33%	8.33%	8.33%
n) Acquisition premium net of control premium	$i - [(f - h)/g]$	20.00%	20.00%	20.00%	20.00%	20.00%	20.00%
o) # shares		1,000	1,000	1,000	1,000	1,000	1,000

shareholding. In fact, for the reasons already discussed in section 11.7, the (indivisible) value of private benefits generates a leverage effect on the percentage representing the acquisition premium.

This phenomenon is clearly observable in Exhibit 15.14, which shows the changing in premiums, depending on the different acquired fraction of capital of the same company.

Also, the data relative to the control premiums are sensitive to the fraction of capital acquired. Therefore, they should be normalized using the procedure illustrated in Exhibit 15.6.

Finally, the observable size of acquisition and control premiums depends on the kind of value expressed by the market prices.

To avoid duplications or deficiencies in estimate, premiums should be applied to a base value coherent with the notion of value expressed by the market.

15.11   ESTIMATING THE VALUE OF CONTROLLING STAKES: AN EXAMPLE

The following example refers to the estimate of the fair market value of a 35 percent stake in an Italian hi-tech listed company. The valuation was requested by the board of directors in order to assess the fairness of the stake's value as reported in the balance sheet.

Considering that, apart from this stake, the shares of the company were widely held, one could assume that the stake allowed *de facto* control. The following information is useful for the estimate:

- Stand-alone value, calculated through the DCF method (entire equity): €1,850 billion.
- Strategic value: based on Mergerstat data showed an average takeover premium of 44 percent at industry level.
- Dealing with a limited share of the capital (35 percent), large enough to allow the control, the analyst decides to include a further control premium. This assumes that the takeover premium obtained from Mergerstat would essentially measure only the strategic value of the businesses. In fact, based on the analysis discussed in section 15.8, the measure of the value of control in the United States was much more limited (1 percent) in comparison to the international average (16 percent).

- In order to avoid duplications, the takeover premium is adjusted taking into account the control premium in the United States, assumed to be 3 percent.
- The analyst has assumed a 10 percent extent of the value of control (as a percentage of market capitalization) on average rebated to the sellers. This percentage is further reduced to 5 percent considering the ownership structure of company.[13]

On the basis of those premises, the calculation of fair market value of the stake may be represented as follows:

1. Stand-alone value (100%)	€1,850 bln
2. "Strategic" fair market value:	€2,608 bln

$$a \times (1 + \text{adjusted takeover premium})$$
$$a \times [1 + (0.44 - 0.03)]$$

3. Proportional value of the stake:	€913 bln

$$b \times 0.35$$

4. Control premium (percentage value of control scaled to the size of the stake):	14.3%

$$0.05 \times \frac{100}{35} = 14.3\%$$

5. Fair market value of the stake:	€1,044 bln

$$c \times (1 + d)$$

15.12   MINORITY DISCOUNT

The expression *minority discount* indicates solely the adjustments, in terms of value, due to the exclusion from control, distinguishing those components from the one related to the marketability of the stake.

---

[13]In particular, in the presence of other shareholders entitled to the shares of importance, there is considered a limit to the possibility of extracting private benefits.

If the control premium refers strictly to the presence of private benefits,[14] the minority discounts should have the same dimension and opposite sign to such benefits. An example could clarify the problem.

We assume that the control premium for a 35 percent stake is estimated to equal 30 percent.

This implies that the value of the private benefits, related to the entire business capital, can be obtained as:

$$0.3 \times 0.55 = 16.5\%$$

Thus, a 16.5 percent share of the cash flow related to private benefits will be stolen from shareholders excluded from the control. As a consequence, the measure of the discount would remain constant and equal to 16.5 percent, independently of the percentage of capital to which the minority participation refers.

In other words, the measure of the discount should always be expressed by the percentage obtained comparing the amount of private benefits and the total value of the equity.

This reasoning appears realistic in the case of a valuation of a stake of a certain importance (indicatively, 30 to 40 percent of the equity). In practice, however, it is difficult to accept that a share of 40 percent should be treated in the same way as a share of 10 percent or 5 percent.

In fact, there are sound reasons for the differentiation, motivated by the fact that, in general, regulations and company statutes allow a certain protection scaled to the held fraction of equity. This implies that the ability of the controlling shareholder to extract private benefits is more limited in the presence of minorities of importance or of those comforted with more effective protection mechanisms.

The empirical studies on the subject of minority discounts provide unconvincing results, because of both the difficulty in gathering extensive databases (the transactions of minority shareholding blocks in unlisted companies are rare and undisclosed) and the lack of a comparison term for measuring the discounts (we have no indications on the value of the companies involved in the transactions).

Thus, the only feasible solution consists in inferring the size of the minority discount from the studies on the control premium, in particular from the methodologically sound researches mentioned in section 15.8.

It is worth underlining that the issues discussed in this paragraph rely on the assumption that the base value on which the discounts are applied

---

[14]We refer here only to the private benefits that the controlling shareholder can steal from minority shareholders.

incorporates the cash flow derived from prospective private benefits (if it can be assumed that these would take place starting, for example, from a stand-alone value calculated using the normalization of the prospective business relations with the controlling shareholders). Alternatively, the estimate of a minority discount would not be justifiable.

15.13   DISCOUNT FOR THE LACK OF MARKETABILITY

The most significant empirical research on the discount for lack of marketability has been conducted in the United States using three distinct approaches:

1. The analysis of the spread between the prices of the "restricted securities" and the same company's share prices (referred to the shares freely marketable)
2. The analysis of the prices of purchase and sale issued by market makers (the bid–ask spread) for securities characterized by different levels of liquidity
3. The analysis of spreads between the prices of transfer of "blocks" of shares and the corresponding market prices

The restricted securities, according to US laws, can be sold only through private placements, but cannot be sold on the market for a period of two years.

These securities are treated with a significant (30 to 35 percent) discount with respect to the freely marketable shares issued by the same company.[15]

The findings obtained from the other two types of analyses are less convincing. In the case of the sale of share blocks, for example, the analysis allows the appreciation of the intrinsic difficulty of selling large blocks of securities, but not of the difficulty of selling shares of unlisted companies. Analogous considerations can be referred with respect to bid–ask spreads.

As a consequence, we believe that the available empirical results can only constitute the starting point for analyzing the discounts applied in concrete negotiations.

In general, an average discount of 30 percent seems realistic according to the practitioners' business valuation literature. Experts suggest that the

---

[15]For an analysis of the empirical research on liquidity discounts, see S. Pratt, pp. 90–110.

measure of the discount should be scaled in function of the characteristics of the shares to be valued, taking into account particularly:

- Characteristics of the firm assets
- Company size
- Soundness of the business
- Overall profitability
- Stake size in comparison with the entire equity

Without reliable empirical research on the issue, the matter can only be treated by applying sound common sense and by relying on the experience of analysts and practitioners. Nevertheless, one observes general acceptance of the fact that the liquidity discount should be higher in the presence of business assets lacking an autonomous market value, as well as in cases of distressed companies.

Exhibit 15.15   Levels of value

Levels of Value	Perspective	Estimation Method
a) Value of acquisition (investment value) of majority stakes	Specific strategic buyer	DCF of specific buyer with valuation of synergies and of private benefits
b) Value of acquisition (investment value) of the entire equity		
c) Probable market prices (fair market value) of majority stakes	Generic strategic buyer	Modified DCF in function of general and "endemic" synergies
d) Probable market prices (fair market value of the entire equity)		Deal multiples
		Stock market multiples + premium of acquisition
e) Stand-alone value	■ Current shareholders ■ Financial buyers	■ DCF stand-alone ■ Stock market multiples
f) Value of non-marketable minority interests in a stock-market	Financial buyers	DCF stand-alone—minority discount
		Stock market multiples—monirity discount
		DCF adjusted in flow and/or in discount rate

15.14   DEFINITIONS OF VALUE AND ESTIMATION PROCEDURES

Exhibit 15.15 connects the various notions of value discussed in this chapter along with the different perspectives of estimation, the bases of calculation of premiums and discounts, and the valuation model applied.

Exhibit 15.15 identifies six levels of value: three refer to the entire equity (entity level) and three to stakes of different dimensions (shareholder level).

The levels of value are ordered in a decreasing scale: this implies that the total value of the shares decreases from the higher to the lower level. In particular, the frame of the table assumes that the investment value is larger than the fair market value. We know that this holds true exclusively for potential buyers who are able to create an amount of value bigger than the merger synergies usually returned to vendors as a function of their negotiating power.

We assume also that market price is a good approximation of the stand-alone value.

## CHAPTER 16

Valuation Considerations on Rights Issues[1]

16.1 INTRODUCTION TO RIGHTS ISSUES

One of the options available for a publicly listed company willing to raise equity by issuing new shares is to do so by offering preemptive rights to current shareholders. Equity offerings of this kind are commonly referred to as *rights issues*, due to the fact that existing shareholders are granted rights to subscribe for new shares proportionally to their current stake in the company and can either exercise such rights or sell them to other investors.

The price at which new shares are issued (*subscription price*) is set in advance by the issuer at a significant discount to the reference share price before the announcement of the offering terms. Preemptive rights can only be exercised during a limited time window (*subscription period*), during which the rights are detached from the shares and trade separately on the same stock exchange. For this reason, the first date of the subscription period is called *ex-right date* and the share price after detachment of the rights is also referred to as *ex-right price* (where "ex" stands for excluding). Unexercised rights at the end of the subscription period are often auctioned in a coordinated placement to the market called *rump placement*.

Investment banks can play an important role in rights issues, particularly as underwriters of the newly issued shares. In this case, the underwriting banks, often organized in a syndicate, guarantee the full proceeds to the issuer and commit to purchase any unsubscribed shares at the subscription price. On the contrary, in a non-underwritten rights issue, under specific market conditions, there is the possibility that some of the new shares remain unsubscribed.

---

[1]This chapter has been authored by Amedeo Giammattei and Giuseppe Sica

From a valuation perspective, there are three main questions to be analyzed in relation to rights issues:

1. How is the subscription price set by the issuer?
2. What is the value of preemptive rights granted to existing shareholders?
3. What is the impact of pricing on existing shareholders?

The next pages aim to provide simple answers to the above questions.

16.2   SETTING THE SUBSCRIPTION PRICE

A necessary condition for a rational investor to exercise preemptive rights and subscribe for new shares is that the subscription price must be below the ex-right price of existing shares. Otherwise, the investor would be better off buying shares directly on the secondary market where they are listed. Therefore, there is a clear incentive for the issuer to set the subscription price at a discount to the ex-right price.[2] Intuitively, the discount should be large enough to ensure that the ex-right price will stay above the subscription price until closing of the subscription period. On the other hand, if the market believes the discount is too large, it could be read as a negative signal on the expected evolution of the share price of the issuer.

16.2.1   TERP and Discount to TERP

As mentioned in the first section of the chapter, the subscription price is announced by the issuer before the start of the subscription period. Therefore, when setting the terms, the issuer can only estimate what the expected ex-right price will be, based on the reference share price before the announcement of the terms (*cum-right price*). The expected ex-right price is called *Theoretical Ex-Right Price* or, in short, *TERP*. The discount applied on the subscription price is commonly expressed as a percentage of TERP (*discount to TERP*). An alternative way to express the discount is as a percentage of the cum-right price (*gross discount*).

There is a simple formula to compute the theoretical ex-right price:

$$TERP = \frac{(n \times p) + (N \times p)}{n + N} = \frac{(n \times p) + S}{n + N}$$

---

[2]The issuer might also decide to set the subscription price at a premium to the current price if, for various reasons, it does not want to incentivize existing shareholders to participate in the offering.

n = number of outstanding shares before announcement
p = reference share price before announcement (cum-right price)
N = number of new shares issued
P = subscription price
S = rights issue size $(N \times P)$

In other words, TERP should be equal to the market cap of the issuer at announcement, plus the expected proceeds of the rights issue, all divided by the total number of shares outstanding after issuance of the new shares.

The discount to TERP and the gross discount are computed as follows:

$$Discount\ to\ TERP = \frac{TERP - P}{TERP}$$

$$Gross\ discount = \frac{p - P}{p}$$

It is possible to express the subscription price in terms of TERP and discount to TERP, and the number of newly issued shares as the ratio of the proceeds from the rights issue to the subscription price:

$$P = TERP \times (1 - D)$$

$$N = \frac{S}{P} = \frac{S}{TERP \times (1 - D)}$$

D = discount to TERP

As a result, the aforementioned formula to compute TERP can be restated as follows:

$$TERP = \frac{(n \times p) + S}{n + \dfrac{S}{TERP \times (1 - D)}} = p - \frac{S}{n} \times \frac{D}{1 - D}$$

Although less intuitive, this second formula can be useful when it is necessary to compute TERP for given levels of discount to TERP and rights issue proceeds.

Some simple calculations will show that, for TERP to be strictly positive, the discount to TERP must be smaller than the ratio of the old market cap to the expected market cap following the rights issue. On the other hand, if the discount to TERP is zero, TERP will be equal to the reference share price before the announcement, making investors indifferent between exercising preemptive rights and buying shares on the secondary market. Therefore, it is sensible to conclude that the discount to TERP should be set in the following range of values:

$$0 < D < \frac{n \times p}{n \times p + S}$$

Exhibit 16.1   Calculation of TERP[3]

Market cap before rights issue announcement		
Reference share price ($)	p	100
Outstanding shares (#)	n	1,000
Market cap ($)	$n \times p = m$	100,000
Rights issue terms		
Rights issue size ($)	S	20,000
Discount to TERP	D	25%
TERP ($)	$p - S/n \times D/(1 - D)$	93
Subscription Price ($)	$TERP \times (1 - D) = P$	70
New shares issued (#)	$S/P = N$	286
Gross discount	$(p - P)/p$	30%
Expected market cap post-rights issue at announcement		
Shares post-rights issue (#)	$n + N = NN$	1,286
Expected market cap ($)	$n \times p + S = M$	120,000
Equivalent to	$NN \times TERP$	120,000

The example shown in Exhibit 16.1 will help to clarify the concepts we have addressed in this chapter so far.

It can be noticed that for $D = m/M = 83\%$, $TERP = 0$. Therefore, in this example, any value between 0 and 83 percent would be accepted as a discount to TERP. In the next paragraph, we will discuss the factors considered by the issuer in the choice of the exact level of discount to TERP within the range of acceptable values.

16.2.2   Setting the Discount to TERP

As already mentioned, the issuer faces a trade-off between two contrasting needs in the choice over the level of discount to TERP. On the one hand, the company wants to minimize the probability that the ex-right price might go below the subscription price during the subscription period. On the other hand, the issuer does not want to communicate lack of confidence to the market by setting a discount to TERP which could be perceived as disproportionately low. Finally, additional constraints faced by the issuer are the willingness of investment banks to underwrite the rights issue below given levels of discount to TERP and the cost of underwriting corresponding to different values of discount.

In this context, the size of the rights issue, the market environment, and the level of discount set for previous offerings are all important elements to be taken into consideration by the issuer when pricing the rights issue.

---

[3]Totals may not reconcile due to rounding differences.

Size of the Offering As far as the size of the rights issue is concerned, one could expect the discount to TERP to get bigger, the higher the amount of proceeds to be raised in the offering. Intuitively, this is due to the fact that a larger offering would normally lead to a higher level of uncertainty regarding the outcome of the issuance. In analyzing the actual amount of risk associated with the size of the rights issue, the following factors should also be taken into account:

- *The relative size of the offering vs. market cap before announcement:* More indicative than its absolute size, it also makes a comparison with previous (if any) rights issues.
- *The relative size of the offering vs. average daily volumes traded (ADTV):* Liquidity of the stock is an additional element to be taken into account when assessing the risk associated with the size of the offering.
- *Precommitments from major shareholders to exercise their rights:* The announcement that some existing shareholders have committed to use their rights reduces the amount of rights to be placed in the market and decreases the level of uncertainty associated with the offering. The amount of proceeds linked to a lack of commitment from existing shareholders is also referred to as *market risk.*
- *The capital structure/level of capitalization following the rights issue:* If the level of capitalization after completion of the offering is perceived by the market as inadequate, it is likely that investors will be less eager to exercise rights and the risk of not achieving a successful completion will be higher. This effectively results from the fear of possible future capital increases and is especially true for financial institutions subject to capital requirements.
- *The time frame linked with a rights issue:* All else being equal, a shorter timeframe reduces the risk of significant price fluctuations and might lead to a less conservative discount to TERP. Such time frames are often dictated by national legislation and may vary significantly from one country to another.

Market Environment Market conditions are also an important component influencing the level of discount to TERP. Differently from the size of the offering, the issuer has less control on this characteristic, especially when the need to raise capital does not leave much flexibility on timing. In particular, the following factors will need to be carefully analyzed:

- *Historical and implied volatility of equity markets:* A higher volatility in the stock market will add risk to the offering and will normally require a larger discount.

■ *Historical and implied volatility of the specific stock:* Similarly to the previous factor, risk increases with a higher stock volatility, but the impact on the level of the discount might be even stronger in this case.

■ *Market sentiment on the company and the sector:* A negative outlook on the sector and specifically on the issuer will make subscription of new shares less attractive and will potentially induce the issuer to increase the discount. Vice versa, a positive market sentiment toward the sector and the company issuing new shares might provide more flexibility to the issuer on the level of discount to TERP.

■ *Relative valuation vs. peers:* An attractive valuation of the issuer with respect to comparable companies will provide higher incentives for investors to subscribe for the newly issued shares and increase the chances of successful completion of the offering. For this reason, rights issues are often announced by the issuer together with the presentation of a new business plan, also with the aim of highlighting the strengths of the company and its potentially attractive valuation.

Previous Offerings The level of discount in previous rights issues, especially if peers' previous issues are available, provides relevant guidance to the issuer regarding the proper level of discount to TERP. On the other hand, it is also an important reference for investors who will check how the discount compares to previous offerings and, in case of divergence, will try to understand the underlying reasons.

It goes without saying that any benchmarking with respect to previous offerings will need to take into consideration comparability across the different dimensions discussed earlier and in particular:

■ Rights issue size as a percentage of market cap
■ Market risk as a percentage of rights issue size
■ Market risk as a percentage of market cap
■ Time frame
■ Market environment at time of issuance

Exhibit 16.2 summarizes how the different factors analyzed above may influence the level of discount to TERP set by the issuer.

16.3 VALUE OF PREEMPTIVE RIGHTS

In a rights issue, existing shareholders receive preemptive rights to subscribe for new shares at the subscription price. The reasons for setting the subscription price at a discount to TERP and the factors driving the level of

Exhibit 16.2 Influence of different factors on the level of discount to TERP

	Discount to TERP	
	Lower	Higher
Rights issue size		
Rights issue size as a percentage of market cap	Low	High
Rights issue size as a percentage of ADTV	Low	High
Market risk as a percentage of rights issue size	Low	High
Market risk as a percentage of market cap	Low	High
Level of capitalization post-rights issue	Adequate	Inadequate
Timetable	Short	Long
Market environment		
Historical and implied volatility of equity markets	Low	High
Historical and implied volatility of the specific stock	Low	High
Market sentiment on the company and the sector	Positive	Negative
Relative valuation vs. peers	Attractive	Unattractive
Previous offerings		
Discount to TERP in comparable offerings	Low	High

discount were analyzed in the previous section. Our focus will now shift to the valuation of preemptive rights. In particular, we will show how to compute the expected value of rights at announcement of the terms and how such value should change during the subscription period based on the evolution of the ex-right price.

16.3.1 Theoretical Value of Rights at Announcement of the Terms

At announcement of the terms, the issuer communicates the size of the rights issue, the subscription price, and the number of newly issued shares to the market. Since one right is usually attached to each outstanding share, the ratio of new shares to old shares (*subscription ratio*) defines how many rights need to be exercised to subscribe for one new share. For instance, in an offering where the subscription ratio is 1:2 (one new share for two old shares), the subscriber will need to own and exercise two rights in order to subscribe for one newly issued share at the subscription price.

On the ex-right date, an investor willing to buy a share in the company will have two options:

- Purchase one share on the market at the ex-right price.
- Purchase the number of rights required to subscribe for one new share and pay the subscription price.

The two amounts should be the same or an arbitrage would be possible. If (A) was greater than (B), there would be a clear incentive to buy rights, and exercise them paying the subscription price. This would lead to an increase in the value of the rights toward the equilibrium price. Vice versa, if (B) was greater than (A), there would be no incentive to purchase rights and the resulting decrease in the value of rights should again adjust their price toward equilibrium.

At announcement of the terms, the ex-right price cannot be observed but can be estimated by computing TERP as was previously shown in the chapter. Therefore, one way to estimate the expected value of one right at announcement is to use the following equation:

$$TERP = R * VR + P$$

R: number of rights required to subscribe for one new share

VR: theoretical value of one right

Solving for VR:

$$VR = \frac{TERP - P}{R}$$

By definition, as one right is attached to each outstanding share, the following should also hold:

$$VR = p - TERP$$

Finally, the value of one right can also be expressed in terms of cum-right price and subscription price, leaving *TERP* out of the equation, proceeding as follows:

$$VR = p - TERP$$

$$VR = p - (R * VR + P)$$

$$VR = \frac{p - P}{R + 1}$$

The example in Exhibit 16.3 and 16.4 will show how the above formulas can be used to compute the theoretical value of rights at announcement of the terms.

Exhibit 16.3 Calculation of the theoretical value of rights at announcement of the terms

Market cap before rights issue announcement		
Reference share price ($)	p	100
Outstanding shares (#)	n	1,000
Market cap ($)	$n \times p = m$	100,000
Rights issue terms		
Rights issue size ($)	S	20,000
Subscription ratio (new shares/old shares)	SR	1/2
Rights required to subscribe 1 new share (#)	$1/SR = R$	2
New shares issued (#)	$n \times SR = N$	500
Subscription Price ($)	$S/N = P$	40
TERP ($)	$(n \times p + S)/(n + N)$	80
Discount to TERP	$1 - P/TERP = D$	50%
Gross discount	$(p - P)/p$	60%
Theoretical value of rights at announcement		
Value of one right ($)	$(TERP - P)/R = VR$	20
Equivalent to	$p - TERP$	20
Equivalent to	$(p - P)/(R + 1)$	20

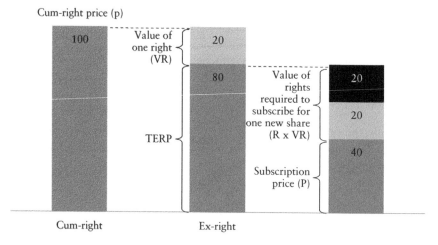

Exhibit 16.4 Separation of rights ($)

16.3.2 Theoretical Value of Rights During the Subscription Period

On the ex-right date, rights are detached from existing shares and start to trade separately on the same stock exchange. For the whole period in which rights are trading, the stock price is referred to as the ex-right price. The ex-right price will evolve from its theoretical value (TERP) during the subscription period as a result of new information flowing to the market. However, the following equation should be satisfied throughout the period in which rights are trading since an arbitrage would be possible otherwise:

$$ERP = R * VR + P$$

$$VR = \frac{ERP - P}{R}$$

ERP: Ex-Right Price

The examples in Exhibits 16.5 and 16.6 will show how the value of rights is expected to evolve in case of positive and negative share price evolution after detachment of the rights.

In reality, small differences between the levels at which rights are traded and their theoretical value can be observed. Among other factors,

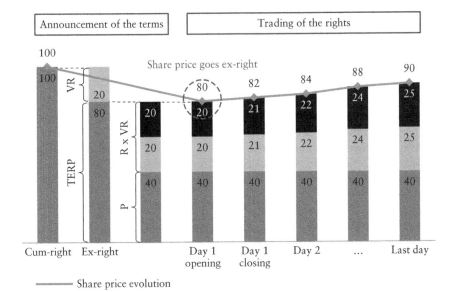

Exhibit 16.5 Separation of rights and positive share price reaction ($)

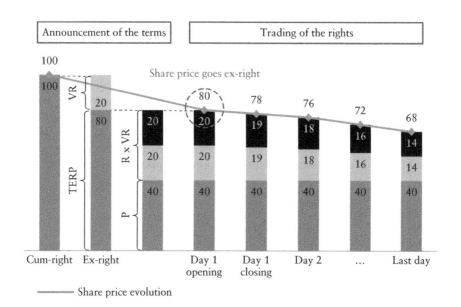

Exhibit 16.6 Separation of rights and negative share price reaction ($)

this can be due to the time value associated with rights, although such component is limited since the subscription period normally lasts only a few weeks. Discrepancies could also be the result of low liquidity in the trading of rights.

16.3.3 Impact of Pricing on Existing Shareholders

Provided with an understanding of the value attached to preemptive rights, it is now possible to discuss the implications caused by the subscription price set by the issuer to existing shareholders. This is equivalent to analyze whether the choice of the discount to TERP is neutral for current shareholders. Neutrality can be assessed under different dimensions. The focus of this section of the chapter will therefore be shareholders' net worth and dilution.

Shareholders' Net Worth Before announcement of the terms, the net worth of an investor whose only asset is a shareholding in the company is the following:

$$nw = ns * p$$

nw = net worth preannouncement
ns = number of shares owned

At announcement of the terms, the expected net worth of the investor will be equal to the sum of the expected value of its shareholding and the expected value of rights.

$$NW = ns * TERP + nr * VR$$

NW = net worth post announcement
nr = number of rights assigned

Assuming that $ns = nr$ (as one right is normally assigned to each existing share), and considering that $TERP + VR = p$, it is possible to express NW as follows:

$$NW = ns * (TERP + VR) = ns * p = nw$$

It can be noticed that the level of net worth post-announcement is expected to be the same as before. In addition, such level does not depend on the discount to TERP set by the issuer.

Exhibit 16.7 compares the net worth of an existing shareholder before and after announcement of the terms for different levels of discount to TERP.

From Exhibit 16.7 it is also possible to appreciate how the lower value associated with the shareholding as a result of a larger discount to TERP is compensated with a higher value of rights.

Dilution The only way for an existing shareholder not to be diluted in a rights issue is to fully exercise his/her rights and subscribe for newly issued shares pro-quota. It is easy to show that the amount of cash that the shareholder needs to invest not to be diluted is independent of the discount to TERP and is equal to the portion of total proceeds corresponding to his/her shareholding in the company:

$$C = P \times N \times sh = P \times \frac{S}{P} \times sh = S \times sh$$

C = cash outlay not to be diluted
sh = investor's shareholding in percentage terms

Any shareholder who is not willing to invest an amount of cash equal to C will be diluted as a result of a rights issue. The question is whether the extent of such dilution is impacted by the level of discount to TERP. As a larger discount to TERP results in a higher number of newly issued shares for a given amount of proceeds, one could be inclined to think that the dilution borne by an investor who does not intend to invest any additional cash in the

Exhibit 16.7 Shareholders' net worth should not be affected by the level of discount to TERP

		Case 1	Case 2	Case 3
Market cap before rights issue announcement				
Reference share price ($)	p	100	100	100
Outstanding shares (#)	n	1,000	1,000	1,000
Market cap ($)	n × p = m	100,000	100,000	100,000
Rights issue terms				
Rights issue size ($)	S	20,000	20,000	20,000
Subscription ratio (new shares/old shares)	SR	1/5	1/4	1/2
Rights required to subscribe 1 new share (#)	1/SR = R	5	4	2
New shares issued (#)	n × SR = N	200	250	500
Subscription Price ($)	S/N = P	100	80	40
TERP ($)	(n × p + S)/(n + N)	100	96	80
Discount to TERP	(TERP − P)/TERP = D	-	17%	50%
Gross discount	(p − P)/p	-	20%	60%
Value of one right at announcement ($)	(TERP − P)/R = VR	-	4	20
Investor's net worth before announcement				
Shares owned (#)	ns	100	100	100
Net worth ($)	ns × p = nw	10,000	10,000	10,000
Investor's net worth at announcement				
Value of shareholding ($)	ns × TERP = V	10,000	9,600	8,000
Rights owned (#)	ns = nr	100	100	100
Value of rights owned ($)	nr × VR = VRO	-	400	2,000
Net worth ($)	V + VRO = NW	10,000	10,000	10,000
Delta net worth ($)	NW − nw	-	-	-

company is higher for increasing levels of discount to TERP. In order to show why this is not the case, the concept of tail swallowing will be introduced.

In a tail swallowing, an existing shareholder decides to finance the purchase of new shares through the sale of rights. In particular, it is possible to compute the maximum number of new shares that can be bought in a cash-neutral transaction as follows:

$$NS = \frac{nr \times VR}{TERP}$$

NS: new shares that can be bought in a cash-neutral transaction

The shareholding of the investor in percentage terms following the tail swallowing can be computed as:

$$SH = \frac{ns + NS}{n + N}$$

SH: investor's shareholding in percentage terms following the tail swallowing

Simple calculations will show that SH is not impacted by the level of discount to TERP and can be computed as the ratio of the value of the investor's

Exhibit 16.8   Discount to TERP and dilution

		case 1	case 2	case 3
Market cap before rights issue announcement				
Reference share price ($)	p	100	100	100
Outstanding shares (#)	n	1,000	1,000	1,000
Market cap ($)	$n \times p = m$	100,000	100,000	100,000
Rights issue terms				
Rights issue size ($)	S	20,000	20,000	20,000
Subscription ratio	SR	1/5	1/4	1/2
(new shares/old shares)				
Rights required to subscribe	$1/SR = R$	5	4	2
1 new share (#)				
New shares issued (#)	$n \times SR = N$	200	250	500
Subscription price ($)	$S/N = P$	100	80	40
TERP ($)	$(n \times p + S)/(n + N)$	100	96	80
Discount to TERP	$(TERP - P)/TERP = D$	-	17%	50%
Gross discount	$(p - P)/p$	-	20%	60%
Value of one right at	$(TERP - P)/R = VR$	-	4	20
announcement ($)				
Tail swallow for an existing shareholder				
Shares owned (#)	ns	100	100	100
Shareholding at	$ns/n = sh$	10%	10%	10%
announcement				
Rights owned (#)	$ns = nr$	100	100	100
New shares bought in a cash	$nr^* \, VR/TERP = NS$	-	4	25
neutral transaction (#)				
Shares owned after tail	$ns + NS$	100	104	125
swallowing (#)				
Shareholding after tail	$(ns + NS)/(n + N) = SH$	8.33%	8.33%	8.33%
swallowing				
Equivalent to	$ns^* \, p/(n^* \, p + S)$	8.33%	8.33%	8.33%

shareholding before the rights issue to the expected market cap of the issuer following the rights issue:

$$SH = \frac{ns * p}{n * p + S}$$

Therefore, in terms of dilution, existing shareholders should be theoretically indifferent among the different possible levels of discount to TERP, even when they are not willing to participate in the offering.

Exhibit 16.8 compares the shareholding in percentage terms of an existing shareholder following the tail swallowing for different levels of discount to TERP.

In reality, other considerations might come into play and lead shareholders to prefer a higher or lower discount to TERP:

- Lower dilution for those investors who may not be familiar with the concept of tail swallowing (e.g., retail investors) in case of a lower discount
- Reduced execution risk associated with a higher discount
- Lower underwriting fees possibly associated with a higher discount (which reduces the risk borne by the underwriters)
- The possibility to appear stronger than other companies who have gone through the same process in previous years as a result of a lower discount to TERP

16.4 CONCLUSIONS

This chapter was meant to provide a simple explanation regarding the pricing of rights issues, the valuation of preemptive rights, and the implications that the pricing of new shares might have on existing shareholders.

It was shown that setting the subscription price at a discount to the theoretical ex-right price is critical for the successful completion of an offering. The level of the discount should be high enough to be confident that the ex-right price will not go below the subscription price during the subscription period. At the same time, the risk of sending a negative signal to the market by choosing a disproportionately high discount should also be avoided. The main elements to be considered by the issuer to determine the discount are the size of the offering, the market environment, and the levels of discount set in previous rights issues.

One way to estimate the theoretical value of preemptive rights is to do so by assuming that there should be no difference between buying a share by paying the ex-right price or by purchasing rights and paying the subscription price. If this was not the case, arbitrageurs could exploit such difference to lock in a profit and prices would adjust accordingly until the imbalance is eliminated. Among other factors, the time value of rights and low levels of liquidity could cause the price of rights to diverge from their theoretical value.

The level of discount to TERP should not have an impact on the net worth of existing shareholders. As a matter of fact, for a higher discount, the expected reduction in the value of their shareholding should be compensated with a higher value of their preemptive rights. In terms of potential dilution, a shareholder who does not intend to invest his/her own cash to participate in the offering should also be indifferent with respect to the discount level. As a matter of fact, after tail swallowing (i.e., financing the purchase of new shares through the sale of rights), the investor's final shareholding will be diluted but the extent of such dilution will not be affected by the level of discount to TERP. Therefore, the subscription price should be set to guarantee the successful execution of the rights issue, but it should also be theoretically neutral for existing shareholders.

A final remark should be made with respect to the diffusion of rights issues. Countries differ greatly with regards to the options available to perform an equity offering. In some jurisdictions, under certain conditions (e.g., above a certain percentage of the company's share capital), a rights issue becomes mandatory. In other jurisdictions, companies have the possibility to issue shares without granting preemptive rights to existing shareholders. Such differences might at least partially explain why rights issues have been much more common in Europe than in the United States.

## CHAPTER 17

Carbon Risk and Corporate Value[1]

17.1   WHY CARBON RISK MATTERS

As climate change and global warming are addressed by tougher regulation, new emerging technologies, and shifts in consumer behaviors, their materiality on the valuation of many industries and companies appears severe. In some sectors, the shocks are going to be profound. According to some estimates,[2] the impact of high carbon price on the cash flow of utilities, industrial companies, and airlines will be substantial and pose serious risks to companies and investors.

As a first step in our analysis, it is necessary to provide a definition of carbon risk(s). Carbon risks principally encompass policy and legal, technology, market and economic factors as well as reputational risks. Those various risks, which have carbon as a common element, may translate to asset risk to financial intermediaries and investors.[3] It is worth recalling that

---

[1] The author of this chapter is Gianfranco Gianfrate. This work was (partially) conducted while the author was a Giorgio Ruffolo Fellow in Sustainability Science at the Energy Technology Innovation Policy research group at Belfer Center for Science and International Affairs, Harvard University. Support from Italy's Ministry for Environment, Land and Sea is gratefully acknowledged. I am also grateful to Pietro Paletta, who provided assistance in the collection and elaboration of the data.
[2] See for example, "How Climate Change Could Affect Corporate Valuations," *McKinsey Quarterly*, n. 29 (Autumn 2008).
[3] Carbon risks differ from the so-called physical climate risks, which are risks associated with "physical impacts from climate change that could impact carbon assets and operating companies. These impacts may include physical damage and/or capital expenditures necessary in response to variations in weather patterns (such as severe storms, floods, and drought) and 'slow onset' impacts such as sea level rise, desertification, etc." (UNEF). Of course, whereas physical climate risks generally negatively affect operations (e.g., an asset cannot operate due to physical impacts), nonphysical carbon risk factors influence the overall risk profile of companies.

the definition of risk in finance is related to the variability of an expected outcome, and that the direction of such variability does not actually matter. Better-than-expected outcomes translate to risk from a financial standpoint just as lower-than-expected ones do.

Therefore, carbon risks do exist not only for companies whose performance is negatively affected by an increase of carbon price but also for companies that are positively affected in scenarios with carbon becoming more and more costly (see Exhibit 17.1). As a consequence, there are valuation implications of carbon risks for companies that have direct or indirect exposure to GHG emission constraints, such as those in the fossil fuel industry or that are heavily reliant on fossil fuels. But there is a valuation impact also on "low-carbon" companies such as renewable energy—which are usually referred to as a potential "hedge" against carbon assets—because, in many ways, policy and market risks for low-carbon assets are negatively correlated with those of high-carbon assets. In fact, carbon pricing is on the whole positive for wind energy and negative for oil and gas. It is worth

Exhibit 17.1 An overview of the main carbon risks relevant for companies

Category of Risk	Definition	Nature of Impact	Examples
Policy and Legal	Policies or regulations that could impact the operational and financial viability of carbon assets	Impacts physical carbon assets and companies that own/operate assets	Fuel-efficiency standards for personal vehicles; emissions trading systems; USEPA regulations targeting air pollution, and GHGs from power plants
Technology	Developments in the commercial availability and cost of alternative and low-carbon technologies	Impacts technology choices, deployment, and costs and demand profiles	Energy storage technologies; advances in renewable energy technologies, carbon capture and storage; alternative fuels
Market and Economic	Changes in market or economic conditions that would negatively impact carbon assets	Impacts physical carbon assets and companies that own/operate assets	Changes in fossil fuel prices; changes in consumer preferences

Source: UNEF

noting that low-carbon assets also face many of the same types of risk as carbon assets (e.g., policy and market/economic risks) but the nature and direction of these risks is different and often symmetrical from those facing carbon assets (e.g., the risk that industrial or innovation policies supporting renewable energy are discontinued or not enacted).

In this chapter, we will discuss how the approaches to corporate valuation discussed so far can be specifically applied to the carbon risks and to other climate changes risks. Therefore, this chapter serves as an opportunity to wrap up the main ideas and tools presented throughout the book.

17.2   FROM CARBON RISKS TO CARBON PRICING

In order to determine the impact of carbon risks on the value of corporate assets we need tools to quantify such risk in a "language" that is consistent with companies and with the "ingredients" of the valuation process. The price of carbon is such a tool. Carbon prices translate into corporate costs for companies whose operations produce carbon emissions. If carbon price increases and companies are not able to translate (quickly and/or effectively) such increase to price to customers, then—all else being equal from an operations and financial point of view—there is a reduction of the cash flows which in turn is reflected in a lower corporate value. The opposite can be true for those companies that benefit from carbon price increases.

Therefore, it should be a surprise that the phrase "put a price on carbon" has become increasingly popular as the debate about how to address climate change quickly moves from theory to action.

17.2.1   Carbon Pricing in Practice

From a practical point of view, there are several possible ways to price carbon, and they all tend to lead to the same result. The various possible approaches try to quantify and capture the *external costs* of carbon emissions—costs that society pays in other forms, such as droughts, heat waves, damage to cultivations, health care—and tie them to their sources just through a price on carbon.

The objective of carbon pricing is to shift the social costs of damage back to those who are responsible for them, and who can actually curb them. In this way, polluters are ultimately left with the decision on whether to discontinue their polluting operations, to reduce emissions (e.g., by adopting cleaner technologies), or to continue to pollute and pay for it. Therefore, the price of carbon provides an economic signal to polluters who can decide for themselves how to respond. In this way, the global and local environmental goals are expected to be achieved in a flexible way. Moreover the pricing of carbon also has the advantage of stimulating technology and operational innovation, fostering the economy transition toward a low-carbon configuration.

There are two main approaches for pricing carbon: carbon taxes and emission trading systems (ETS). The former consists of defining a tax rate on greenhouse gas emissions or—more frequently—on the carbon content of fossil fuels. Following this approach, the overall emission reduction associated with the carbon tax is not predefined (but it can be estimated) while the carbon price is.

With the latter approach (also known as cap-and-trade system), the objective is to cap the total level of greenhouse gas emissions. The firms that perform better than expected in reducing the emissions can sell their surplus allowances to the larger emitters. In this way, the firms that are more effective in reducing the emissions get rewarded while the least-effective ones get penalized. This is a market mechanism where the interplay between supply and demand for emissions allowances is reflected in a market price for greenhouse gas emissions. The caps ensure that the required emissions reductions will progressively take place by keeping all the emitters within the boundaries of the preallocated carbon budget.

The choice between carbon taxes and ETS systems (or the coexistence of the two) depends on national policymakers and economic circumstances. According to the World Bank, 40 countries have a carbon pricing system in place, and that number is expected to increase significantly over the next few years following the climate change agreement (COP21) reached in Paris in 2015.

17.2.2 External versus Internal Carbon Prices

Many companies around the world are using an *internal carbon price,* which is different from, but in relation with, carbon expressed in terms of taxes or ETS prices. Internal carbon price can be a powerful tool in ongoing business strategies. For instance, carbon pricing can be embedded and drive business planning. In fact, many companies acknowledge the process of ongoing climate change—including extreme and unpredictable weather events—as a key relevant business factor for which they wish to be prepared.

Preparedness includes use of an internal carbon price, based on the business assumption that addressing climate change will be both a business cost and possible business opportunity, regardless of the regulatory environment.

The companies that adopt internal carbon prices are the ones that expect an eventual regulatory approach in some form to address climate change. Therefore, companies cite use of a carbon price as a planning tool to help identify revenue opportunities and risks, and as an incentive to drive maximum energy efficiencies to reduce costs and guide capital investment decisions. Those companies deem it prudent and useful to use the concept

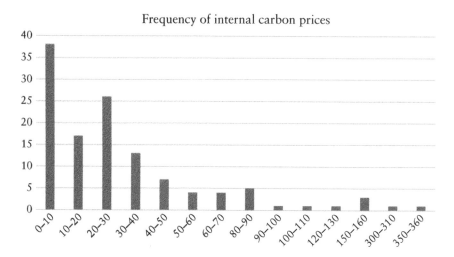

Exhibit 17.2 Frequency distribution of internal carbon prices (in $) per ton of CO_2

of a carbon price as part of their planning for achieving reductions in greenhouse gas (GHG) emissions.

By analyzing the data gathered by the Carbon Disclosure Project (CDP) issued in 2015 (see Exhibit 17.2), prices used range from US$0.95 to $360 per metric ton of CO_2, and companies use varying terminology, such as *internal carbon price; shadow price; internal carbon fee; carbon adder;* or *carbon cost.* Companies that have international operations are especially sophisticated in pricing carbon as a response to the regulatory environments in which they operate. This is particularly true for European and Australian companies that operate in jurisdictions where GHG emissions reductions are compulsory and covered by mandatory cap-and-trade programs or carbon taxes.

CDP shows that companies have also set internal targets for GHG emissions reductions, in terms of either absolute tons or carbon intensity, and use an internal carbon price or gauge to evaluate return on related investments, or to incentivize employees to meet established corporate targets. With this background, utility and energy companies are the most likely to employ internal carbon prices for strategic operational decision making, as they make long-term plans to meet energy and electricity needs, load factors, and amortization of plant investments and costs.

It is worth noting that even the highest value in the range used to internally price carbon by US companies appears significantly lower than most estimates produced by climate change specialists. For example, in 2015 the United States Environmental Protection Agency (US EPA) released some estimates[4] of the social costs of carbon (SCC), which include scenarios with costs very far from the ones currently used by US companies. The SCC is an estimate of the monetized damages associated with an incremental increase in carbon emissions in a given year. It is intended to include (but is not limited to) changes in net agricultural productivity, human health, property damages from increased flood risk, and the value of ecosystem services due to climate change (see Exhibit 17.3).

17.3 INCORPORATING CARBON RISKS IN CORPORATE VALUATION

What are the strategies to incorporate carbon risks in corporate valuation? Throughout the book we have discussed the possible ways we can adjust

Exhibit 17.3 Estimates of the social cost of CO2, 2015–2050[5]

Year	5% Average	3% Average	2.5% Average	3% 95th percentile
		Discount Rate and Statistic		
2015	$11	$36	$56	$105
2020	$12	$42	$62	$123
2025	$14	$46	$68	$138
2030	$16	$50	$73	$152
2035	$18	$55	$78	$168
2040	$21	$60	$84	$183
2045	$23	$64	$89	$197
2050	$26	$69	$95	$212

Source: United States Environmental Protection Agency, 2015

---

[4]Those estimates are intended to allow US government agencies to incorporate the social benefits of reducing carbon dioxide (CO_2) emissions into cost-benefit analyses of regulatory actions that impact cumulative global emissions. Therefore, they represent a useful and reliable guideline of the current administration's range of carbon valuations. The future policies adopted by the government are likely to assume such range of valuations and to price the carbon accordingly for US companies.

[5]Exhibit 17.3 shows the social carbon costs (SCC) according four different discount values to be used in regulatory analyses. Three values are based on the average SCC at discount rates of 2.5, 3, and 5 percent. The fourth value, which represents the 95th percentile SCC estimate across all three models at a 3 percent discount rate, is included to represent higher-than-expected impacts from temperature change further out in the tails of the SCC distribution.

the value of companies for their risk. Technically, the riskiness of the equity (or of the corporate assets) is encapsulated in a single number: either higher discount rate or lower cash flow (Damodaran, 2012).[6]

There are more informative ways to treat the relevant risks incorporated in corporate assets such as carbon risks. We can, as discussed in the first four chapters of this book, quantify the value of companies in a certain number of scenarios, rather than synthesizing the different outcomes in a single expected value.

Depending on the level of uncertainty, on the information available, and the time and effort investable in the valuation, it is possible to choose one of three DCF approaches:

1. Standard DCF, to be preferred when uncertainty is limited and there is a clearly dominant likely scenario.
2. Scenario-based DCF to be used when there is significant amount of uncertainty and there is one or more scenario(s) that are alternative to the most likely one and that could have extreme—either positive or negative—consequences for company's value. Usually two extreme scenarios are worked out: one optimistic and one pessimistic.
3. Stochastic simulation DCF to be used when detailed data are available (or assumed) regarding the probability distributions of key variables affecting future cash flows. This approach, as discussed, is mathematically complex but it can be handled by software packages easily available.

The increasing relevance of carbon risks for companies will require more and more often nonstandard valuation processes. Given the great uncertainty of future carbon prices a scenario-based DCF or a stochastic simulation are the two approaches to be preferred especially for companies whose operations are particularly exposed to carbon risks.

17.3.1   Scenario-Based Valuation and Carbon

Scenario-based valuation requires at least two scenarios, but very often consists of three: a best case, a most likely case, and a worse case. To gauge the effect of risk on value, expected cash flows are estimated under all scenarios. The valuation outcomes can be treated in two ways. They can be considered

---

[6]A third possible approach is the application of a discount factor as in the cases of discounts for lack of liquidity/marketability.

as a measure of the "value at risk" providing information on how the corporate value would be affected in case certain exogenous factors do happen. For example, assuming that there are three scenarios and that the company value is $100 million under the most likely scenario, $120 million under the optimistic scenario, and $70 million under the pessimistic scenario, we can conclude that with regards to the value under the most likely scenario, there is a 20 percent upside risk and a 30 percent downside risk. Alternatively, we can synthesize the scenario results by weighting the probabilities attached to each scenario. In this case, assuming that the most likely scenario has 50 percent probability and the other two scenarios have 25 percent probability each, we can conclude that the expected value for the company is $100 million × 0.5 + $120 million × 0.25 + $70 million × 0.25 = $97.5 million.

Scenario analysis particularly fits corporate valuation sensitivity to carbon risk, as climate change experts usually do use scenarios to forecast the consequences of certain climate policies (or lack thereof). Scholars, academic journals, think-tanks, and governmental agencies produce abundant wealth of data, often encapsulated in scenario frameworks, about carbon prices. The estimates of the social costs of carbon released by the US EPA presented in Exhibit 17.2 are just one among many available.

Provided that there are reliable estimates about the cost of carbon, in order to build a scenario-based valuation for a company, it is necessary to identify other relevant factors (if any) around which comprehensive scenarios could be built. For example, for energy and utilities, usually there is a strong correlation between revenue growth and national economic growth. However, depending on the specific circumstances, other factors such as geographical expansion or the adoption of a new technology could be considered.

The second step is usually to determine the number of scenarios to be worked out. Two is the minimum number, and some corporates prepare and work on 20 different scenarios. The choice about the number should actually be a function of how different the scenarios are, how accurately they can be forecasted by analysts, and the amount of time and resources that can be invested in preparing them.

Once the number and the drivers of the scenarios are set, the cash flow should be estimated under each scenario and, if appropriate, probabilities should be attached to each of the scenarios.

To illustrate how scenario-based valuation should be used when scenarios are built around carbon (and maybe other factors), we assume that we are interested in valuing an electricity utility. The valuation is in real terms, which is equivalent to a case with the expected inflation equal to zero,

Exhibit 17.4 Cash flow estimate

Current Cash Flow	
Revenues per MWh ($)	100
MWh sold	1,000,000
Total revenues ($)	100,000,000
Costs per MWh ex. carbon ($)	30
Costs except carbon ($)	30,000,000
Carbon costs per MWh ($)	34
Carbon costs ($)	34,000,000
Cash flow ($)	36,000,000.00

and we assume a cost of capital insensitive of the various scenarios equal to 5 percent.[7]

The company currently sells 1 million MWh at a price of $100 per MWh. The costs for the company (excluding carbon costs) are equal to $30 per MWh, while the carbon costs are the factor scenarios are going to be built around. For sake of simplicity, we assume that EBITDA is an accurate estimate of the cash flows to firm, being the amount of investments exactly equal to the yearly depreciation (the input is presented in Exhibit 17.4).

The company is unable to pass any increase of costs to its customers. As a consequence, given also the absence of inflation, the price per MWh is expected to remain $100 in future.

On the basis of these assumptions, and assuming a real growth rate of 3% per year, the standard DCF valuation of the company would be:

$$W = \frac{Cash\ Flow_1}{Cost\ of\ Capital - g} = \frac{\$37,080,000}{2\%} = \$1,854\,million.$$

Out of the possible factors around which it would be informative to build scenarios, in this case two are picked. One is the carbon cost/price, the other the expected growth (in real terms) for the company.

---

[7]Such assumption is in fact unrealistic and made here for sake of simplicity. Especially in case of extremely high carbon prices, the level of risk for the company—and, as a consequence, its cost of capital—would increase significantly.

As for the carbon cost (per MWh), $34 is assumed as the most likely (moderate) scenario two other scenarios are deemed worthy of consideration:

- An optimistic scenario with carbon price at $15;
- A pessimistic scenario with carbon price at $60.

For the real economic growth, while the historical average rate of 3% per year is assumed as the most likely, two alternative scenarios are considered as well:

- An optimistic scenario with a growth of 4.5% per year;
- A pessimistic scenario with a growth of 1.5% per year.

By using the assumptions discussed before and the input in Exhibit 17.4, we obtain nine cash flow estimates (shown in Exhibit 17.5) depending on the possible combinations of the three GDP growth rates and of the three Carbon prices.

The value of the company can be computed under each scenario by discounting the estimated cash flows.

The further step consists of estimating the probability associated with each scenario, as shown in Exhibit 17.6.

Each cell of the table in Exhibit 17.6 reports the joint probability of a certain combination of the carbon price and economy growth scenarios. For example, the probability of having a carbon price equal to 60$ and a high growth rate of the economy is equal to 10%.

The last step of the valuation scenarios-based is the multiplication of the valuation of the company under each cash flow scenario times the prob-

Exhibit 17.5   Cash flow estimates under scenarios

	Low Carbon price (15$)	Moderate Carbon price (34$)	High Carbon price (60$)
High (real) economy growth (4.5%)	$57.48 million	$37.62 million	$10.45 million
Average (real) economy growth (3%)	$56.65 million	$37.08 million	$10.30 million
Low (real) economy growth (1.5%)	$55.83 million	$36.54 million	$36.54 million

Exhibit 17.6 Probability of each scenario

	Low Carbon price (15$)	Moderate Carbon price (34$)	High Carbon price (60$)	*Sum*
High (real) economy growth (4.5%)	5%	5%	10%	*20%*
Average (real) economy growth (3%)	10%	35%	10%	*55%*
Low (real) economy growth (1.5%)	5%	10%	10%	*25%*
Sum	*20%*	*50%*	*30%*	*100%*

ability associated to that specific cash flow estimate. By computing the sum of all the products of cash flows by their probability, we finally obtain the expected value which is the scenarios-based company valuation.

17.3.2 Stochastic Simulation Valuation and Carbon

We will now run a Monte Carlo analysis on the same data. For details on this method, we invite the reader to look back to Chapter 4 dedicated to this topic. The data are the same we have just examined through scenario analysis. We have three sheets in the Excel file: the baseline sheet for our valuation, a sheet containing historical data on the US real GDP growth, and a sheet containing historical data on carbon prices. As explained before, we need to identify two important elements for our Monte Carlo analysis:

- The set of assumptions
- The set of forecasts

The assumptions we need in this setting will concern the expected real GDP growth rate and the expected carbon costs. Since we have historical data on both variables, we would like to fit our probability distribution to the historical one. There are two main ways to do this. The first one consists of the analyst personally analyzing the historical distributions, guessing the theoretical distribution that would fit the empirical one best. The second approach, which is the one we will consider in this exercise, is to let Crystal Ball find a suitable distribution based on the provided data. We will illustrate this method in this section.

To set our assumptions, we will need to proceed in the same way we have described in Chapter 4. First, we need to select the cell whose value will vary according to the assumed distribution. Second, we need to click on the "Define Assumption" icon:

We will then select the "Fit distribution to data" option. Excel will then prompt us to select the data on which we should base the distribution:

We can then click on the "Range" button and select the historical data in the "US real GDP growth rate" tab:

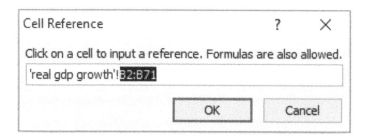

For the US real GDP growth rate, Excel is not able to fit one particular distribution to the data as suggested by the following message:

By clicking on "OK," we prompt Excel to show all the possible distributions that it deems reasonable for the data together with all the parameter values related to them. It is then up to the analyst to pick the one he or she deems best:

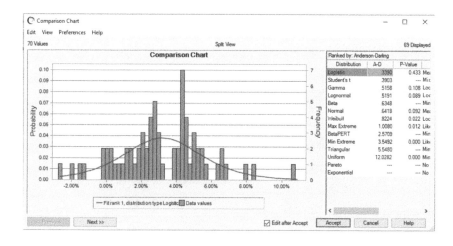

We will pick a logistic distribution centered on about 3 percent as our best fit to the data. We therefore click on "Accept," prompting Excel to show the distribution for the expected US real GDP growth rate:

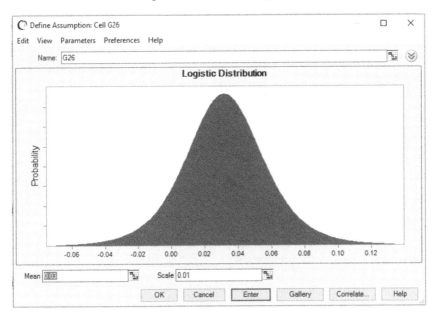

We then select the expected carbon cost cell and click on "Define Assumption" and "Fit distribution to data" again. Excel is able to find the best-fitting distribution without the analyst's intervention in this case, suggesting a lognormal distribution:

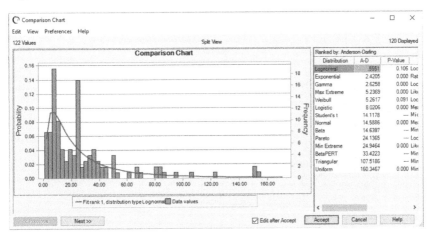

By clicking on "Accept," we once again obtain the distribution of the new values drawn from the selected distribution:

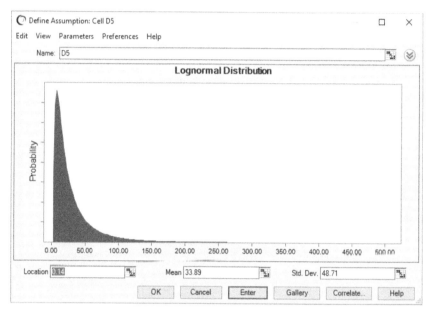

Next, we need to set our forecasts. We will select the expected amount of carbon sold, the expected revenues, the expected total costs, the total carbon costs, the expected cash flow, and the valuation value as our forecast cells. The sheet will differentiate between the assumption cells and the forecast cells by marking them with different colors: All assumptions are green while all forecasts are blue.

12	Forecasts		
13	Real expected GDP	3%	probability from distribution
14	Mwh sold expected	1,030,000.00	
15	Revenues expected ($)	103,000,000.00	
16			
17	Total costs ex. carbon ($)	30,900,000.00	
18			
19	carbon cost	34.00	probability from distribution
20	Total carbon costs ($)	35,020,000.00	
21			
22	Expected cash flow (FCF1)	37,080,000.00	
23			
24	**Valuation**		
25	Discount rate	5%	
26			
27		1,854,000,000.00	
28			
29			

Finally, we simply need to select the number of trials and initiate the Monte Carlo simulation by clicking on "Start." We will first run it with 1,000 trials, obtaining the following results:

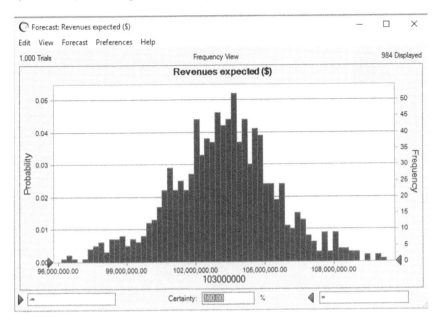

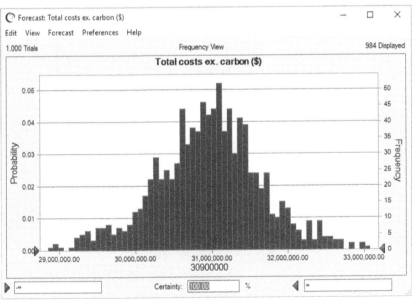

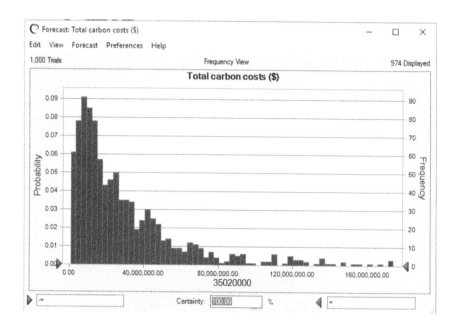

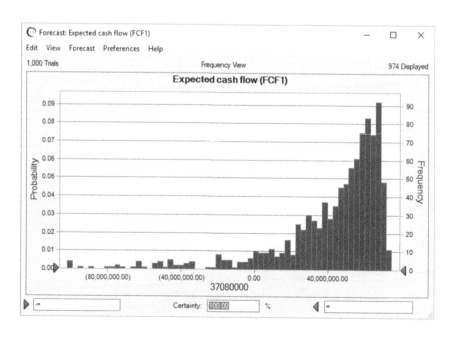

Thus, we reach a distribution of valuation values equal to:

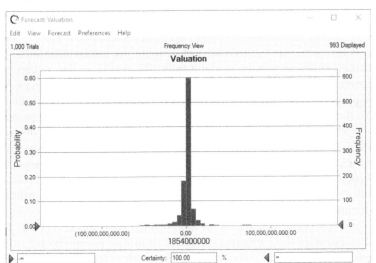

We can then see that the distribution is clearly centered on a value very close to the one in the base scenario. However, the values drawn can vary consistently.

To obtain more consistent values, we finally run another Monte Carlo simulation increasing the number of trials to a million. We obtain the following value distribution:

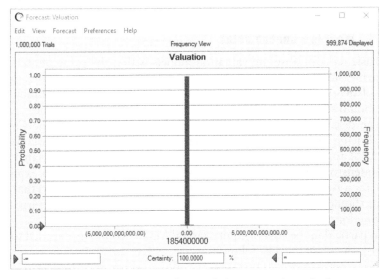

which gives probability 1.00 to values tightly centered on the base scenario.

17.4 CARBON BETA

Our discussion so far has relied on the assumption that financial markets are correctly pricing carbon risks and incorporating them in the price of traded financial assets. However, this assumption might not hold true because financial markets may be irrational and not fully efficient. This element can be relevant, especially for the estimation of the cost of capital when using CAPM.

In particular, the beta might not truly reflect the exposure of the company to the amount of risk that cannot be diversified away. Underestimating carbon risks can be even more costly for non- (or not-enough-) diversified investors. In those situations, it can be advisable to compute the cost of capital with the inclusion of an ad hoc estimation of carbon risks. Koch and Bassen (2013) have proposed an interesting approach to this estimation conundrum: they carried out an empirical analysis of European utilities by introducing a *carbon beta* concept.

By using an asset-pricing model to adjust the corresponding cost of capital, they estimate the company-specific carbon risk premiums for utilities, defined as the incremental return that shareholders require to hold a risky, carbon-intensive utility stock rather than a risk-free security. In order to carry out this estimation, returns from the market of European ETS have been considered. Such a market has proved relatively inefficient over the last few years, but its flaws are expected to be fixed in the near future.

More importantly, cap-and-trade systems are gaining momentum in various regions of the world as a tool to address climate change; therefore, the higher number of ad hoc markets pricing carbon expected to be available in future will provide further data points needed to model the carbon beta.

17.4.1 What Is a Carbon Beta?

The basic tenet of absolute valuation models is that the value of any asset can be measured as the present value of all its future income streams (in the form of dividends, cash flows, or economic profits). The discounting rate used should specifically reflect the risk associated with that income.

The discounting rate is usually estimated on the basis of the Capital Asset Pricing Model (CAPM). The assumption of this research is that popular CAPM applications do not wholly embed the carbon risk associated with CO_2-intensive operations. Therefore, a multifactor model, which explicitly estimates a *carbon risk premium* and the company's sensitivity to that premium, should deliver a more precise estimate of the stock's return, thus allowing for a more accurate measure of the cost of capital.

In particular, the cost of equity capital for any company exposed to carbon risk can be derived as follows:

$$\mu_i = r_f + \beta_{iM}(\mu_M - r_f) + \beta_{iCO2}(\mu_{CO2} - r_f)$$

If compared with the traditional one-factor model (μ_M being the market return and β_{iM} the stock sensitivity to the market return), this equation features β_{iCO2}, which is the stock sensitivity to the carbon factor, and $\mu_{CO2} - r_f$ that is the carbon risk premium. In the first attempt to estimate carbon beta by Koch and Bassen (2013), the monthly excess return of the EU ETS[8] carbon futures was used as a proxy for carbon price risk factors. In practice, the regression equation for an asset-pricing model comprising carbon risk would be:

$$r_{it} = \alpha_i + \beta_{iM}\, r_{Mt} + \beta_{iCO2}\, r_{CO2t} + \varepsilon_{it}$$

where r_{it} are the monthly[9] returns of stock i, r_{Mt} and r_{CO2t} are respectively the monthly excess returns of the market portfolio M and of the EU emissions allowances, respectively. β_{iM} and β_{iCO2} are the unknown parameters estimated using an OLS regression. If carbon price risk affects the equity returns of the observed companies, the beta coefficient of the carbon ex-post returns should be significantly different from zero.

A multifactor asset-pricing model that includes a carbon beta can be an effective tool to assess carbon risk materiality in terms of corporate value. This approach could be potentially extended to other environmental-related sources of risk, such as other pollutants or water.

17.4.2   Carbon Beta: An Application

In order to show how to estimate the cost of capital adjusted for carbon beta, we have focused on the European utilities sector, under the assumption that we intended to value a large player in the European electricity market. We have first identified a set of 23 comparable companies on the basis of their industry/business model, geography, size, and profitability.

We have collected weekly data from April 2005 to December 2011. This time frame almost fully covers the period (also called "II Phase") when the ETS market worked at its historical best, expressing meaningful prices. For the regression analysis, which is based on the ordinary least squares (OLS) approach, we have computed the individual stock returns, the

---

[8]European electric utilities—which are mandatorily participating in the EU Emissions Trading Scheme (EU ETS)—have shown to be significantly exposed to carbon risk. Such risk mainly consists of the price risk resulting from companies' need to buy carbon dioxide (CO_2) emission allowances in the EU ETS markets. Therefore, companies have to shape their industrial portfolio to comply with the restrictive emission regulations reflected in the EU ETS.
[9]Of course, the returns could alternatively also daily or weekly depending on the nature of the analysis and on the judgment of the analyst.

carbon returns, and the market returns with the methodology discussed in Chapter 5. In particular, market returns have been calculated with reference to the MSCI European index and carbon returns have been obtained from the prices of the futures related to the ETS allowances traded on the European Climate Exchange (ECX).

The results from the regression are shown in Exhibit 17.7. Overall, the average β_{iCO2} for the entire sample is equal to 0.03, and such coefficient is statistically significant. As a result, we can affirm there is a sensitivity to the carbon price factor.

Interestingly, we can obtain information at a more granular level by grouping the utilities in our sample on the basis of the carbon emission intensity of their operations (measured as CO2 Kg/MWh). By using this segmentation, we notice that the β_{iCO2} is above 0.03 (statistically significant) for utilities with the highest carbon-intense operations. Whereas the carbon shrinks to 0.02 for average emitters (and loses statistical significance), β_{iCO2} is above 0.06 and regains statistical significance for utilities with the relatively lowest carbon intensity.

These results are consistent with the view that carbon price risks have a symmetrical impact on the utilities that are the best and the worst in terms of carbon intensity. For the former, there is a carbon price risk associated with their role as sellers of allowances, thus a risk affecting potential revenues; for the latter, there is a risk as buyers of allowances, therefore a risk that could affect their costs. Carbon risks do exist and are relevant for both of those categories.

Moving from the estimation of the betas to the definition of the cost of capital, we can compute our K_e adjusted for the carbon risk as:

$$K_{eCarbon} = R_f + \beta_m \times (R_m - R_f) + \beta_{Carbon} \times (R_{Carbon} - R_f)$$

The missing element in this formula is the risk premium for carbon. As a possible estimation strategy, we could extrapolate the excess returns of carbon by using the time series of the annualized ETS returns observed in the phases when the ETS market was working efficiently. This approach delivers an R_{Carbon} of about 9 percent in Koch and Bassen (2013). The risk-free rate over the period analyzed was around 1.5 percent, considering the 10-year-maturity German sovereign bonds as a proxy of the relevant risk-free rate. The equity risk premium ($R_m - R_f$) for European companies is assumed to be 5 percent.

As the company's operations have a high level of carbon intensity, we use the betas obtained by analyzing the high-emitters subsample of comparables. We eventually obtain a K_e adjusted for the carbon risk as:

$$K_{eCarbon} = 1.5\% + 0.654 \times 5\% + 0.034 \times 7.5\% = 5.02\%$$

Exhibit 17.7 Carbon beta of European utilities

	Intercept			MSCI Europe			Carbon			adj. R^2
	Coeff.	Err. std.	Stat t	βM	Err. std.	Stat t	βCO	Err std.	Stat t	
Only high emitters (>500 kg CO2/MWh)	0.000	0.001	0.083	0.654	0.022	29.292	0.034	0.015	2.297	0.728
Only average emitters (from 300 to 500 kg CO2/MWh)	0.000	0.001	−0.512	0.668	0.022	29.978	0.000	0.015	0.011	0.730
Only low emitters (<300 kg CO2/MWh)	0.001	0.001	0.840	0.694	0.025	27.446	0.058	0.017	3.414	0.707

The alternative estimation of the cost of capital using the CAPM would have led to a K_e equal to 4.77 percent.

The implication of using a carbon-adjusted cost of capital versus a single-factor asset-pricing model might not be negligible in terms of corporate value. In this example, if we assume an equity-side DCF valuation with an FCFE equal to $100 million and a perpetuity with no-growth situation, we would obtain an equity value of $2,096 million using the traditional CAPM cost of capital (Equity value = 100/4.77%) and $1,990 million using the carbon-adjusted cost of capital (Equity value = 100/5.02%). This implies a dollar amount difference equal to $106 million of overestimation of the equity value if carbon risks are not taken into account—that is, 5 percent of the total value.

17.4.3 Conclusions on Carbon Beta

As the example clearly demonstrates, the carbon beta approach relies on the existence of a liquid market for carbon allowances as well as on the assumption that stock markets are not pricing correctly the information about carbon and, more generally, climate change risks. Both elements are highly debatable in theory and practice. Still, the idea of adjusting the cost of capital directly using the price of carbon expressed by trading platforms has its merits. The more markets are established to trade carbon permits, the more room there will be for techniques to disentangle the sources or risks for companies and for stockholders.

Index

Printed and bound by CPI Group (UK) Ltd, Croydon, CR0 4YY

23/04/2025

14660992-0003